To Roger & Denise
from

NINE LIVES
~ *Through Laughing Eyes* ~

First published in 1993 by
Invicta Publishing
21 Manor Road
Milford on Sea
Lymington
Hampshire SO41 0RG

All rights reserved. No part of this book may be reproduced, transmitted or stored by any means without permission in writing from the Publishers.

© Lt.Col. Robert Butler, MBE, MC

ISBN 0-9522491-0-3

Printed by BluePrint
Severn Place
East Road
Cambridge CB1 1HY

Nine Lives, Through Laughing Eyes

I	Childhood to Sandhurst	3
II	A subaltern at Napier Barracks, Shorncliffe	14
III	Palestine 1938–9. Skirmishes and serious thoughts	27
IV	Malta 1939–43. Blissful peace and salad days	49
V	Malta: The phony war	63
VI	Italy takes the plunge	67
VII	The Luftwaffe turns on the heat	75
VIII	Farewell to Malta. Egypt and South Africa	95
IX	Return to the Queen's Own for the Aegean Campaign	109
X	Farewell to the Aegean. Life at 64th General Hospital	130
XI	A 'Gabardine Swine' in Cairo and Jerusalem	141
XII	Ten months in wartime Britain	160
XIII	Burma. War, peace and strange adventures	170
XIV	The long, long trail to Jhansi	190
XV	Life at the War Office and at Fulmer, Bucks.	201
XVI	Journey to Addis in Wonderland	217
XVII	About horses and Holletta	229
XVIII	Addis incidents	256
XIX	Drive to Massawa	267
XX	Back to Shorncliffe, Korean training, Rugby	282
XXI	Joint Services Staff College	296
XXII	The Mau Mau Campaign	301
XXIII	Solo to Cyprus	331
XXIV	Full circle, return to the Queen's Own	337

Author's Prologue

During my life I have been subjected to three strong influences. Firstly, early tuition in general physics, which began when I was seven and which awakened my young inquisitive mind to independent thought and inventiveness. Secondly, chance encounters with various religions, and experiences which tested certain beliefs and created others. Thirdly, my involvement in a considerable number of incidents which, had fate decreed otherwise, would have cost me my life.

Over the years I have sketched out two books, one on the philosophy and religion which has developed as a result of my experiences, and the other my life story which has been so often filled with amusing and exciting events.

When I began to set down the story of my life, I soon realised that my thoughts on Matter, our Creation and on religions generally, all evolved from personal experiences during my lifetime. It seemed that if I slotted them in at the appropriate places, they would enrich my autobiography as much as the adventures and that both are inter-dependent.

I am hoping to enable readers of all ages, and all walks of life, to experience the events about which I write, through my eyes and my pen. When I explain simple terms or facts concerning specialised activities such as yachting, horses, soldiering, or flying, it may bore those who are experts in those fields. But not everyone has been a yachtsman, horseman, soldier, or owned an aircraft.

The excitement and suspense of some of the engagements and skirmishes in which I was involved in Palestine in my early twenties, and later in other theatres of operations, must have made an everlasting impression on my subconscious mind, because I still seldom dream without finding myself in some military situation.

If I appear light-hearted in the early chapters which describe my younger days, my reaction is that we were all young once, but as responsibilities are thrust upon us, we mature to meet them. The discerning reader will observe the growth of my own sense of responsibility as the story of my life unfolds; seen mainly through laughing eyes.

When I was living at Flagstaff House in Cairo in 1944 and saw General Gammel jump onto General 'Pop' Dowler's back as we went into dinner, dig in his heels and say "Come on Pop, give me a piggy-back", I realised that we are all young at heart and that this included generals!

When, after an interval of several years I met Major-General Norman Wheeler in his London office, as chairman of a large Public Company after his retirement from the Army, the first thing he did was to walk to a mahogany cabinet, get out two glasses and a bottle of sherry, and announce "We will now sing 'The Fireman's Band'". His mind had shot back 35 years, and for the moment we were both subalterns. In the interim years he had not only commanded a regular division, but also held the appointment of Chief of Staff, Rhine Army.

It is a medical fact that when one looks back to the days when one was young and carefree, one unlocks the area of the brain which stored those youthful memories, and momentarily carries its youthful mantle.

I believe that we are influenced by what we experience, hear in discussions, and what we read, whether in novels or serious works. I could not begin to list the names of the many men with whom I have discussed serious matters, from a former Prime Minister to a loyal sergeant who kept me aware of what the more responsible working men were talking about over their pints of beer; but I am deeply indebted to them all and to the authors of the countless books which have also added to my knowledge and, hopefully, my wisdom.

Chapter 1

Childhood to Sandhurst

My earliest memory, unusually early I am told, is of lying in my pram and seeing the ceiling move as the pram was pushed towards the front door and of seeing and feeling everything tilt as the pram passed over the front doorstep and descended eight inches into the front porch. I grew up in a doctor's house in London. My father was an exemplary doctor, a G.P. and a qualified surgeon who operated once a week at the West London Hospital. He was also a keen natural scientist and had an observatory containing an 8" astronomical telescope built in our garden. This round and rotating aluminium monster was not to my mother's taste and was eventually painted 'garden' green.

As soon as my sister Mirabel and I had grown out of the kindergarten stage we had a succession of French-Swiss governesses, due to my father's conviction that the best way to learn a language is by 'doing what comes naturally' when one is very young. We both went at an early age to Le Lycée Français in South Kensington, where I was put, quite happily, into a class of French children. I remember my first report from Madame Champignon contained the comment 'ecriture deplorable'; it still is. As soon as we spoke French fluently we started to have German-Swiss governesses and began to speak German. The result of speaking German so young, albeit nursery German, has meant that I have always been at home speaking that language, whereas Spanish, which I learnt at Oundle and in which I reached a high standard, I lost in about two years through lack of use.

The stream of violent events which have made my life so exciting at times began when I was only seven. My mother, sister and I were waiting for a bus at a road junction, when a light lorry with solid rubber tyres turned into the road we were facing. I noticed that its front wheels stayed on full left lock, so that instead of straightening out, it continued its left hand turn towards us. The next thing I remembered was waking up to find myself flat on my back looking up at the dried mud which lives under all motor vehicles, about three inches from my face.

I was one of three human skittles, bowled over in a row. Mirabel and I had been knocked down by the side of the lorry as it scythed us down, breaking one of Mirabel's ribs and clouting the side of my face and ear, all of which went black and blue. My mother, who was standing a little to our left, was run over by both front wheels as the lorry completed its U turn, one just catching a big toe and the other running over her shoulder, breaking her collar bone in two places. The middle section was depressed downwards and forced out of contact with the two side pieces, and it took much time and pain before the bone completely knitted.

A long court case ensued with my father, who was the only member of the family not to finish under the lorry, being awarded the lion's share of the compensation. He had borne the cost of many weeks in a nursing home for my mother, had to claim for his own legal costs and had sent the three of us away for four weeks to convalesce. I was bottom of the scale for the wounded with £15; but it had grown enough by the time I was commissioned to buy my first motor car. During this holiday I rode for the first time. My pony danced around a bit and somehow I controlled her. My mother proudly told me that she had heard a man say "one day that boy will make a fine jockey". Thanks to some starvation in Malta in 1942 he proved right because my stomach shrank, I lost two stone, and I have been unable to eat a large meal ever since. I could get my weight down to nine stone four and ride (overweight) on the flat.

One of my father's distinguished patients was Dr. Chaim Weizman the Russian Jewish exile who was a brilliant physicist and became a don at Cambridge. He was biding his time before emerging as the leader of the Zionist movement, and destined to become the first President of Israel. His son Michael was roughly my age and we became firm friends. We used to meet escorted by our respective governesses, and sail our boats together on the Round Pond in Kensington Gardens. I had been given a scale model of Britannia, King George V's J Class yacht, which sailed beautifully and which I still have in my workshop. When the King had Britannia converted from a gaff-rigged cutter to a Bermudan-rigged sloop, my father made a new mast for my model, and my mother made new sails; so that my model remained in every way a correct replica of Britannia.

My father was keen to pass on to me his interest in every form of science. From the age of seven I had to appear at his bedside, fully dressed at a quarter to seven to learn all about Matter down to the Atom; then indivisible! Because my father went there, I started my serious schooling at the City of London School at Blackfriars. They then took boys at prep-school age into the Junior School. After a couple of years, because I showed a great interest in science, I was allowed to go into the science side and at the age of eleven began to study chemistry and physics. At that age, if one is really interested in something, one can learn very quickly, and for a short time I became a 'child wonder' – three years below the average age of my form.

I used to spend all my pocket money on buying retorts, test tubes and other laboratory equipment. I eventually started to sell my lunch tickets for this purpose and subsist on a bar or two of chocolate. My subsequent problems at the dentist certainly testifies to this malpractice. I designed and built a small rocket-powered aeroplane, for which I manufactured my own explosive, which did succeed in taking off.

As a result of all this, my parents decided that I should be sent to Oundle, which was then the leading public school for the sciences. I was to have a special entry at the age of thirteen, the normal age then being fourteen. This proved an absolute disaster which neither Oundle nor my parents seemed to have foreseen. Because I was only just thirteen I had to go to The Berrystead, the Preparatory house at Oundle, and boys from The Berrystead were only allowed into classical forms. I had to take a special exam in the middle of the summer term of 1928 and was given just three weeks of Latin coaching in the Easter holidays to reach a standard which other boys would have reached after three years of Latin. From being three years younger than the average age of my form, I became one year older.

This total 'loss' of four years was equivalent to an entire public school normal life of fourteen to eighteen and I was utterly depressed. Had I done one more year of science and gone to Oundle at the age of 14, I would have arrived having already taken my School Certificate.

Before leaving for Oundle I had lovingly sealed the glass stoppers of the bottles of all my chemicals to prevent deterioration. In the event, I never looked at them again. By the time I reached the age when I could restart science I was fifteen years old and had to begin at the beginning with $2H + O = H_2O$. My brain virtually went to sleep for two whole years and this general shock to the mental system was something from which I do not believe I ever recovered. I bowed out of science and capitalised on my modern languages which came to me easily and effortlessly.

Apart from this tragedy I enjoyed everything else about Oundle School. Every other day was a half holiday when one played games in the afternoons and did what one liked in the evenings; although we were always given more prep to do on those days. The layout of the school was and still is, like a mini-university, which meant walking several hundred yards from one set of classrooms to another, and the distances from some Houses to the Great Hall were more than a quarter of a mile. I spent many evenings at the studio, where the art master was quietly helpful and made us feel welcome.

Because Flight Lieutenant Atcherly, one of the Schneider Cup pilots, was an Old Oundlelian, he arranged for the senior boys in the O.T.C. (Officer Training Corps) to fly at R.A.F. Wittering. As I was being strapped into my seat the attendant Aircraftsman asked "A straight flight

My first term at Oundle

"I always loved horses"

Sir?" I replied "I think so". The result was that he fastened the straps rather loosely over my schoolboy's narrow shoulders. After a while the pilot asked me if I would like him to loop the loop and I said "yes please". This we did and it was a great thrill. He then asked me if I would like to do a slow roll, and again I said "yes". As we slowly rolled upside down, instead of being pressed hard into my seat, as one is in a loop, I dropped into my loosely fitting straps and nearly slid through them. He then flew upside down for a few seconds and below me I saw the spire of Stamford Church pointing at me, as I desperately hooked my toes into the side of the fuselage and clung to my seat with my hands. I still nearly slid straight out. When he completed the roll I was rigid with fear, and the moment I got out after landing I parted with all the gorgeous strawberries and cream which they had so generously given me for lunch.

Oundle then excelled at games as well as work. In 1928 we won the Public Schools Athletics Championship. In 1929 our rugby side was unbeaten and in our final match against Blackheath they paid us the compliment of turning out seven ex-internationals. When K.C. Fyfe left at the end of the Summer term of 1932 he got his Blue as a Freshman that same year and his Scottish Cap in January 1933, when he won the Calcutta Cup for Scotland by scoring the only try of the match. Duncan Shaw who succeeded him as Captain, left the following year and also got his Scottish Cap in the following January. In 1934 we provided four out of the sixteen oars in the Boat Race. But sport was no detriment to our scholastic achievements. In those days most leading schools averaged around thirty Higher Certificates at the end of each school year. Oundle regularly got over a hundred.

I gained some kudos at Oundle when Dr. Weizman was invited to lunch by the Headmaster, Dr. Fisher. He had been one of Dr. Weizman's pupils when an undergraduate. After lunch Dr. Weizman asked to see me and I was duly summoned. I felt rather smug as he greeted me with great warmth in the Headmaster's study, whilst Dr. Fisher seemed to be treating him with a deference which almost amounted to awe. He brought me news of Michael, whom he had visited at Rugby during the week-end, and was now on his way back to London.

My friendship with Michael continued during our school-days and during my time at Sandhurst, when he was at Cambridge. His wealthy father had given him a superb Railton straight-eight, which I once drove all over London at high speeds whilst he was amorous in the back seat with an attractive blonde girlfriend of mine. She told me that she fought a successful retreat and bought time as long as she could because she knew how much I was enjoying myself at the wheel. Through Michael I met the Marks and Sieff families, and I remember a dance given for the young Hannah Marks.

Michael had inherited his father's brains and would have become a famous scientist. In the event World War II occurred, he joined the Fleet Air Arm and was killed whilst leading a flight of Swordfish in a torpedo attack on a German battleship.

Although I was two years younger than Mirabel, but from the age of 15 was taller than her, I became involved in her parties, as they often needed a spare man. I became the owner of a dinner jacket and then tails, and we used to dance in London at minor night clubs like the Kit Kat, presided over by Roy Fox and his orchestra. My father was very generous in lending us his car, which I learned to drive at 17. We tended to be in trouble if we were too late home, although we were given latch keys.

Having become somewhat precocious by rubbing shoulders with these older people, I sometimes went to a party without Mirabel, and one night after returning late on my own, my father withdrew my latch key. It was then that I became an expert cat-burglar and found that I could get into the house however much he locked it up.

More and more windows were locked until I was forced to climb up over the roof of the garage and worm my way round the side of the house to the back, over a conservatory where there were only four inches of firm going without treading on the glass, and then climbing in through the loo window. In the morning my father found me asleep in bed and demanded in some perplexity "how the devil did you do it?" I foolishly told him, and the next time I did this I found the door to the outer lobby of the loo locked on the landing side. He obviously expected that I would have to spend the rest of the night sitting in the loo or shout for help and reveal the exact extent of my lateness.

I foiled him again my managing to worm my way round to Mirabel's room, climb onto her window-sill, raise the lower half of her sash window, climb through, and move across her room and out of the door without waking her. When my long-suffering father found me in bed after discovering the outer loo door still locked, he just could not believe it and I thought it best not to tell him my exact route.

My ability to move as silently as a cat has never left me. When I later did some game stalking in the Northern jungles of Burma, whilst a guest of Major Finch, who had taken over 'Elephant Bill's' famous Elephant Company, his second-in-command, Claude Hann, an Anglo-Burman, told me that he had never before met a white man who could move as silently as the cat tribe. It is not all that difficult if you wear crepe soles, your eyesight is good enough to avoid treading on a single twig or dry leaf, and of course have had plenty of practice at moving silently at night when you are young!

In my last year at Oundle I pulled myself together and started to work, moving from the Modern VI, to which I had drifted after my temporary disenchantment with work, to the Army Class to prepare myself for my Army Entrance Exam. I cashed in on my modern languages, based on the groundwork which my parents had so painstakingly provided and passed high enough to have gone to Woolwich. I did not, however, wish to become a Sapper or a Gunner, but wanted to join a County regiment. In those days entrance to Sandhurst and Woolwich was through the Civil Service Examination, plus an interview by an Army Board and a practical French oral examination, which took place on the afternoon of the same day. Whilst waiting for the interview I got into conversation with a boy from Marlborough and we decided to have lunch together and to speak nothing but French in preparation for the afternoon's oral. We both came equal top out of all Army and Civil Service entrants, which shows the importance of taking time to refashion the shape of one's mouth to achieve correct French pronunciation. I finished my years at Oundle as fifth School Prefect, Head of my House, and a Company Sergeant Major in the OTC, the highest rank which one could attain except in the Summer Term. All this seemed to impress the Selection Board.

I remember being woken up by my mother during the Christmas holidays in which the list of successful Sandhurst entrants was published in The Times, shouting "you've passed, you've passed and so high too." She then admitted that she and my father had looked up and down the bottom half of the list several times, and decided that I had failed, before starting to look at the top end and finding that I had not.

I went to Sandhurst in January 1934 and as a former Company Sergeant Major in the OTC, foolishly felt that I had little to learn in the way of foot drill! In those days, we did not go to Sandhurst after other-rank service, and were told to report in a cloth cap, hacking coat and flannel trousers. The motley crowd which was to form the Junior Division of No.3 Company were told to fall in and were quickly sized. Our Company Sergeant Major, 'Biff' Bowen, was a very heavily built Scots Guardsman with enormous shoulders and rather a small head on top of which was perched his Scots Guards cap with its peak near his nose and his eyes barely visible beneath it. I thought he looked a priceless joke and looked forward to ribbing him, knowing that I was now a gentleman cadet. I nudged my neighbour. Bowen of course missed nothing and said "You sir, the gentleman I'm pointing at, what's your name sir?" I realised at once that irreparable damage had been done. I squeaked out my name in a weak falsetto. CSM Bowen then inflated his chest like an enormous bullfrog "Quartermaster Sarn't Lynch, Sarn't Riley, Sarn't Vine, 'ere at the double." When they had all assembled and were facing us, he pointed firmly at me. "See that gentleman there", he said, "that's Mister Butler; remember 'im!" They were used to this, and I don't remember any of them ever victimising me; but he never forgot, because I had mocked him, and it hurt his pride.

I had to be careful on every drill parade after that never to put a foot wrong, and it was not until a year later in my senior term that he finally got me as we were being marched across the drill square and the cadet in front of me drifted back a bit until we were doing a Flanagan and Allen act, my toecaps literally touching his heels.

It was my fellow cadet who had fallen back from his correct dressing who was at fault, but Bowen must have noticed the martyred look I was wearing and chose to halt the squad and ask me what I was doing. I replied "I was correctly dressed by the right, what the hell do you expect me to do?" "Oooh! So you swore at me, did you sir? Come 'ere at the double." I felt that an injustice was being done and doubled with very slow, short steps. However much he bellowed at me to get a move on, I refused to increase my pace and he gave up. At the end of the parade he sent for me and charged me with insubordination, and achieved what he had been plotting for so long – Three Extra Drills from the Company Commander; and he was the duty CSM for the first one. This was enlivened by Peter Starkey. Biff Bowen bellowed "Mister Starkey, sir, is there any reason why you cannot 'andle your rifle like all the other gentlemen?" "Yes, Staff," replied Peter in a very quiet voice, "I have only one thumb". It was the first time that I had ever seen Biff Bowen at a complete loss.

There is a lesson to be learned about the imposition of rigid discipline on young cadets. I do not believe it is a good idea for future officers to enter the rough and tumble of the barrack-room with men who they may one day command. There should always be a slight mystique about being an officer and entitled to a salute if men are going to entrust their lives to such people in battle without question.

It is therefore of paramount importance to select and train individuals who will be worthy of this trust. It is also important for cadets to feel the hand of persecution and even a tongue-in-cheek petty injustice. I abhorred injustice and nearly decided to abandon a military career when I was persecuted by a cadet under-officer. I felt that I did not want to be involved in such a system, but knew that my fees had already been paid by my parents and felt that I could not let them down.

In the event I later learned that having injured my knee in a bicycle crash, I was missing a few parades 'on the square' and that it was felt that I must pay for this welcome relief in another fashion. Although, because I was able to clean my kit to a high standard during these parades, and it was undoubtedly the brightest, I was told at a kit inspection that I had the filthiest kit in my section and had let the others down by preventing it from being the best in the platoon. Nothing could have been more calculated to make one feel small. I was sentenced to cleaning my kit to a strict timetable during every waking hour of an entire weekend. Frequent inspections were made to ensure that I was polishing my scabbard rather than my boots or belt etc. My old servant 'Speedy' said "don't let them get you down Sir, your kit is as bright as anyone can get it, 'ave a tin of polish open and a duster in your 'and, and the right bit of kit in front of yer and read a novel". I blessed him.

Later, as a major sitting in judgement over my own men, I 'knew the feeling' of one or two men who had got into the bad books of my Sergeant Major and told him to lay off them and give them a grain of encouragement; and it worked.

During my senior term at Sandhurst, I had a lot of fun. Although cars were forbidden, even to seniors at that time, many of us hired them for special occasions and drove up to London or collected our girlfriends for events like the June Ball. I once was taken as a passenger up to London by a fellow cadet who was dressed in tails and was going to an Old Boys Dinner. We got caught up in several traffic jams and started to run late, until about halfway up Piccadilly, well short of the Circus, John Forte said "I'm going to be late Robert, if I get out and run it will save the time it takes to drive all the way round the Circus and back to Jermyn Street, so will you take over and leave her outside those flats opposite No.17". I duly slid across into the driving seat and when the traffic began to move, felt for the gear lever. Wherever I put it, the gear knob wobbled at least six inches to right or left and seemed to me to be still in neutral. There was nothing to indicate the gear positions on either the top of the knob or at floor level. I tentatively tried one position and the car bucked back a foot. I hastily tried another and it jerked forward irresolutely, obviously in top gear. I moved it into third and kept it firmly in that gear as we wound our way round Piccadilly Circus but had no sooner turned into Jermyn Street when a Police car signalled to me to stop; which I did with some relief. "What do you think you're doing?" said a blue figure in the window. "Have you got a licence?". Fortunately I did have my driving licence and explained that I was driving a strange car, and the problems I had encountered. I asked him if he would be so kind as to park the car for me. He got in, made the same mistakes that I had, and managed to tap the car behind us – to my great delight. Nevertheless, I was charged with careless driving.

I was sensible enough to give my home address and not 'The Royal Military College, Sandhurst', but I still had to appear at Marlborough Street Police Court and was lucky enough to get the case heard on a Wednesday which was our half day. A friend of the family, Teddy Tapp, had witnessed the policeman hitting the car behind mine, and very kindly volunteered to be a witness in my defence. We both stood for a whole afternoon in Marlborough Street Magistrate's Court and my case never came up. Teddy apologised that he could not expect his firm to subsidise my welfare any further, and so on the following Wednesday I was on my own. Mr. Sandbach, who had already become one of London's best known Magistrates, listened to my woeful tale with great patience and dismissed the Police case against me on payment of ten shilling costs. This sum represented my whole week's spending money, but in those days ten shillings would buy a hundred and twenty penny buns or ten gallons of petrol – around £20 today.

An incident at Sandhurst which has remained firmly fixed in my mind and influenced my thinking may seem trivial; but I do not believe it is. I was always a keen rugby player, from the first moment I ran with a rugby ball. At Oundle, because I was relatively tall and had stamina, I was cast as a break-away forward. They thought I would put on weight and grow into the part; but I never did. The best I managed was to play for the 2nd XV. When I went to Sandhurst, I was asked if I played Rugby Football and said "yes". I was then asked where on the field, and replied "wing forward". The cadet in charge of No.3 Company's rugby looked me up and down and said nothing. I was not given any sort of trial and resented it. I knew that I was sprinter, had won the 100 yards championship for my age at the City of London and likewise in my first year at St Anthony House at Oundle, and would have preferred to have been cast as a three-quarter. At Sandhurst I took the plunge and asked if I could have a word with our Rugby captain and explained how we had been made to play out of position at Oundle in practice games to gain experience and that I would like at least to be tried once as a three-quarter. He was most understanding and agreed to give me a trial.

On the day in question he was thoughtful enough to seek me out and tell me that he could only watch the game for the first ten minutes; he was the Sandhurst hooker, and had a scrum practice that afternoon.

As I went onto the field and saw him standing on the touch-line I thought "sod it, what hope have I got to impress him in so short a time". I was so keyed up mentally that when I reached my position for the kick-off, playing left centre three-quarter, I dropped on one knee and pretended to adjust a boot-lace. In fact I was praying with all my heart and soul that I would play well in the first ten minutes.

The opponents kicked off and I did not have to move very much to get under the ball, catch it cleanly and begin to sprint like a scalded cat. I avoided their forwards, cut through their backs, side-stepped and wrong-footed the full-back and scored between the posts. About five minutes later there was a scrum in the middle of the field. We hooked it, and the ball went from scrum half to stand-off half to me, and once more I ran straight through the opposition and scored between the posts. A minute or two later my selector had to move off. I did not score again but did not have a bad game and subsequently played for my Company. I am certain that I drew inspiration and strength from my prayer and it began a belief that the Creator is a part of us because we are a part of Him. The prayer I offered up may seem in hindsight to have been flippant for such a minor matter, but it was not for something bad or wrong, and it was offered up with tremendous feeling. I have never heard of any other case of someone catching a ball from the kick-off of a rugby game and scoring a try between the posts, no-one else having touched the ball.

At the end of each Term at Sandhurst we sat for exams to pass into the next senior Term or suffer the disgrace of dropping a Term. Having passed in fairly high, mainly on the strength of my marks for modern languages, I managed to drop a hundred and twenty places at the end of my first Term. This was duly celebrated by a punitive visit to the Commandant, General Sir Reginald May, at the beginning of my Intermediate Term. He was a charming man, but I was unaware of this when I was marched into his office, where he demanded to know why I had been so idle in my Junior Term. I was able to take him aback and force him to smile at my reply that not many people could have afforded to drop a hundred and twenty places without dropping a term. Although I never managed to pull up all my lost places, I regained around forty-five in my Intermediate Term and forty in my Senior Term, earning undeserved praise for my steady improvement.

On 29th August 1935 I was commissioned into The Queen's Own Royal West Kent Regiment, and posted to the 2nd Battalion at Napier Barracks, Shorncliffe, Kent.

Chapter II

A subaltern at Napier Barracks, Shorncliffe

During the summer of 1935 my father had bought a Harrison-Butler 7.5 ton cutter called the Phoebe. She was moored at Bosham, in Chichester Harbour, and I spent some of my last weeks before joining my Regiment sailing her single handed. Sailing had been my father's one and only sport and we had had a lot of fun together. During this period, with the help of a mutual friend, Tom Debenham, we sailed the whole length of the South coast, round the South Foreland and North Foreland, across the Thames Estuary where we had to thread our way through all the sandbanks on the blackest of nights, and thence to West Mersea, to which island my father had retired earlier that year from his London practice. Apart from the harrowing experience of identifying the myriad of lights blinking a variety of colours and frequencies in the Thames Estuary, the thing I remember most is being becalmed in a wind against tide situation off Dungeness Point. We had previously had a strong following wind which had built up quite a sea, and when this dropped we just wallowed with the boom dangling aimlessly from side to side. My father had a stomach of iron, but Tom and I were reduced to helpless seasickness and since we were now actually being drifted slowly backwards, I suggested that we should anchor, leave my father aboard, and sleep on the shingle under our upturned dinghy above high water level. We slept like tops and returned on board having re-gained our sea legs.

The time eventually came for me to join my Regiment in a splendid little sports Morris 8 which a cousin had sold me for a generously low figure. I felt a great sense of symbolic pride as I walked for the first time through the swing doors of an Officers' Mess. Before this moment, although commissioned, I had not felt that I was a proper Officer!

In 1935, regiments varied in the way that they greeted new officers. Some made them welcome at once into their new home, some played practical jokes on them, such as one of the Second Lieutenants pretending to be the Adjutant and telling him that the C.O. wanted to see him straight away, etc. etc.; others ignored new officers for the first fortnight. My Regiment adopted the third course and I was told by the Orderly Officer who was on duty in uniform on that first Sunday evening, in an otherwise

"...to join my Regiment in a splendid little sports Morris 8"

"Sailing had been my father's one and only sport and we had had a lot of fun together"

empty Mess, that the form was that I should only speak when I was spoken to by my senior Officers, including my immediate neighbours at the dinner table.

I found this idea rather tiresome but was lucky enough to be joining with two other friends from Sandhurst, Mike Read and John Morton, and when they had duly arrived and gone through the same performance, we got into one of our cars and drove down to Folkestone for a glass of beer. My Company Commander was a gallant war time entrant from World War I and the holder of a DSO and an MC. He showed more warmth than the subalterns but everybody referred to me as Butler. My Batman, Private Stubbings, provided a standard of valeting that had become the norm in my Regiment and was of a high standard than I have ever encountered before or since. Bath run at exactly the right temperature and depth, toothpaste spread on toothbrush and laid across tooth-mug containing the exact quantity of warm water. All clothes meticulously brushed, folded and ironed when required. He was extremely intelligent and I very soon recommended him for the rank of Lance Corporal and only four years later he became a Sergeant commanding one of the sections of my Carrier Platoon in Malta.

When my first fortnight was over and intercommunication was eased, I still remained Butler; until playing for the Regiment at rugby football, a fairly senior subaltern, Tony Martyn, shortly to become Adjutant, shouted "Well tackled, Robert". This small gesture of acceptance meant more to me than I can describe. I can only say that I felt the same glow which I experienced when I landed safely after my first solo flight 27 years later. The rest of the Mess soon followed his lead and there began for all of us a long period of light-hearted approach to soldiering.

The Battalion Rugby side began to take things seriously as the draw for the Army inter-Regimental Cup was published, and we found ourselves drawn against the Devonshire Regiment stationed at neighbouring Dover. John Whitty stopped playing for Richmond for a couple of weekends and decided to abandon his normal position of flanker which he played at Army and Club level and play stand-off half for the Regiment. We put in some practice together and soon worked up a good partnership. He had very good hands, and as I had adopted the then current style of flinging myself at full length on the ground as I passed, I was able to shoot out long and accurate passes. The advantage of flinging oneself at full length is that the opposing side have no target to aim at. We finally met the Devons on our own ground and were narrowly beaten in a very close match.

That evening a few of us were invited by the victors to join them at a party at the flat of one of their older subalterns who was married 'off the strength' and allowed to live out with his young wife in a flat in Dover. I had never met him before the match and would never have recognised him, or found his flat, had I not been taken there by John Whitty.

When we arrived, there was a loud buzz of conversation and around a dozen thirsty subalterns tucked into some draught beer which our host had thoughtfully provided. After half an hour there was a knock on the front door and as I was standing nearest to it I opened it about two inches and shouted "Sorry chum but there's a party on here" and slammed the door. There was a loud banging and another guest near the door opened it again, and let in a character carrying some bottles – it was our host, Pat Leeper, who had gone off for further supplies! He was highly amused, pulled my leg, and we were not to know that we would meet again fourteen years later in Africa.

Life for a subaltern was very frustrating in those days, when the men were undergoing what was known as 'individual training'. They worked in small squads under Sergeant Instructors and all one had to do all day was drift from one squad to another, spending a few minutes with each and trying to look important, returning at intervals to the outer Company Office where the Company Clerk, in my case Private Poffley, would supply welcome cups of tea. At 11 o'clock it was in order for us to return to the Mess for a cigarette and a cup of coffee. One of my friends from Sandhurst, who had gone into the Grenadier Guards and had a great sense of humour, told me that when he was being briefed by his Adjutant, the latter remarked with a bored drawl "I believe that in Line Regiments, in the middle of the morning, the Officers return to the Mess for tea and biscuits; in the Brigade of Guards we partake of port and plum cake".

Presumably to nurture my sense of responsibility, I was made 'Silver Officer' and became the most junior and unimportant member of the Mess Committee. My main duty was to check the silver at irregular intervals, to ensure that it was properly locked up every evening, and that it was only cleaned with soap and water, not something like Brasso, which would have made it shine like chromium and add a year's wear every month. It is quite surprising how soap and water kept the silver looking bright and naturally shiny once it had been brought to a high state by Goddards Plate Polish, which was only used under my supervision when some item which had been out of use for some time was brought into action.

These duties meant that I was quite frequently behind the 'green baize doors' and a keen observer of what went on behind them. One development which was proceeding behind the green doors was the maturing of a very large Stilton cheese which one of our more elderly members had been given as a Christmas present. Seldom did a day go by when one or two majors or senior captains did not take a peep at this monster, to feed it with port or stick a silver probe in to ensure that the port was getting well down into its innards. At last the great evening came when the Stilton was to be given its first sight of our dinner table and conversation about it became almost obligatory. Sergeant Baseley, the Mess Sergeant duly appeared at the appropriate moment, but empty-handed and white faced. "Where's the cheese?" demanded the President. "It's gorn Sir" replied the unhappy Baseley. An enquiry was later held; there was talk of putting the entire Mess staff under arrest, and anyone who had been in the kitchens that evening was questioned. Eventually the culprit was narrowed down to a defaulter who was doing 7 days C.B. and had been cleaning out the larder as part of his punishment. He was asked if he purloined the Stilton. "Waddit look like?" he demanded. It was duly described. "Oh that" he replied, quite unperturbed, "it smelt something 'orrible so I chucked in in the dustbin".

Our social life, however, was far from boring. With a Cavalry regiment also stationed at Shorncliffe, together with a horsed Gunner regiment, there was no lack of horses and one could rent a good hunter for fifteen shillings a month. There was good hunting to be had with the East Kent and there was also the Shorncliffe Garrison Drag Hunt. In those days the Infantry were still horsed, and in battle the CO, the Adjutant, all the Company Commanders, the Platoon Commanders of the Machine Gun Company, the Signal Officer, the Horse Transport Officer and all their orderlies were mounted. It was for that reason that so much time was spent at Sandhurst teaching us to be good horsemen. By the time we joined our regiments we could mount and dismount at the canter and go down a line of jumps without stirrups and with arms folded. My Company Commander, having gone straight out to France in World WAr I, had never learned to ride and always took his leave at a time when our annual manoeuvres took place. This suited me well, as I found myself the senior subaltern in the company when Peter Buckle went out to India to join our 1st Battalion and Jimmy Goater allowed me to ride his charger and treat her as my own for free.

There were all sorts of drinking dens in those days, the best ones being in Dover. These were perfectly harmless places where one was able to drink endless glasses of beer after the pubs had shut at eleven o'clock. The best one was known as The Round House, and was once raided when quite a few captains and majors were imbibing. Luckily, I was not amongst those present on that evening.

We soon got to know some of the local residents who had attractive daughters. I will never forget the evening when two or three of us were invited to a drink party at a house on the Folkestone-Dover Road. The generosity of our young hostess was such that everything became lit up except the rooms. We were invited to play sardines. I had not played this game since we were children, and I well remember waiting with bated breath, often in cupboards, with about five other children whilst the last and sixth finally unearthed us. Playing for the first time as a twenty year old, I found myself playing to a new set of rules. Apart from this, I was unused to the strong cocktails which I had so readily accepted from my generous hostess. I accordingly felt that it would be prudent for me not to seek out the first sardine, but a bed on which to lie until my nausea had worn off. This I did, and came round twenty minutes later to find that I was not alone. I eventually ran her home. We decided that my presence would not be welcome at that hour and I risked my career with a back door smuggle into the Mess. When it came to running her home I slipped on pyjamas, carpet slippers, a camel-haired overcoat and a cap. So far so good, but it was not when my car (always nearly empty) ran out of petrol on the way back to Shorncliffe and I had to abandon it and walk for two miles through, mercifully, deserted streets with my striped pyjamas and bedroom slippers very prominent below my coat. It also taxed my fieldcraft to the full to avoid the guardroom, the sentries, anything else that moved, and to make it to my room.

In February 1936 I caught a very bad chill on an exercise, which finished up on my chest, hospitalised me and eventually led to my being sent to Osborne House, Isle of Wight for six weeks convalescence. It was like living in a very expensive hotel in Royal surroundings. We dressed for dinner and were not supposed to leave the grounds thereafter. I was the only 2nd Lieutenant there. There was one senior lieutenant and we and a few captains sat at what we called the cads table. It was not unknown for one or two of us to change after dinner into more informal attire and to slip down to the local, which was only a few hundred yards from the Lodge gate, and enjoy a few quiet beers. We were often joined by one or two majors. Just as we felt that they were older than God, so they must have felt about the many retired officers who must have represented a sixty percent majority. Many readers may be unaware that in those days every regiment was permitted a fixed number of captains and majors, hence irrespective of age or ability, subalterns had to work their way to the top of the roll and then wait for someone to get an extra-regimental appointment or to retire before they even became a captain. When I joined, the senior subaltern in my regiment was thirty five years old.

During my stay, the original Queen Mary sailed for the first time to her home port of Southampton from Scotland and I spent my last few shillings buying a ticket on a pleasure steamer to go out and greet her. As the then largest liner in the world she was an awe inspiring sight as we looked up at her from only twenty feet above the water. As I walked back from the jetty at East Cowes, I was nevertheless slightly regretting the fact that I would be broke until the following Wednesday, when my next monthly pay became due. On arrival at Osborne I was greeted by another inmate with the news that I had won the patients' Grand National sweep which we had organised. Only now as I type these words do I wonder for the first time if they had cooked the result, to help the only 2nd Lieutenant whose pay barely covered the mess bills. The £9 prize was more than half a month's pay.

On returning to Shorncliffe I was faced with my first confidential report. My light-hearted approach to life had not escaped the attention of my Commanding Officer, and he expressed the opinion that I should settle down a bit. Unfortunately, though neither my Brigadier nor the General Officer Commanding Eastern Command had ever met me, they felt it their duty to pitch in on the side of the law and piled on the agony. The General went so far as to say that if my conduct did not improve and produce a better report next year, my retention in the Army must be in doubt. I took this report to heart and proceeded thereafter to take my soldiering a trifle more seriously.

My Regiment was detailed for duties at the 1936 Aldershot Tattoo shortly before Whitsun, and we all found ourselves in a tented camp near Rushmoor Arena. I had only nine months service and was still a little wild. A firm called John Gardiner did the catering and the standard, both in quantity and quality was, even in those days, beyond belief.

I remember starting my breakfast with porridge or cold cereals and lashings of cream, followed by an enormous pile of scrambled eggs, surrounded by rashers of bacon and sausages, and then crowned with a fried egg or two, followed by two or three slices of toast, butter and marmalade. I am now a small eater and just cannot comprehend where it all fitted into me, as in those days my waist was only 28 inches and I have just measured my original Sam Browne belt to get the figure right. I could certainly not get it round me today, even on the last hole.

We were responsible for providing two companies of Eighteenth Century Infantry to do historic musketry drill, and in another setting, to storm the stockades of a rebel Burmese village, the dusky inhabitants of which were portrayed by the Royal Ulster Rifles, with whom we were brigaded in Kent and later in Palestine. We left there in the same troopship, and memories of certain evenings on board, such as when we were granted formal permission to sing their 'Firemans Band' remain evergreen.

I found myself in charge of one of the ladder parties and had to be first up the ladder to exercise my authority as an officer, albeit for them of the wrong regiment, and see that they did not repeat their efforts to push the ladders over and cause a lot of broken necks and legs, which they had attempted to do at the first rehearsal.

The tattoo week ended at Whitsun and we subalterns all got well and truly plastered on returning to the Mess tent after the final Saturday night's performance. I was Orderly Officer the following day, and had already asked my batman to give me an early call, whilst the rest of the subalterns would be enjoying a good lie-in. The next thing I remember after falling into bed in my tent was being shaken by the shoulder by an angry 'Captain of the Week' who demanded to know why I was not supervising the men's breakfasts.

I peered at him blearily and saw a cup of cold tea perched precariously on my folding canvas chair alongside my camp-bed. I explained that my batman seemed to have inadvertently failed to ensure that I was properly awake when he called me. This was nothing but the truth because my last memory was of falling asleep in the dark. It was, however, not enough to avoid a formal visit to the Adjutant's office and being awarded two extra Orderly Officers, effectively gateing me for the rest of the Whitsun weekend.

On my first afternoon as a free man once more, I drove into Aldershot to put a couple of gallons of petrol into my car, down to half a gallon, and make me fully mobile on my first night of pubbing since the Tattoo finished. I was in no hurry on that warm afternoon and was dawdling along at about 30 mph as I approached an unsigned cross-roads of whose existence I was completely unaware. The right hand side was concealed by a copse. As I approached the copse, I thought I could hear a car approaching at speed. I braked and came to a complete halt, but the 4 seater Ford 8 Saloon, which had made the noise, made no apparent attempt to brake but struck my front offside wheel and crushed it right up against the engine.

In those days cars had fixed front axles with a wheel at each end, hence my nearside front wheel finished up a good foot clear of the left hand side of my car, like the wheel of a side-car. My coupé had a fabric body consisting of ¾" x 1¾" timber framework, and had I braked 1/100th of a second later, I would have been sent right through my car and out the other side, impaled on the bonnet of the Ford which, on impact with my engine, did three lengthways, end to end somersaults and then rolled onto its side. The occupants – five in a four-seater – were so tightly packed that when their car stopped somersaulting and rolled onto its offside, the upper side doors opened like hatches on a submarine and out they climbed, shaken but relatively unscathed.

My hood was down; and having seen their car doing its PT exercises one foot in front of my face, like a gymnast doing a front somersault over a gym horse, I was propelled over the left-hand corner of my windscreen onto the tarmac road. My right leg was badly damaged in the knee area and the funny bone of my right arm was crushed. I was off-duty for two months, the first as a bed patient at the Cambridge Hospital, Aldershot. I remember, when I was taken down to the theatre for a minor operation on my knee, being mildly surprised to note that the surgeon was sporting brown boots and spurs beneath his white coat. Doctors were technically mounted officers in those days, but as they had no horses I thought this was carrying things a little too far. Bits of bone have been coming out of my elbow at irregular intervals ever since, and the lightest knock on it is never appreciated – I hit it against the bedroom door only this morning; but those bits of bone could not compare with the larger pieces which would have been scraped off the Ford's bonnet if it had hit me a split second later.

There is no justice in this World. The fact that my car was still on the cross-roads and the Ford on its side a good forty yards down the other road meant nothing. I was one against five and had been driving too fast, whilst they, in spite of the evidence for all to see, had been driving carefully. A passing motorist drove me to the Cambridge from whence I telephoned a garage to remove the remains of my car, which was a complete write-off. The Police never came near me, but my insurance company asked me to find another to cover the (Third Party only) risks of a twenty year old subaltern who had only been commissioned – and a car owner – for nine months. It was not easy!

Every cloud is said to have a silver lining, and in my case the reward came very soon after my return to my Regiment. Whilst I had been away there had been endless route-marches to prepare both officers and men for a four day march from Shorncliffe to Falmer Camp, near Brighton. Not only had I missed this training, but my right leg was still as thin as a broom-stick. It was however the last year before we lost our horses; to be replaced by 15 cwt trucks and the like. My gallant Company Commander, Jimmy Goater, always took his annual leave when we went on manoeuvres. So though still a 2nd Lieutenant, as the senior subaltern of my company, I found myself temporarily in command and able to ride at the head of my men. It was perfect bliss.

By this time command had been taken over by Lt. Colonel Victor Palmer who hence took me over after my 'reform'. From the very first, I had always had a feeling of rapport with him which I knew he shared, and except for one incident I gave him no cause for complaint.

This incident occurred the day after all training was halted by foot-and-mouth disease and we had nothing to do. That evening, we decided to have a drink in every pub in Lewes. Six of us got into two cars which we left in a central car park in Lewes and began our evening, not having reckoned on the large number of pubs there seemed to be. The odd subaltern would have a White Horse Whisky statue, won from some bar, in his room at Shorncliffe; since the White Horse of Kent was our cap badge, this seemed a proper symbol. On that evening we felt we should all go back with a white horse, and as we worked our way around Lewes we gradually accumulated them without being detected at the time.

Eventually, however, some telephoning took place between publicans and they must have arranged a reception committee at our next port of call. Only one or two had arrived before we got there, but I sensed that trouble was brewing and made a quick plan. It was obviously imperative for two of us to get back to our cars and drive to some pick-up point to collect the remainder. I organised myself and the other driver to lead the party out and turn away from the town so that the four passengers would screen us from behind. We darted into a gateway and they continued on and the ruse worked, the toughs followed the group of four. John Morton and I slipped back into the town and safely got to the car park to find two policemen already standing guard over our cars. The Battle of Lewes, as it later became known, was lost. We were all gated until our final departure by road for Shorncliffe and Victor Palmer had to go and make the peace with the Chief Constable for Sussex to prevent six of his officers being charged with theft.

On our return to Shorncliffe, we all had to parade formally, wearing our swords, at the Commanding Officer's office. There, after giving us one hell of a rocket, Victor Palmer allowed his face to soften. "It is only right," he said, "that young officers should have high spirits, there would be something wrong with the Regiment if they hadn't. The mistake you made was to be so foolish as to allow the name of the Regiment to be involved." 'Boots' Stanyon had worn a Regimental blazer. Boots was always getting into some sort of trouble. He was popular and intelligent, but alas, mischievous. We passed into Sandhurst in the same term, but he dropped a term through idleness and joined the Regiment with the next batch of officers. he had won a half-blue for Cross-Country and took over the training of the Cross-Country runners under the guidance of RSM Pond. He was a hard drinker and fond of the ladies.

Many years later, when we both served at the War Office, I asked Boots why he didn't get married and his reply, tongue in cheek, was "I think it unfair for me to confine the pleasure I give to only one woman, hence I prefer to bestow it upon as many as possible."

One evening we had a beer drinking evening in Sandgate, and when our favourite watering hole, The Royal Kent Hotel, closed its bar we decided to go to one of those harmless joints which do no more harm than to serve drinks after hours, probably with no licence. We duly mounted the steps to 'Auntie's' and prepared to knock on the door. I noticed that the fresh air had not improved Boots' sobriety and gave him a careful inspection, straightening his tie and telling him to keep his mouth shut. When my knock was answered and 'Auntie' appeared at the door I was amazed at her look of horror and the speed with which she slammed the door shut. I turned round to Boots and found the answer. He was flat on his back; out cold. We did not have enough money for a taxi, and so I had to bring him round, get him to his feet, and cajole and support him all the way up Sandgate Hill to our barracks at the summit.

One weekend before this episode, one of my friends, Mike Grove, asked me if I would make up a four with him as he was going over to Bolney to see his girlfriend, Elizabeth Anley, who had a friend staying with her. We had done a lot of training, including day and night exercises and I replied that I wanted to catch up on my sleep. He pointed out that I could have a good sleep in the car, and that he felt sure that I would enjoy meeting Phoebe Sawyer, whom he had met before. I duly slept and he woke me up when we arrived to find them having tea on the lawn of their lovely house. Phoebe had just come back from a holiday in the Channel Islands and was blonde, bronzed and beautiful. We spent a pleasant afternoon and evening, drove to a roadhouse for a swim, and before we finally left for Fulmer, I sensed that something important had happened to me.

Phoebe lived at Bishopstoke, nine miles from Winchester and many miles West of Bolney, whilst I was stationed 50 miles East of Bolney. I afterwards realised that a casual relationship would be impossible and that I should dismiss the episode from my mind. In December of that year Mike Grove told me that Elizabeth had asked him if I would like to join their house party for the New Year and to go to a New Year's Dance with them and that Phoebe would be there. His actual words were "she said 'use Phoebe as bait'".

I saw that Fate had taken a hand and decided that I should try and see her at least once before this golden opportunity, so that we would already be better acquainted. How could one possibly ask a strange girl to a dance in Shorncliffe with nowhere to put her up, or to know what sort of dances were taking place in her own part of the world? I suddenly remembered that Sandhurst always had a Christmas Ball which young officers often attended, and that Camberley was only forty miles up the road from Bishopstoke. I accordingly invited her to this and she replied inviting me to stay the night and to stay on for a second night and escort her to a Hunt Ball just North of Winchester. We had a wonderful weekend and at the end of it, the New Year's Eve party to look forward to in only twelve days time. We never looked back.

1937 was quite a year for me. I ran the Battalion's rugby team and in April switched to athletics. I had won a Half Blue for athletics whilst at Sandhurst and also became Officer I.C. Athletics. John Morton had won a

Blue for the 100 yards and long jump and L/Cpl Watts was an Army champion at the Discus and Javelin and also put the shot for the Army. We also had a number of Army runners and a well-balanced supporting team. Apart from training the Battalion athletics team, with much assistance from the RSM who took on the long distance runners, I ran for the Milocarians – an Officer's Inter-Service club which was then one of the leading athletics clubs in the country. Against Oxford University I was asked to run the 220 yards and the quarter mile consecutively, which I found a terrible strain. I spent ages digging my holes and taking off my sweater and slacks before the second race, but my heart was still racing when the starting pistol went. However, it stood me in good stead as far as training was concerned, and I won the Kent quarter mile two weeks later.

It was during this Spring that Phoebe came and stayed with me and my parents for a few days. On one sunny morning whilst we were sailing in a West Mersea Sprite I asked her to marry me and she accepted. We both realised that, since marriage for officers below the age of 30 was frowned upon in those days, and indeed if one was given permission to do so no marriage allowance was paid, we had a hard road ahead if we were going to pull this off. I knew that Victor Palmer had got married as a very young officer at the outbreak of World War I and that he was likely to have a certain sympathy for my cause. I determined to be a model officer and to win his support. As a Second Lieutenant, to ask for even his permission to get engaged would have risked a rebuff, and so my tactics were to let it be known that I had made my choice, simply by asking her to Regimental dances and other functions. The finals of the Eastern Command Unit Athletics Championships took place at Colchester that year, no more than twelve miles from my parents' home. It was natural that she would stay with me and attend them and, I am pleased to say, see me being presented with the trophy which my Regiment duly won.

Later on that year we heard we were being posted to Palestine in December and that our First Battalion, then serving in India, was taking over our Barracks in Shorncliffe. Those officers and other ranks in India who had served less than three years abroad were dropped off at Port Said when their troop ship passed through, and we were to meet up with them in Haifa. An equal number from Shorncliffe were to remain to join the First Battalion when they arrived, and I was to be one of their number. I was very flattered when Victor Palmer sent for me and said he would like to take me with him if I would agree to make the change.

Phoebe and I had agonising talks about this choice. An overseas tour in those days was for six years; with one paid leave home after three years. It seemed an impossibly long wait to ask anyone to face. As against this, I felt that I would mature more quickly in an overseas active service station, and that perhaps in three years, as a full Lieutenant, I might be able to pull it off. John Whitty, who was a great friend of mine, had managed to get married after only four and a half year service, so Phoebe and I gambled on my being able to do the same.

Only those who have had the experience can know the pain of parting when it is for an indefinite period. Three days before I was due to sail, Alison Wolfe, a very close friend of Phoebe, whose parents lived at Fair Oak Lodge near Bishopstoke, was getting married. Phoebe was a bridesmaid, and I had been asked to be an usher. Although normal leave had ceased, Victor Palmer turned up trumps and allowed me to attend the wedding. It was the last time I wore my scarlet full dress uniform.

That evening, a Saturday, we joined the Wolfe's family celebrations and dined and danced at the Polygon Hotel in Southampton. The next day we drove down to a beach and picked a spot where Phoebe would stand and wave when the Troopship California passed by on the morrow. It was a very sad day, and we eventually said our farewells at Winchester Station in the late afternoon before my return to Shorncliffe.

On the following morning my Regiment entrained for Southampton, and about four hours later I saw the Sawyer's house nestling among the trees of Bishopstoke from my carriage window. By the time we had embarked and got under way, it was too dark to see the shore! We passed the returning First Battalion in the Troopship Dunera in mid-Mediterranean with appropriate exchanges of signals.

Chapter III

Palestine 1938-39.
Skirmishes and Serious Thoughts

On arrival in Haifa on 14th January 1938 we felt like the poor relations, as the ex-Indian contingent, who had been dropped off by the Dunera were all in Khaki drill with brown knees whilst ours were still white from an English winter. It was two days before the Indian tailors had fitted us out in similar attire. It seemed a miracle to me that they could fit hundreds of men so quickly, and in the case of officers in measured and tailor-made uniforms. On the square outside the tailor's rooms countless yards of wet drill material were laid out to dry in the sun, so that it would be pre-shrunk before being made.

The Other Ranks had to undergo some ribbing for a few days with jibes such as "get your knees braan", but we quickly merged into an extremely competent battalion. We soon became involved in actions to enable the fulfilment of the Balfour Declaration, actions against trained freedom fighters sent across the border from Syria and Iraq and irregular bands recruited from the locals who, quite naturally objected to handing over their land and that of their forefathers to Europeans whose ancestors had left Palestine voluntarily, some possibly around 1,000 years earlier. The Balfour Declaration was in any event in direct contradiction to the promises of Lawrence of Arabia, which were to reward them for their help to us in defeating the Ottoman Empire. I could not understand, even as a 2nd Lieutenant, why Whitehall did not take advantage of Lord Balfour's carefully chosen words that we would find a home for the Jews, who so badly needed one, provided that this could be achieved without detriment to the current occupants of the land. It was patently obvious that just because we had defeated the Turks in World War I and administered Palestine for a mere twenty years, we had no moral right to disinherit Arab families from the land which they had inherited from their fathers, grandfathers and countless earlier generations. The British Army was constantly employed in those days of Empire as the peacemaker (jam in the sandwich) between rival factions, frequently taking stick from both sides. Although it is essential that orders are obeyed instantly and without question in battle, I firmly believe, however, that no soldier should act against his conscience in matters affecting civilians, that he should explain the reasons why he feels that an order is wrong or grossly unjust and, if possible make an alternative suggestion. Sometimes an order has emanated high enough up the chain of command to be beyond reach; but one can always do one's best.

An example of this cropped up in the Autumn of 1938, when I was commanding a detachment based on the coast near Sarafand. We had learned that some illegal immigrants were in ships lying just over the horizon, waiting to come in and land after dark. Since there was a dusk to dawn curfew, and anyone moving at night risked being shot, anyone landing on the beaches in my area were to suffer that fate. I was not prepared to walk forward in the morning and find dead and wounded women and children lying on those beaches and ordered my outposts to set their sights at a thousand yards, and to aim high if they heard any movement. In this way any unwelcome arrivals would be harmlessly warned what awaited them there, and give them a chance to re-embark or try their luck elsewhere. To my great relief no-one tried to land in my sector.

✧

Palestine during the winter rains could be fairly inhospitable. The paths in the villages became rivulets and the tracks, which we then used when off the few tarmac roads, became quagmires. Many could only be used by three tonners which had been converted to half-tracked vehicles by laboriously fitting tracks round the two close-coupled rear wheels on each side. The temperature could be quite warm when the sun was out and bitterly cold, especially in the hills, when it was not. We wore normal service dress jackets and khaki drill shorts, with long putties and Regimental coloured hose-tops. Later, when the weather became hotter, we wore Khaki drill shirts and shorts and the now obsolete Solar Topee helmet.

Very soon after our arrival my Company was sent down to occupy the hilltop villages dominating the stretch of the main railway line between Haifa and Jaffa to put a stop to the constant blowing up of the trains. Favourite ways of the terrorists were either to put a large bomb in one of the culverts under the line or to put a small bomb under a join between two rails, which would be detonated by a nail sticking up between those rails. Every inch of the line had to be examined at first light each day before the first train came through. Each of our three platoons was allotted a length of line about five miles long, and we would walk southwards the whole of our length, inspecting both rails and all the culverts, and then get a ride back on the first Northbound train. To provide additional security, a small 'box-car', propelled by a Ford V8 engine drove ahead of the first train to use the line each day.

The Emergency Platoon turning out for action. Victor Palmer in plain clothes and white jacket on left and Tony Martyn on right of the group.

A Ford V8 engined box-car which used to patrol areas of line where no troops were available. It was rather a suicidal task.

The village of Irtah and its surrounding territory was my first independent command and I was filled with pride when I surveyed the twenty five square miles of countryside over which, at night when curfew was in force, I had free rein to patrol where I wished and to open fire at anyone who moved after dark. We sometimes fired the odd shot up one of the narrow streets to remind the villagers of our presence, but concentrated on patrols and laying ambushes on the inter-village tracks in the hills above us. On this first detachment, which was for me the first of a number of unrewarding operations with little excitement, we nevertheless achieved what we had been sent out to do, as there was no blowing up of the railway line during our period of occupation of Irtah.

On our relief by another Company from Haifa we returned there and entered the normal life of a battalion which always had a certain number of troops on detachment, as we had been, and usually two Companies in the barracks, one of which was known as the Emergency Company. This Company was at thirty minutes notice and one of its platoons known as the Emergency Platoon was at five minutes notice. Every now and then one of my fellow subalterns had a brush with an enemy patrol or flushed out a gang by a night search of a hill village and after two or three months one of us was even wounded. After six months I was still awaiting my baptism of fire and was getting quite desperate. I even got one of my Lance Corporals who was a marksman to put a bullet through a Players cigarette tin which I placed about a yard behind me with my two feet spaced well apart so that the bullet passed between my calves and I could tell what the crack of a bullet was like when it came really close!

Our enemies were not often the villagers, but uniformed armed gangs who came over the Syrian border via Transjordan, as it then was. A few villages used to support the gangs willingly with food and armed men. Some villages which were located up in the hills ran their own local armed gangs, and though I did not blame them politically, I had no hang-ups about tackling them when they attacked women and children in Jewish colonies, an experience yet to come.

On one or two occasions when we arrived they actually held women and children in front of them as shields. Eventually we became more and more hardened, and any group of Arabs carrying weapons were automatically enemies. Apart from our patrols having progressively more skirmishes and minor engagement with armed gangs, our resolve to subdue them hardened when Squadron Leader Alderson was killed and his young daughter wounded on 18th February. They had been travelling in an unescorted car on the main coast road about twelve miles south of Haifa, just West of a track which led up the hazardous Wadi Mughar, which led deep into the Carmel hills.

Moving up the track leading to Wadi Mughar behind the Police tracker dog

Sappers blowing up the house indicated by tracker dog

I will describe the ensuing actions by the Security Forces, as they were typical of an incident of this kind. The Wadi led to Ijzim, a village which had a reputation for aiding and hiding armed gangs. Being in our Battalion Area, a small command group and two companies, including mine, were sent off from Haifa with a small section of Palestine Police, including a highly trained Doberman Pincher tracker dog and handler. On arrival at the entrance to the Wadi, we found that local Police had already put a soup-plate face downwards over the most prominent foot-print.

These dogs are highly intelligent and have a sense of smell surpassing most other tracker dogs. They can memorise the smell of a footprint which has been thus covered, up to around 24 hours. They do not amble along sniffing the ground like a Bloodhound, but take the scent of all the other footprints about 2 feet above the ground at a very fast trot. The handlers had to be extremely fit to keep up with them and the soldiery had an impossible job keeping up with them until we learned the hard way, and used gym-shoe patrols carrying the minimum of equipment; usually just a rifle and a cotton bandoleer of ammunition.

On this occasion we were slightly delayed by the knowledge that we were entering dangerous ground and hence the need to have patrols moving along the higher ground dominating the track. To no-one's surprise we were led into Ijzim, which was duly surrounded, and where the dog 'pointed' to one of the houses. This was eventually blown-up by the Sappers as a punitive measure and the villagers fined collectively through a lump sum to be collected by the village Mukhtar or Headman. All the men found in the village were lined up, squatting in rows. The dogs were trained to sniff each man in turn as they moved along the front of each row and to pass their suspect and continue to examine the others, to make sure that there was not someone else with a similar or stronger smell. They would then pass along the back of the row and place their paws on the shoulders of their suspect. On this day the dog drew a blank and the village was given a punitive search, which meant that items within the houses were not replaced in the precise positions which had earlier prevailed; we were told to turn the place upside down. Every soldier was searched by his platoon commander before leaving after such searches to ensure that no looting took place, and in my Regiment we prided ourselves that it never did.

I volunteered for every operation going and after six months was still unblooded even though the whole battalion less one Company was surrounded once whilst searching a village called Tamra at the Western edge of the hills South-East of Acre; my platoon having been sent out on a wild goose chase to the South of Haifa on that day.

The battalion fought quite a notable battle. Our Commanding Officer had done all the right things whilst searching the village and picketed the hill above it, withdrawing the picket only after the motorised column had driven off on its way home. He had however not deemed it necessary to picket the low mounds between which the track ran to the Acre-Nazareth road, as no force of battalion strength had ever been attacked in such semi-open country.

The terrorist command had however come under more co-ordinated leadership and a capable tactician named Sheik Abbu Dorah was now in charge of our area. When he realised that our battalion column must return along that long winding track later that day he laid on the biggest operation to date and organised local gangs from as far away as Safad and Jenin about thirty miles away to come in local buses with their rifles hidden under their voluminous clothing. As the last of our men came down from the high ground above Tamra the low mounds which dominated the track became alive with hostile riflemen on all sides and the whole battalion column found itself in a monstrous ambush. They inflicted heavy casualties on the terrorists but not without loss to ourselves. Two Military Crosses were awarded, one to our Medical Officer for tending some of the wounded under fire and helping to carry two of them to safety. Needless to say, for quite some time anyone who had not been at Tamra was almost a non-person and I was one of them.

However, not long after the Tamra battle one of our patrols found itself surrounded two miles into the hills behind the village called Ijzim, about twenty miles south of Haifa, and I was appointed Commander of a two platoon rescue column. We scorched down the Haifa-Jaffa road with all drivers' accelerator feet hard down on the floorboards and turned up the Ijzim track. I was leading the column in a khaki painted Austin 7, which in those days was the standard vehicle for junior commanders. As we approached the outskirts of the village I halted my small force and got out to have a peep at the situation, which by then had advanced two hours since receipt of the SOS wireless call to the battalion. As I stepped down onto the sandy track, a bullet kicked up the dust about nine inches from my foot. I shall always remember the surge of exaltation which encompassed me; at last I had received my first baptism of fire.

We had soon shaken out and made for the olive groves on the high ground which dominated Ijzim and from whence the firing had come. The gang, as we often called the opposition, had seen our move and withdrawn further up the slope and taken up a position behind a low stone wall in an olive grove beyond about two hundred yards of open grassland. As soon as we broke cover to cross this open ground they all let loose with everything they had and I remember looking left whilst a low humming noise came past me, and saw my batman, who was on my left, looking right. We both winced as we realised that one of these very heavy solid lead dum-dum bullets which could be fired from a shotgun had just passed between us. If one of these hit one's shoulder, for example, it would take it clean off. I decided that the best way to avoid getting hurt was to fix bayonets and charge, and this we did. The Arab fire immediately became more erratic as we raced forward to the wall and when we reached it they had all taken to their heels. We tried to pursue them for about 100 yards but in the light sandals which they wore and with no equipment like we had they quickly outdistanced us and got away through a series of olive groves and broken ground.

I returned to make contact with the subaltern who had been caught by surprise and made the SOS call in the first place; we conferred and decided to make much of our departure and leave him to pick his own ground for a possible ambush that night in case the gang returned to the village. He would pick a strong position from which he would be happy to take them on. In the event the gang made themselves scarce and were not seen again. I led my small column back to Haifa in a glow of elation. I had at last broken my duck!

Having at last got off the mark, fate decreed that I should become involved in a series of engagements and skirmishes, both by day and by night, and I will select a few to give readers an idea of their almost infinite variety. Late one afternoon, when I was 'standing by' in Haifa as Commandeer of the Emergency Platoon, I was sent off with orders to drive up Mount Carmel and proceed south along the Carmel Range past a village called Daliyat El Carmel, where the track ran along high ground with good visibility to the eastern side which sloped down to the Plain of Esdraelon. Firing had been heard in the foothills. We halted at a good vantage point on a ridge and could hear firing in the distance. With my binoculars I spotted some tiny figures dressed in white moving southward along the lower slopes on a course parallel with our own. We would be unlikely to be able to close on them now that we had left our vehicles, which we always did whenever we halted, so I got one of my platoon to fire a shot at about a thousand yards range to see what the reaction was. Innocent villagers would have just melted away. These were certainly villagers as armed bands from Syria wore khaki, but they took fire positions and started to shoot at us. With a thousand yards start we would never catch them, so we started a long range rifle duel. With both sides now having taken cover behind rocks and boulders, neither side could really see the exact location of his opponents. We could however see the odd puffs of smoke. By now we had learned that our opponents were bad shots at long range, whereas most of my men were certified First Class Shots and a few were marksmen. I reckoned that several of my chaps could hit a target at that range if only he could pin-point it. I accordingly ordered the men to concentrate on the exact position of any puff of smoke with great accuracy and to aim just to the left of the rock or bush from whence it came whilst I danced up and down on a prominent rock to entice them to try their luck and do some shooting. Nothing came within ten yards of any of us but we later learned that two of them had been wounded, from a report in the Arab Press which concluded that "the Officer responsible for firing on innocent villagers must be punished"!

✧

Early one afternoon, about ten days later, I was sent off to the Northern end of the Plain of Esdraelon to a remote village where a gang had been reported. This area is on the terrorist route from what was called the Trans-Jordan in those days and now called Jordan, to the Acre area where a number of Jewish colonies had sprung up to the North between Acre and the Lebanon frontier and includes the village of Tamra (of the big battalion ambush) and more excitement to follow. We debussed from the Haifa-Acre road and set forth into the wilderness.

We spent several hours combing an area in the foothills which consisted of jagged boulders, prickly pear cactus, and an occasional patch of flat earth seldom more than fifty yards square which sometimes was used for growing a tiny crop of oats, water melon or perhaps barley by local Arabs. Where there was a more prominent hill, there would be a small Arab village, often with the houses forming the outer boundary touching each other and with a protective mass of prickly pear cactus growing right up to their outside walls; so that apart from two or three tracks leading in, the village was a mini-fortress.

When no more than two hours of daylight remained I abandoned my search of the few areas of concealment and the small villages in the area and led my hot and weary men back towards our trucks, which had come as far as they could before the size of the rocks on the track we were using prohibited further motoring. When we reached the flatter terrain nearer our transport, we came upon one of these open fields with water melons growing and decided to slake our thirsts. Our bayonets were the flat sword-like type as used with the Lee Enfield rifle and were sharpened for active service. One stroke would slice a water melon neatly in half and then to segments. Just as we were tucking into the crescent shaped slices the ground all around us became peppered with little spurts of dust, followed by the sound of a fusillade of shots. We had been well and truly caught in the open and in no time had each found an indentation in the ground, a small rock or some other kind of cover and were lying flat and returning the fire from the village which I had completely ignored on our way back as we had already inspected it on our outward patrol. It was now

"With a protective mass of prickly pear cactus growing right up to their outside walls… the village was a mini-fortress"

obviously occupied by what I estimated to be around twenty riflemen. Being in wireless touch with my headquarters, I asked for another platoon to be sent out to a spot near where my trucks were parked, but out of view of the village. It was my plan to get two of my sections round the back of the village, using a shallow wadi to avoid observation and set up ambushes to catch the gang when it reacted to an advance from the new platoon by vanishing through the rear of the village. I accordingly worked my way back to explain my plan to the new Platoon Commander whilst my third section kept the enemy under occasional single shot rifle fire to hold their attention, and keep their heads down to prevent them from seeing too much, but not enough to scare them off! All this took time and the new platoon arrived much earlier than I expected, was seen from the village, sprang our opponents before my chaps had finished the encircling movement and they got clean away. It was nevertheless an exciting afternoon with bags of noise, a spice of danger and not a single soldier getting hit; although one truck had two bullet holes in it. If our opponents had been better shots they could have killed or wounded several of us when they first surprised us and fired their volley at what were stationary and unsuspecting targets.

When we left Shorncliffe, it had been made clear that no wives would be able to join us. But since we were one of the two battalions which were posted as part of the normal Palestine garrison, as opposed to those on a short-term emergency tour, Victor Palmer allowed his heart to soften, and an increasing number of wives came out to join their husbands.

Inevitably we became more professional, and instead of constantly seeking action, began to relish more and more the little free time we had. The pressure on junior commanders was mounting, and as the organised Arab resistance gained momentum and more and more outposts had to be manned and mobile columns found, all subalterns became absorbed. The situation was eventually alleviated by the promotion of platoon sergeants of initiative to a new rank known as Platoon Sergeant Majors (Warrant Officers Class III).

Victor Palmer encouraged any of us who were in barracks and not on stand-by to go into Haifa for dinner, or play skittles at a well known restaurant called Pross's run, not unexpectedly, by an extremely likeable and portly old German called Herr Pross. On Saturday nights one also danced at Pross's. There were a few English girls and young wives to liven things up, Margot Cox, the daughter of the manager of Barclays Bank being a popular favourite, who soon got married.

At week-ends the British community would also foregather at the tiny Haifa Yacht Club, which was very near Peninsular Barracks and a very popular focal point at weekends for those of us not on stand-by. We had acquired one of the local 16' one-designs which we renamed Marina after the wife of our Colonel-in-Chief. Because I was lucky enough to have done a lot of sailing since my early youth, I was put in charge of Marina and we had some quite good racing. Sometimes when we were not racing, especially in the very hot weather, one of us would slide overboard naked with a rope and have a tow. If one arched one's back and raised one's shoulders it was possible on a breezy day to become a human surfboard. Disporting himself thus, Tony Martyn, our adjutant, once got severely mauled, in an area of his body which he would never have selected, by a very poisonous jellyfish.

Once when taking Harold and Daphne Scott for a sail we became becalmed in the lee of HMS Malaya, and with no steerage way the tide gently drove our bow against her hull under the supercilious eye of the Officer of the Watch. I took a little ribbing for ramming one of HM's ships, but it broke the ice, and we got to know them quite well. I managed to get my own back when I won a crate of beer off one of her officers for surviving a complete circuit, around 1 1/2 miles, of Haifa Harbour towed by their speedboat standing on a surfboard by balance, with no hands.

Sometimes the Navy sent a shore party on one of our operations to practice firing their portable 12 pounder guns such as seen in competition at the Olympia Tournament. On one such occasion they accompanied us to Shafr Amr, on the edge of the bad lands. The plan was for us to occupy the old Turkish fort and fire our mortars and the gun at irregular intervals throughout the night at various track crossings. I privately thought it a useless exercise, as after the first salvoes any terrorists would soon get the message.

In the event, one of the mortars had a faulty charge, and the bomb landed in a courtyard near the edge of the village, injuring several villagers including a girl of about 12 who had a hole torn in her back so large that her lungs were flapping in and out of it. I managed to get a shell dressing secured over it firmly enough to stop any bleeding and to settle down her breathing rate. I then wirelessed for an ambulance but could not get the civilian ambulance service to come out until first light because of the risk of terrorist attack.

I begged my own commander and the Naval gun crew commander to abandon the firing on the grounds that enough punishment had already been inflicted on harmless villagers, but my pleas fell on deaf ears and the guns crashed every fifteen minutes throughout the night. I was not even allowed to remain in attendance on her in case I was carved up. She was still alive when the ambulance arrived and I saw her safely off. She died later that morning in hospital. I will never forget the simple gratitude of her family for my ineffective efforts or how strongly I despised those who would not, not could not, amend a useless plan to save the life of an innocent young girl.

For a few weeks in September 1938 I was posted to a company which was based in the old walled town of Acre, of both Biblical and Crusader fame, which lies at the Northern end of Haifa Bay. To the North, the main Haifa-Beirut road ran to the Lebanon frontier and therefore carried traffic tempting to the terrorists. This road was flanked by a number of new Jewish settlements, which lay between the road and the sea-shore. Gangs would cross it from the comparative cover of the olive clad lower foothills and shoot up these settlements which were protected by armed Special Constables, drawn from their residents. To the North-East lay the higher foothills which rose gradually to the snow-capped heights of Mount Hermon, near which we had a permanent heliograph station which could link up Battalion Headquarters with all its outposts. Not so far from Acre, in the lower foothills and on the edge of the plain stood the danger villages of Tamra, Sasa and Shafr Amr. Excitement was guaranteed!

One evening about an hour after sunset a report came through on our operational telephone that a colony about five miles up the road was under heavy attack. I was commanding the so-called emergency strike force, which on this evening amounted to no more than two sections carried in fifteen hundredweight trucks. One of these sections was made up from a mortar detachment who, although used to rifles, had little experience of infantry night operations in local conditions. However, off we went and roared up the Haifa-Lebanon road, the adrenalin running as it always did. The first thing that happened was that our friends from over the mountain had put out an ambush party about a mile South of the attacked colony, knowing full well that any rescue forces must come from the Acre direction. Fortunately, everyone always seems to shoot high at night and no one was hit with their first volley. We were all out of our trucks and lying flat on the tarmac road in one second and the next volley also missed us. However a tarmac road is a most inhospitable surface to try and get tucked into and one's chin can dig no hole in which to hide one's head. I simply said, "Load, get ready to move, move". And we surged forward across a ditch and, in pitch darkness, found ourselves at a low wall from behind which they had laid their ambush. We were just able to pick out ghostly figures fleeing as hard as they could go.

Once more I tried the tactic of feigning a complete halt with sporadic firing whilst leading my second section, the mortarmen, quietly and in single file on a right hook to encircle them. This looked like proving a success as they had fallen back to an old Roman aqueduct about 100 yards further on and were returning the fire from my left hand section. We gradually crept up into the darkness which was relieved by sporadic shafts of moonlight until we were about 50 yards behind them and 25 yards to their left. I then halted and signalled to my batman, who was just behind me, to get the mortarmen to fan out quietly so that we could get in a good first volley. We were still unobserved and I could see the figures lining the aqueduct and hoped to point out specific targets to each man as he came forward. My batman put a stop to my splendid fantasy by a hoarse whisper, "There's no one behind me Sir, they must have got lost".

Every man in my own platoon had by then proved himself and had confidence in me. I felt very let down by these temporary substitutes. We slipped back to locate them and they had, after losing touch, sneaked back to the others near the road. The enemy was surprisingly quick to react and redoubled their fire when a moonbeam lit us up. I felt that having lost my opportunity I should get back to the trucks and hurry North to the besieged colony we had been sent out to rescue. Our enemies were well trained and persistent and before we had driven off they had resumed their position behind the roadside wall and the first arrivals got in a few shots before we left in our vehicles. When we reached the colony, the main force of Arabs had withdrawn back into the foothills east of the main road. The Jewish defenders reckoned that all the shooting which they had heard less than a mile away probably gave the impression that more than only 16 men were in the rescue party.

A week or two later, after I had left Acre, I was having a drink at the Haifa Yacht Club with a dear old retired brigadier who loved the Palestine climate and lived just off the Acre-Lebanon road. He told me that the entire scenario which I have just described took place on his land, and no more than 200 yards from his house. The aqueduct was only 50 yards away and he heard the shattering first arab volley and rushed up on to his flat roof, from which he witnessed the whole action, even seeing the arabs running forward again from the aqueduct when I withdrew back to my trucks.

All military intelligence arrives with varying degrees of reliability, and it is essential not to over-react. Before leaving Acre I became involved in an example of the reverse. Not for the first time, a large gang had been reported in the bad lands South of the Acre-Safad road. Bill Heygate, my temporary company commander, muttered "usual time-wasting rumour I suppose", and sent me off on a reconnaissance patrol with two weak sections, totally about ten men in all in an armoured 30 cwt truck. These were very primitive vehicles and were no more than a wooden sided truck with 3/16th inch armour plates screwed on outside to form a small square sanger and a similar makeshift arrangement to protect the driver, who also had an adjustable armoured flap which he could lower to a slit if the truck came under fire. We had a Lewis Gun pointing over the front plate, which turned the assembled outfit into a sort of armoured car. Off we set along the Safad road at a sedate pace and keeping a sharp look-out. Suddenly, rounding a bend well short of the Birwa track we found ourselves looking at a subaltern's dream. Between eighty and a hundred armed and uniformed guerillas were spread out and moving away from the road at a range of no more than a hundred yards. Because the top of a thin sheet of armoured plate is an inhospitable surface to rest on, when on the move, the men all sat on their bottoms on the wooden floor, where they could see nothing, whilst I and my senior corporal stood holding on to the top of the front panel, with the Lewis gunner between us with his gun resting on a pad made from a folded sandbag. Lookouts to the Left and Right were provided by the other corporal and a lance corporal.

The truck screeched to a halt and I shouted to the gunner "sights down, fire controlled bursts" and bellowed to the squatters to man the right hand panel to capacity and for the odd two or three for whom there was no space to keep watch to our left and rear. Meanwhile there was an ominous silence from the Lewis Gun, followed by repeated clicks as the gunner repeatedly cocked the gun and pulled the trigger to no avail. All this only took a matter of seconds, during which the guerrillas had spotted us and were making for a hedge and bank behind which they had a very good fire position, covered by about half a dozen who dropped on one knee and gave them covering fire.

I realised that the gun had been incorrectly assembled and that we were in an awkward situation with only five riflemen able to man the right panel and presenting a silhouetted target like five green bottles sitting on a wall. The rear armour was in two panels, hinged on the outsides, thus forming two doors held together by a rough catch. I decided to get all the riflemen out and deployed in the best possible fire positions whilst the gunner and his number two stripped down the Lewis gun, protected by the armour, and tried to get it going.

Meanwhile, the men covering the main body of the guerillas had joined these behind the bank, and I was faced with a rifle battle with numbers of around ten to one against. The reader must remember that we knew that most of them were appalling shots and that some of their old Turkish rifles even had no backsights. I realised however that a few might have British Lee Enfields like our own; looted from Allenby's troops or even issued to them by Colonel Lawrence a mere twenty years earlier; hence the odd marksman amongst so many might start picking us off. I had borrowed a rifle from the gunner's number two and called a corporal and four men by name to follow me at the crawl as soon as I began to move, ordering the other corporal to take over, cover our move, thereafter to conserve ammunition and fire only at identified targets.

As soon as my small party had reached the cover of first a ditch and then some bushes which obscured us from the guerillas, we got up and ran as fast as we could for about a quarter of a mile to some scrub on some slightly rising ground which I judged to be on their most likely line of retreat and from whence I felt that I could pick some good fire positions to ambush them. After about twelve minutes we cautiously made our way back towards the truck.

A view to our left opened up after two hundred yards and we dropped to a crawl and I edged forward to have a good look around and saw the most amazing sight. The party which we had first seen must have joined up with their high command, and the scene was reminiscent of pictures of Waterloo, with two or three leaders mounted on horses surrounded by a small group on foot on the summit of a low mound, and below it a very large number of khaki clad riflemen. It was far too large a force to take on with six rifles and no automatic weapon and my first priority became to get this vital information back to Acre and thence to Battalion Headquarters.

It appeared that Abu Dorra was now openly commanding a large uniformed gang, and in the ensuing days the whole of the bad lands became a hive of activity with motorised columns roaring round the roads and tracks, often with the help of RAF reconnaissance planes, in attempts to encircle him. He eventually made it up into the higher hills, probably by night. The Lewis gun was found to have its 'Right stop pawl' and its 'Left stop pawl' reversed through an assembly error after stripping and cleaning. Disciplinary action was taken; but an error in design which made such a mistake possible should surely have been corrected in a weapon which was used throughout World War I and into World War II. Ours could have inflicted heavy casualties on our first sighting. This was our role once contact was made, so that the terrorist gangs would be driven back into the inhospitable rocky hills and, hopefully, out of Palestine. Only then could the Arab villagers and the Jewish settlements in the area have a chance to live in peace and begin to understand one another.

On returning to Haifa I had the satisfaction of becoming a full Lieutenant. In those days it meant much more than it does today, because not only was one beginning one's fourth year of service, but a Lieutenant was a far more important person, since he could have up to 15 years service (our record was 22 years) and often held higher local ranks when serving away from his regiment. Whilst we were in Haifa the system was changed from the number of captains and majors per regiment to the 'number of years service' system. I was soon given command of a detachment at Nathanya on the coast and well South of Haifa, and for the first time, an officer under command. Denis Jackson had won a commission through the ranks of the Grenadier Guards and Sandhurst, and was in fact a few months older than me.

By this time I had gained more experience than there is space to describe in detail, and was told to teach him the many things he would never have learned with his regiment or at Sandhurst. We were based on a squadron of Royals who were kind and considerate hosts. There were some marshes nearby and a lake which provided some good duck shooting. The guests at the one hotel in Nathanya included some officer's wives of the Royals who were literally 'following the flag' and since I was making use of the free hand I had been given to concentrate on the silent night patrols, we were able to enjoy afternoons on the beach as if we were in a small peacetime resort. The hotel held dances on Saturday nights.

Night patrols were the only means of obtaining success in that flat coastal plain area as the enemy could not move around in it by day; but even so, success could only be attained by endless patience and the ability to move in complete silence with no speech and all instructions by touch or the occasional whisper in the ear. We wore gym shoes, woolly 'cap comforters' and had blackened faces and carried only rifles and cotton bandoleers of ammunition. As we ghosted slowly along a track leading to a village south of Nathanya one half-moonlit night I heard the banging of a rifle butt on a wooden door. A gang was surely trying to get the villagers to open up and give them food.

I made a quick plan and ordered Corporal Greenyer to take his section along the track which we were using until he was about 50 yards from the village, which consisted of no more than a dozen houses, where he was to prepare an ambush position.

I led the remainder silently round to the far side of the houses and we managed to creep up to within 50 yards of the figures which were moving on to the next house. I ordered my bunch to take independent aim and fire the moment I fired the first shot. At that moment my batman, Pte Wallington, who always accompanied me on all operations, whispered in my ear "I think they're Corporal Greenyer's chaps Sir". I didn't believe him. Corporal Greenyer was a reliable man who had been firmly told to halt clear of the village, but I just could not run the risk of shooting up and killing half my own force. I whispered, and it took time, to let all my chaps know that I was firing a Verey Light and that they must open fire the moment we established identity. These fireworks, fired from a pistol, which light up the area extremely well, take time to whoosh up to the height where the white ball lights up and by the time it did the entire gang had scattered and not a shot was fired. Corporal Greenyer had seen them too, but had held his fire until they cleared the village. They had left by a third track, which in the dark, we had not seen. We had done all the spadework, gained surprise, got our adrenalin working, and achieved nothing; but the fact that I can remember every tiny detail fifty-two years later indicates the mental concentration which such incidents engendered.

In the Autumn of 1939 Major General Bernard Montgomery came out with sufficient troops to raise our strength to approximately a division. He was already a strong character with a clear mind which concentrated on essentials. He realised that owing to the Arab scouts and look-outs, when we surrounded a village for a search operation, even at night and with great caution, any gangs spending the night there melted into the darkness and went elsewhere, so that the subsequent searches were fruitless.

He therefore ordered a change in our tactics which was for us to descend on every village in a prescribed area on the same night. Any gangs leaving for another haven would thus find us awaiting them there too. My Regiment carried out such an operation on 25th October in the Tamra area in conjunction with the Royal Ulster Rifles and the Hampshire Regiment. I was sent up to the hill overlooking Tamra from the Eastern (or enemy) side, commanding a platoon from another company. By this time, because of the call on the services of junior commanders, this had become the norm. The view from the East was of a high barren plateau with little cover and gently undulating hills. In the immediate vicinity, however, there was a valley which ran from lower ground to the left or North and ended up on the right or South side. The high ground on which I was situated hence continued round to my right in the form of a horseshoe or punchbowl, with the far side of it about six hundred yards away, from which it stretched into the middle distance. In the bottom of the valley there was a steep rocky wadi with plenty of scrub and scarab trees. From the plateau in front of my positions a track led across the plateau to the lip of the horseshoe from whence it wound down to the bottom of the wadi, became hidden from view, re-appeared and wound its way through my positions and down into Tamra behind us. All my posts were well concealed and within earshot, the left hand section being across the track but not quite, the right post at the top of the wadi and just below the crest, and the centre section and my platoon headquarters half-way between them.

In the early afternoon I spotted some dust drifting from the track about a mile to the South East and realised that there must be people moving on it. As soon as I had identified some horsemen I sent a runner to crawl to my Right section to warn them and ordered silence, no movement and no firing until my Left section, to which I was going to crawl, opened fire.

Meanwhile all our eyes were on the approaching figures which turned out to be three horsemen and one man on foot. All were bristling with arms and one of the horsemen was carrying an unfurled banner, floating in the light breeze. As they approached the rim of the valley and began the descent I whispered "range 600". It seemed ages before they had zigzagged down halfway to the wadi and I breathed "range 500". Their descent continued towards the wadi where they would be lost from sight until they re-appeared on the track quite near us, and it occurred to me that they might well turn to the North and completely disappear down the wadi out of our view. I quietly said "range 400, fire". The Lewis gun roared into life and we saw the dust kicking up on the slope above their heads. It is very difficult to judge ranges when looking down a steep hill, and one should also reduce range on one's sights firing steeply down hill; because firing, even to infinity straight downwards needs no deflection at all between line of barrel and line of sight.

I had blown it; and the horses pranced about as the riders leaped for cover and out of sight. I then realised that even if they had not decided to turn down the wadi to our left, they were most likely to now and would all get clean away.

I handed my revolver to the No.2 and grabbed his rifle, told them to fire occasional shots into the trees and scrub into which they had disappeared, and called to Corporal Phillips to follow me. I could not have had a better companion for our mad scramble down the hillside to a point on the wadi below where our enemies had vanished, he had a magnificent physique and had served with Wingate's Special Night Squads.

Major General Orde Wingate, who later made his name as leader of the Chindits, was then a captain living in our mess. It was he, even in those days, who had the acumen to appreciate that there were few fighters who were equal to those on the North West Frontier, either at concealment or as marksmen, and that our local enemies did not match up to them. He accordingly broke with tradition and started operating at night, which was never done on the North West Frontier of India.

As soon as we dropped into the dry stream-bed we crept silently back up it towards the spot where the Arabs had vanished. They had not thought of making use of this obvious escape route and before we reached them they had started to fire back at my section which had first opened fire. When I took the first he was unaware of our presence. Corporal Phillips got the second and the other two ran up the wadi, one nipped into some overhanging foliage and I told Phillips I would take him on and to go after the fourth in case he got away. My one-to-one duel with the chap in the undergrowth was a little hazardous because he could see me, but I could barely make out his exact position. I eventually fired five shots at him, never certain that I had hit him and each time moving in closer. When I reached him I found that he had been hit by all five bullets, one of which had ricocheted off the barrel of a 9mm Luger pistol, still held in his hand. I kept it as a souvenir. The fourth man got away up the valley and was killed by my Right section at the head of the wadi.

The total haul included a large assortment of weapons, a rebel banner with the Sword of Islam on one side and the Mosque of Omar on the other, documents and posed photographs of various rebel groups of great value to Military Intelligence and a quantity of medical stores. The leader of the group was Nur El Ibrahim, one of the known and wanted rebel leaders. It was uncanny to see many of these photographs on the front pages of London newspapers in the next batch of airmail. Montgomery visited us in Haifa to hear my personal account of the action.

More and more positive operations co-ordinated by higher command continued until our departure in March 1939, and I have tried to give the reader a worm's eye view of a cross-section of actual events as seen by a participant.

Phoebe and I had corresponded frequently and regularly throughout the fifteen months of campaigning and I was well aware that before I asked Victor Palmer for permission to get married, it was essential for me pass my promotion examination to Captain. I accordingly studied the Manual of Military Law and the other subjects for my written paper. We had become experts at map-reading and I was no longer afraid of a Tactics paper. Victor Palmer was aware that I had put in a lot of mileage on operations and sent me off to Beirut for a week's unasked-for leave. It was wonderful to relax and not have to carry a Colt .32 even in plain clothes. I went from Beirut up to Damascus for a couple of days and was fascinated to see our opponents buying guns and ammunition openly in the bazaars. With my extremely fair hair they could not miss recognising me as a British Officer in plain clothes and, although we were both on neutral ground, looked really sheepish and embarrassed.

Another pleasant windfall was a trip to Egypt as officer in charge of an escort party to some soldiers who were being sent to Cairo for long-term prison sentences. I had to hand them over to another escort from Cairo at the canal town of Ismalia. Someone tipped me off that the train from Haifa to Cairo only waited for twenty minutes at the station on the Eastern side of the canal and that unless the ferries performed a miracle, it was impossible to hand over the prisoners and get back in time to catch the train back to Haifa. The trains only ran once a week. I duly packed a lightweight suit, pyjamas etc in a suitcase and took care not to rush the handover. I then made a distress call to Tony Martyn and asked him for instructions for my return. There were no road convoys crossing the Sinai Desert that week, so I was able to spend a whole week enjoying visits to the pyramids, the Gzira Club and many other less salubrious spots where spectacles of which I had heard tell really could be witnessed.

Shortly before we left, 'Monty' attended our last Church Parade and presented some of us with Certificates for Distinguished Conduct in Action. He made an extremely complimentary speech which he finished by saying "You leave here as the best battalion in the British Army, and if anyone questions this, tell them I said so". Abu Dorra also managed to get a last minute message to us on the quayside, bidding farewell to "brave opponents and clean fighters". With such praise from both sides of the house, Victor Palmer had every right to be a very proud man.

We came away with a DSO, 5 MCs, 2 MMs and 37 Mentions in General Orders for Acts of Distinguished Conduct in Action; but left behind eleven of our men whose names are carved on the oak lectern in the garrison church at Shorncliffe, it having been moved from Peninsula Barracks chapel when the British Mandate over Palestine ended in 1948.

We sailed on 22nd March 1939 in the troopship Dunera together with the Royal Ulster Rifles and Brigadier Jack Evetts who had commanded our brigade throughout our tour and would appear from nowhere with a butt-holstered 9 mm machine pistol on his arm on countless occasions. I was entertained by him and his charming wife in Haifa and met him again in the sixties, when we had both retired from the army, so more of him later.

We had been close friends of the Ulsters ever since we had been brigaded together in Kent; ourselves at Shorncliffe and them at Gravesend. The subalterns of our vintage went on the same Brigade Young Officers Tactical Course.

For both battalions to be shut up in the same troopship was lethal and much liquor was consumed. We had a stop at Alexandria where short shore leave was granted. John Whitty and I enlivened proceedings with a horse-drawn gharry race. He and three others tried to persuade their driver to overtake the one in which I, Mike Read and Mike Rickord were travelling and I persuaded our driver not to permit this. Both drivers entered into the spirit of the ensuing race, with cracking whips and loud exhortations. Eventually, when we were neck and neck, an approaching car forced the over-taking driver to close the gap between us and, at an exhilarating speed, the gharries got their wheels caught up and John's overturned.

No-one was injured and even the horse, on whose head one of the drivers was sitting, was only being restrained for his own good to prevent him from jumping up and getting even more tangled in the general mess until things had been lifted away. It did not cost us all that much when we all shared the bill.

After resuming our voyage, one of the evenings the subalterns of the Queen's Own were granted the unusual distinction, by the subalterns of the R.U.R., of being permitted to sing 'the Fireman's Band' on appropriate occasions! I probably drank a little less than most because I was trying to cram two years of study for my promotion exam into five days. We duly arrived in Malta and I had to take my written exam on the following morning. After a week or two I learned that I had passed. Another obstacle to an early marriage had been overcome.

"At an exhilarating speed, the gharries got their wheels caught up and John's overturned"

Chapter IV

Malta 1939–43. Blissful peace and salad days

Malta was one of the finest peace-time stations one could wish for. A glorious climate, within reach of the United Kingdom, by boat to Syracuse, train to Rome, Paris and Calais; a friendly population and the enlivening company of Naval and RAF officers and their wives. I should perhaps add the wonderful parties which the former gave under snow-white awnings aboard their ships, matched at times by the French Navy.

I was faced with the impossible task of getting our athletes fit in far too short a time. The Governor, General Sir Charles Bonham-Carter, was one of our regimental 'Old Boys', which is why he had worked at getting us this posting, little thinking that if war came all our careers would be damned, since we would be out of the main stream of the promotions which arise from expansion. Knowing our reputation for athletics in Eastern Command in 1937, he had boasted that no-one would have a look-in at the forthcoming Fortress championships once we were on the scene, and made this clear to me when we met at a welcoming cocktail party he gave for us.

I did my best in the short time available, but being fit to travel great distances over rocky hills is no substitute for work on the track. In the Battalion Sports I thought that I might have a go at the Battalion quarter mile record, as having had my tonsils out in the middle of the 1937 season, I missed the Battalion Sports that year, but managed to run over three seconds under the record later in the season. Pte. Wallington, my batman, also got into the final and drew the inside lane. I, on the other hand, drew the outside lane which meant that I was furthest forward and could see no-one. Wallington sportingly offered to change places, knowing that the best he could hope for was fourth place, but I felt that I must refuse, and finished only equalling the record. This three second difference made it quite clear to me that we were all still unfit and in for a hiding, which we duly received from the Suffolks, who had been in training long before our arrival.

We were due to take over from the Suffolk Regiment in St. George's Barracks, the plum site in the island with its own private bay, St. George's Bay and wonderful views in every direction. Because we arrived a few weeks earlier than expected, we went temporarily into St. Patrick's Barracks which was just adjacent but consisted of single-storied accommodation and did not have such a splendid mess as St. George's. The Suffolks had been our friends and rivals at athletics in Eastern Command, when they were our runners-up and we had got to know a number of their officers. This was useful to me, because although I had not yet plucked up courage to broach the subject of marriage to Victor Palmer, I knew I had to do so soon, as he was being relieved in June by Lt. Colonel 'Nobby' Clark, whom I had never met.

On the military net the good news was that I was being appointed to command the battalion's new acquisition, the Bren Carrier Platoon. I was sent on a course, together with my prospective platoon sergeant and two corporals to learn the driving, maintenance and inspection of a Bren Carrier and all the tricks of the trade to ensure that all grease points really had been serviced, etc. The Bren Carrier Platoon with its automatic fire power equivalent to that of a whole company, was the most prestigious command for a subaltern and I felt extremely honoured.

As soon as our carriers arrived we ran our own courses to train our men, who were hand-picked for their intelligence and mechanical aptitude. One of them was my old friend and former batman Stubbings, now a corporal. It soon struck me that since the carriers had to be able to operate widely dispersed, they lacked communications and should have been provided with wirelesses. I, therefore, made every single man learn semaphore, and to encourage them, whenever we took to the road for the drivers to practice, the carrier commanders were allowed to chat to each other by semaphore, saying whatever they liked. They soon became very accomplished and semaphored to each other as individuals as a matter of course even from ground to ground positions.

The Army in Malta, with its Naval connections, was well provided with six oared coxed gigs; and the battalion took over six from the Suffolks. As I had been so useless at cricket when at Oundle, I used to row there and found myself Officer i/c Rowing. Each Company had a gig, with two for H.Q. Company, and one of these I hijacked for the Carrier Platoon and coached its crew. I must emphasise here that I have always aimed at being a jack of all trades. I only ran the rugger because John Whitty's time was absorbed playing for the Army and Richmond. Harold Scott who ran the cricket played for Sussex, whilst Roddy Fyler and Robert Moss, neither of whom came out to Malta or Palestine, both played tennis for the Army; so I was a medium sized fish in a very small pond in the activities I ran.

In our social lives there was an indefinable spirit of gaiety amongst the young, perhaps engendered by the distant threat of war. We did not know how distant it was, but we did know that it was real. Denis Jackson, known as are most Jacksons, as Jacko, and I gave a bachelors party to repay the endless hospitality we had received from young marrieds and the daughters of prominent Maltese families. It was a scavenger party, no different from many others except perhaps for some of the items to be scavenged, each scoring varying points dependent on the acquisition difficulties likely to be encountered.

In Malta most dogs have fleas, and one item was a flea in an Eno's bottle. Another was a goat's brassiere. There was only one small herd of cows on Malta, owned by Freddy Trigona, but goats abounded and lived on anything including newspapers. They had been bred for the size of their charlies and all the best ones had to wear brassieres to prevent their nipples trailing in the dust. The problem here was to get one without hindrance from the goat's owner. In those days honour meant more than money and I doubt if any were bought. The road stud was produced by Vivian Muscat, whose partner had dug it out of the road outside her father's house. He was the Chief of Police!

The highest points were awarded for a road roller, to be delivered at the rendezvous where drinks and small eats awaited, before the deadline of 7.00 p.m. The score for that simply read on the acquisition sheet – you win. I believe three were on their way before the deadline, but none arrived at our picnic spot on a hill overlooking Salina Bay.

It was incredible what excitement the party produced and the speed at which cars were driven to win the prize; a three foot, brightly painted, statue of a black footman carrying a card-tray on his head. It was duly unveiled and presented to the unlucky winners to prolonged applause. We wanted to have an unusual prize and we did. We found it in a third-rate antiques shop.

When I was not working or engaged in some form of sport, I was scheming to get married. Firstly, I had to make sure that Phoebe and I could live and hold our heads up financially in local conditions. These were ideal, with petrol at 11p a gallon (at the 240 pence to the £1 rate), and I sounded out one of the Suffolks I had run against us in 1937 on the cost of renting a house and furniture. Johnny Tyndall had married Elizabeth Bulteel, who had been at school with Phoebe and they had a house in Balzan, only about 2 miles from St. George's Barracks, which was a miniature palace. It had a wide stone hall running through to a courtyard which contained a gazebo, reached by an ornamental wrought iron spiral staircase. Looking through the double doors which opened onto this courtyard one saw further wrought iron gates in an archway with a view through an orange orchard to a marble statue at the far end, the path being bordered with white arum lilies.

A wide and shallow-stepped staircase led with two landings to the first floor which had a spacious drawing room with hand-painted ceilings and walls.

"…a spacious drawing room with hand-painted ceilings and walls"

"…a typical Maltese balcony overlooking the front door"

"…a view through an orange orchard to a marble statue… with white arum lilies"

"…a courtyard which contained a gazebo"

It had a typical Maltese balcony overlooking the front door. From it a door led through to another sitting room or study, which in turn led on to the flat roof of our garage, which had space for two cars. The beauty of this roof was that a vine had been trained to spread on overhead wires to provide a shady hot-weather outdoor room and was automatically the place where one could sit for drinks, or coffee at any time of the day. The cost of this piece of paradise was to be £3.10.0. a month for rent and £5 a month for all the furniture. I decided that the finance was on and set about stage II, getting the blessing of two lots of parents and Victor Palmer. I decided that my parents had no right to object to a man, shortly to be 24, getting married, and that hence I could say that they had no objection.

I then tackled Colonel Sawyer, a formidable character who had won two DSOs and a French Croix de Guerre in World War I and devoured subalterns for breakfast. Whilst in Palestine I had kept Phoebe's parents softened up with the odd case of Jaffa grapefruit to remind them of my continued existence, and wrote to him that since my parents had no objections to my marrying Phoebe, could I have his consent, providing that my Commanding Officer approved? The tension for the next few days was such that I could hardly eat or sleep, but on the fifth day came a warm reply that he had come to realise that her happiness lay with me and that he and his wife were happy to send their good wishes and blessing.

I then wrote to my parents telling them of my intention to marry Phoebe, and that I had won Colonel Sawyer's approval and wasn't I lucky. They wrote their congratulations and finally I was in a position to ask for an interview with the C.O. on the following morning. This Tony Martyn duly arranged for 11.00 am. Having explained to Victor Palmer that both my parents and Phoebe's had agreed to our marriage, I formally asked for his permission. He replied that he would give my request careful consideration and would see me on Sunday morning at the same time. I blurted out that if I was going to run the 100 yards, 220 yards and the 440 yards on Monday, I would need some sleep, and had not been getting much; but he was adamant and dismissed me. I felt that all was lost. On Sunday, when we were both in plain clothes, he simply said "You know perfectly well that I cannot stop you from getting married", then after a short pause "but I can refuse you permission to live out of the mess". A long pause whilst my whole world seemed to fall in ruins, then, with a twinkle in his eye which he had so far managed to keep quite hidden "but I have no intention of doing so." I felt like jumping over his desk and banging him on the back. Having reported with complete accuracy his every word, I just do not know what I said or did. I presumably stumbled out some muttered thanks. He then said "let's go to the mess and have a drink."

In next to no time I had telegrams humming to England and applied for four weeks leave in the U.K. There were difficulties because the War was a foregone conclusion and it was just a matter of when. Regulations regarding leave off the island were tightening, but somehow I made it, and booked through Syracuse via the SS Knight of Malta, Rome, Paris and Folkestone.

Victor Palmer, having taken the plunge and given me the green light, was most supportive and was one of those who trundled down to the Knight of Malta to give me an extremely alcoholic, and hence jovial send-off. I seem to remember an attractive member of the Secretariat sitting on my knee to no-one's apparent surprise except mine, because I had never taken a girl out, even for a drink, during my bachelor's weeks in Malta.

The thing that stands out most from the long train journey that followed was being treated very rudely, almost to the point of being refused food, by the waiters in the restaurant-car between Sicily and Rome, until they discovered that I was not a German but an Englishman, when they could not do enough for me. Strange, I thought, since the so-called Axis had already formed, but it did show that the hearts of the Italian people were not behind the Axis.

I had enjoyed the rich scenery of Sicily as the train bore me to the train ferry at Messina, the line passing round Mount Etna and the vines and olive groves that encompass Taormina. In due course the novelty wore off, because after crossing by train ferry to Italy, the railway runs for much of its length between Messina and Rome along the Western Coast, providing one with an endless panorama with the June sunlight creating sparkles on the blue wavelets off places such as the bays of Salerno and Naples. The changes at Rome and Paris were just the usual scuffle, with rather a heavy suitcase which had to contain a variety of clothes including my dinner jacket. My morning coat was fortunately at home at West Mersea.

My next vivid memory is of seeing the cliffs of Dover and Folkestone on the horizon for the first time since 1937, and seeing Phoebe standing clear of everyone, seemingly on the roof of one of the harbour buildings at Folkestone.

We wondered if we would be shy after so long a separation, and even if we would each feel that the other might think that expectation had been greater than realisation. But it was not to be, and in no time we were in her mother's Morris 8 saloon heading for Bishopstoke.

In 1939 there were no motorways and few dual carriageways, but there was also far less traffic. The trip from Folkestone to Bishopstoke involved driving through Ashford, Maidstone, Redhill, Reigate, Dorking, Guildford – near which we stopped for a dinner à deux in the Hogsback Hotel – Farnham, Alton, Winchester and a fairly late warm welcome at Asfordbye, the Sawyer's home in Bishopstoke. It was a Friday evening. With only four weeks leave in the U.K., into which we had to try and cram all wedding preparations, a wedding and a honeymoon, it was essential to get things moving very quickly and Colonel Sawyer was slightly stunned, when he and I were having a quiet whisky in his study after the ladies had gone to bed, that the first of the banns would have to be read 'the day after tomorrow' if we were going to get in the requisite three before the wedding. He finally settled for this and eventually agreed that we could be married by Special Licence in the event of my receiving an early recall. I made it clear that I was not leaving for Malta without Phoebe, a feat that the young man who left England less than two years earlier would never have achieved.

Phoebe and I drove up to West Mersea, in Essex, to stay with my parents as soon as items like her wedding dress had been sorted out for our wedding on 24th June. We also toured around, staying with close friends and aunts from both families and eventually the eve of the great day arrived. My parents came down and stayed with the Sawyers for the night and met them for the first time; and my Best Man, Mike Read, who was on an M.T. course near Aldershot, was also present, he and I having had an alcoholic bachelors party with a few Royal Ulster Rifles friends the previous evening. Their Regiment had not disembarked in Malta like ourselves but carried on to England.

After dinner Mike and I went off to stay with the Wolfes, who lived only two or three miles away. That morning I had insisted on driving from their house at Fair Oak to Bishopstoke Church, which was no more than two hundred yards from Asfordbye, at exactly 30 mph so that we knew to the second how long it took.

On our wedding day Mike and I lunched with the Wolfes, who generously fortified us in the traditional manner and then went off to the church in their second car, leaving their chauffeur and their Rolls for our own dignified arrival.

Unfortunately, one of my father's patients, who was a clairvoyant, had read my palm in 1937 and had clucked and said "You poor boy, you're going to left at the altar." I only half believed her, but I could not forget her words, and was determined not to be one of those bridegrooms who waits for hours. For this reason, I arranged with Phoebe that she and her father would arrive at the church at one minute past three and I would arrive at one minute before three; hence our careful timing on the Friday morning.

We duly left Fair Oak Lodge at the correct time, but after about a minute I sensed with a deep feeling of certainty that Colonel Sawyer, who had a reputation for catching the train before the one he intended, was going to beat the gun. I told the chauffeur, who was dawdling like a snail, to get a move on. "I know just how you're feeling Sir" he said in a soothing voice as he slowed down even more. "I'll get you there on time."

As we drove up to the church I saw a large car pulled up and a flash of white as the back of a slim figure entered the gates of the churchyard. Mike Read and I were out of the car before it even stopped and running for the gates. By the time we reached them the bridal party had entered the porch and the vicar was standing facing us and pointing to our left, where there was another entry via the Vestry. We hopped over gravestones and dashed into the first door. The interior seemed in a terribly untidy state and there were dusty old organ pipes leaning against the wall. I made for the door handle leading into the main part of the church and found it locked. I couldn't believe it. We had lost all this time and would have to dash back and follow the bride up the aisle. As we ran out I saw another door beyond that which we had first entered. We ran in and made for a second inside door which I tore open to find myself roughly opposite the first pew on the bride's side. We stepped back, straightened our ties and walked forward slowly and as nonchalantly as possible past the front row of pews and across the aisle to the bridegroom's side. Out of the corner of my eye I saw Phoebe and her father about to take the first steps forward to the music of the Wedding March.

I looked to my front until almost the last moment, when I half-turned to see the last few paces of her entry. We used to have a private signal to indicate pleasure or dissatisfaction, which was to touch the corner of our mouths with one finger and move that corner almost imperceptibly up or down. I moved mine up and dreaded getting a down so early in our lives. Terrible as Phoebe must have felt she gave me an up to her eternal credit.

She is however a woman; and when we had gone through the ceremony, signed the Register, stood for a photograph outside and were finally alone in the bridal car she began to let fly. I stemmed the flood of words and told her firmly that no-one was more sorry than I, but that I had taken every step to keep to our agreed programme and that I never wanted to discuss the matter again. By that time we had driven the 200 yards down the hill to Asfordbye and were being helped out of the car. Apparently no-one realised that I had not been just behind that door waiting for my cue and all had thought that a most wonderful feat of timing had been achieved. We used the modern Wedding Service which let me escape comparison with "a brute beast that has no understanding", but omitted the need for Phoebe to promise to obey me, and she never has.

The subalterns of the Royal Ulster Rifles at the reception duly embarrassed us by insisting that Mike Read and I joined them in singing the 'Fireman's Band', since the occasion was, to their warped way of thinking, deemed appropriate. It was a harmless drinking song with no rude words and doubtless stemmed from the dim mists of time in far off Ulster. One of them became a Major General, Normal Wheeler, who died two weeks ago. He had always remained a close friend of mine, but I had not seen him for a year or two. He was one of those who succeeds by sheer quality of results and I do not believe he ever had a single enemy.

We borrowed my mother-in-law's Morris 8 for our honeymoon which began at Grosvenor House. I had cunningly arranged (I thought) with Phoebe's brother Jim, to keep the car hidden away until just before our departure; so that it did not get doctored in any way; hence it was not until we were driving through Winchester that I noticed someone pointing at us. I pulled into a narrow side street to have a look, and they had tied a white satin shoe, which made no noise, on to the rear bumper.

We then had an uneventful journey to Park Lane, where we were able to dine and dance in luxury and comfort. Even in those days of so-called peace, violence was in the wings. The IRA blew up the letter box during the night just outside our hotel, and in the morning the papers were full of the tragedy of the submarine Thetis, with pictures of its tip showing above the water before it finally sank with heavy loss of life.

Apart from Grosvenor House, which I had pre-booked, we wanted to drive down to the more beautiful parts of the Thames Valley until we found an attractive riverside hotel. We can be forgiven for not having wanted a twin bedded room, but this is what we were offered time and again, from every small riverside town from Sonning, where we first hit the river, down to Marlow. We were young and shy and did not at first have the courage to ask for a double bed, but found fault with the view or found some other pretext for turning down a series of 'twins.' At the Compleat Angler at Marlow we finally struck gold and the situation was perfect with views of Marlow Weir, a golf course near at hand and an aura of warm luxury. It has now grown much bigger and the service more impersonal, but when we went there for our Golden Wedding they augmented the champagne and flowers that our children had surprised us with, adding more flowers and gratuitous drink.

Alas, we were not to be allowed to see out the week. All those on leave in the U.K. were recalled to Malta and on Monday 26th June I received a long telegram from John Whitty, who was acting Adjutant, telling me that the Governor had personally intervened to allow me 7 clear days between our wedding and return to Malta. We drove back to Asfordbye on the afternoon of Tuesday 27th and caught the afternoon boat-train from Victoria on Wednesday 28th. After three days and two nights in sleepers, we arrived in Malta on the evening of Saturday 1st July 1939.

We had an hour or two in Paris before boarding the Rome Express, and the same in Rome before boarding the train down to Syracuse. In Paris we

"At the Compleat Angler at Marlow we finally struck gold and the situation was perfect with views of Marlow Weir"

drove around in a taxi and took photographs including the Eiffel Tower, the Arc de Triomphe, the Place de la Concorde, etc for our newly started 'album of our life'. In Rome it was so hot and sticky that we decided to go to a good hotel and have a bath, reluctantly contenting ourselves with tempting peeps of ancient Roman monuments from the windows of our taxis to and from the stations.

We arrived in Syracuse in time for a late lunch and indulged ourselves by sharing a litre bottle of strong red wine on an outdoor terrace under a hot sun. We both fell into a stupor in deck chairs during the crossing to Malta and felt very bedraggled as we collected our luggage before disembarking. I had not expected, as an 'illegal immigrant' married-off-the-strength, to be met and had thought in terms of taking a taxi to our hotel, where we would be staying for the period before moving into our house. There was. however, quite a reception party of the younger officers and their wives on the quay with news that Colonel Nobby had laid on a party in our honour at his house for ALL the married officers and their wives and that they were expecting us about twenty minutes ago. The Knight of Malta had, as usual, docked a bit late.

I was filled with pride that my Regiment had pulled out all the stops to make Phoebe welcome, and I know it was a great relief for her to feel she need not feel lonely, but had been adopted into the heart of the 'marrieds' where rank, other than the Colonel's, was ignored. Many of the younger wives remembered Phoebe from the dances I had taken her to when I was subtly introducing to the Regiment at Shorncliffe.

There followed a few carefree months of peacetime soldiering. In pre-war Malta we had a whole-day holiday in the middle of the week as well as Saturday and Sunday, so our memories of those days were of wonderful picnics at little bays where one could swim, and the usual social round of tennis and golf at the Marsa Club and drinks on board H.M. Ships. Before we moved into Casa Tre Chiese we experienced a real heatwave, 119° in the shade, and conditions with the dampness of sea air almost unbearable for a few days. On one such afternoon it was so hot that we filled our bath with tepid water from the cold tap, one could not call it cold water, and without drying just lay on the stone floor of our fairly spacious bedroom in the Modern Imperial until the water evaporated, when we would walk into the bathroom, lie in the water and return to the stone floor in a repetitive routine. There was a knock on the door of our adjacent sitting room and a maid announced Mrs Clark. We mumbled that we were just finishing changing and were with her in about forty seconds, and were composed and offering her tea. I never heard anyone call her by her Christian name, and doubt if any but Nobby knew it. She was warm and kind, but being our parent's generation, we looked up to her as a mother figure rather than a friend. Because no-one could sleep in the incredibly hot nights until the small hours, the Maltese used to sit out in the streets on their doorsteps if they had no access to their roofs. Some would form string bands and stroll, literally at snails pace, through the streets playing haunting melodies on their violins and guitars.

Phoebe and I had both fallen asleep one night under our sandfly net, which did not help much in a heatwave, but was a real necessity, and heard a haunting tune so far away that it was barely audible. It gradually came nearer and it seemed to us both that it was almost unreal. Eventually it became more and more audible until we realised that it had reached the end of our street. All the members of the band, or orchestra, were in plain white shirts, white slacks and white shoes. Their progress so slow that they took about half a minute to pass the window of our Maltese balcony which by now we were both manning. Their sound decreased as slowly as it had arrived until, straining our ears, we could no longer hear it. We had never heard the tune before but were both utterly bewitched by the experience. It was not until thirty years later that I heard it played on a record and was able to discover the name of the tune, Cittara Romana, which I now play indifferently on the piano, one of the many trades at which I am a jack but no master.

When the great day came for our move into Casa Tre Chiese and we settled into our little palace I felt that I really was keeping Guy Sawyer's daughter 'in the manner in which she had been accustomed.' Pte. Wallington was far too young and bright to be a married officer's batman, away from the cut and thrust of a soldier's life in barracks; so I looked out for an old sweat who would like living out, would avoid inspections and parades and enjoy the quiet life. This admirable vacancy was filled by Pte. Charley Farley, he really had been christened Charley, who had joined the Regiment before me and was one of those dropped off from the 1st Battalion when they passed through Port Said from India.

Whilst our Mess Sergeant, Mess Corporal and senior wine waiters all had a livery consisting of dark blue tail-coats with light blue facings, the colours of the two regiments which formed The Queen's Own Royal West Kent Regiment, with light blue stripes down their dark blue trousers; junior waiters and officer's batmen, when doing Mess duties, wore high-necked jackets with trousers as described above. In the evenings, officers batmen living out wore this form of dress, whilst wearing khaki drill shirt and slacks in the daytime. We had taken on the Tyndalls cook called Guisseppa, whom they referred to as Zebba, and for the first year I thought that was her name. They recommended her as a well trained cook who knew her conventional European cooking.

Since our foreign tour had four more years to go, we had sent off from Asfordbye two crates containing our wedding present silver and china, etc.

together with some of Phoebe's clothes and our golf clubs and tennis racquets. With the permanent stream of shipping calling in at Malta in those pre-war days, this had arrived before our move.

When we sat down to our first dinner, the table had been perfectly laid by Farley, with the silver cleaned and a general air of opulence. The meat course had been professionally arranged by Guisseppa with creamed potatoes in feathered blobs, each decorated with parsley surrounding the sliced meat. The standard of both cooking and service was impeccable and we both felt we were starting our proper married life on a nigh note.

Because our house was only a few hundred yards from St. Anton Palace, the Governor's main residence, and Peter Buckle had taken over the job of ADC from Geoffrey Elliott, we were nice and handy for making up the numbers if required, at short notice. A memorable occasion was when Air Chief Marshal Sir Robert Brooke-Popham flew in for a night with the Bonham-Carters on the way to take up a senior Air Appointment in Whitehall after being the Governor-General in Singapore. We duly turned up in diner jacket and long dress and were introduced to him as Sir Robert Brooke-Popham, but without the rank.

For the first month after our arrival Phoebe was always treated as the honoured lady, and referred to by Mrs. Nobby as 'our bride', to Phoebe's embarrassment. On this occasion the label persisted inasmuch as she was placed on the right of the guest of honour. He told her that he was utterly exhausted after his long flight from Singapore and she innocently asked him if he had ever flown before. He turned towards her and gave her a stony look. She was sublimely unaware that apart from being an Air Chief Marshal, he was one of the first Englishmen to have ever held a Pilot's licence. Brooke-Popham had a reputation for dozing off at conferences and this habit asserted itself after dinner, when sitting on a sofa with Lady Bonham-Carter, who was not only an extremely attractive woman, but also a polished hostess and conversationalist; his head sunk forward and he dropped off. Lady B.C. flashed a dazzling smile to us all and shrugged her shoulders. So it was fifteen all between the two most honoured guests.

✧

The one thing that did not quite marry up to 'the manner in which she was accustomed' was our family budget. Having organised the budget to the last penny, after paying my mess bill, club subscriptions, the rent, the hire of the furniture, the four gallons of petrol we would need for local running about, the batman's and cook's pay and our food and drink, we only had six shillings a month left, i.e. one and six a week. This, in spite of the fact that we drew part rations 'in kind' once a week and the cook sergeant always ensured that we had generous quantities of sugar, bread etc and a jolly good joint of beef. We could be seen in all the best places; but not doing much.

We would go down to the Marsa Club and play tennis, and afterwards sit out on the terrace and have a pot of tea; but no cakes. When we got back to Casa Tre we would perhaps cut ourselves a slice of bread and butter. If we had to overspend, we would dip into our £200 of capital, which called 'the false teeth and baby fund', but we never showed a chink in our financial armour.

It was obviously necessary for us to give a drinks party as a housewarming, and this we did unstintingly with lashings of Cointreau in the White Lady cocktails and good eats. I remember finding that it took longer than I expected to squeeze all the fresh lemons, and that our first guests, the Maltese ADC to the Governor, Edgar Salamone and his wife arrived whilst I was still at it and dashing upstairs to grab my jacket when I heard the knock on the front door.

Chapter V

Malta, The Phoney War

The three months of gay frivolity soon came to an end and the declaration of war on 3rd September 1939 by Neville Chamberlain found us already at our battle stations. My Regiment had been allocated an area from the Southern outskirts of Valletta to the coast due South of it, and Eastwards to Kalafrana Bay and its South Eastern promontory. Towards the end of August barbed-wire defences were being erected round the whole coastline of the island and on 24th August we moved into our battle positions. I had just been given command of 'A' Company, though still a lieutenant. Battalion Headquarters was at Tarxien (pronounced Tarsheen) and my headquarters, being the mobile counter-attack company, was sited in the area of Bir id Deheb, slightly to its South.

It was not long before we got the feeling that Italy would not join her Axis friends yet, and so since the war failed to erupt into the Mediterranean, our state of readiness was reduced from full alert with dawn and dusk 'stand-to', and we eventually returned to St. George's Barracks. Before returning I had my first taste of practical Military Law, when I was asked to defend a private soldier who arrived late back from a local pass in Valletta and was charged with being absent without leave from his company, which, technically, he had been. I am not keen on the modern legal system whereby the defence exceeds its proper role of ensuring that the alleged wrongdoer receives a fair trial, but with money and a reputation at stake, moves heaven and earth to get him off, whether he is guilty or not. It is frequently necessary to have details of the guilt to produce the best defence. In this instance however I had a sympathy with the alleged wrongdoer because, although he arrived late at his Company H.Q. and had duly been booked as absent, he had arrived inside the Battalion area at Tarxien before 22.00 hours and had persuaded one of his friends, an unpaid Lance Corporal King, to run him out to his company.

My first act on the opening of the Court Martial was to ask if the case of the Private who had been late could be taken first. I was defending them both and saw how I could get the Private off if I put the blame on the Lance Corporal for not immediately reporting him within the Battalion area. Having done this, I then pleaded that the Court could not punish the

Lance Corporal because he had already been punished by the C.O., who had relieved him of his stripe; and he was charged as Private King for using a vehicle without permission. Tony Martyn, the Prosecuting Officer, argued that this was not a punishment and that the C.O. could hand out and take away an unpaid stripe at will and need give no reason. I then took the unprecedented step of calling the Colonel as a witness for the Defence. Tony tried to block this, but the President of the Court said that it was legal and adjourned the Court until the morrow.

My first question to the C.O. was "Before the circumstances which resulted in this Court Martial, was the defendant an unpaid Lance Corporal?". "Yes". "Was he then allowed to go into the Corporal's Mess?" "Yes". "Is he now allowed there?" "No". "Was he on the roll of Unpaid Lance Corporals in which the names rise, as vacancies occur, until the unpaid Lance Corporals become Paid Lance Corporals?" "Yes". "Has he been struck off that list?" "Yes". "Was he marched into your office dressed as a Lance Corporal, and charged with an offence?" "Yes". I then turned to the Court and pointed out that Private King had suffered several forms of punishment as a result of losing his stripe and had lost it after being charged with a military offence. The Court was closed for consideration of the evidence, and on return ruled that he had already been punished and could not be re-tried for the same offence. Both defendants were hence unpunished. Nobby Clark was very generous afterwards and bore me no grudge. I doubt if there are many cases where the Commanding Officer of a Battalion is called as a witness for the Defence!

Having triumphed with my first attempt as a defending officer, I was much sought-after by those remanded for trial by Court Martial and never lost a case in Malta. Eventually I was declared 'unavailable' unless the accused was being prosecuted by the Judge Advocate's Department and was entitled to a barrister. I still got them off and though ribbed by my brother officers, was never under hostile pressure from the subsequent C.O.s or Adjutants. Later on some of the Regiment's underworld repaid their debt to me when I was asked to unravel some serious skulduggery. Later still, after my eventual return to England, I enrolled at Gray's Inn because I felt that a leg wound which I subsequently suffered would jeopardise my military future after the war and that I might have a reasonable chance of success at the Bar. Fortunately, it proved unnecessary.

During this period of battle stations but no war, Phoebe remained at Casa Tre, but slept the odd night with the Allfreys at St Paul Ta Tarja near Naxxar (pronounced Nashar). Their house, apart from overlooking a reservoir, had a wonderful view right across the plain of Mosta whose church had the second largest unsupported dome in the world, and one could see the high ground on which stood the ancient capital of Citta Vechia, also called Medina.

Whilst communications with the U.K. were still open, Tony Martyn's wife Jean invited her younger sister Mary Laird to come out and stay with them. Mike Read was rather lost in the mess after I got married, because John Morton had been left in Jerusalem, Mike Grove, Mike Archer and Paul Crook had gone home with many others to stiffen up and train the Territorial Army and the new recruits pouring in to bring Territorial and Regular battalions up to strength. It soon became a routine that Mike would come and have Sunday lunch with us and after a while we used to ask Mary Laird to make up the foursome. After a few months they got engaged and for their wedding Phoebe and I acted as the parents of the bridegroom, gave a champagne lunch for Mike and the ushers, and I was his best man. On the evening before the wedding a large party of bachelors took him round the drinking haunts of Valletta. At a late stage of the evening Willie Tuffill, who had been my company commander at Tamra and was currently acting Adjutant said "Letsh ring up ole Jack Coe" (our quartermaster) "and tell him ish garash ish on fire". We duly crowded round a telephone box where he delivered his garbled, but quite clear message – that we were all rather plastered and that there was no fire. We all felt rather crestfallen, as people in that state do, and I brightened the party by suggesting that we ring Dick Allfrey, charming but more gullible than the wily old quartermaster, and tell him that the reservoir near his house was in danger of bursting. "But let me do it" I said "and I'll put on a Maltese accent." "Meester Allfrey?" I said "Zee dam by your house is cracking and you must all move out before you are flodded."

The top wall of the reservoir was at least fifty yards below Dick's house and I didn't think he would swallow it. However, I had the feeling he was a person who might; so within a minute of putting the 'phone down I rang him back to tell him it was just a hoax. He said very curtly "I've heard about the dam" and slammed the 'phone down. We all felt we had been foiled again and had one final drink before dispersing to our beds.

The following morning I arrived in barracks to find chaos in the Orderly Room area. Dick had got everyone up and dressed the night before, including his baby son and nanny, and had driven down to spend the night with friends who had not been best pleased to have unwanted guests at eleven o'clock at night. He was demanding to see the Colonel. Willie Tuffill, acting as Adjutant was occupying the outer office and insisting that the Colonel wasn't in. The real Adjutant, Tony Martyn was, of course, acting as 'Father of the Bride' and was going to give Mary away. Their house was in the usual turmoil on such occasions. Willie, never letting on that he was one of the guilty idiots, managed to stall Dick with the assurance that an enquiry was in hand and that dire punishment would be meted out.

Eventually I was despatched with an enormous bunch of flowers to crawl, to eat humble pie and not to say that I thought he was an absolute idiot to think that water would run up the hill at his house. In my own defence, I did murmur that I did not think he had believed my story, which was true, and that when I rang up to tell him we were joking I had thought he was just angry when he slammed the 'phone down, also true. In fact he had been too busy packing things up and just thought it was someone else ringing up to warn him of the impending disaster.

It took a lot of persuasion. He wanted the whole wedding cancelled because Mike Read, the bridegroom, was also one of the villains. Sense eventually prevailed, but only by a whisker, and the wedding went off without a hitch. Remembering what had happened when Mike was my best man, I had our car followed by another in case of puncture or breakdown. Within forty eight hours, restoration of our relations with the Allfreys was restored and the warmth which had previously existed between our families was cemented by future events.

The phoney war continued, although mid-week holidays ceased, but at weekends we still went on picnics and enjoyed a happy social life.

Around this time petrol for all private cars was suspended and most cars, including ours, were taken over for Army use and painted to look like the stone walls which lined every road in Malta. Because there were only two motorcycles in Malta they were not withdrawn and were allowed a small petrol ration. The smaller of the two belonged to our Maltese Liaison Officer, a Captain Parnis-England. In spite of his name he was very Latin and very wealthy. When he discovered there was another, better motorcycle on the island, he bid for it and got it, and I managed to get in the first offer for his. Being mobile made a great difference to our lives and although my motorcycle only had a 150 cc engine, I soon designed and made a well sprung rear seat cut from an old mattress and mounted it on the small luggage carrier. Phoebe and I became the only people on the island below the rank of Lieutenant-Colonel to be power driven on all social occasions except for Parnis-England.

Chapter VI

Italy takes the Plunge

When Italy finally decided that the Axis would beat the Allies and proudly entered the war on 11th June 1940, she celebrated by a fairly heavy bombing raid on Malta. She had probably gleaned sufficient information from Italian sympathisers that we had only three outdated Gladiator fighters to oppose her bombers, and attacked in formation at an altitude that even these could not reach in the time available between the first radar warning of their approach and their arrival over the Grand Harbour. A straight line down the middle of the Grand Harbour passes between Marsa township and the Marsa sports ground, with the Marsa Club at its centre, and thence through Luqa aerodrome.

By this time we had regretfully abandoned the wonderful cricket, polo and rugby ground, together with a very pleasant golf course and transferred this possible landing area into a death trap covered by mass cross fire from automatic weapons and old lorries and every other form of junk ironmongery lay everywhere to impede progress of gliders. At Colonel Nobby's insistence, I had one man in a vertical round hole covered by a 40 gallon drum with an anti-tank rifle and incendiary bullets. The man had to be a volunteer and we all wished him luck and shook his hand before the first air raid. In fact, short of a direct hit he was in the safest place for miles, a deep but small hole and sufficient head cover to protect him from the shower of jagged shrapnel which descended upon us from the many Anti-Aircraft guns. After a few near misses on some of our larger and open posts, everyone was volunteering to change places with him.

✧

A few days before this first air raid on 11th June 1940, Phoebe went into the King George V Hospital, Valletta when Christopher began his first violent movements. I was naturally worried that she had to move into a potential target area and was relieved when I heard on 12th June that she had gone back to the Allfreys for the night.

All through the first breakfast-time air raid on 13th June I was thanking God that Phoebe was safe at St Paul Ta Tarja. The Marsa was bombed and one man was killed. It was my first experience of being bombed from the air and I found it extremely frightening. It was frustrating to have to crouch in a slit trench and to be able to do nothing more positive than to hope and pray. When the dust settled, the telephone rang at my headquarters, and Harold Scott, who was commanding Headquarter Company said "congratulations you lucky man, you're the father of a bouncing son."

Later on that day, I got permission to slip into Valletta to see her. Although Phoebe was less than two miles away, we had, of course, been standing to in our battle positions, ready to repel an air invasion and I could not just wander off! She had been rushed into hospital by Bridget Allfrey during the night and gave birth to Christopher shortly before the raid. Within a very short time they were both carried into a rock cave beside the hospital which had been enlarged into a bomb-proof shelter. Water was streaming down the roughly hewn, porous sandstone walls. She was on an army stretcher, covered with a brown army blanket, with Christopher by her side.

She looked up at me pleadingly and said "please, please darling somehow get me out of here." At that moment I was so touched that I could have moved mountains. I went straight up to the hospital which had been part taken over by the Army and demanded to see the Commandant, who was a full Colonel in the Royal Army Medical Corps. He received me with great understanding and courtesy, and when I told him that the hospital should be moved out of what was obviously a target area at once, instead of telling me to get out replied very quietly "and where to?" I had not thought about this, but my Guardian Angel replied for me "to Boschetto of course, it's miles from any target area and a lovely cool spot for a hospital in summer." Within 24 hours they were all there or had been dispersed to other suitable sites away from target areas.

Malta was to endure over 3,000 air raids, and during the most prolonged session, lasting for a week in October 1942, a total of over 1,400 bombers dropped their bombs into a target area not much bigger than that which bounds Hyde Park and St James's Park.

Because the Italian bombers attacked from such high altitude their bombing was extremely inaccurate and although they were obviously aiming at the Grand Harbour and Luqa airfield, bombs were liable to fall half a mile wide in any direction. Civilian buildings fell victims to many direct hits, and as the Maltese houses are built of the sandstone of which the island consists, the blocks, usually around eighteen inches by twelve inches, needed two men to life each one away. A heart-breaking task when it was known that someone was alive beneath the rubble. Another snag was that the upper floors were made of metal girders with flat stone flags, around 3" deep, laid end to end with ends sharing the top of each girder.

Blast effect often caused these blocks to jump up and land diagonally, to fall through between girders and bombard the floors below.

When Phoebe was fit to leave the temporary hospital at Boschetto, she moved in with the Allfreys on a semi-permanent basis, and she, Bridget Allfrey and Daphne Scott all shared a large bedroom like a small school dormitory. We three husbands were extremely relieved that our wives were as safe as was possible. Any living in the Sliema and Valletta areas were always at risk from the overs or unders of a stick of bombs.

Phoebe has reminded me that they all got quite used to going through Sliema and catching a ferry across to Valletta for shopping. They all kept their fingers crossed as the so-called ferries, which were no more than the Maltese version of a gondola, were pretty slow, and because the Sliema embarkation point was very near the Manoel Island submarine base, it was unhealthy to be caught in one during an air raid.

As time wore on we got more and more used to doing whatever we wanted to do during air raids and even played rugger during alerts until we heard the A.A. guns open up. Sometimes play could not be resumed until we had all formed a line abreast and walked the length of the ground, picking up all the bits of sharp edged shrapnel which had rained down upon us. During much of the period when the Italians were the sole enemies over our air-space, our A.A. Artillery still had the support of only three fighters. These Gloster Gladiators were outdated bi-planes very little more advanced than the fighters operating at the end of World War I. They quickly became known as Faith, Hope and Charity. We knew the pilots personally from social contacts in the pre-war days and felt very integrated with their varying fortunes. They could never climb high enough to take on enemy fighter cover and were slower than the bombers. They did, however, find that if they climbed high enough to get above the bombers without getting shot down by the enemy fighters, they could dive down and attack them. By keeping one very good eye on their mirror, they could, if set upon by the enemy fighters, judge their moment to do a tight turn which the faster enemy fighters could not possibly match and then get the hell out of it. I remember seeing one Gladiator dive into a formation of bombers and, seemingly floating motionless, have a go at no less than three of them. After a while the news spread like wildfire that a new Gladiator had been found in a packing case at Kalafrana or Hal Far. This 25 per cent increase was most welcome. I never saw all four in the air together. Perhaps we always left one in reserve.

In the course of time a small number of elderly Hurricanes arrived and the Italians began to show more respect towards our air defences. It was not until the Luftwaffe took a hand in January 1941 that we realised how weak our air defences really were, emphasised by the increasing shortage of

A.A. shells as more and more shipping was sunk. Much has been written about the Malta saga, so I will confine my writing mainly to first-hand accounts of events which affected me, my family or close friends. The Luftwaffe was drawn into the air battle for Malta when the Germans realised that too much use was being made of Malta's dockyards for the repair of warships, climaxed by the arrival of H.M.S. Penelope.

By this time we had become so blase about air raids that when on 24 hours leave we would take our drinks on to the roof of the Union Club in Valletta and watch the bombing. Because the Luftwaffe was far more accurate than its Italian allies, the target areas became more lethal and risk to roof watchers was minimised. Later I will inform readers what it was like to be in the heart of the main target area.

A French regiment, Les 2 Regiment de Tirailleurs Algerienes, consisting of three battalions of Infantry limped into the Grand Harbour after an unfortunate collision at night and in fog with the bows of one of the two ships carrying them badly crushed. The bows had buckled into folds and split open, so that one could see a crushed body in each fold. Because of my familiarity with their language I was appointed liaison officer, and was able to arrange the supply of their most important requirements. The siege had not yet started and there was no shortage of food or drink or dockyard expertise. I ended up as an 'Officer Honoraire des 2 Tirailleurs Algerienes', and was presented with an official document and a gilt and nickel badge which all members of the Regiment wore on their left breasts where British Generals wear their Orders of Chivalry. I took mine off as soon as they sailed, but it was quite fun to wear it later in Cairo, where a motley crowd of officers from Tientsin to Timbuctoo were displaying everything under the sun on their uniforms.

✧

Our ability to requisition the Marsa Club which was in the middle of our area as our Officers Mess was one of those strokes of luck that doesn't happen often. Rather than risk losing the entire cellar stocks to the fortunes of war, the club offered to sell them to us and we made no difficulties. As imported drinks became scarcer, we really appreciated our good fortune, but it became increasingly expensive to refresh ourselves as modest wines gave way to more expensive vintages and, in due course, champagne went the same way. Eventually we were down to liqueurs and became experts, if not connoisseurs, at mixing extremely palatable liqueur cocktails. Crème de Menthe, so much despised as a tart's drink and known by them as 'Sticky Greens" were quite acceptable when frappé with Crème de Cacao and ice.

Once the Italians had digested the fact that we had some Hurricane fighters, air raids diminished and hence the need for Phoebe, Christopher and Polly his nurse to impose any longer on the kindness and warmth of the Allfreys. For a while we shared a house, on a fifty/fifty basis, with Desmond and Joan Wakeley in Sliema; but some distance from the Manoel Island base. Whilst there I was posted as Senior Staff Officer to be commander of a small composite force which was to be established in Gozo to counter a possible invasion of that island by the Italians. Landing craft had been photographed in Sicily. As this was for an indefinite period, it seemed a good opportunity for my family to move there away from all bombing unless Gozo really was attacked. Gozo was very picturesque and much more unspoilt than Malta. The architecture of the churches and larger buildings was similar, but the coast was broken by a number of beautiful little bays and creeks, some of which could only be reached by boat.

I was not allowed to live out, but had the odd afternoon free when we could sail our 12 foot International dinghy to picnic on the uninhabited island of Comino, which lies between Gozo and Malta. Two events stand out in our minds. Wearing only bathing dress and shorts, we visited an old ruined fort and explored the semi-dark interior. When we left and saw ourselves in the sunlight we discovered that we were both black with fleas from above both knees to our toes. We tore down the hill, screaming, shouting and laughing, and into the sea, rubbed them off with our hands and could see them all around us like a form of scum. The second, and more pleasant experience, was sailing into a tall narrow cave with plenty of clearance above the mast until the lack of breeze brought us gliding to a ghostly halt deep within its silent and dark interior.

This little period of semi-paradise was ended when I was posted to St Paul's Bay as Chief Instructor of the Command Tactical School. There was little point in Phoebe returning to the bombing inferno of the Valletta/Sliema area, so she, Christopher and Polly remained in Gozo for the time being whilst I looked around for somewhere suitable to live, St Paul's Bay being out of the main target area. I was lucky enough to find a house just across the bay from the school and as there was a small wooden jetty near both our house and the School, I was able to sail to work each morning in our dinghy once my family was safely installed.

The Commandant of the School, George Newall, had served his first twelve years in my regiment, and being a bright up and coming officer had received accelerated promotion into the Cheshire Regiment and we had tremendous rapport. He was always impeccably dressed and wore a monocle which was always in position. Some people suggest that he even slept with it. He was, however, not much of a small boat sailor. One day we asked him to dinner and to spend the night with us. We duly sailed across, he with a small suitcase with his night things, and we took the opportunity of first sailing along the bay to have a closer look at the statue of St Paul which stands above the spot where the Saint was washed ashore during his voyage through the Mediterranean to spread the Gospel.

The following morning we duly embarked in my dinghy and made a fast trip across the bay to the jetty which was only fifty yards from the School. I was not holding on as I was planning to drift a few yards down to make fast. George duly stepped on to the gunwale, allowed the dinghy to shoot outwards, and promptly fell into the water. He was never quite submerged and was still smiling as he swam, stick in hand, fore and aft hat on head, and monocle firmly screwed into eye back to the jetty. I just couldn't believe it.

Our life at St Paul's Bay, following on as it did from Gozo, was the extension of an oasis of peace in a desert of fear and danger. At weekends we used to hire a flat-cart and pony and go for picnics with Polly, Christopher and a new acquisition, Jane, an adorable little Maltese terrier puppy. These terriers are like tiny little white poodles. We just kept her clipped in the summer and fluffy in the winter. Christopher adored her. A Maltese flat-cart was rather like a gate screwed down onto a wooden axle with normal wooden cart wheels. A plank or two was added to prevent one from falling through, and one could sit with one's feet dangling down, or with one's knees up or on top of a whole pile of crates which could so easily be accommodated on the flat upper surface and lashed down with ropes between the gaps. At different times we had used all three systems, the last for our eventual move back to Sliema.

Some of our picnics were up winding narrow lanes to hilltops crowned with little clusters of trees standing beside some of the rare patches of grass, so prized in Malta's countryside. Jane was soon joined by a tame half-grown rabbit which Polly had somehow acquired. He soon became quite humanised, fearless and house-trained. Because Jane had never learned to hunt and George, named after my boss, had never learned to run away, he used to chase her all over the house. Surely this emphasises the importance of the military quality of high morale, which George undoubtedly had.

Looking back on those days, I have a strong feeling that Nobby Clark was being kind to me. As a young captain he had got me some interesting jobs outside the battalion, but whenever the Regiment was liable to fight, he gave me command of a company; at the outbreak of war, on the entry of the Italians, and now in the late Autumn of 1941, the command of 'A' Company once more, since our brigade was earmarked to carry out a landing behind Rommel's lines in North Africa.

Another move was required and I looked for a house in the Sliema area but on the North East side, as far as possible from the Grand Harbour and Luqa airfield. I found one at Sacred Heart Avenue in St Julians, known as 'Snob's Alley' because of the number of senior officers who lived in it. The rental for the house was double the norm because it had a concrete air-raid

"...a house just across the bay from the school ... the statue of St Paul which stands above the spot where the Saint was washed ashore"

shelter in the basement. It was a large semi-detached house with a road running down to the shore on its open side. The other half of the 'semi' was occupied by Mike and Mary Read. Theirs was 'Juba' and ours 'Tana', both named after African lakes. There was a hole in the wall between the two cellars which enabled them to share our shelter.

This set-up seemed fairly suitable since during our period in Gozo the Luftwaffe produced a completely different situation from that under the Italian high level attack. They went for military targets, and their near misses were measured in a few hundred yards rather than a mile or two. We once went to the Union Club in Valletta whilst H.M. Illustrious was being bombed. The towns of Senglea and Vittoriosa were decimated, but we, less than a mile away, took our drinks up on to the roof and had a sad, but grandstand, view.

The eventual move was helped by John Symons who commanded a Gunner regiment and lent us a 3 ton lorry to move our furniture and cases of belongings. The day before the move there was a terrible gale and our dinghy broke away from her moorings and was blown inland to the head of the bay. I stripped and put on some bathing shorts and ran down to save her from being broken up by the waves which were breaking onto the shelving shore. I eventually manhandled her, after a real struggle, to a stone wall nearer our house and further out than the breakers, and made her fast to a ring. By the time I got back to the house, I was so numb with cold that neither hot drinks nor endless blankets could thaw me out for over an hour.

Next day I led the flat-cart which carried the human cargo of 3 civilians, who could not be seen in the Army vehicle, in 200 yard bounds, on the motor bike. Although I was well wrapped up with jerseys and a heavy Melton overcoat, it did no good to the chill I had sustained the previous evening, and I had to go straight to bed in our new house under orders from our Medical Officer.

Christmas 1941 was fairly jovial and being back amongst our many friends there were the usual parties. We still got one 24 hour leave each week and used to try and co-ordinate with our friends so that, where possible, we men returned on the same day. Back in the Mess we had been enriched by a trickle of high quality wartime officers. Roy Cooke had played rugby for the Barbarians, Surrey and Richmond; and also taught me how to eat glass, although it was some time before I plucked up courage to do it; John Browne who was in my House at Oundle and had joined my family for a sailing holiday one summer; Jimmy James who later became the senior Civil Servant administering the Metropolitan Police; Philip Mackie a young actor who later became a successful author and playwright, to mention but a few.

Chapter VII

The Luftwaffe turns on the heat

The year 1942 opened with renewed attention from the Luftwaffe, and our twin Lewis Gun posts on Luqa were daily under attack. My Company Headquarters, which was a hut in a quarry just clear of the airfield, was blown away, fortunately when I was going round my posts, and a new one was prepared, cut horizontally into the rock-face so that it could take a direct hit above it. Sandstone is fairly soft and can be worked even with a saw until it has weathered for a while. Tunnelling was not too difficult and thus saved countless lives throughout Malta. It was ironic that once installed in a really safe hidey hole, I felt it my duty to leave it just when we needed each other, to walk round my open posts and make for the nearest when the dust began to fly.

Being stationed in the midst of R.A.F. territory, I inevitably got to know quite a few of their officers, and before leaving Malta I had probably used their mess longer than any of them. One of them organised flying lessons for me in a Miles Magister trainer. I was not doing too badly with take offs, landing, and climbing stalls, but in the course of two weeks both the remaining Magisters were destroyed by bombs and I was left with my hunger for flying whetted but unfulfilled. I sometimes invited some of the pilots to drinks at Sacred Heart Avenue when I was on a twenty four hour leave. I remember Adrian Warburton as a fresh faced Pilot Officer when he arrived in Malta. He became a legend as a Photographic Reconnaissance ace. By 1943 he had risen to become a Wing Commander with two DSOs and three DFCs, and his face, deeply etched with character lines from endless hours of flying, looked the face of a man ten years older and fitted his rank. He was eventually reported missing whilst on a mission over Southern Europe. His parents lived at West Mersea only a few hundred yards from mine. I also met Air Vice Marshal Hugh Pughe Lloyd who was later most kind and helpful to me in Cairo. Whilst stationed at Luqa, four incidents stand out more than any others in my memory. One afternoon, during an air-raid when we were manning all our posts, we spotted a twin-engined bomber heading for us with a fighter on its tail. Their speed and rooftop altitude made identification difficult and we at first assumed that it was a German bomber being pursued by one of our fighters. We were just preparing to engage it with our ten pairs of Lewis Guns when the pilot of the bomber did one of the tightest turns I have ever seen from such an aircraft. The fighter overshot it and we saw the R.A.F. roundels on the wings of the bomber and the Luftwaffe crosses on the fighter. It was a Maryland light bomber, converted to photographic reconnaissance, being chased in by an ME 199 which continued its pursuit as the pilot of the Maryland weaved and evaded, then made the mistake of turning back towards the sea, where he lost all his A.A. protection and was shot down. We saw one parachutist float down, but knew that there was a crew of two. It was Arnold Potter who was the observer bailing out with valuable photographs of the Italian fleet. Only a few months earlier we had met him having a few days leave near St Paul's Bay, and had kept up with him, and had asked him to be a godfather to another bambino now on the way. We later heard the whole story of how his gallant pilot had played for time, whilst he got all his valuable photographs into waterproof covering, before safely delivering him into the sea – and then died with his plane,which by then, had been badly shot up. Gillie Potter, as he was known, survived the war and went back to Wellington to continue teaching mathematics.

As I have earlier pointed out we were on a direct line with the length of the Grand Harbour and got all its overs as well as the bombs intended for parked aircraft round the outskirts of Luqa airfield, which, of course, is where my posts were sited. We had every kind of experience. One day an enormous 2,000 pounder landed very near my own private gunpit and failed to explode. Had it been a time-bomb it would have been necessary to evacuate a very large area, because such brutes were designed to make, and did make, the most enormous craters. Acting on impulse I ran forward to it and pressed my ear hard against it to hear if it was ticking. It was silent. Then I began to think. "If it goes off now" I reasoned "I will feel nothing and there will be nothing of me to feel with, but the moment I leave it and get a few yards away, if I am not killed by blast I could have a complete leg or shoulder blown off or even the lower half of my body". It was a terrible thought, and for a few moments the brute became my friend and I found great difficulty in leaving it. Commonsense prevailed in the end and I tiptoed away for about thirty feet and then sprinted like mad for the safety of my gunpit and telephoned for a bomb disposal party. I have a picture of my entire company sitting in one of these huge craters, photographed on a sunny afternoon when the lunchtime raid was safely over and there would normally be around three hours to the tea-time one.

A week or two later, one of our own fighter pilots who had been badly shot up and could not lower his undercarriage, decided to do a belly landing on the grass quite near my command/observation/gun/post, which

Gigantic bomb crater near one of our beach-posts

"*I have a picture of my entire company sitting in one of these huge craters*"

was situated just above my underground headquarters. I ran forward towards it as it skidded to a halt and was joined by Corporal Greenyer, who commanded the nearby section manning twin Lewis Guns. Before we reached it flames had begun to engulf it and when we finally arrived it was an inferno. The pilot seemed to have his legs trapped and was struggling to get out. We mounted the wings, one each side and managed to get the canopy open, grabbed hold of his shoulders and pulled with all our strength. He never spoke but moved his torso forward and back a few times. We could not free him and were eventually driven back by the heat. I believe that he must have been unconscious from the heat and after a few seconds even dead. The fire truck then arrived with a crew, in asbestos clothing, who sprayed the pilot and plane with foam. When finally extricated by them, the pilot was found dead. Apart from a few singes, Corporal Greenyer and I were unscathed and I will never know how much real burning I would have been able to endure if the trucks had not taken over and we had found ourselves able to move him. I have since wondered if his harness was still fastened, since it would have been until after the crash. Corporal Greenyer and I never forgot those moments when his body was still rocking to and fro even after being covered with foam. We both prayed that if he was alive, that he was at least unconscious. Corporal Greenyer was later killed on the Rhine. I met him quite by chance on a platform at Waterloo Station whilst I was at the Staff College, Camberley early in 1945. He was then on his way back to his Unit in Germany as a Company Sergeant Major and wearing the ribbons of the Distinguished Conduct Medal and the Military Medal, a cheerful and gallant warrior if ever there was one.

I nearly preceded him to the Great Club within a few hundred yards of that crashed aircraft about five weeks later. After the destruction of my headquarters hut and in an effort to maximise my survival chances, I sited a new private post just above my office. It was on a jutting out spur of the quarry with the airfield to the East and vertical quarry faces to the West, North and South. It was a modern example of those castles on the Rhine which can only be attacked from the rear and looks down at the enemy on the other three sides. I had thus decreased the chance of a near miss by three to one – I thought – as on three sides any bombs would fall harmlessly down into the quarry. The bottom sandbags were about a foot from the lip of the quarry.

In February the bombing continued to intensify. The Luftwaffe had the Island under tight siege to restrict its use as a base from which to attack the ships supporting Rommel by our submarines and from our aircraft. Food was getting very short as their bombers not only attacked the convoys trying to supply us, but the individual ships alongside the quays of the

Grand Harbour. Civilians were given slightly more bulk in their rations than the Services, so that they would feel less hungry. We had more proteins, such as the occasional half tin of sardines and a bigger ration (half a tin) of bully beef and M & V (a horrible stew or carrots, beans, potatoes and bits of gristly meat). I have always been a fastidious eater and in spite of being hungry I hated M & V and would swap my ration of half a tin for a slice of bread and half an ounce of real butter. Bully and Spam were highly edible and I would in the course of a week go without two half tin rations of each and take one tin of each home on my 24 hour leave. Phoebe thought I had just scrounged them from the cookhouse.

One morning when I was manning my twin Lewis Guns with a Sergeant Parnell who had served with me since I first joined the Regiment, we spotted a formation of JU 88s carrying out a really low level shallow diving attack on us. From the moment they left the Grand Harbour my eyes were on the leader waiting for his bomb doors to open, but they never did, and he began to climb. Suddenly Parnell shouted "down Sir" and pulled me to the ground. I just caught a glimpse of a bomb coming straight for us, and in about two-tenths of a second it exploded against the Northern side of the quarry a few inches from the lip. Jane, was was having a week with me for her health and fresh air, was blown right round the inside of the circular pit and finished up on an open shelf let into the inside wall to retain oddments like binoculars and map cases, etc. We were dazed, cut and grazed and I suffered a burst left eardrum, which was found to have two tears across it. Two seconds later, as I was about to remark how incredibly lucky we were, an enormous piece of rock came flying in from the next bomb of the stick which had landed down in the quarry below us, like a Laurel and Hardy film. It picked my left lower ribs as its target and broke a couple. The two Lewis Guns, which were on a raised mounting with an all-round traverse, took the full force of the blast and were twisted round each other like two giraffes being amorous. Sergeant Parnell who had saved my life was unscathed.

The airfield's Advanced Dressing Station was tucked away in a nearby part of the quarry, and after handing over to my Second-in-Command, I went there to have my ribs strapped up and my left ear examined. I was naturally shaken by what had been almost a direct hit and felt I could do with a cup of coffee. Jane also needed a break and might have vanished in panic, so I put her on her usual travelling place, the petrol tank of my motorcycle between my knees, and rode home to St Julians for an unauthorised twenty minute coffee break. It was quite extraordinary to be sitting in a peaceful drawing room, about three miles away and twelve minutes later, with a cup of coffee in my hand. The doctor on duty in the ADS, and who strapped me up, was Captain Jack Kempster RAMC. He often played bridge in the evenings at our Mess in the old Marsa Club which was over a quarter of a mile off the deadly line of the Grand Harbour/Luqa. A few years ago we bumped into him at the Royal Lymington Yacht Club, where we are members, and he had called in on a passage to Spain. He came to our house and was most knowledgeable and helpful about some of our shrubs. He amused himself by delivering people's yachts to other countries. Tragically he was later drowned in the Bay of Biscay in a moderately big sea. His only crew was a youth in his late teens who shouted that the tea was ready, and receiving no reply, discovered that the cockpit was empty. I understand that he had a pretty gruelling time all on his own until being spotted and someone being put aboard to help him into port.

On Saturday 14th March to 6.00 pm on Sunday 15th March I was taking my 24 hours leave at Sacred Heart Avenue. Christopher heard my motorcycle coming because Phoebe always told him to listen for it, and because Parnis-England lived nowhere near us, he had never seen another. He was ready to run down the steps to greet me and I was early enough to see something of him before he went to bed.

We had a typical siege meal that evening, which Phoebe had cooked as appetisingly as possible, given the ingredients she had available. We had parted with Guisseppa when we left Casa Tre and Phoebe had been the head cook ever since. We had an early night as Michael was now five months on the way. When I was on leave I thought it prudent not to go down to our shelter, which Phoebe, Polly and Christopher normally did, because I felt that I dare not get the shelter habit. In any case I did not remember any bombing in our area whilst I was at home. Around seven o'clock on Sunday morning the sirens went and distant sounds of bombing could later be heard, but we took no notice until a stick of bombs started coming down very near us and finished beyond us. The glass of the windows blew in and I jokingly shook the sheet and counterpane of my twin bed to project the fragments onto the floor, and said "weren't we lucky, now let's try and get some more sleep." Phoebe said "I think the house has been hit". I replied "nonsense" and got out of bed and walked to the door. When I opened it there was no house. We were in the corner room of the first floor and no other part of the house was standing. There was a mound of stone blocks over where the shelter was and I called back "don't worry darling, the shelter was built for that, we'll soon get them out."

We could not get down until someone produced a long ladder, by which time we had flung on some clothes. Phoebe was taken to Brigadier Ivan De la Bere's house which was only two houses away down Sacred Heart Avenue, and I set to work organising people to lift the heavy square sandstone blocks away from the shelter. Taking two men to lift each block, it was nearly eleven o'clock before we got to the roof of the shelter. For a

*"Christopher heard my motorcycle coming because Phoebe
always told him to listen for it"*

few moments I was elated and then began to wonder when I saw a huge crack in the roof. When the last stone was pulled clear and I was able to look down through the crack, I saw Polly sitting, crouched protectively forward, on a chair in one corner with Christopher peacefully cradled in her arms. They were both dead, and from their positions appeared to have died instantly from the concussive effect of blast. I walked down to the de la Beres', but did not have to tell Phoebe anything. She just looked at my face and with a choking sob ran into my arms.

By this time arrangements had already been made for us to stay with the Governor at St Anton Palace, whatever the outcome of our rescue efforts. Because we lived opposite Sacred Heart Convent, run by a medical Order of nuns, which gave our road its name, the bodies of Christopher and Polly were taken there, firstly to the Casualty Theatre and then to the Chapel. Someone drove us to the Dobbies at St Anton where Lady Dobbie was warm, welcoming and tactful. Mike and Mary Read, who often used the shelter when Mike was on leave, were spared, although when the bombs got nearer they leapt out of bed and were on their way down to the shelter when it was hit. Life at St Anton Palace was not all a bed of roses. Although the Dobbies were kind and thoughtful, they were strict Plymouth Brethren and disapproved of many of the pleasant things in life. On the first evening, having been told to ring for anything I required, I rang and asked for a small whisky. Most hosts would have seen that I had had several already, but I was told that sherry would be served in the drawing room at seven-thirty. the A.D.C., who had taken over from Peter Buckle, did his best to cheer us up but he had an uphill task. Phoebe was, very rightly, determined to do everything in her power to avoid losing Michael, already quickened and only four months from birth.

One of the Dobbies practices was to take no cover but to rely upon the Lord to preserve them. We should have gained high marks for having adopted the same system ourselves in Sacred Heart Avenue, but I could not understand why the Lord should have selected Polly and Christopher, for whose safety I had prayed every night, to the exclusion of ever praying for myself or Phoebe. I did not believe that God had selected Christopher but that such matters were chances run by everyone under the Laws of Nature. The Padre assured me that God had selected Christopher because he loved him so much, but it seemed to me if he was in such detailed control, why had he allowed him to come to our evil world at all, even for 21 months to be killed by a bomb; it seemed a funny way of loving.

✧

General Dobbie might have felt differently if his house had had a direct hit. Much time was devoted to prayers and he spent too much time (I thought) in St Anton Palace and not enough at his Headquarters as Commander-in-Chief. He once asked God during prayers to ensure that a convoy, which was struggling to reach us, but still one day's steaming from us, would arrive safely and lift the siege. I felt that he was the one person who should have been co-ordinating the efforts of the various organisations which were necessary to make the complete combined operation a success, and guiding them to that end. In the event, there was a mix up in the handover of air cover to our aircraft from those operating from North Africa, which left the convoy unprotected for a vital period, during which the Luftwaffe wrought havoc with them. Because the Grand Harbour was already fairly full of ships, some were diverted to Marsa Scirocco Bay, but the heave A.A. Batteries needed to protect them there had not been sited round the bay, hence they took more stick after anchoring. The few ships which limped into the Grand Harbour lay unloaded for some time because the Maltese dockers refused to unload them. British troops eventually did the job. But who but the Governor should have foreseen this civilian problem and ensured that these ships were unloaded at once and not later? I was not a Dobbie fan, and was delighted to hear later that Lady Dobbie had abandoned his principles when a stick of bombs rained down near St Anton Palace whilst she was graciously dispensing tea in the guardroom. She was last in a mad rush to get under the guardroom table, and her rear end was not properly under cover. I was later told that an edict had been issued after this incident that in future it was to be ladies first under the table!

We often hear of clairvoyants and some people are sceptical about them. Phoebe, every now and then, dreams something which then takes place the next day. Only last week she dreamed about someone we had not seen for some time and bumped into her in the High Street of Lymington on the following morning. A few days before the bombing of 'Tana' the submariners who lived in a small Mess near us asked Phoebe if she would like to swap our single beds for a large double bed, and she agreed wholeheartedly. On the night of Saturday 14th March she dreamed that she had met them and told them that there was now no point in swapping beds.

✧

The aching sorrow occasioned by Christopher's funeral was only superseded by the earlier visit to the little Chapel in Sacred Heart Convent, just across the road from 'Tana', where he lay in peace in a tiny coffin. He was unmarked except for a small graze on his forehead which had a small bandage round it. Ultimately left alone with him, it was the first time I allowed myself to break down and sob. An instinct told Phoebe that if she came with me, the expression of her anguish would result in the loss of Michael, and this I fully understood. It was eventually decided that Phoebe should be flown to Alexandria, where she had an aunt who lived in very luxurious surroundings. The necessary exchanges of letters took quite a time, as most mail came and went by submarines.

After around a week we visited the ruins of our home and found a few items worth saving. Amongst them was the photograph album of our married life to date, starting with our wedding and short honeymoon, and including pictures of Paris, Rome and Syracuse, which were all part of it. The album had been picked out from the fallen masonry, but being of the padded variety, and well made, the pictures within were mostly unscathed. We still have it in a drawer of Phoebe's desk.

Time hung heavily upon us at St Anton Palace until the night arrived when I was lent an Army car to drive her to Luqa for a night flight to Egypt. The Wellington bomber was empty except for the crew and two pregnant Nursing Sisters. They sat in a circle on wooden crates. After we had bid a sad farewell and she had climbed in, I remembered that I had a light novel in the car and ran back for it. The Wellington taxied away to the far end of the runway and I jumped into the car and drove along on the grass and jumped out as it slowly turned at the far end. I ran to the rear turret and the tail gunner rotated it and put out his hand for the book when he saw that I was holding something up.

I stood dead behind the turret as the pilot revved up his engines, to protect me from the slip-stream as she slowly began to roll. I knew that this was the beginning of another indefinite separation, the first since our marriage. I had not realised that great flames shoot out of the engines on full thrust at night and genuinely thought that the one on the port side to which I had moved, was on fire. Memories of the last fire in which I had been involved came flooding back to me and I began to run like a fiend. The Wellington soon gained speed and climbed up into the darkness with the flames getting smaller as the slip-stream dowsed them and I stopped running, blessed my luck for having been completely alone and felt a complete Charley.

When I got back to St Anton I found that Phoebe had left a touching little note under my pillow. Next morning I thanked my hosts for their hospitality and rejoined my Company which had been moved to the Marsa area.

Phoebe and I were able to carry out a steady but irregular correspondence as Aunt Ray, who lived at Bulkeley, Ramleh, just East of Alexandria had many contacts with the Navy through her family's cotton and shipping interests. I was spoiled with expensive cigarettes in those round sealed tins, State Express 555s, Players No.3 and Churchmans No.1 being then my favourites. I am now a non-smoker and have been for twenty years, but we did not then know the damage which tobacco can do to one's lungs and heart.

I learned in due course of Phoebe's adventures in the Wellington; bumpy clouds and the nausea provoked, the kind and thoughtful second pilot who handed them a tin hat as a basin to be passed around; of the officer in Cairo who would not listen to her explanation that she had left Malta with express permission to stay with her aunt, and said "Woman don't argue, do what you're told, report to the Continental Hotel from whence you will be evacuated to South Africa", and her decision to walk out and take a taxi to the station and a ticket for Alexandria. It was only five days before they caught up with her and she was then able to point out that she was too late in her pregnancy to be allowed on a ship.

Michael was, therefore, born in Alexandria in great luxury but not without a few hiccups. Her British doctor vanished without a word when Rommel's guns began to be heard in Alexandria, and a Greek doctor had to step in at the last moment to do the necessary.

✧

On returning to my Regiment I found that my Company had been moved from Luqa Aerodrome to the Marsa. My Company Headquarters was under the Grandstand of the race course, and we were being given a break from being in a red hot target area. I installed a Vickers 'K' gun in my private slit-trench outside the grandstand. It had been presented to me unofficially for my earlier efforts at Luqa on behalf of the R.A.F. It fired more bullets per second than two Lewis Guns, had much better sights and was normally used by 'side gunners' in big bombers. For the first two weeks after the tragedy of Sacred Heart Avenue I regretted that we were not in closer touch with the enemy and wanted to get one in my sights at close range.

On my third day after Phoebe's departure there was an air raid warning and I climbed into my extremely narrow personal slit-trench and dropped the K gun into its small mounting which I had hammered into the South facing parapet. A low flying ME 109 came in from the West, rather surprisingly, and was engaged by our Bofors and I saw a bit fly off it and opened up myself at about 200 yards range. Drum Major Watts, who had been passing by when the sirens went, had joined me in my trench. At almost the same moment the pilot had bailed out and he started to float down. "Go on, Sir" shouted the Drum Major. "He's already a prisoner" I replied with a smug feeling of self-righteousness, and realised that my judgement was beginning to return to normal.

Two or three days later it became my turn to have 24 hours leave. I had never before had to think where to go and felt completely lost. I remembered that I had a few water colours and a block of water colour paper. I decided to return to painting, which I had kept up intermittently since the Oundle days. It was a good way of passing the time. We were all in a comparatively low state of health and many of us were suffering from the local enteritis, known as 'Malta Dog'. I developed bacillary dysentery and then amoebic dysentery on top of it and was due to go to hospital. 'Bosun' Pulverman, who initially recruited me into the Regiment whilst at Sandhurst, had just taken over from Nobby Clark. He flattered me a bit by asking me to take sole charge of all the working parties who were going to build the fighter pens on Luqa airfield to protect the next batch of Spitfires which were soon expected.

I was still only a Lieutenant (Temporary Captain) and it was a daunting task because two other regiments were also supplying working parties, one from another brigade, and several parties would be in charge of officers senior to me. I felt that I should not turn it down in spite of my physical weakness plus the dysenteries. Bosum had beseeched me and promised me that as soon as the pens were built, I could go to hospital for a complete cure, followed by leave.

My job was to inspire the working parties to give everything they had in them to complete dozens of fighter pens before the arrival of the Spitfires which had already left the U.K. in an aircraft carrier. The men obviously wanted the fighters to be protected, but they were physically weak and tired after so long on inadequate rations. The original plan to use sandbags was soon abandoned as they ran short almost at once. We were reduced to using empty petrol tins, of which there was an almost inexhaustible supply. The tins, which had to have their tops cut off with tin openers or powerful pliers, were filled with earth and daubed with mud as a camouflage. They were 'in section' like a pyramid starting with a base of ten tins and finishing up with four. Their view from above would have looked like an open figure of six with the vertical line curved round to the right thus effectively closing the entrance from bomb fragments, providing the aircraft was tucked up into the circle of the curve. The planes would have to be manhandled in on a circular route.

I briefed all the officers on the first morning at daybreak on the exact size, shape, construction and location of each pen and left them to get on with them, walking round to see that they had got the hang of it and to try and gauge their effort. I detected no deliberate shirking, but I formed the impression that much more could have been achieved when we knocked off after eight hours work. Most pens had only the bottom ten tins in position and a varying number of the next layer of nine. On the next morning I told them all that they could fall out when they had completed a total of four layers which meant completing nine, plus eight and seven. They were all packing up by half past eleven and moving off. They had proved my point for me and had put on more tins in around half the time. I knew that I must retain their confidence and not go back on my word, but subsequently saw to it that they retained the incentive of going when they finished, before their eight hour stint expired; but had to get really stuck in to achieve this.

On that second day at around midday Brigadier Pearce Smith, our neighbouring commander, came to see how his men were getting on. They had all left by then and he approached me with great vigour and a face almost purple. His brigade were all terrified of him, but I had been given a free hand, and made him aware of this in firm but polite terms, pointing out my intention to go on squeezing more and more work out of them each day as they became more skilled at the job.

I heard no more from him, but I know that he must have had a go at my brigadier because as part of the citation for my M.B.E. was the sentence "His co-operation with the R.A.F. and the many senior officers with whom he had to deal was admirable"!. Apparently I had between 1,400 and 2,000 men under me at varying times, but no mention was made of the bombing. This may have been because during the months I served on Luqa airfield, I never once saw a senior officer there during a bombing raid.

I was in due course allowed to go into hospital and get proper treatment for my amoebic and bacillary dysenteries. By this time I was in a really bad way and had become incredibly sore. The tedium of hospital was lightened by the presence of one of Phoebe's thirty-two first cousins, Neil Campbell, a submariner similarly afflicted. We were not strictly bed patients as we spent the whole time running in and out of the ward anyway, and we spent almost the entire daylight hours playing bridge in our dressing-gowns. Playing constantly like this did an enormous amount of good to my bridge. I remember teaching someone who wanted to learn by sitting him behind me and explaining my play aloud even to my opponents as I played a hand, such as: "In order to make this hand I will have to take one finesse. I feel that George on the right here must have the King of Clubs from the calling, so I shall play my Queen from dummy through him and if he does not put the King on I shall let the Queen ride.".

Meanwhile, the operation to transfer a powerful force of Spitfires to Malta had begun, which was to be followed by the most exciting air battle that the World had ever seen. Not only was it exciting, but it lifted the hearts of the civilian population by removing the constant nagging fear which we had all endured and enabled our Air and Naval forces to resume really effective attacks on Rommel's supply lines to North Africa. Subsequent strategical studies have suggested that it superseded Stalingrad and the Battle of Britain as the turning point of World War II.

I wrote a Paper on this as an exercise whilst at the Joint Services Staff College in 1953. In those days, memories were much fresher and with no apology, I enclose a text of the paper with a few editorial editions to correct factual dates and details. I was lucky enough to be discharged from the hospital shortly before the decisive battles and was able to witness them from my new Headquarters at the Marsa. This article was the only descriptive account in the Memorial Book published on the 50th Anniversary of the lifting of the Siege in 1992.

THE DECISIVE AIR BATTLE FOR MALTA
10th May 1942

In April 1942 Malta was in a sorry plight. Several weeks of heavy bombing without a single day's respite had made the garrison weary, dispirited and somewhat 'bomb happy'. Rations had been cut to an extremely low level and the morale of both civilians and those members of the Services who did not have the fortune to be taking an active part in the Island's defence, was low.

Every ship of a convoy which had set out for Malta from Alexandria in March had been sunk, either en route or within twenty four hours of arrival in the Grand Harbour. As a result of this tragedy there was a dearth of every form of material which we of the garrison required to carry out effective and energetic defence. There were very few fighter aircraft and those that remained were worn out and slow. There was very little petrol to keep these few aircraft in the air and they were forbidden to tackle enemy fighters. This was bad for the morale of their pilots, and gave a corresponding fillip to their German opponents who sometimes indulged their Teutonic sense of humour by giving aerobatic displays to anger the helpless garrison. The powerful anti-aircraft defences, capable of putting up a barrage which must at that time have been second to none, were largely silent. Certain guns only of each site were manned and some sites were forbidden to fire at all unless they themselves were the target of air attack. Those guns which did remain in action were limited to a very small number of rounds per day.

A large number of the civilian population had lived a termite existence in rock caves for months, some children who had been born in these underground shelters had never seen the light of day. Many of the Maltese who only went to ground between air-raid warnings and the 'all clears' nevertheless spent periods as long as twenty four hours in their shelters. The Germans arranged these long alerts by sending reconnaissance planes and single nuisance raiders between the big raids, thus ensuring that there was a hostile aircraft on the radar screen right round the clock.

It was at this stage that the War Cabinet decided that an adequate force of up to date Spitfires, fitted with long range tanks, would be shipped in aircraft carriers from Gibraltar to a point West of Malta, from which they could fly to the Island. The part which the soldiers in Malta had to play to ensure the ultimate success of this operation was to construct more dispersal areas and sufficient splinter-proof pens. A vicious circle soon began. The fighters could not arrive until their pens were ready and it was almost impossible to build the pens with constant air interference, which only the arrival of the fighters could curb. We Infantry turned ourselves into Sappers, working in hundreds on every airfield throughout daylight hours at the construction of fighter pens from every conceivable material. When all normal materials were quickly exhausted, we used old petrol tins filled with earth and painted with mud in an optimistic but unsuccessful effort to camouflage them from the prying eyes of the Luftwaffe.

Kesselring, seeming to sense what was afoot, ordered attacks on the empty pens and the cratering of the runways. Work continued however until all airfields were ready. In this final phase of preparations a fine example of Inter Service co-operation began. Firstly, the R.A.F. trained a large number of Infantry to assist in rearming and refuelling fighters. Next, line communications were established by the Infantry from the control rooms to the proposed squadron dispersal areas on each airfield. These were reinforced by wireless nets and again by military dispatch riders.

In the case of my regiment at Luqa, the C.O. sat alongside the Controller in the control tower and a company representative was located in each squadron dispersal area. Communication to flights was by motor-cycle dispatch riders and by runners to individual fighters in pens. These pens were manned by our own soldiers who re-armed and refuelled them as they returned from their sorties. We did everything except fly the planes and service the engines but were not oblivious of the fact that we were only the administrative tail of fighting weapons manned by gallant young men. Some of the non-flying wartime R.A.F. officers did not match up to the high quality of their flying brothers and exercised a weak and inefficient control over their ground staff. A substantial number of these took advantage of the lack of roll calls and got shacked up in Maltese villages. When things hotted up at Luqa they tended to fail to make an appearance, and it was for this reason that so many Infantrymen were needed to step in. Lines were also laid to concealed rendezvous about two miles from each airfield where lines of lorries awaited, loaded alternately with stones and soldiers. A call for three lorryloads of stones would thus bring six lorries, three of stones and three of soldiers ready to unload them at speed into bomb craters on the runways. Motor rollers, driven by us, stood by on the airfields to level the surface as soon as each crater was filled. All was now ready for 'der Tag'.

The first real trial of strength was a bitter disappointment. The fighters that arrived were hustled into their pens and made ready to take the air once more. It was decided however not to risk more than half in the air at one time. The result was that when the Luftwaffe appeared in great strength, the number of Spitfires in the air was insufficient to enable them to hold their own, and they therefore received a terrible mauling, whilst most of those on the ground were severely damaged. Hopes had run so high that the gloom which descended once more was deeper than ever.

The next operation was now planned to take place on 9th May. This time no mistake was to be made. All the new aircraft had to be prepared to take the air in defence of the island within ten minutes of landing, and experienced pilots who knew the area stood by in some pens to take them over from the ferry pilots. The Senior Controller was now a skilful Battle of Britain Controller. Every aircraft on the island which could get airborne was to be put into the air – no juicy targets on the ground. Although stocks of A.A. ammunition were pitifully low, every heavy and light anti-aircraft gun was allowed full operational freedom.

A tremendous atmosphere of expectancy pervaded the whole Island, and rumours of what was afoot seeped down to the Maltese in even the deepest caves. The planes duly arrived on the morning of May the ninth and were quickly made ready for the air by the R.A.F. groundstaffs and the newly trained soldiers. Hot drinks were taken round the pens for the incoming pilots and those waiting to take on the Luftwaffe. The enemy duly came to investigate and was appalled by what it saw. Squadrons had taken off from every airfield and were flying purposefully at three different levels. The Luftwaffe withdrew and went back to do some thinking, and were punished by our Spitfires on their way home.

May the tenth dawned warm and cloudless and I was only one of thousands who flung on their clothes with a feeling of uncanny excitement. A showdown was inevitable and it seemed certain it must come that day. The atmosphere of confident elation which had started on the previous day had taken hold on the entire civilian population. When the air-raid warning finally sounded men, women and children, instead of going to their shelters, solemnly climbed up onto their roofs. Out of holes in the rock came people, some of whom had not surfaced for weeks. And quietly they waited. Formations of new Spitfires which had taken off before the sirens went were already high in the sky, and lower down at bomber level were the patched-up Spitfires and Hurricanes of earlier days, waiting to take their revenge.

The familiar ominous drone began to swell from the direction of Sicily and all eyes turned to meet the oncoming enemy. With a deafening roar the Grand Harbour barrage opened up in full voice. We had almost forgotten what these gunners could do, so long had it been since they had last been allowed to fire without restriction. About a minute later the guns of Luqa Aerodrome defences opened up with the Luqa barrage and the battle was on.

Within a matter of minutes the sky was a mass of whirling aeroplanes. The enemy bombers were jettisoning their bombs anywhere, and although it thus became much more dangerous for people away from the target areas than during a normal raid, the Maltese just didn't seem to mind. Parachutes started floating down in all directions. The German fighter cover was being chased all over the sky by planes which really had the legs of them. The war-weary old Hurricanes tore into the bombers and took their long awaited revenge. The gunners put up such a thick barrage over the Grand Harbour that it looked like an enormous eiderdown. I saw one formation of six JU 87's try to dive through it. The first three disintegrated and bits of engine, tail and fuselage went spinning down into the water. The last three pulled out and dropped their bombs blindly through the barrage.

The flat rooftops of all the towns were now black with people waving handkerchiefs, shouting, pointing at the descending victims and making that rather rude sign of contempt which is peculiar to the Maltese. Sixty-nine German aircraft were lost in this battle, which exceeds the final proved figures of German losses for any day during the Battle of Britain.

The evening reconnaissance over Sicily that day reported a veritable boat-race going on in the Sicilian Channel as large numbers of defeated aviators, whose aircraft had been ditched on the way home, rowed northwards like mad in their little rubber dinghies.

From this unforgettable day onwards Malta never again lost her local air supremacy. The constant strain on morale of being the helpless underdog who had insufficient means to hit back and redress the situation, was finally over. The battle was a wonderful feat of organisation and Inter Service co-operation which, in addition to the Royal Artillery and Infantry had also called for substantial use of major units of the Fleet.

I am fortunate to have a copy of the log of one of the RAF Pilots who flew a Spitfire from the US Carrier Wasp and submit this extract.

9 May 1942

"Took off from the Wasp at 06.30 hrs. Landed at Ta Kali at 10.30 hrs. The formation flew too fast and got his navigation all to hell, so I left them 40 miles West of Bizerta, 5 miles off the North African coast, and set course for Malta, avoiding Pantellaria and Bizerta owing to fighters and flack being there. I landed during a raid and four 109s tried to shoot me up. Soon after landing the airfield was bombed but without much damage being done. I was scrambled in a section of four soon after this raid, but we failed to intercept the next one, though we chased several 109s down on the deck.

Ate lunch in the aircraft, as I was 'ready' till dusk. After lunch we were heavily bombed again by six JU88s.

Scrambled again after tea – no luck again. One 'Spit' was shot down coming in to land and another one at the edge of the airfield. Score for the day, seven confirmed, seven probables and fourteen damaged for the loss of three 'Spits'.

The tempo of life here is indescribable. The morale of all is magnificent – pilots, ground crews, Army; but it is certainly tough. The bombing is continuous, on and off all day. One lives here only to destroy the Hun and hold him at bay; everything else, living conditions, sleep, food, and all the ordinary standards of life have gone by the board.

It all makes the Battle of Britain and fighter sweeps seem like child's play in comparison but it is certainly history in the making, and nowhere is there aerial warfare to compare with this."

After the decisive air battle of 10th May 1942 the siege was not automatically lifted and we continued to remain hungry; but morale was high, because the drone of Spitfires climbing up in formation to meet the enemy preceded every air raid, because we knew we were now winning the war, and in North Africa the Eighth Army was building up to defeat Rommel. My Regiment was withdrawn into reserve and we were billeted in St Julians in a number of houses either fully or partially taken over. My Company Officer's Mess was in a house which we shared with the civilian owners. The lady of the house was English, married to a Maltese who was not on the island. She had one daughter who lived with her. We kept to our own part of the house and only met them when we asked them in for a drink or vice versa. Due to the rationing, this was not very often, but the arrival of occasional merchantmen, always after searing air and naval actions, had led to a small increase in rations.

One of the most notable convoys was codenamed 'Pedestal', and resulted in three supply ships and an oil tanker the 'Ohio' getting in. The latter had been repeatedly hit and was only afloat because a destroyer had been lashed to her on each side like a pair of water wings. The captain of 'Ohio' later came to live in our village of Sway. He was awarded the George Cross for his leadership, courage and determination. The convoy arrived on the feast of the Assumption of the Virgin Mary and is still the subject of an annual service of remembrance on the day of 'Santa Marija'. This convoy is still referred to in Malta's history as the Santa Marija Convoy.

Two or three weeks before Christmas 1942, I was surprised by a visit from Bobby Radcliffe our Brigade Major. As a close friend of the Dorset

Regiment I was delighted to see him, but was taken aback by his opening remark "I want you to paint a couple of pictures for Joan". Flattered though I felt, I could not resist raising my eyebrows. "Of course I would pay for them" he hastily added. I could have fallen on his neck. Someone was actually prepared to give me money for my pictures. I immediately agreed a ridiculously low price. To my amazement, a trickle of orders came in from all sorts of people who hadn't liked to, but now felt free to ask me to paint local scenes which they would like to remember in post-war years. I was thrilled. I had become a professional artist.

By and large, we were being given a long and well earned rest after the poundings and loss of life at Luqa and round the Marsa. Christmas was celebrated with what then seemed quite plentiful food and drink. After Christmas, rations continued to improve and my first priority was to get my men fit for a land battle in North Africa. Stationed as they had been on Luqa airfield, they had not walked further than the distance from their fire posts to their sleeping shelters for months. We had in fact been prohibited from giving them any unnecessary exercise as the number of daily calories in their diet was so low that they would have suffered from effects of malnutrition.

I was now able to take my men on exercises, mainly 'advance to contact', which I felt would be our role in North Africa, penetration from the beach to a few miles inland, then some digging-in and quick preparation of defensive positions. On a small island like Malta, with restricted terrain for deployment, I picked a circular route which had two places wide enough to deploy on either side of the road and the third large enough to dig-in in company strength. At the first two places I arranged for my batman, Pte Charley Farley, who was a marksman, to go ahead as an unseen enemy and fire two or three live rounds into the ground, a few yards clear of the leading scouts to cause a halt and deployment. The odd bullet which hit a stone and made a whaang noise was a bonus, and reminded them that we would be facing not just that, but more. I felt that the small risk of a casualty was worth the benefit to the realism of the training. No-one questioned this or even knew about it until after it was over. After three such exercises, lengthening the distance each time, I felt my chaps were beginning to become soldiers once more. I learned, after leaving Malta, that I was the only commander who had carried out any serious training for what would have been a very testing operation. The others proved to be right because the operation was cancelled!

By an extraordinary chance I achieved a lasting benefit to my personal military skills which stood me in good stead some eighteen months later. I had always been a useless pistol shot because I have small hands and could never get my trigger finger right round the trigger of my .38 revolver. One afternoon, when I was on leave and window-shopping in Valletta, I spotted an old 9mm Luger going for a song in a junk shop. I bought it and found that the barrel was interchangeable with the damaged one I had collected at Tamra. I managed to get some 9mm ammunition from the R.A.F. and practiced snap-shooting at a small target which I had rigged up. The butt fitted my small hand perfectly and I became a crack pistol shot. I handed my .38 revolver to the Quarter-master and never used one again.

Chapter VIII

Farewell to Malta. Cairo, Alexandria, Sarafand and South Africa.

Early in 1943 I learned that I had been allocated a vacancy at the Staff School at Sarafand at Palestine. After nearly four years in Malta, I could hardly wait to shake its dust from my feet. The many happy memories had been blurred by tragedy, pain and months of hunger and poor health.

My swan-song was a Court Martial in which I had been asked to defend five men accused of stealing a load of flour for sale on the black market. It was a big occasion and the Judge Advocate General's Department was prosecuting. The defendants were therefore entitled to a barrister to defend them but asked for me. After I had studied the full details of the case, I accepted the challenge. They were billeted in Sliema where even most large town houses formed a solid phalanx. In their case their billets were separated by a small courtyard from a building used for storing flour. One of the soldiers was walking out with a Maltese girl whose father was a baker. He had suggested that they should pick the weak cement from one of the roughly bricked-up windows of the flour store and that he would come along with a lorry and collect the bags of flour which they were to pass through to the courtyard. He would pay cash in notes.

The operation would have probably worked if one of the love-sick soldier's four friends, who were to receive a handsome cash bonus, had not suddenly got cold feet and reported the plan in secret but still pretended to his friends that he was with them.

I felt that if I had been commanding that company, I would have had them all up in front of me and charged with that wonderful and all embracing military offence of 'Conduct to the Prejudice of Good Order and Military Discipline' and roasted them in a way that they had never been roasted before. I certainly would not have allowed them to go on and commit an offence which could have been prevented, which is what then took place.

The baker was duly detained that evening after the men were all due back in their billets and a plain-clothes Maltese policeman took his place in his lorry, together with a wad of paper cut to the size of Maltese pounds with a few real ones on top, held in position by elastic bands. The company commander organised a squad of officers and sergeants, all wearing gym shoes, to observe the crime taking place, and when the agreed number of bags had been passed through the window of the flour store into the courtyard and the lorry drew up, a whistle was blown and in came the heavy squad.

In the darkness and confusion all the five slipped back to their beds, fully dressed and pulled off their shoes and socks. Since many soldiers in those days considered pyjamas sissy, it was not unusual for men to sleep in day clothes. In spite of having had complete knowledge of the attempted coup beforehand, the officers and sergeants had blown it. Only by going to the known men and taking their racing pulses were they able to extract confessions, and at the expense of revealing that they knew all about the proposed deal the whole time.

I found myself, for once, really in sympathy with the would-be crooks and studied all the legal aspects with great care. They were charged with "stealing 20 bags of flour".

I was lucky enough to strike gold at the first session. The legal definition of stealing was to "remove and carry away". The blundering forces of retribution had struck before a crime had been committed: the flour was still on the premises.

I have a feeling that the Court shared a certain distaste for the methods adopted by the Prosecution. They could not call my 'clients' as prosecution witnesses but could only rely on the man who had grassed, and was not one of the accused, to relate the hatching of the plot.

Under my guidance, my clients kept very quiet and all pleaded Not Guilty. At the close of the Prosecution I rose with quiet dignity and pointed out to the Court that none of the accused had any case to answer since none of them had been found guilty of any crime. They had admitted to me that they realised that they would have been in the wrong to accept money for moving bags of flour from one part of the premises to another as part of a shady deal, but they were not accused of this, and the fact remained that they had not removed anything from the premises, which was what the Prosecution should have proved to sustain a case of stealing, nor had they received any money!

The Court was adjourned and only took 20 minutes to deliberate and re-open with a verdict of Not Guilty.

Old Bosun Pulverman apparently strode up and down his office when he heard the verdict, muttering "how on earth did he do it". He never said a word about it to me, and when we next met it was about four months later in Cairo, where he had been appointed an Assistant Adjutant General and played a major part in getting me four weeks leave in South Africa, whence Phoebe had been evacuated with the recently born Michael.

✧

Although we had gained a fair mastery of the sea and air in the Eastern Mediterranean by the time I sailed from Malta in late February 1943 one did not talk about shipping movements too much and I slipped away on a fairly small cargo steamer with no more than a dozen other service passengers and few goodbyes. I had gone down to just over nine stones and put on a whole stone in the five days it took us to reach Alexandria. The food was probably normal wartime Merchant Service fare, but the delight in eating things one had missed for so long was unbelievable. My main memories are of eating eggs and bacon for breakfast on the morning of our departure and of being able to *spread* butter *on* the bread rather than scrape a miserable amount across it.

I can only remember three or four officer passengers, with one of whom I made firm friends. Tom Blackwell was a most unusual character who had held a commission in all three Armed Forces. Firstly, he had been commissioned in the R.A.F. as a pilot. He was then assigned to an aircraft carrier. Then all R.A.F. officers flying in H.M. Ships were transferred to the Royal Navy and moved their wings from their Airforce blue breasts to their Navy blue sleeves. He then had a bad crash into the sea and was so badly concussed that he was invalided from the Service. After lying low for a few months in England as a civilian; during which time he discovered that he could do anything except have a drink, which made him pass out or behave very strangely. He then joined the ranks as a private in the Royal Engineers having said nothing about his previous service.

He very soon won a commission as a Sapper, became a skilled bomb disposal expert and was, not surprisingly, sent to Malta. During his eighteen odd months in Malta he won the M.B.E. and the George Medal for his brave and hazardous work. We teamed up and shared carriages and taxis on our onward journey from Alexandria to Cairo and were finally booked in at the Continental Hotel one morning at about 9.30 am.

I told him that I was going straight to Air H.Q. to see if Air Marshal Hughe Pughe Lloyd could fix me a trip to South Africa during the two weeks before my course started. He remembered me well and was most sympathetic. He said "I can certainly get you flown down to South Africa on almost any day, but there are virtually no vacant seats back to Cairo before your course starts. I will do it for you because of the circumstances, but it must be your choice". I felt that I had no choice but to accept the disappointment and to express my very real gratitude for his willingness to support me had I elected to make the wrong moral decision.

I returned to the Continental at around 11.00 am and found Tom Blackwell in the lounge bar having a soft drink. "I've failed to pull it off" I said "I'm going to get drunk." "Why don't you have just one beer to keep me company and I will monitor your behaviour after half a bottle and stop you finishing it if you behave strangely".

He passed the test and said "I not only enjoyed it but I feel absolutely fine. Perhaps my brain has recovered". We then proceeded to drink large bottles of beer all through the morning, through the lunch period without having any lunch and finally after being warned that last drinks were being served at two-thirty, we bought three large bottles each and stood them behind the sofa we were sitting on and pretended from two-thirty onwards that we were just sipping the last dregs of the lunch-time drinks. Around four o'clock it looked as if we were coming to a halt when I remembered, from my pre-war visit from Palestine, that the Services were honorary members of the Gezira Sports Club, and that the bar there opened at five o'clock. A short taxi drive later and we were drinking beer quietly and purposefully at the Gezira Club. Neither of us got unsteady. We were just enjoying, for the first time for years, the freedom to have a few unrationed drinks. At around seven we took a taxi back to the Continental and continued our quiet enjoyment until, at eleven, the bar was finally closed. We then remembered that we had not had a morsel to eat since breakfast, but decided that we were not hungry and went to bed. For me this set up a record which I have never broken; twelve hours of non-stop drinking with no food. Tom was thrilled that the three years of non-drinking had given the part of his brain which had been injured time to recuperate.

The next day I telephoned Phoebe's Aunt Ray in Alexandria and arranged to stay with her for a week. I said farewell to Tom and we warmly wished each other luck. Regrettably I have never seen him since.

Aunt Ray was a very warm and kind hostess and my week of really graceful living was just what I needed after the deprivations of the last eighteen months. I did not weigh myself again, but I do not think I went up beyond my pre-war weight of just under eleven stones. My stomach had shrunk, and although I enjoyed the varied and delicious meals which were served, I could not eat large helpings and still cannot. I am, therefore, not like many septuagenarians, who resemble a potato on two match sticks, but have kept my figure – well almost!

The time came for me to make tracks for Sarafand; by train to Cairo, and thence across to Ismalia and on to the famous trans-Sinai railway which had provided me with that week's leave in 1939. The course was of intense interest because we in Malta had become right out of touch with much modern equipment and its strange terminology. When I first read in an exercise that a unit was to be supported by three bull-dozers, I couldn't believe my eyes or begin to picture what these people would look like. They are in fact earth moving machines, but I took time to enter this new world. I felt like the Royal Welsh Fusiliers must have felt when they returned from years in Jamaica wearing pig-tails, to discover that the rest of the Army had given them up some years earlier. We had some very interesting lectures, one of which was given by a Major Grant-Taylor on pistol shooting.

He had been commissioned into my Regiment in World War I and became a crack pistol shot. Between the wars, as a civilian, he taught the Chicago Police battle firing with revolvers involving keeping a low profile, if necessary by lying down; but the main lesson was that if you point at something with your index finger from any position, even if you hold your pistol centrally in front of your stomach, the line of the finger is aligned exactly on the object you are pointing at. This of course exactly coincided with what I did in Malta when I could not get my finger round my revolver's trigger and changed to a Luger which enabled the bone of the index finger which joins the knuckle to point in the same line as the barrel. I had thus, quite by chance, taken the right step in Malta to be a good pistol shot. He said that if you had a nice big target and stuck a black mark, no bigger than a postage stamp, in the middle and then pointed your pistol at it, it should not take more than four or five shots before you hit it every time at twenty feet.

All my life I have found that I feel like a five minute doze after lunch, and even longer if the lunch is generously lubricated or I am listening to a lecture which does not hold my attention. One afternoon the Commandant himself was holding forth and his voice gradually faded away, but never completely, because when he suddenly raised it and said "what do you think Butler?", the message came through, but I hadn't the foggiest idea what he had had been talking about. I brazened it out by saying very politely "I'm sorry Sir, but I was in a coma"! Loud laughs all round saved the situation.

During the weekends we made trips to Jerusalem to visit the Holy Places including The Garden Tomb, unearthed by General Gordon after much research and careful measuring. I believe it to be the actual tomb of Jesus. Every detail fitted, including the groove outside the vertical rock face in which the flat round stone door would have rolled like a giant coin. One tends to team up with someone on courses and my most frequent companion was Dickie Green who had already seen a lot of action with the 8th Army. I learned a lot from him and he reappeared forty years later at a party given by the Wakeleys. He finished up by living only three miles from Sway. There was no shortage of food in Palestine such as we had in Malta or even in England and both food and drink were of a high standard.

"During the weekends we made trips to Jerusalem to visit the Holy Places including The Garden Tomb"

One evening during dinner in the Mess, a telegram was handed to me by a waiter with the news that I had been awarded an M.B.E. This was a complete surprise to me, and no-one else knew the contents of the telegram. I wanted to jump up and shout "Yippee", but felt that this would be rather overdoing it. I did however have such a strong urge to do something that I picked up and consumed my entire wine glass except the stalk, firmly chewing it and fearlessly swallowing it. When my neighbours and those sitting opposite me said "we know you're mad Robert but what on earth did you do that for?" I was able to reply quietly "I've just heard that I've got an M.B.E." I later found that I had many friends indeed when I reckoned the cost of the evening to my wine bill.

Having once eaten glass and survived, I just couldn't stop doing this trick. One evening at a restaurant in Tel Aviv we heard an American officer at another table say to his friends "gee did you see that guy? He must be Jesus Christ". When my Regiment left Malta, my 'glass master' Roy Cooke joined Special Forces and very regrettably, was killed in Italy. At the end of the course, apart from one or two officers who were posted North or East, i.e. to Haifa or Paiforce in Iraq, we all got onto the 'Sinai Queen' to report to Cairo for our postings. Dicky Green reminded me quite recently that we all lined up and fired a live salvo from our revolvers as a salute to the Staff School as the train chuffed past it. I said "what on earth did we do such a stupid thing as that for?". He replied "we did it because you made us."

On reaching Cairo most officers made their way to the Military Secretary's Branch for their staff appointments. I went straight to the Adjutant General's Branch to see if I could now get leave in South Africa, be re-united with Phoebe and see my ten month old son Michael for the first time. Bosun Pulverman, now firmly installed in Cairo, pulled out all the stops and organised me "four weeks leave in the station", which meant that however long it took me to get there and get back, I would have a month in East London where Phoebe and Michael were living in great comfort at the King's Hotel, right on the waterfront with her suite overlooking the Indian Ocean.

I only had to wait a day or two before reporting for a flight in a twin engined Lockheed Lodestar to Pretoria. Because we had such a full load of passengers, we carried little fuel and had to stop at numerous places along our route. I had never been to any part of Africa before, with the exception of Egypt, and it was for me a really thrilling experience to be able to visit such places as Luxor, Wadi Halfa; Khartoum (night stop); Malakal, Juba, Sudan (night stop); Entebbe, Uganda; Nairobi, Kenya (night stop), Dodoma, Tanganyika; Kasama, Northern Rhodesia; Ndola, Northern Rhodesia (night stop); Lusaka, Northern Rhodesia; Bulawayo, Southern Rhodesia; and finally Pretoria in South Africa. We had by then been flying together for five whole days and had hopped our way across the arid deserts of Egypt and the Sudan, the lush tropical forests of Equatorial Africa and the semi-tropical and temperate areas of Southern Africa.

The aircrew were friendly South Africans, who let me fly a large numbers of hours on dual control, and the passengers a mixed bunch of South Africans returning on leave and British Servicemen being posted to appointments in South Africa.

Although we only managed to get a feeling for the places where we night-stopped, we were nevertheless able to see the ancient monuments of Luxor, which the pilot circled slowly at low level, and to get the jungle atmosphere in the Equatorial belt. During our second night stop at Juba I saw wild elephants for the first time, coming down to drink the waters of the Nile. We rarely lost sight of that great river which painted a wide green strip through the yellow sands of the deserts of Egypt and the Sudan, seeming, once we had gained altitude, to stretch to eternity. At Ndola in the Rhodesian copper belt we saw for the first time a really sophisticated European township, beautifully laid out and cultivated, with bright green lawns and the large splashes of scarlet which seem ever present in Africa's gardens. I noticed how relaxed, helpful and happy the African staff of the hotel were and now wonder if they fare so well now that they are back into the hands of the sons of the cruel and bombastic leadership who failed to bring them into the Twentieth Century, or even to invent the wheel, which existed in civilised countries thousands of years earlier.

After the farewells of passengers and crews at Pretoria Airport I made for a hotel for the night and got the hall porter to look up the best train for East London. This left on the following day and followed a route through Kroonstad, Bloemfontein, Springfontein, Queenstown and King Williams Town, a rather small and lifeless little dorp where Colonel Sawyer had once been stationed in the South African War and Phoebe spent a few weeks before negotiating the move to East London.

The entire route, until we dropped down to King Williams Town, was between 3,000 and 6,000 feet and so although the sun was warm, the air was cool at night. The high veldt is wonderful country for Europeans owing to the moderate climate, but before the early settlers opened up the area it was virtually uninhabited except by the Hottentots and the Bushmen nearer the Cape. The Looney Left who misguidedly protest that the Bantu tribes from the North were dispossessed of their land have been deliberately misled by forces attempting to destroy a civilisation and replace it by the strife-torn corrupt regimes which can be seen in every single country which has been handed back to Black rule. The Looney Left turn a blind eye to the millions who have died from internal strife since the withdrawal of British Administration. I have seen so many

African countries during and after British Administration, and can bear witness to a dramatic fall in the standard of living and rise in the death rate through tribal wars and the violence without which the African seems unable to live when no European restraint is exercised. The tragedy is that the figure 'millions' is no exaggeration. The million figure has been topped in a number of countries including the Sudan, Nigeria, the Congo, Angola and most probably Uganda.

✧

I had telephoned Phoebe the arrival time of my train at East London, and after two whole days and one night in a sleeper, I arrived at around six thirty in the evening to be re-united with Phoebe and see Michael for the first time. We had a wonderful four weeks in East London, where Phoebe had made a number of friends in the hotel amongst other British Servicemen's wives and some of the South African residents in the area. The coast from Durban down to Cape Town is largely populated by former United Kingdom expatriates.

The climate in late May, being only three weeks from the shortest day in the Southern Hemisphere, was like a late Autumn day in England and we wore clothes appropriate to those conditions. We bathed once or twice, but it was a quick in-and-out effort. We had many picnics and visits with Michael to a local park called the Glen, which had pleasant lawns sheltered from the wind on which a rug could be spread for picnics in the sun. Phoebe told me that there was an unpleasant character who, seeing a few unescorted mothers and children lying around on rugs, would creep through the surrounding shrubs and expose himself. They called him 'Ben of the Glen'. I was always hoping he would appear whilst I was there so that I, a rugby playing 28 year old, could sort him out. I regret to say that not once did Ben appear whilst I was in East London. Michael was only ten months old and therefore not yet walking. He had blonde hair and looked not unlike Christopher at that age. One afternoon a plane flew low over the town and Michael burst into tears. We did not then know, as we do now, that children hear from an early age inside the womb what is going on around them. He must have shared our conversations at the time of our bombing in Sacred Heart Avenue, heard the planes and the bombs, and was now voicing his fear and general disapproval. We decided that we might not get another chance for some time to provide him with a younger brother or sister, and took the steps required. The war could easily have gone on for another three years during which we might have been parted.

Whilst I was there the Rotary Club of East London asked me to lunch as their guest of honour and to give them a talk on the siege of Malta. The

Xhosa warrior in the Transkei

A typical Xhosa hut in the Transkei

"Once more I was reunited with Phoebe and Michael, the son I had never seen"

Phoebe and Michael picnicking on the beach

dining room was packed to capacity and those unable to get seats listened from an adjoining room. They were a touchingly appreciative audience.

On the twenty-eighth day of my stay in East London I set forth for Durban under orders from the British Military Mission for a sea passage to Egypt. Phoebe decided to accompany me in order to extend our leave together, and Michael was put in charge of another refugee from Egypt who was a qualified nurse. It was to be a most interesting trip as there was no direct rail link between East London and Durban; hence we boarded a train which took us as far as Umtata, the capital of the Transkei, a native territory; we then went by bus to Kokstad at the Northern end of the Transkei and from there by train to Durban. The Transkei was a living reminder of the natural laziness of native Africans. Mile after mile of wonderful grassland which could have produced fertile crops were left uncultivated. Dotted about were Xhosa villages about two miles apart, and round each village about three acres of cultivation, mainly maize, was visible. The men sat around in small groups smoking, and a few women could be seen tending their crops. The Transkei could obviously have supported ten times the number of Xhosa living there and I realised then and am even more certain now that the so-called 'land hunger' of the Bantu is not for land, but for the good things of life which organised civilisation provides. After our bus drive from Umtata to Kokstad we took a taxi from the bus stop to the station, to find that the daily train to Durban had already left. We asked the taxi driver to take us to a comfortable hotel and this he did. It was incredibly British, with roaring log-fires and an enormous Royal Coat of Arms in bas-relief over the fire place. As soon as the sun went down it became bitterly cold and we realised that we were at a fairly high altitude. Next morning we were thrilled to find white hoar-frost on the branches of the trees outside our windows and on the lawns beneath them. I had not seen such a sight since the winter of 1936-7, more than six years earlier.

We went for a walk into the countryside and soon found ourselves looking along a really picturesque valley dominated by a snow-capped Mount Curry; another big surprise. After lunch I sketched it as the basis for a water colour.

We realised that day that we were indeed going to provide a companion for Michael and Kokstad has always had a warm place in our hearts. We returned to it and stayed at the Royal Arms thirty years later whilst driving from Cape Town to Johannesburg by the so-called 'garden route' as part of an extended Southern African holiday. I gave my daughter Jill the picture of Mount Curry when she married and it hung in her house until destroyed by fire in 1980.

After an uneventful but very beautiful journey through highland scenery down to Durban, I reported to the British Army Headquarters and was told to go on indefinite leave, since the enemy submarine campaign had seriously affected our shipping schedules. Durban being some 300 miles nearer the Equator was far warmer than East London and very much warmer than Kokstad. We stayed for a week near the beach, but found it very humid and moved up to a very comfortable hotel on the Beria, a long ridge on the inland side of Durban around 200 feet higher than the town and more airy and cooler. The weeks rolled on as the submarine campaign continued, but we did not complain. The Kew Hotel had been a fine mansion with a pillared porch from which an earlier generation could have descended from their carriages on a rainy day without getting wet. It overlooked Mitchell Park on its North Western side, which contained a small zoo whose variety of wildlife included a female Indian Elephant. Nellie was eighteen years old and I tried to make friends with her including visiting her in her stable, where I would feed her with oranges. I had always wondered how strong the two finger-like tips of her trunk were, knowing that the main trunk could lift quite large sawn-off tree trunks. One day I thought I would test the strength of her 'fingers' by holding on to an orange to see how strong a pull they could muster to release it from my grasp. She released it in a flash, tossed it into her mouth and, all in the same movement gave me a mighty back-hander across the chest as the trunk came forward again. It was not painful like a punch from a boxer but a gradual acceleration which sent me somersaulting through the air for about five yards. It was then that her Indian keeper said "It was luckee Sahib that you were both owt of dors or she might have keeled you by crushing you against the wall of her stable. She has already keel two keepers". I paid her no more personal calls, but was able to get an interesting job after I had retired by adding at the foot of my C.V. "even if I do not suit you, it is not often you will have had the opportunity of meeting someone who has been knocked down by an elephant, kicked by a bee and flown the Sahara in a single engined aircraft." I got the interview and the job, and was later elected onto the Board. The bee story is simply that, as an animal lover I found a bumble bee in our drawing room on an Autumn evening and felt it kinder not to turn her out until next morning. It rained for the next two days and I used to ferry her on a piece of paper from one vase of flowers to another. Eventually she had taken all the nectar available and so, having made friends with her and called Beatrice, I ferried her onto a piece of paper with some runny honey on it and watched her drink it through a magnifying glass. A little tongue about an eighth of an inch long came out of her proboscis into the honey. The magnifying glass also picked up a host of tiny mites in the fur on her neck and back. I dipped a cocktail stick into the honey and with the tiny point I was able to lift the mites off one by one. Beatrice found this disturbing to her gastronomic treat and being now a trusting friend she put up one of her back legs and gently pushed my hand away.

✧

After three weeks at the Kew Hotel and still no sign of Allied shipping, Phoebe began to worry about Michael. He was very young to be left too long and yet old enough to be mentally hurt. She therefore decided to go back to East London to collect him. I could not leave Durban as I was permanently at twelve hours notice. There were all sorts of complications as our finances were fully stretched and in order to be able to live at a reasonable hotel in Durban for an indefinite period we abandoned the scheme whereby the Army took full responsibility for her and received a generous allowance in lieu. I, in the meantime, painted and sold pictures of wartime Malta which I could do from memory of some that I had already painted there, and they all sold. I was also commissioned to paint a large picture of the hotel by the proprietor.

The cost of a single room with a child was far more than half the cost of a double room without a child, and Phoebe would have had to move to a small grotty hotel for the rest of the war, and no-one could guess for how long that would be. I therefore moved heaven and earth to get her re-accepted onto her original scheme, being then able to plead the compassionate reason that she was now pregnant. I was able to leave with peace of mind knowing that they also allowed her to return to the King's Hotel in East London and her circle of friends. My lasting memory of Michael was of his ability to stand, which he had learned to do during his five weeks of absence and we still have a photograph of him standing up, holding onto a tap in the garden. I saw him take the odd step but regrettably just missed seeing him string a few together. Before my ship even arrived, I was put at four hours notice and ordered to the Army Camp.

It was most unpleasant being at sea in the equatorial area of the Indian Ocean with a complete black-out enforced. We had to wear shirts, open-necked, for meals, but after dinner when every aperture was closed, we sat bare-chested and wearing only shorts. I played a bit of Bridge with some quite good players and soon realised that I had a very great deal to learn about that fascinating game.

As we ploughed our way North we crossed the Equator and the heat continued to increase the whole way to the Red Sea. She was a dry ship and in the end I decided to give up drinking endless and unnecessarily expensive soft drinks, playing bridge or even reading in that hot and steamy environment, but preferred the fresh air of the dark decks. There one could feel the soft movement of the air, caused by the ship's progress, watch the stars, lean over the rail and see the phosphorescent flashes as the water sluiced along our side, and commune with Mother Nature.

One of my fellow passengers had been the British Resident in Basutoland and he honoured me by presenting me with a carved hardwood walking stick, which he informed me was a chieftain's emblem of office, and even passed to another would be presumed to have been presented only to people worthy of commanding instant respect and obedience!

Chapter IX

Return to The Queen's Own for the Aegean Campaign

In due course we passed through the Suez Canal, disembarked, and in my case, made my way to General Headquarters in Cairo for my first proper staff posting. I was startled to learn that I was not getting one but being posted back to my Regiment which was by now up in the Lebanon, having done both combined-operation training, involving storming ashore from landing-craft, and mountain warfare training. "I can't say any more old chap, but I'm sure you will never regret it" said the Military Secretary's representative.

Another trip on the Siniai Queen, but this time on Northwards through Haifa and eventually by road to my Regiment which was bivouacked under olive trees on a hillside between Tyre and Sidon. As I got out of the fifteen hundred weight truck which had driven me from the rail halt along a dusty track up the hillside and entered the battalion area, one of the first people I recognised was Farley. I shouted his name and he came running over. I never asked him if he would like to be my batman once more. He simply said "you're to command 'A' Company Sir, I'll make the arrangements for my transfer from 'C'". He guided the truck to Battalion Headquarters and dropped me off and then took it on to the officers lines, where he had already organised a tent for me. We had so many shared memories from the days when he had replaced Wallington as my batman in Casa Tre to the morning I embarked from Malta for Alexandria. He had adored Christopher and on more than one occasion we had found him inside Christopher's playpen, playing with him as an overgrown friend.

The Bosun had been replaced by Lt-Colonel Ben Tarleton, (RNF) who overlapped with me for a few weeks as Second-in-Command and C.O. designate before I left Malta. He greeted me very warmly and at the C.O.'s conference next morning told those assembled how pleased he was that another senior officer had returned for the mystery operation for which the battalion had been training. I had never before felt the slightest bit senior but reflected wryly that it was only a few days before my twenty eighth birthday, and that in the Eighth Army quite a few battalion commanders were by then around that age.

I was delighted to get back to the last Company I had commanded in Malta. The key personnel were however different except for my old friend CSM Spooner; my 2 i/c being Bill Grimshaw, and the platoon commanders 2/Lieuts Hewett, Groom and Johns. After only a day or two we received orders to move to another set of olive groves, this time just South of Haifa. We sensed at once that we were due for a move by sea, and rumours were rife. One was that we were going to help Tito's forces in Yugoslavia. Percy Flood, who had been my first Sergeant Major when I joined my Regiment and had slaved his guts out to keep me out of trouble, had by this time become Captain Flood, and the commander of 'B' Company. They had been sent off to the island of Castelrosso just off the Turkish coast and East of Rhodes. We then began to wonder if we were going to have a crack at Rhodes or Crete.

Finally Company Commanders were given the confidential information that we were embarking in Haifa on 19th September, and ammunition, stores, provisions and nothing heavier than 3" mortars were assembled for movement to the docks. We still had no idea of our destination. Whilst riding through the streets of Haifa on a motor-cycle on the eighteenth, a hornet collided with one of my bare knees and managed to get its sting well in before I brushed it off. By the time I had got back to my camp bed, which was under an olive tree protected by a green sand-fly net hung from a branch, my knee was the size of a football and I was feeling quite dizzy. In those days they did not seem to have anti-hystamine remedies and all that the Medical Officer (M.O.) could do was to tell me to keep lying down with a pillow under the foot to reduce circulation. The pain was considerable and walking was out of the question. Ben Tarleton came to see me next day and was wondering if I would have to be left behind. It was then the nineteenth of September. I assured him that in a day or two it would be better and that we must have at least two days in hand before we landed anywhere, so he abandoned any idea of appointing someone else to take over 'A' Company.

Meanwhile we learned that our complete 234 Brigade was embarking in destroyers for this still unknown destination, the other battalions being the 1st Durham Light Infantry and the 2nd Royal Irish Fusiliers. I still could not walk but was driven down to the docks in a 15 cwt truck in the evening, after dark, with the rest of my Regiment. In those days every care was taken to conceal military movements from the enemy. We did not discuss our plans, options and destinations in public, let alone broadcast them on civilian wireless frequencies; a practice which helps only to fill the pockets of the reporters, but can be of great value to the Intelligence Branch of the enemy.

Once inside the dockyard gates, which were well guarded, and with minimum lighting, our weapons, baggage and stores were loaded on to two destroyers, A and C Companies in HMS Faulkner and HQ and D Company in HMS Frobisher. I began to feel sleepy, my leg having kept me awake most of the night, and having seen my own stores aboard, I fell asleep on a bale of something unknown. Eventually CSM Spooner roused me and told me that we were boarding and on I limped. We left well before midnight, and although crowded were well fed and looked after by the Navy. After we had been at sea for about an hour, with all lights doused and no sounds but the humming, the vibration and the crashing of a destroyer travelling at speed, the Captain's voice sounded on the loud speakers. I should here inform the reader that we had served on numerous islands and that there were in those days two fine regiments, The Queen's Own Royal West Kent Regiment and The Queen's Own Cameron Highlanders. The Captain's first words were "I am now able to inform you all that your Brigade is about to occupy the islands of Samos, Leros and Kos". One of our cockney wags immediately interjected in a loud voice "what's this 'ere, going to another f…ing island, might as well call us The Queen's Own f…ing Islanders"!

The overall picture was that since Mussolini had been overthrown twelve days earlier, a large number of Aegean islands were garrisoned solely by Italian troops and were technically now Allied islands. The Joint Allied Command believed that the Germans had their hands full now that the Italian front had opened and that the main attack on French had yet to take place. It appeared unlikely that the Germans would deem it advisable to divert reserves into a sideshow which could be dealt with later if they triumphed in the two main theatres. The Joint Allied Command took a very logical gamble, hoping that the seizure of the three main Italian held islands along Southern Turkey's Western coastline would tempt Turkey to enter the war fully including the use of her airspace. The large island of Rhodes had however already fallen into German hands. It was the only island which had a small established ascendancy over the Italians. We were thus left with only the airfield at Kos to provide our air cover.

Like all good soldiers, they soon found themselves somewhere to sleep, and in my own case, I managed to rest my leg on a haversack and do likewise. After spending the daylight hours of the twentieth at sea, my birthday,we slipped through the narrows between Karpathos and Rhodes that night and early on the morning of the twenty first we entered the imposing harbour of Leros, which has the space and depth to accommodate an entire fleet. We were ferried ashore and spent a few hours loading our supplies, stores and equipment onto a cargo boat named the Eolo, the rest of the Battalion from the Frobisher doing likewise. The Eolo could only carry Battalion Headquarters, HQ Company and two rifle companies, one of which was A Company. We embarked that evening and after steaming all night we arrived at Vathi, the capital of Samos around 8.00 am the following morning.

As we rounded the horn of cliffs which mark the North East corner of Samosto enter Vathi Bay we were met by the most moving reception that could possibly be imagined. All the church bells, including the little chapels up on the hillsides began ringing and out of literally every house, again from sea level right up the steep slopes which surround the bay, people were waving sheets and handkerchiefs. An enormous crowd had gathered on the tiny quayside, and as the Eolo slid alongside we were greeted by cheers and prolonged applause. Ben Tarleton stepped ashore to be handed bouquets of flowers and to be told by the Mayor that a large tobacco factory had been put at our disposal as a barracks. This was certainly not the assault landing we had been trained. Ben Tarleton had given provisional orders that we would carry our kit bags and march as an ungainly body up the road to our new abode. He came back on board and said "I am afraid they expect a bit of pomp and circumstances, so we will have to leave our stores and kit for the moment and march to attention with rifles at the slope."

We formed up on the quay, and instinctively the troops straightened their jackets and made the best of themselves before we moved off. Throughout all this the bells continued and the sheets continued to wave wherever one looked.

We moved off as crisply as I had ever seen us and I am sure that I was not the only soldier who had a lump in this throat as we marched over the flowers which cascaded onto the road in front of us. It was now three days after my brush with the hornet in Haifa and though it was still painful, it was down to half its swollen zenith. Nothing would have stopped me from leading A Company through the crowd at Vathi. It was the Greek's way of indicating to their former Italian conquerors how glad they were to be rid of their yoke. Little did we, or they, then know that Samos was to return to Axis rule in eight weeks time, and that all those who had openly welcomed us would be shot by the Germans.

Ben Tarleton's first task was to make contact with the Commander of the Italian Division and sound out his loyalty to the new Italian Government which had broken away from Germany. He said that two of his brigades would obey his orders but that the third, a Black-Shirt Brigade, was still un unknown quantity. Their commander had apparently expressed strong views about Italy changing sides twice in two wars. Both he and his subordinate commanders, though unlikely to attack us independently, would most certainly be unwilling to fire on German troops if they attempted to restore Axis control over the Island. Even without German help, they outnumbered us three to one.

Meanwhile, the Italians loyal to Their Divisional Commander were for the most part friendly and helpful and we were provided with rations and a surprisingly large number of lorries. As soon as we had settled down in our tobacco factory, which exuded a pleasant aroma of turkish cigarettes, Ben Tarleton decided to send a motorised column through the area occupied by the Black Shirts. To make this more effective we made use of a cross-roads which was out of sight of their positions to go round a second time, our leading vehicle having reached it only a quarter of a mile behind the tail vehicle of the column. As commander of A Company I soon closed up and hopefully our column seemed twice as long as it really was; talk about endless Roman soldiers marching across a stage in a theatre and running round back-stage to keep the column going!

After a few days in Vathi where we sorted ourselves out, during which time a Brigadier Baird arrived as Military Governor and set up a headquarters, we were ordered to take up a defensive position on the high ground which overlooked Vathi to the North and Pythagorian to the South. We had a spell of useful training, and I emphasised the importance of good communications. We practised our wireless sets from platoons to Company Headquarters and our rear-link wireless to Battalion Headquarters even on route marches so that correct wireless procedures and changes of frequencies would become second nature. My knee had still not gone down to normal. The pain had gone but it still itched interminably.

At first it was warm enough for us to hang our sand-fly nets, which were vital, under olive trees as we had in Syria and Palestine, and we enjoyed drinking the famous Samos wine in the evenings. The Company officers mess consisted of no more than a small circle of tiny folding camp stools and the odd rock or tree stump on which to balance a plate. One evening the geese from Northern Europe began to fly over us and the column continued Southwards for just under three days.

Then, one day the rains came and we went into billets in the villages within our operational areas. My first night, within five minutes of getting into bed I found myself itching. I turned on a torch and found at least ten bed bugs crawling around. I destroyed them and turned off the torch. I had the same experience five minutes later and conducted another search including looking under the mat; no dice. The third attack prompted me to look behind an ornamental mat hanging on the wall alongside my bed. It was absolutely crawling with them, a nest right alongside a handy source of food. The worst thing about bug bites is that they sting like hell when they occur. The good thing is that they do not last like a flea bite, so in the morning there is no problem. My predecessor was a harder drinker than me and used to go out like a light and never noticed them. He couldn't believe it when I ribbed him for enduring them.

O.C. 'A' Company in Samos.
"At first it was warm enough for us to hang our sand-fly nets, which were vital, under olive trees"

Things soon began to hot up on the islands to the South of us and it was not long before Kos was attacked by first-class German troops from the Greek mainland. As the only Allied airfield for supporting 234 Brigade was on Kos, we lost all effective air cover and the Navy, which had been making extensive use of Portalago Harbour in Leros began to suffer severe losses from German air attacks and, surprisingly, German naval forces which had been moved to the Aegean. No longer could we expect to be supplied by normal sea routes or even destroyers carrying food. The Green population of Samos were already down to empty larders and another Malta situation seemed imminent. Our temporary solution, made at a high political level, was to be supplied by caiques to and from small Turkish ports. At one point, Turkey was no more than half a mile away, and our troops supervising this secret lifeline wore borrowed Greek jackets and no British insignia.

We received a visit from a German Bomber which dropped a stick of bombs to remind us of the German presence. The next downward step to our fortunes was the heavy bombing of Leros, followed by news that German landing craft had been sighted. It was decided that since Samos was a far larger island than the others, should be invaded in overwhelming strength we would take to the hills and join the Greek guerillas who had never bowed to Italian rule. They lived in a large expanse of mountainous terrain which was in effect a high plateau with near vertical sides and only one viable path of access. This looked like another goat track on the lower slope, but if followed, led through a narrow cleft between steep rocks from which two men with a light machine gun could hold up an army – memories of Horatio and others of his ilk.

❖

Increased air activity by the Luftwaffe rammed home to us the seriousness of the loss of Kos and its airfield on 3rd October, which left the whole brigade with no air cover whatsoever. The bombing of Leros could be distinctly heard. We did not know then the punishment being meted out to our Navy who sustained devastating losses. Some of the remnants of the D.L.I. from Kos managed to get to Leros to support the R.I.F. and our B Company was sent there from Castelrosso. The Leros garrison was also reinforced with 1st Kings Own and 4th Buffs, who lost an entire company when the vessel carrying it was sunk with all hands. The stage was now being set for our entry into the battle. First we moved out of billets and took up battle positions in slit trenches on Dhimitrios Ridge. By then the weather had broken and we were pretty sodden most of the time. I managed to get a couple of camouflaged ground sheets fixed up as a roof over a tiny shepherd's hut about 8 feet by 6, and found half an hour to paint a quick water colour of it one afternoon, with the high plateau to which we had planned to retire in the background. On 11th November a Major General Hall arrived with an appropriate headquarters as General Officer Commanding Aegean. The days of bombing of Leros were inevitably followed by a full scale invasion, and this took place on the following day and was seen from an observation post on a high point in our area. On that same night my company and D Company were ordered to embark for Leros on two minesweepers from Pythagorian, then known as Trigonion. Both these names were derived from the fact that Pythagoras was one of the leading founders of modern trigonometry. For the first time in the war we were issued with proper battledress. In Palestine and Malta we had worn Khaki Drill in summer and K.D. with service-dress jackets in winter. We were immensely proud to be dressed like the rest of the British Army, and must have been the last troops to abandon the old fashioned pre-war Service Dress. The large ocean-going minesweepers which were to carry us to Leros were dancing around like small rowing boats in the gale which had got up and we had quite a job embarking. We had barely got the last of our equipment on board when orders came for us to disembark. The Navy had calculated that the time already lost plus the time that would be lost disembarking in Leros and the reduction in our speed during the thirty mile trip to Leros would not allow the minesweepers time to reach the safety of Turkish waters before dawn after disembarking us on Leros. Not a single vessel was allowed to remain in the Leros harbour of Portalago in daylight as it would most certainly have been sunk by the Luftwaffe. We accordingly returned to our sodden slit trenches (and snug shepherd's hut).

The Southerly gales continued all night and all next day, so the minesweepers were sent round to Vathi in the North of Samos which was sheltered from the Southerly gales, for us to embark the following afternoon. Most of my company got some sleep that night, but I and my headquarter staff had the job of organising the removal of stores and getting them back to our headquarters up under the trees of Dhimitrios Ridge, by which time, after someone had brewed up some tea, we saw the sky lightening in the East of the Turkish hills. I snatched a few hours sleep that morning and then it was time to go down to Vathi for a briefing conference, followed by orders to get back to my company and prepare to embark again – that evening from Vathi quay.

We re-loaded our stores and equipment and trundled down the picturesque mountain road through the Scotch Fir copses which make Samos so attractive. The seas were so heavy off the headland North East of Vathi harbour that only one minesweeper managed to get round it. I was duly embarked with my company and all its stores, weapons and ammunition, together with some anti-aircraft gunners and large quantities of anti-aircraft and other ammunition urgently required in Leros. The news from Leros was difficult to come by, but we gathered that the fighting was of the utmost ferocity and that we were liable to be thrown into it immediately on arrival.

At least two thirds of my men had campaigned in Palestine and most of the other third had undergone the heavy bombing in Malta, during which time we had a two year period of air raids.

I do not remember having any other feelings but complete calmness and looking forward to doing what for all my military life I had been training to do. I think this rubbed off on my men who were quietly cheerful. The rapport between officers, N.C.O.s and men was perfect. As soon as we were once more embarked and I had been designated O.C. Troops, I told the ship's Captain, a Lieutenant R.N.V.R., that I was going to have a solid three hours sleep as I had had little the previous night and would get no more that night once we had disembarked. I told my company to get their heads down wherever they could so that we would give a good account of ourselves in the morning. I was given the Captain's bunk and after I had walked round and seen everyone settled I turned-in myself and went out like a light. The minesweepers tossed and rolled but not as badly as some of my father's sailing boats!

Suddenly I awoke as I sensed a change in the engines and that we were circling. The wind and the seas were abating and I rushed up on deck and onto the bridge to see what was going on. The Captain told me that he had inadvertently circled the wrong island, but had now identified it and was setting course once more for Leros. I was not impressed. I asked him to give me a call half an hour before we reached the entrance to Portalago and returned to my dreams.

The next thing I knew was that I was being shaken by the shoulder by an agitated Lieutenant who said "I've found Leros Major, but it's now too late to go in and we'll have to go and lie up in Turkish waters until tomorrow evening." I silently cursed but felt a surge of sympathy for him and accompanied him up to the darkened chart-room where we selected the best place to lie up under camouflage nets trying to look like a rock. I pointed out that it was no use looking like a rock except among other rocks and we picked a rocky bit of coast to the South East named the Gulf of Manalya. I added that this would enable us to make for the cover of a tiny island between Leros and the Turkish coast which we could use as a sight shield from observation posts on the high ground on Leros when daylight dawned.

We were caught by the morning twilight but reached the Eastern side of the island before it was full daylight. We then kept the island between us and Leros until we were virtually invisible in the early morning mist. The wind had now completely dropped and the sun rose in all its magnificence behind the Turkish hills to the East and soon caressed us with its warmth. Most of my troops who had not had such a warm nook as I had, and were still damp, found sunny corners on the deck to dry out.

The area of Turkey which we had to approach to keep our island between us and Leros was a long sandy beach which stretched as far as the eye could see to the North and South; but it was unbroken by any rocks and about five to seven miles North of the rocky bays of Manalya, amongst which we had agreed to lie-up. I wondered when the Captain would turn South East to get there. He was standing facing forward with his hands on the bridge rail and I was standing tucked in one corner at the back. I went forward and said "I think we are far enough from Leros now to turn to the South East and get amongst our rocks." He did not move a muscle or answer me. He might have been in Madame Tussaud's. Once more my heart bled for him and I believe he was half stunned by his serious navigational error. I will not name him. I went back to my corner, took a bearing on two prominent mountains that we had seen even from Samos, and one on the South tip of Leros, which projected from our friendly island, plotted them on my small scale map and went forward again with the words "I have just verified our position with bearings on Leros and those two mountains. I know that my compass looks small but it has served me well in the past. We are here" and I indicated the dot on my map where the three lines roughly intersected "don't you think we should bear away from the coast now?" No reply; by then we were so close to the shore that the water was already losing its Mediterranean blue and showing yellow, so I said "look if you're to hit the beach for Christ's sake slow down or we'll never get her off." Two seconds later we hit the bottom at least a quarter of a mile from the shore, the bows rose up and we came to a standstill.

I was in an extremely sensitive position, having sailed my father's second yacht single handed, and navigated the waters of the North Sea and to ports on both sides of it, I was a reasonably experienced seaman and had in my earlier days been an expert at going on the mud, getting her off and ultimately of avoiding it altogether. My friend simply put his engine into full astern and stirred up a lot of sandy water but made no movement. I then very politely and quietly intervened and suggested that we got all the men near the stern, floated the bow, towed it round with the launch so that we pointed downhill, then moved our human ballast towards the bows to take the weight off the stern, then with the launch going flat out and pointing seawards and the engines at 'full ahead' we should give it a go. We got off at the first attempt, but instead of then quietly stealing along the coast to the cover of bays and rocks, he anchored about a further quarter of a mile away from the shore and set about trying to disguise his vessel as a rock in the middle of open water with green and brown scrim. Later when I was in hospital in Alexandria, a wounded Beau-Fighter pilot told me that he had spotted us on a mission to dive-bomb and machine-gun the German positions on Leros and had seen us through the camouflage and assumed that we were Germans. He had decided to shoot us up on the way back. In the event he had no ammunition left or we would have been a sitting duck.

My tactful approach to the Captain succeeded in persuading him that I did have experience of seamanship and he took my advice from then on with the sincere friendliness with which I offered it. I was senior to him in rank, and as O.C. troops had some responsibility for getting my troops and the valuable A.A. ammunition we were carrying to Leros quickly and safely.

I was more than aware that it would be unusual, to say the least of it, for a pongo to start telling a Naval Officer what to do with his own ship, but I did suggest that I worked out our navigational plan for taking her into Leros that night; timed so that we moved the moment the light began to fade, stole North along the Turkish coast, circled to the North of Lipsos which is North of Leros, and then descended on Leros from the North in full darkness.

I drew the whole trip on the chart with distances, bearings and timings pencilled in and then planned a trip ashore in Turkey. We had left Samos for only a four hour trip and our minesweeper did not carry enough drinking water for all those extra mouths. What I would call a large 'dinghy' was tied astern the launch and some clean and available vessels which would hold water were put aboard. We removed all badges of rank and any military insignia, and set off for Turkey. Leaving the launch in shallow water with its Bosun, we rowed the dinghy ashore. Aware that the coast could well be mined, we moved inland with considerable caution until we bumped into two Turkish soldiers on look-out duty. They pointed their rifles at us and we duly raised our hands above our heads whilst I shouted "English" and then hopefully, "Inglese". I did not know a word of Turkish, but in due course, in exchange for some packets of good quality cigarettes, they filled up all our vessels and gave us two more petrol cans which had been used for water and did not smell. After much goodwill, sign language, smiles and handshakes all round we made our way back to our minesweeper.

At tea time the troops all had a proper evening meal because I had no idea where their next meal would come from, and shortly before sunset we weighed anchor and proceeded Northwards along the Turkish coast and thence on the three successive bearings I had plotted on the chart. As we had been under wireless silence since leaving Leros waters in the small hours of that morning, we had no idea how the tide of battle was swinging. I did not know if we would be fired on as we entered the entrance of Portalago, or whether if we did get through, the Port or Northern side or the Starboard or Southern side of the huge bay would be in enemy hands. Our minesweeper, whose name and number I just cannot recall, was armed with three Oerlikon 20 mm cannons, so I suggested that as we approached the narrows from the West, one should be pointing forward, one Starboard and third to Port. My men would man the rails on both sides with their Brens and be prepared to return fire from whichever direction it came. If we were fired at from the Starboard side we would race for the quay on the Port side. If we were fired at from the quay we would run for the shallow waters on the Starboard side and when she ran aground attempt to wade ashore from the bows, a look-out having tested the depth with a long boat-hook.

It was by then a fairly dark night, but we picked up the skyline of the island and reduced speed and moved South towards Portalago Harbour which is roughly in the centre of the Western shore, keeping about two miles off the shore. The Northern side of the harbour entrance is guarded by Mount Patella, which is over 800 feet high and when finally spotted abeam, we began our turn in. I do not need to tell you that excitement was tense and all our throats were dry.

To our relief, although in a way it was something of an anti-climax, we spotted a tiny winking light approaching us and this turned out to be a small motor boat manned by the Navy coming out to guide us in. Both sides of the vast harbour were still in our hands, but the land battle was not going entirely our way and I was required to hand over to Grimshaw for supervising our disembarkation and proceed at once to Fortress Headquarters. It was around 2300 hours on 14th November, and I was bundled into a jeep and taken up a mountain road to the tunnel in Mount Meriviglia which the Italians had scooped out of the hillside from West to East, and Brigadier Tilney met me and fell on my neck. I was just what he needed; a Company Commander of seasoned troops from a regular battalion, who were not yet battle exhausted, and who could attack and capture Mount Rachi, which a composite battalion had failed to gain that same morning in a dawn attack. I was told that my men were being taken up to an assembly area where they would be given a hot breakfast, and I was given some late supper and retained there until dawn, so that I could look down on Rachi Ridge and see the ground over which I was to fight between my start line and my objective. Although bodies are normally recovered during the night, there were still a few khaki-clad ones around to be seen through my binoculars that morning, which did not do much for my appetite.

Eventually Major George Jellicoe of the Special Boat Squadron (an offshoot of the S.A.S.) appeared to give me further details of the ground, since he had come round the Western side of Rachi Ridge in the darkness and reported probable gaps in the German positions on that side. If I had had more time to plan my own attack I would probably have elected to do a left hook and attack Rachi Ridge from the West, but my start line had already been predetermined and I was ordered to attack from South to North through the Regiment on Point 103 who were to hand my company some grenades which we lacked. 'H Hour' was to be at 0800 hrs.

I then scrambled down to the mountain road and was driven to the assembly area where my men had been fed. I was shattered to learn that all the wireless sets which provided my Company to Platoon links had been rendered unusable by the salt spray they had endured during the storm between Samos and Leros. I was to have no forward link, but the set that worked back to Battalion H.Q. was working, and would enable me to talk to the C.O. when he arrived. There was just time for me to have a word with my men before taking my platoon commanders and C.S.M. Spooner off to a view-point from which I could point out the actual ground to them whilst I gave them their orders. Just before they dispersed I received a message that 'H hour' had been postponed until 0830 hrs. It says much for British Army training that we all went through the processes before battle just as if it had been an exercise in England; and because we had been conditioned to intensive aerial bombardment in Malta, we took little notice of the close attention of the Luftwaffe which had started at first light.

When we reached the area behind the start line, the occupants told me that they had no grenades to spare, and it had been hinted that I might not receive any fire support. We accordingly adopted a square formation with two platoons forward, the third platoon prepared to give fire support to the right hand platoon and the two bren guns of Company Headquarters supported the left hand platoon. The fighting of the previous two days had been so intense that nothing else could apparently be spared to support us either.

At 0830 we moved forward in complete silence and I began to think that the enemy had abandoned the highest bump on Rachi Ridge, which was our objective, during the night. Not until Hewett's platoon was within fifty yards of the crest did all hell let loose from the German position. I saw Hewett's leading right section almost on top of them when his men started going down and Hewett was killed. I decided to run forward so that there would be an officer on the objective and as Company Commander, I would be well placed to marshal my second wave in. I paused in my tracks to look over my shoulder to see how my second wave was faring and saw that they had passed through the start line and were beginning to come down the little saddle which separated the start line from the Germans. At that moment, the enemy machine guns switched their fire onto this second wave and I saw my old friend C.S.M. Spooner and several of those with him fall. He was in fact killed instantly. Those in the second wave who had not breasted the rise took cover. Once the Germans had their heads up and were not fired on they had complete fire superiority over the saddle and anything that moved on the forward slope of our start line Point 103 was mercilessly machined gunned. I turned my attention to Hewett's other sections and saw the left hand one go round the left of the German position and vanish. His middle section were crawling about right under the noses of the Germans and I joined them. I told them to worm their way round via the left and attack from there whilst I remained fairly central to marshal the others in when they arrived. They never did. I was beginning to feel isolated as the only live person on the front apron of the German position. My nearest neighbour was a dead subaltern of the Royal Irish Fusiliers who must have been lying there since their attack the previous morning. A silence fell on the immediate area. Since the left side of the objective seemed the only entry point I crawled round to the left feeling extremely lonely. I gingerly stood up and moved forward in a crouched position until I was suddenly confronted by a German light machine gunner lying completely in the open but just over the crest. The military term is 'a reverse slope position'. We both saw each other simultaneously and I thanked my stars that I had played scrum-half for my Regiment for a whole season. I flung myself to the ground, shooting my feet rearwards at the same time so that I fell full length. His stream of bullets crackled a good two feet above me and I wormed backwards as fast as I could. He never fired a second burst and his job had obviously been to protect his right flank and not to expose himself by crawling forward. I then wormed my way across the front of the German position until I was in front of their forward strong-point, a stone sangar. They seemed to have no idea that I was there and no-one fired at me. I was to be on my own there for nearly three hours. I still had my Luger which I had acquired in Tamra in Palestine and had managed to get a supply of 9 mm ammunition for it whilst in Samos. It was then much used by Axis troops, but rarely in our Army. I wriggled into a natural hollow a few inches deep, alongside one of the outcrops of rock which dot all those hillside fields. It was about eight inches high and had a base around three feet by two.

The next time their machine gun was poked through the slit they had made in the rough stone sangar I was already in the aim position and let fly. A long burst was later directed by them across the valley to where my second wave was still lurking. The sun was out and I repeatedly tried to flash a reflected beam at them by using the base of my wrist-watch. I also hoped that if they got their act together and continued the assault that any covering fire that they planned would take my unwilling presence into account! In between times I kept the dark slit in the stonework, which was no more than thirty feet from me, covered with my Luger. I got in three shots altogether and they all went through the slit, or they would have ricocheted all over the place. Always the face vanished and a machine gun would be poked out to fire blindly across the valley. I suppose a 9 mm pistol shot close-to would sound not unlike a sniper's rifle from one of our people across the saddle.

Meanwhile communication between me and the rest of the world was nil, and the first thing to prove it was a series of soft crumps behind my old start line followed by the whistling down or our own mortar bombs all round me. I nestled into my hollow, dug my face into the earth and eased my tin hat back to protect the back of my neck. The mortar team which had come to support us after we had left our start line was from our friends the Royal Irish Fusiliers. They took their time, and the attack seemed to last till all eternity. They were aiming at the stone machine gun-post, and I was literally part of the target. When the last of the bombs landed and I had counted up to twenty I gingerly raised my head and looked around. The nearest bomb had landed just the other side of the little outcrop, about four feet from my head. Our 3" mortar bombs were designed to explode when the elongated nose hit the ground, thus showering metal pieces outwards with a flat trajectory. The tail-fin of the bomb lands in the centre of the shallow crater and there it was.

I felt that I would be in an extremely uncomfortable position if Ben Tarleton mounted a battalion attack to compensate for 'A' Company's inadequacy and wormed my way round to the right to see if there was any chance of shooting up the men manning the post from that side. I had already seen no entrance to the left. I thought I might apply Major Grant-Taylor's principle of surprising them from the rear and shooting them in the order in which they moved. I hastily dismissed the thought that they might all move at once! I soon found that I was out of luck, as that flank was also guarded by a single light machine gunner lying in the open slightly back in a reverse slope position. I somehow managed to repeat the gymnastics I had rehearsed earlier on the left, missed his stream of bullets and wormed my way back. For the first time, the men in the post spotted me. I fired two shots at faces which appeared, then a plastic grenade was lobbed over the top and rolled towards me.

I remembered an old Charlie Chaplin film as I leaped out of its way and lay down to my right. I knew that another would come down there and that I would have to go and lie down in the wispy cloud of dust which the first had created. After this had happened and I ran back to the right again, I knew that next time there would be two simultaneously, one each side, and there were. I ran back about fifteen yards and took cover behind a pile of small rocks just before they took courage and popped their heads up and managed to be down before a long burst of machine gun fire began to tear into my little mound of rocks. These are made by the local farmers who walk round every month or so and pick up any stones and small rocks which have worked their way to the surface.

The whanging and pinging that followed was most disquieting, as bits of stone and bent bullets sailed over my head and my cover began to erode. I decided that it was time to make a move. I rubbed all the chinagraph markings of the battle plans off my map, and took a large swig from an Eno's bottle of Italian brandy which someone had pressed into my hand when I disembarked at Portalago, and began to run like a madman down the Eastern side of the ridge towards our own positions. In the course of the morning I had worked my way across from the Western side.

It was downhill and I went like the wind, weaving left and right, and every German who saw me had a go. Eventually I just had to have a breather and flung myself down as if I had been hit whilst my heart raced and I puffed and panted. The firing stopped and I sighed with relief. Then some vicious opponent fired a single shot and a bullet hit between the underside of my wrist and the ground on which it lay and flung my whole arm up in the air, as if in a sort of gesture of surrender. "Damn" I thought "now the beggars will know that I'm alive after all" and off I set once more aiming more down-hill and out of their line of sight.

I eventually made my way round to the rear of my held-up second wave and climbed up to them to everyone's surprise. On my way up I encountered an officer of the regiment who had felt unable to spare us any grenades. He was shouting "the Jerries are coming, the Jerries are coming". I pointed my Luger at his midriff and told him to go back to his men, or else. He said "don't be a fool, I'm carrying an urgent message". I reflected that his presence in the front line would probably do more harm than good and allowed him to proceed. All the racket he had heard was the Jerries firing at one frightened Butler.

The machine-gunning had alerted both sides as I crawled forward for the last fifty yards and when I reached Bill Grimshaw he looked a bit shifty but I simply told him where I had been all the morning, asked why there had been no look-out who would have seen me and my signals, and then took stock of what we had left. The answer was one platoon and Company Headquarters, less their dead and wounded, some of whom were still unrecovered on the slope that faced the enemy.

I got on to the only wireless set that worked, the set to Battalion Headquarters, and managed to raise the Adjutant, Donald Cropper and then Ben Tarleton. I told him that I could divide my remnants into two weak platoons but that with all my subalterns and my CSM killed or wounded, I and my second-in-command Grimshaw would have to command them. I said that I was sure that a left hook would take the position, and that I would support them in with my own Brens which I would deploy to the right so that they could keep up fire to the last moment. I asked for smoke and for continued use of the Royal Irish Fusiliers mortar detachment, which had so nearly written me off that morning; all good chaps who said "Sorry Sorr" when I recounted my experience of their morning's firing. There was only one 25 pounder gun left in action and I was given its support to fire smoke. I said that we could attack at 1430 hours, and we did. The two wounded subalterns were Johns who was temporarily blinded by the flash of a near miss from a bomb and Groom who had a flesh wound in the calf. It was bandaged with a field dressing and he seemed to be walking alright, but said he couldn't face the walk. I put him in charge of the Bren Guns. My instructions were that the guns would fire in turn, never together and that the one firing would rake the ridge in front of us its whole length, to be taken up by the next etc., until we took the position. The moment we were seen on the position I wanted them up there at the double. At 2.30 the mortar, the 25 pounder and the first Bren opened up, and off we went at a fast trot with bayonets fixed. I took them all well down the Western side of the saddle and then we turned in and rolled the position up from left to right. Unfortunately I was shot in the thigh, right through the sciatic nerve, and bowled over; and Grimshaw had a nasty wound in the wrist which hit bone. We did however clear the entire position, and seeing no signs of movement from my Bren gunners, I sent a runner back with orders for them to join me at the double to defeat the inevitable counter-attack. The runner returned to report that the C.O. of the regiment through which I had attacked had refused to allow my men and their Brens to leave his Battalion area. I was absolutely shattered. I had been obliged to leave my Brens to provide my covering fire because the men of the regiment supposed to support me had been fighting more or less continuously for three days without sleep and seemed reluctant to put their heads up; and now their C.O. was keeping my men and their Brens to protect his own positions.

 I crawled forward on my elbows to look to the North and, taking a peep over a low wall, whilst one of my chaps put a field-dressing on my leg, I found that I could see to the far end of Leros. The appearance of my head produced streams of German bullets from every direction which clattered against the two foot thick wall. I was down to about twelve men with only rifles and bayonets, both Grimshaw and I were wounded, and in my case I could only proceed on hands, bottom and one leg.

 My Regimental History states "Major Butler, who had himself been badly wounded in the knee in the final assault, realised that he had insufficient men to hold the position and as his requests for reinforcements were unanswered, he ordered a withdrawal to Point 103". The truth is that I never asked for any reinforcements, but for my own men and my own Bren guns to join me on the objective which we had captured with such heavy loss of life, and could have held with my eleven Brens and the 22 men who manned them against anything the Germans threw at us. With no automatic weapon, however, and the Luftwaffe's air supremacy, it was only a matter of minutes before we would be bombed out of existence, and my survivors would have had short shrift from the Brandenburgers, who would not have appreciated being thrown off Point 100.

I took my remnants almost straight down the Western slopes of Pt. 100 before turning South towards our own positions. I had been so preoccupied by the prickles which were assaulting my bottom that I was quite taken by surprise to find us being machine-gunned from the air. Now that I was no longer effectively controlling a military unit I was able to take these things in. One of my men said "they've been at it all day Sir, haven't you noticed?" I honestly hadn't, and even to this day my memories are crisp and clear about the ground and the ground battle and only hazily do I remember the odd aeroplane. Our tin hats screened us from the sky unless we made the mistake of looking up, which we were trained to avoid.

As we got further down the slope I spotted a couple of jeeps on the mountain road which led back towards the valley in which Battalion Headquarters had been sited. Both jeeps carried stretchers but only one was used, for me, as I was the only walking wounded who couldn't walk. The worst injured of the others climbed into the spare seats of the jeeps and the others walked on down to Battalion Headquarters. My jeep turned off at a cross-roads called "The Anchor" and went on down to Portalago. As I made myself comfortable on my stretcher which was laid across the back of the jeep, over where the rear seat is situated, I thought my dangers for the day were now over, but my feet stuck out on one side and my head on the other and on that narrow road, bounded by uneven stone walls, I missed decapitation by inches at least twice and had to plead with the driver, when in doubt, to keep to the left and let the walls hit my feet.

Down at Portalago the quayside was littered with stretchers each bearing a wounded soldier awaiting evacuation. This could not take place until at best an hour after darkness, as the naval vessels to evacuate us could not leave their hiding places in the surrounding islands until darkness had fallen. A Medical Officer appeared and insisted on giving me a shot of morphine. I was in no pain whatsoever as my leg was completely numb and remained so for nearly three weeks. He then said "We can't have senior officers lying around out here, I'll get you moved to the hospital". He indicated a buff coloured building which had already been bombed and its nearest door was hanging drunkenly by one hinge. I said "please leave

My objective skylined at the top of Rachi Ridge, and the track down which we scrambled onto the narrow road where I was met by a jeep
"...my feet stuck out on one side and my head on the other"

me here with the others, I don't want to go in there and probably be buried with rubble in the next air attack." By now two nights of little sleep, followed by one night of no sleep, followed by more nerve-shattering experiences than one would expect in a decade, plus the effect of the morphia beginning to tell, weakened my resistance and I found myself being carried through the drunken door. My last memory was of saying "I know what's going to happen, the boat will come in and everyone will be loaded on except me because I'll be forgotten." I was assured that I would not be forgotten and closed my eyes. The next I remember was my shoulder being shaken and a voice saying "I'm very sorry Major, but we did forget you and the minesweeper is nearly full, they're now taking walking wounded only." I peered into the darkness which now prevailed.

I felt that I had had enough of Leros, flung off the brown Army blanket which covered me, leaped up onto my good leg and said "I'm walking wounded" and began to hop towards the quay on my left leg. Two of my soldiers who had seen me taken into the dark and unlit hospital appeared out of the darkness. Both had their arms in slings, luckily different arms, so they fell in on either side of me and helped me to the gangplank. I believe we were the last three on board as the gangplank was already being manned. A Naval Officer shouted "find yourselves somewhere to lie down on the open deck, there's no more space below". I settled down on the already crowded after-deck, grateful to be on board at all and hoping we would make a safe passage to Turkish waters. In next to no time an officer appeared and cast an eye over his charges. I thought he looked familiar and then he saw me. "Into my cabin Sir" he said with a broad smile of welcome. He looked relaxed and confident and had obviously overcome the stunned shock that his lapse the previous day had done to him. He came in to see me for a minute or two after we had cleared Leros waters and been at sea for about twenty minutes. He had already heard that I had been wounded, and asked me how we had got on. It was only then that I realised that I had only been on Leros for twenty seven hours. It seemed like two lifetimes. We had left around 2 am and Leros fell in the early afternoon.

◇

When we returned in 1977 I was amazed to see that the door of the hospital was still hanging on one hinge and the interior was still full of rubble. The slit trenches between the trees and the hospital were still as I remembered them and had not been filled in; presumably left as a memorial. I took Phoebe up to Rachi Ridge and found the outcrop of rock which had saved my life from the mortar bomb. I stirred up the earth where the bomb had landed, and out came a bomb fragment over an inch long. It now lives in a glass case amongst other souvenirs and treasures.

In 1988 the forty-fifth anniversary of the battle for Leros was marked by a pilgrimage to that island by British survivors. A service was held at the Military Cemetery followed by a March Past, both attended by Greek service men and guerillas who had continued to harry the Germans from the mountains after our ignominious departure as wounded or prisoners. The salute was taken by Brigadier Jeremy Phipps whose father had been killed as a young Naval officer seconded to the Island Commander to direct the fire from such Naval vessels which had survived German air attacks. He had been sharing a slit trench with Jimmy James, our Intelligence Officer and had just remarked "I had always looked forward to an exciting shore posting, but didn't think it would be quite like this." Two seconds later he was killed outright by a bomb splinter. Jeremy had been one of Michael's closest friends at Sandhurst.

Although many Italian officers had obeyed their orders to transfer their allegiance to the Allies against Nazi tyranny and fought gallantly alongside us, there was not a single Italian present at the ceremony. The Germans had shot all the Italian officers in cold blood as soon as the last of the British had left Leros as prisoners or wounded.

Chapter X

Farewell to the Aegean.
Life at 64th General Hospital

The first thing I did on settling down fully clothed onto the Captain's bunk was to go straight off to sleep. I had been twice wounded, once rather severely, and had received an unasked-for shot of Morphia. I still felt no pain whatsoever.

During the night we were somehow picked off in the moonlight by an enemy bomber who scored a very near miss and we lost a man overboard. I was blissfully unaware of all this. We had been bombed incessantly during the previous 24 hours and my sub-conscious mind was attuned to the noise, but I have a vague memory of it in my sleep. In the morning I awoke to find us in amongst the steep rocky bays we had been heading for two days earlier. I peered through the porthole and saw a destroyer alongside. Before long two men came to lift me onto a stretcher, and carried me onto the deck. It was rather frightening being lowered on the end of two ropes down to a launch and then up from thence onto the destroyer. I felt most insecure. In the destroyer, a room had been set aside as an 'officers Ward'. It was probably the ward-room – pun not intended! We were to be aboard this destroyer for three days and two nights. On the first night we shelled Axis-held Kos. The noise inside the ward-room was indescribable without ear plugs, and everything shook when the main guns were fired. The effect of this was for the German H.Q. on Kos to get the Luftwaffe to come and bomb us, which they did. On this occasion I was awake, and felt very helpless. In due course we made our way safely across the Mediterranean to Alexandria on 18th November 1943, where we were put into ambulances and taken to hospital. I heard a cheerful voice in the bunk above mine in the ambulance call down and say "is that you Sir, it's Wallington here." It is a small world at times, and the voice was that of my old Batman. I later heard that he had been a tower of strength on Leros and had, as the Platoon Sergeant, taken over command of Lt. Jode's platoon when he was wounded, and led them fearlessly and effectively until he himself was wounded. I felt that he should have been awarded the Military Medal. We were eventually trundled into wards at 64th General

Hospital at Ramleh, a few miles East of Alexandria. Wallington, whose wound was healing adequately was fairly soon transferred to another hospital, but I was to remain there until the following March.

The first RAMC officer to examine me was a Captain Dancer, an Irishman with a great sense of humour. Because my wounds were both clean and bleeding when the dressings were put on, under cover of a low wall on the battlefield in Leros, they were nearly healed and only needed covering with dry dressings. There was still no pain and I felt rather a fraud, but I was assured that it would start in around two weeks time, which it duly did. Because a bullet is very hot when it passes through you, when it also severs a nerve, the upper nerves above the injury send messages to the brain that all the areas to which that nerve sends and receives messages below the wound are being burnt. One might just as well have one's whole lower leg in a blacksmith's furnace! Sometimes at night I would put my foot into a basin of cold water as a psychological attempt to ease the burning sensation. It used to work for a while, because the circulation ceased, but it was twice as bad when it was brought back into the bed and warmed up. It had to be kept in a splint to prevent the muscles from assuming the wrong positions, and I had to remain in bed, as although the heart sent the blood down the arteries, the veins, with no message from the brain, were unable to move the blood uphill and back up the leg. It is normally done by minute 'hairs' inside the veins making wave-like movements which massage the blood along. Without this help, the blood can only get back when the leg is lying flat. If I put my foot down it went dark blue and if I held it up in the air it went white.

The process of healing could only be accomplished by the raw nerve-ends growing down the tubes from which the dead nerves below the injuries gradually retreated. I could even feel the vibrations of the trams which ran past the hospital on their way to Alexandria, and if anyone knocked my bed it was, at first, extremely painful. The pain continued for about three months, but one learned to live with it and to control one's reactions. In the end the chap in the next bed and I used to tease one another by jerking each others beds on purpose. John Smith was a major stationed in Alexandria, had broken an arm, and did not relish being jarred. We had both just read 'Snow Goose' by Paul Galico which was around in the Officer's Surgical Ward; a touching story which left one with a lump in the throat, and if either of us failed to keep a stiff upper lip the other would say 'Snow Goose'. I was soon encouraged to get around on crutches, but for periods of not more than five minutes, so that the circulation in the leg was not stopped for too long.

In due course he left with his arm in a sling and came back one afternoon to see me and recount a tale which he couldn't wait to tell. I said

"What are you smirking about?" He replied "I went with my boss to a funeral this morning, and we duly stood at the graveside and took part in the Service. We then took a pace to the rear and my Colonel fell backwards into another newly dug grave just behind us. He landed on his back and for a moment looked like a beetle with its arms and legs in the air. He eventually struggled to his feet and I and another chap each gave him a hand. Just as he was almost out, I felt myself slipping in on top of him, and as my arm has not yet set, I didn't dare risk a fall and let him go. He dropped back down into the bottom of the grave again with his arms and feet in the air and although I shouted 'So sorry Sir' I just couldn't stop laughing uncontrollably. I couldn't face him at the office this afternoon, so I thought I'd come and see you instead." He was welcome.

We had the usual run of hospital visitors, local residents who came in with titbits or boxes of chocolates. One rather over-weight lady could hardly speak a word of English, and every time she came she said the same words at each bedside "You are better yes? 'ave a banana", and her hand would plunge into a voluminous bag and reappear with one.

Amongst regular visitors was Peggy Bavin, who had been at school with Phoebe and who lived in Alexandria because her husband, now fighting in Italy, normally worked there in peace-time as a civilian. She brought me a bottle of whisky one day and I found that if I had one really strong whisky and water, although it did not ease the pain it enabled the brain to do a mental exercise to dissociate oneself from it. I used to be able to think "I'm alright, there's nothing wrong with ME, it's just my leg, what a nuisance it is". I realised that if I kept on doing this all day long, the effect would wear off and I would just become an alcoholic; so every day at 6.00pm I had a happy half-hour and enjoyed a care-free state of mind. Another regular visitor was Phoebe's Aunt Ray, whose house was less than a mile away. The trouble was that she used to appear too soon after lunch when I often managed about half an hour's undrugged sleep. As one was never out of pain, the last thing one remembered was the pain and it was the pain which broke through and woke one up. However well one kept a stiff upper lip when one was fully awake and in control, all of us with nerve injuries tended to let out a groan when they were being woken by the pain, eyes still shut, and not in full control of their faculties. Aunt Ray often hit that moment and I found it most embarrassing to open my eyes and see someone looking down at me when my guard has been down.

Every morning I would have three treatments, a massage to help circulation, a form of electrical treatment which made all the muscles of the leg operate whether the nerves worked or not, as we used to make dead frog legs move with electricity in the biological laboratories at Oundle, and a weaker form of electricity which was applied to the nerves above the wound to try and encourage them to grow down. It was then that I was encouraged to use all my will power to pass messages down to my toes.

Eventually the weak electricity began to get movement, but it was not until the following February that I got my first unassisted twitch. I was giving everything I had to make my toes uncurl and come up and suddenly the toe next to the big toe fluttered slightly. It was a great day and the beginning of the first periods when the pain began to ease. Suddenly I found the pain gone one morning and was over the moon with joy, but after an hour it came back. Gradually the periods of relief lengthened until it was a matter of just sometimes having the pain.

During the worst period, which was in December 1943, it had become almost impossible to make me sleep. They tried all sorts of soporific drugs and finally mixed a cocktail called 'Three Fifteens'. It consisted of 15 grains of Bromide, Opium and Chloral. Those of us who were on various sleeping-draughts were not given them until around midnight, the idea being that if we had them too early we would come round when it was still dark, and that it was better to do so when the new day had dawned.

The most severely wounded officer in the ward was a Lieutenant Rushton, who had received a direct hit on the right buttock from a small mortar bomb. He had lost his right leg and the whole of the right buttock and the problem was to get the enormous wound to heal. The dusty atmosphere of Egypt was full of germs and whatever dressings he had, the wound kept going septic. When the screens were put round his bed the whole ward went silent and we were almost sick with communal compassion when he would cry out "No! No! Colonel Armstrong, please, please stop!" as a hard-faced Lt. Colonel in the Australian Army got out his knife and cut away bits of septic flesh with no anaesthetic. To hear a brave young officer pleading for mercy was far worse than undergoing pain oneself. One day a pot of Penicillin ointment arrived from Cairo and Armstrong put it on his dressings. After two days I saw Rushton's face smiling for the first time and he told me he was completely out of pain. At the end of the third or fourth day the ointment ran out and Rushton's wound deteriorated almost at once. I was so worked up that I threatened to steal a motor cycle and lobby G.H.Q. until some more ointment was provided, leg splint or no leg splint. It was no good. It was an early experimental jar and not generally available. Rushton, who was in his early twenties and had a young wife in England, was eventually flown home. He died a few weeks after his arrival, but at least the couple saw each other for a little while.

The dreaded Armstrong turned his attention to me. I had expressed the view that there seemed no anaesthetic which reduced pain, they just put one out. I wondered if something could not be done to relieve pain whilst one was awake to enjoy it! His response was to make me a guinea-pig and attempt to inject the main sciatic nerve about three inches above the nerve injury. It was a crazy thing to do, because sticking a needle right into the nerve would automatically tear and cut the tiny sensory nerves which surround the main motor nerves, the sciatic nerve being like a cable with numerous small wires within it.

I had asked for something to be done and was not in the position to say "but not that", and was duly invited to crutch my way to the operating theatre. He opened the batting by saying "You'll feel it alright if I hit the nerve and must let me know when I hit it and I will then squirt in some local anaesthetic. I found this far from re-assuring and lost all confidence. To get through my thigh muscle, which was above the wound and had not wasted so much, he needed a long, strong and very intimidating needle. He plunged it in and said "have I reached the nerve yet?" "Yes" I gasped, lying like hell "you are spot on." He duly injected the fluid into me, and to my great relief withdrew his weapon. "You must let me know how long the effect lasts" he exclaimed, and then I can give you a booster. There followed a lot of cunning lying on my part to avoid further dosage. I had to pretend that it had worked, but not well enough to be worth a repeat performance.

✧

My interchange of letters with Phoebe included more and more thoughts about the names of our new offspring, which was due at the end of February. All had gone fairly smoothly with Phoebe's return to her former arrangement, and after a short period of punishment, when she was given a small room with no view of the sea, she returned to the luxury of a suite with balcony. To counter the monotony of hospital life, I decided to gatecrash the Doctors and Sisters New Years Eve Fancy Dress Ball, dressed as the Red Queen. This involved careful planning and the organisation of dressers who could get of bed and use their hands. Having acquired all the necessary gear, after 'lights out' on the great day I stood up in my pyjamas and dressing-gown with my crutches held closely to my side, and a series of sand-fly net rings, which varied a little in size were lowered over my head, the largest at the base, pre-tied together onto two lengths of string, each passing from the bottom front straight up my chest, over one shoulder and down the back to the bottom rear. Two large lengths of red cloth purloined from bed screens were then wound round the rings and fastened with safety-pins, gathered in at the top round my neck. A number of red rubber rings, normally used to cushion sore bottoms, were then lowered over my head, smallest at the top. From all the gold paper and tinsel left over from Christmas, a crown was fashioned round a base consisting of an unmentionable vessel with its handle at the back well camouflaged with tinsel. A slit for me to see was provided by two small balls of red paper on either side of my eyes between the two rings at eye level.

I was able to move my crutches about a foot back and forth and was soon gliding sinuously into a large empty ward which was being used as a ball-room. Picking my moment when people were dancing, I made for the first table with a vacant chair and sat down. The hospital was very large, and I recognised no-one from the Surgical Ward through my tiny aperture. The two couples at my table had no idea who I was, and I could have been a member of the staff. They were amused and helpful, and eventually opened a gap opposite my mouth and poured in a large whisky. I then muttered my thanks and said "I must get out of this", struggled to my feet and retired with dignity, again choosing a moment when people were dancing. No-one was apparently quite sure who the Red Queen was, and the spirit of goodwill prevailed the next day, although some of the surgical staff had done some shrewd speculating. I had also done some speculating because quite a few in my ward had wagered that I would not attend the doctor's Ball, let alone tweak it.

The nights continued to be an eternity and from 10 – 12 pm those of us on the drugs waited in the dark – unable to read and unable talk – for our various knock-outs. I began to think about the 1000-bomber raids which we had started on Germany and reflected that many people whose friends and relations had prayed for them would be killed in Hamburg that night and many evil so and so's for whom no-one had prayed would be spared. I thought about my prayers for Christopher and how I had prayed exclusively for his survival and not our own. I could however not disbelieve in our Creator. If our Creator is not our God who is our God? I had felt His presence and had had prayers answered as if by miracles, and felt that there must be some feasible solution to a problem which has puzzled man since time immemorial. It then occurred to me that one could pray for a state of mind; that one could ask for the strength to accomplish this or to resist that; but that it was not possible to ask for bombs to be deflected or Aunt Agatha's ingrowing toenail to be cured.

I have since read the writings of Lin Yutan, the son of a Chinaman converted to Christianity who became an ordained Christian priest. Lin was also a baptised Christian but eventually allowed pure logic to dominate his thoughts. In his father's youth, sailing ships leaving the Thames for South Africa held a service praying for favourable winds. "Can he really believe" wrote Lin" that God could be swayed into providing unfavourable winds to all the ships going the other way." He eventually became an Atheist. I have come to believe that if the Captain had prayed for the skill to navigate successfully to Cape Town and the ability to overcome any hazards such as fog or storms which his ship might encounter en route, those prayers would have been answered.

Anyone who has studied the Laws of Nature cannot fail to be awed at their logic and their cleverness. They are disobeyed only at our peril. They are the only pointer that God has given us to understand his wishes. He has given us ten fingers and it has taken man many centuries to realise that they point to decimalisation and the simplest method of calculation. There is every indication that we are free to disobey His Laws, but if we go too far, there is no indication that He will come to our rescue. If we foul up our Planet it will be our own fault and no-one else's. One of the most powerful Laws is the Survival of the Fittest. The magic of Creation occurs inside the body of male creatures who turn fluids, salts and minerals into tiny living creatures which in the case of man look like, and swim like, tadpoles. Mother Nature, or God or our Creator has decreed that millions of these tiny living creatures will die each time a man or any other mammal mates, and that only the strongest and fastest swimmers will survive and carry on their line.

Religions which make a fuss about destruction of lives in their most primitive form forget to mourn for the millions who die, in the act of mating whether or not a contraceptive is used. Human life has developed differently in various parts of the world. In some areas, conditions are so harsh that Nature compensates by making the population more fertile. They have endless children to compensate for the high mortality rate. If such people are moved to another zone which is less harsh and has better medical facilities, they multiply like compound interest. If current statistics in this country prevail, the Ancient Briton-Saxon-Norman population will be in a minority in less than a century. Many people in this country would not wish for this to happen. I had better return to the Officer's Surgical Ward at 64th General Hospital.

◆

As I gradually managed to get more and more movement out of my leg, the talk was of providing me with a surgical boot to pick up my foot. The calf muscles, and those which came into play lower down when I tried to put pressure on the ball of my foot, were much stronger than those on the front of the leg which lift the foot up. There was to be a band round my leg below the knee to which a spring would be attached to pull up the front of the boot. After due measurements had been taken, the monstrosity was placed on order. The immediate problem was that if I tried to walk on my right foot, the splint would immediately break when it was rocked forward with weight on it, being designed to support no more than a floppy foot in bed. As time went on the the movement improved, I began to be impatient to get up and about. I counted the days until my boot would arrive and eventually decided that they could be too many, and set to work to invent a temporary solution.

Around this time, in March 1944 John Whitty sailed into the ward, on leave from Italy, dressed as a Lt. Colonel and wearing the ribbon of the DSO next to his MC. "What the hell are you doing in bed" he exclaimed "we'll have to get you out of there." I explained the boot problem and my plans for overcoming it; having already designed an arrangement which was to work successfully for many months. It consisted of a wide dog collar, which one of the afternoon visitors purchased after I had measured my broomstick-like leg. I had then persuaded another visitor to pad it with cottonwool and cover that with soft chamois leather. I had not yet got it back, and the final requirement was for a long length of knicker elastic from one of the V.A.D.s (Volunteer Nurses), so that I could rig up four strands round the ring on the dog collar, which normally clips onto the lead, to the lace showing at the toe end of my right shoe.

In the meantime John got permission to take me out and we went to a hotel which had a bar and more appetising food than that supplied in the hospital. Next day I arranged for us to have tea with Aunt Ray, and he delighted her with his charm and by playing her piano. I had only heard him playing honky-tonk tunes in pub bars before the war, but he played excerpts from musicals including Gilbert and Sullivans with a very delicate touch.

On the third day I arranged to sail the club dinghy of the One Designs at the Royal Alexandria Yacht Club in one of their weekly races. It was a bit hazardous crutching along the narrow floating catwalks, but leaving my crutches on the catwalk alongside which the dinghy was moored, I only had to hop twice to get aboard. Having sailed small boats for most of my life, I had developed a fairly good touch, particularly in light breezes. However, I did not expect much in the club boat with John, a pretty inexperienced crew. As we cruised to and fro before the start, I took stock of my opposition. There were some pretty fearsome local ladies amongst them who looked very keen and businesslike. They obviously knew behaviour of every eddy of wind, from whichever quarter it blew, and seem to curl their lips at the two gauche English strangers.

At last I found that I could do something better than John, who had represented the Army at Rugby Football, Cricket and Golf, was a tap-dancer, piano-player and something of a conjurer, apart from being an outstanding Battalion Commander, and I was determined to pull out all the stops that afternoon. The set course had to be sailed twice, and in the first circuit I was getting the feel of the boat, of the currents and the behaviour of the wind in those parts of the course affected by buildings, whilst John was getting to grips with the jib sheets when we went about, learning to change sides smoothly, and how to turn it into a small spinnaker with the aid of a little pole when we ran before the wind. We slowly pulled up from our starting position of seventh out of ten to about fourth as we began the second circuit.

The wind then became increasingly light, almost dropping completely at times. By this time I was regaining my touch on the tiller and John the art of moving almost imperceptibly or being completely still. For the first time the four leaders, two with tight-lipped dusky local ladies at the helm, began to look back at us as we closed on them. We were, as a pair, perhaps a little heavier than them. This was not a total disadvantage, because if we made the most of a puff and got a bit of speed up, we could freewheel further through a calm patch. This is precisely what we managed to do on two occasions, each time passing two opponents. We got our gun at the finishing line and it was surprising how the local beauties who had so smilingly, but condescendingly, welcomed us when we first appeared at the Clubhouse now found it almost impossible to force even the faintest smile – Very un-British,a I thought, but in those days many of the locals were an odd lot, being a mixture of Egyptians, Greeks, Christian Lebanese with, quite often for the lucky ones, a touch of British soldiers' blood thrown in.

On the next day when John appeared at my ward to collect me, my self-designed surgical shoe was in action. I had quite a job with the final touches. First the foot was too floppy to get into the shoe. It was like trying to push a dead fish into something and I had to cut the comfortable old brown shoe open with a razor blade right up to half an inch from the toe, and then just drop the foot in from the top. The next problem was to get the right tension on the elastic, which had to taut enough to lift the toe up at the end of the step forward but not stay up too firmly. It all worked out in the end and I stained the white elastic brown so that it did not catch the eye too much. The contraption worked perfectly and once more strength built up in the foot, I was able to abandon the slit shoe and later, when I got home to England, to use black elastic when I was wearing black shoes. I still await the arrival of the official 'surgical boot.'

Some of the friends I had made during my months in bed were, like John Smith, doing normal headquarter jobs in Alexandria and lived in flats or shared houses. They rallied round me and John Whitty, and we soon found ourselves being asked to parties in the evenings. The Sisters and Nurses were delighted to see me out of pain and getting my foot going and turned a blind eye if I came in after the official deadline, which I think was 9.00 pm.

The senior Ward Sister explained "but you must ring up and tell us where you are so that we know you are safe. You can imagine how foolish we would feel if you were found in the gutter with your throat cut and we had not reported your absence from here". A few robberies with murder were not unknown at night in the dark streets of old Alexandria. I fully understood and religiously telephoned my whereabouts. Sometimes, when the drinks flowed too freely, John would not deliver me until after midnight, but the Night Sister seemed quite happy.

On one such night John and I found ourselves boarding the tramcar for Ramleh at the same time as Colonel Armstrong. I didn't flinch for a moment, or exhibit any guilt, but sat beside him and introduced him to John, who had been born in Australia and lived there until he came to England to go to Clifton. As two Oz Lt. Colonels they got on well, and I am sure Armstrong was impressed by John's row of medal ribbons. When we reached the hospital John did not get down but went on to the next stop where he was staying in a hotel. Armstrong and I walked in together and said 'goodnight' when we were both inside with no hint or reproach.

On the next evening John and I were off again on the tiles and at around 11.00 pm I telephoned my Ward Sister to let her know of my whereabouts and telephone number. She sounded in quite a panic and said "Colonel Armstrong made a surprise visit to the Ward this evening and wanted to know where you were". I interrupted her with the comment "Well if he knows I'm out that's it. There's no point in hurrying back now." I was of course awash with Dutch courage. When John finally saw me to the steps of the hospital, I made my way to the Sister's cubby-hole and found her in real distress. Armstrong had told her to telephone him every half hour until I came in, so I had no chance of pretending that I had come in at eleven thirtyish.

I solemnly went to bed and wondered what the morning would bring. In no time at all, in fact very shortly after breakfast, three hard-faced doctors whom I had never set eyes on before stood round my bed, asked me a few questions, told me to take my splint off, and the one who had a mill-board with some papers clipped to it did some writing. The leader then said, after no audible consultation between them, that I was being upgraded from 'D' to 'B'. 'B' being fit for duty anywhere except the Front Line.

There was no sign of Colonel Armstrong who had obviously acted in a very underhand manner, not having had the courage to rebuke me to my face on the evening we returned together with John. He was certainly not my favourite doctor, neither was he popular with his fellow doctors. My friend John Dancer, who had first taken off my field dressing, was constantly in his bad books, probably deservedly. He did a wonderful imitation of Armstrong's Australian accent. "Keptin Daanser you hev agine bin consoomin the pieshunts ile."

✧

The coincidences which seem to befall me occurred with John Dancer. A few years ago, when I had my eyes tested in Lymington, our local shopping town, I found myself sitting down in front of John. He had abandoned an orthopaedic for an ophthalmic career, and we had many a jar in the Angel Hotel, about fifty yards from his surgery.

✧

I was shortly informed by the Ward Day Sister that I was being discharged that very morning. As I had lost all my clothes in the Aegean except the battle-dress that I had been wounded in, which had been replaced because it had been ripped open on the battlefield, I had only to pack the contents of my haversack. That I had it was a miracle of administration by my Regiment, because I must have left it at our last assembly point before going into battle, and my efficient Colour Sergeant must have heard that I was wounded and got it down to my stretcher whilst I was asleep. It contained, amongst other things, a few water colour paints and a small 8" x 6" sketch book. I said farewell to the Day Staff of my Ward who had looked after me so well and passed similar messages through them to the Night Staff.

John Whitty arrived, was told the news and said "don't worry, I'll go and book us seats on the next Cairo train and will be back with a taxi." I was then given a posting order to some transit camp in the sand, where walking would have been a problem and my sticks, which now replaced my crutches, would have sunk in. I was then told that I was to appear before the O.C. Hospital, a full Colonel, for an official rebuke. I duly tried to march in in a soldierly manner, but the floor was highly polished and I slipped and fell fairly hard. The Colonel and his Staff Officer came and helped me up. The Colonel reseated himself and a chair was produced for me. I sat on it feeling quite unrepentant, and in any case the sting had already been taken out of the performance by my fall. I said I was sorry but felt that some tolerance should be shown to the movements of comparatively senior officers who could walk, after a fashion, and the interview was terminated.

Chapter XI

A 'gabardine swine' in Cairo and Jerusalem

When I came out John had already arrived back with a taxi and off we went. His first words were "forget about the camp, we'll go and see Bill Oliver who is BGS Ops (Brigadier, General Staff, Operations) at G.H.Q. and he'll soon fix you up with a job". The next morning we went to see Bill, who was in my Regiment. He immediately organised a week's leave for me, and one day later I learned that I had been appointed M.A. to the C in C (Military Assistant to the Commander-in-Chief), probably the most prestigious Major's job in Egypt. I hastened to telephone the Headquarter Staff of 64th General Hospital to let them know of my new appointment, on the pretext of enquiring for some fictitious item that I pretended to have left behind. I also visited a good tailor to be measured for a gabardine service dress jacket and slacks, so that I would be well turned out when accompanying the C in C on formal occasions. This dress was normal for senior officers and their staffs, which is why we were known as 'gabardine swine' by officers with recent experience of the hardships of the desert war!

John, who always seemed to know everybody, had already organised us to stay in a flat which was rented by two ATS officers, one a major and one a captain. Both these ladies had staff jobs at G.H.Q. The flat had three bedrooms, one for each damsel and a double room for guests, which John and I shared. We saw little of them except at breakfast. We spent most of our time being entertained by John's endless friends, either to lunch or evening parties. Although my leg was still weak, it was gaining strength slowly if imperceptibly and we played a few holes of golf at the Gezira Club. As a 5 handicap player John had a lot of useful tips to offer, but with a stroke a hole, I managed to give him some sort of game for about 6 holes at a time. When the time came for him to go back to his battalion in Italy we both had a hunch that it might be for the last time, although neither of us voiced our fears. In his case he made a point of doing all the things he had done before at the end of leaves in Cairo. One of these was to go for a drive in an open carriage with Jules, an old French friend who ran a successful restaurant.

He had to be at Heliopolis Airport at around 7.00 am one morning and dressed and had an early breakfast without waking me. He popped back to our room, we had a firm handshake and he was gone.

From that time on we had running correspondence. He used me as a safety valve when he felt frustrated. He had been offered command of a Parachute Brigade, but turned it down, saying that he would prefer to wait for command of a normal Infantry Brigade.

His Battalion, our 5th Battalion, fought its way up to Florence, and having started its long journey inside Egypt at the Battle of Alamein, they had come a long way and were due to be sent home. Somewhere in Southern Italy his men had 'captured' a piano which was an important item in the Battalion Headquarters three tonner truck. Whenever they were out of the line John used to give his men an impromptu concert, playing all their favourite tunes from memory.

Unfortunately word of their move had got around, and they failed to capture their objective in what was to have been their last attack. The Brigadier was most understanding and told him that he was prepared to capture the position with a night attack by a Ghurka battalion; but that if he wanted to go out on a high note 5/RWK could do it. "We'll do it" said John, and they did. In the morning John and one of his officers from Battalion headquarters went round to see his men on the objective. Whilst he was away, his Adjutant took a telephone call from Brigade "to invite Colonel Whitty to lunch with the Brigadier who had some news for him." He was to be given command of an Infantry Brigade. He never came back. He trod on a concealed mine and most of his leg was blown off and his companion wounded. His main artery was severed and he must have bled to death in seconds. He never learned that his ambition to command an Infantry Brigade was about to be realised. His Obituary in the Times, which described him as an outstanding Battalion commander was headed "A HAPPY WARRIOR."

Before John left Cairo, I had one interview with General Sir Bernard Paget, the Commander-in-Chief of Middle East Land Forces (MELF). He explained that he thought it wrong to have aides de Camp (ADCs) in wartime, "rather a sissy thing to do" he said, "so I have decided to make my ADC a second Military Assistant (MA) and to have two MAs." The young temporary Captain who was his current ADC was entirely unqualified to undertake any serious staff work, a wartime officer whose one qualification was that his father had served with Paget in World War I.

Young as I was, I was a Temporary Major, a Regular Sandhurst trained officer who had qualified at the Staff School in Sarafand. I had also held previous staff appointments in Malta, and had been twice wounded and had been awarded an M.B.E. When I finally arrived to take up my appointment, this young man had re-arranged the furniture so that we were equals but that I was the lesser of the two equals. I found myself doing a lot of the ADC jobs, which obviously had to be done by someone, such as accompanying the General on visits, and meeting V.I.P.s at airports. I did not like to demur openly because if we both confronted the General, the son of his old friend was bound to win. When, however, the General went to visit King Ibn Saud of Saudi Arabia on a goodwill visit, with a superbly finished and polished rifle as a symbolic gift, my young friend changed places, and I was left with the more responsible job of running the C in C's office on my own and dealing with all the mail including sorting the essential papers which should be sent on to him each day. I accepted all this as just part of the rich pattern of life, although in fact I detest injustice in all forms. I lived in great comfort at Flagstaff House with a wonderful view of the Nile from my bedroom window. We two MAs were the only officers living there who were not senior officers wearing red-banded caps. The Chief of Staff, Major General Ballion and the Major General Administration 'Pop' Dowler were extremely friendly and treated me as an equal in the Mess, which was of course no more than the large drawing room of a pre-war stately home.

A lot of amusing incidents occurred, such as, when the General and I got out of the Rolls Royce each morning at G.H.Q., instead of my holding the door for him, he made sure it did not swing on to me as I and my, by now single, stick got out. The same procedure took place when we went up in the lift to his office, when he would pull back the heavy rolling metal door, and I would go in first on his insistence. He was extremely kind and courteous but enjoyed being seen around with a disabled warrior.

We had quite a few exciting moments, such as when the Greek Brigade stationed in Egypt mutinied. Cryptic messages would arrive from Winston Churchill – always urging action. I remember one of them "Where are your 75s?" The French Army used 75mm guns in World War I! It was always a problem to decide whether to wake the C in C up on these occasions. He was fairly irascible, and if one failed to wake him up he said "Why the devil did you wake me up, I could have dealt with that in the morning."

Returning to the Greek Brigade, when we did produce a show of force they began taking the covers off the big guns of their tanks and diplomacy was again required to avoid a set-piece and bloody battle.

Another notable event was the visit of Field Marshal Smuts. I was lucky enough to be present at a formal luncheon, and his breadth of vision was outstanding. He looked into the future and commented that the "yellow peril" would eventually dominate European politics. He could well have been right.

The most amusing incident, but only in retrospect, was when General Paget's Regiment, the Oxfordshire and Buckinghamshire Light Infantry known throughout the Army as the 'Ox and Bucks' was pulled out of the line from Italy and given leave in Cairo. They were going to have a friendly football match against some other regiment, and on that day the Commanding Officer and Second-in-Command were invited to lunch and I laid on the Rolls for two fifteen. As we walked down the steps of Flagstaff House for our journey to the ground, I asked the C.O. on what ground they were playing, so that I could give the necessary instructions to the chauffeur. He went rather white and said he didn't know and turned to his Second-in-Command. He didn't know either. I didn't give them many marks for this but felt that I should try and support them. It was too late to turn back and make a quick telephone call without blowing the gaff, so I decided to try and bluff it out. We all got into the car, and with all three rear seats occupied, I got in front with the chauffeur in front of the glass partition which was wound up. I quickly asked the chauffeur how many football grounds there were, and he said "three, Sir". I said "we will visit each in turn until we find the right one, but don't stop or pause if the first or second are the wrong ones, just drive on, turn at the first convenient turning and weave your way to the next choice until we do find the right one. They're all busy talking and will be unlikely to notice anything wrong."

The first ground was empty, and we glided slowly past it without slowing down. Unfortunately there were no side turnings for some time, and when we eventually turned right into one, the tarmac surface, which had shown such promise, suddenly came to an end and we found ourselves on a rough bumpy earth surface. The environment matched the road surface, mud houses, squalor and the odd camel. I would love to be able to say that one of them stuck his face into the open rear window of the car and burped but, though a possibility, it didn't quite happen. The General wound down the glass partition, turned purple, and barked "do you know where we are, Butler?" "I'm afraid I don't, Sir". "Damn bad staff-work" he barked, and wound up the window again. My cover was by then completely blown and, stealing a sideways glance, I saw the two officers beside him shrugging their shoulders as he was obviously asking them where their regiment was playing. This made me feel a trifle better.

After turning round with some difficulty in the now narrow little street we retraced our steps and after asking several military passers-by, we eventually located the right ground. Our august party was met by one of the senior majors of the Ox and Bucks and led up a long stairway which took us onto the grandstand. On arrival we found that every seat had been pillaged by the locals for firewood, but that one, rather rickety wooden kitchen chair had been provided for the Commander-in-Chief. He looked at it, then at me, leaning on my stick. "Sit down on that chair" he said gently. "I'm sorry, Sir" I replied, "but I just couldn't". "Well we can't just leave it, can we?" he mused, and we finished up by turning its back towards the game and each putting one buttock on the top cross piece, each with the top of the uprights in our crutches. There were some red faces around as the officers of the Ox and Bucks struggled to maintain their composure. When we got back my only defence was that I had imagined that the soldier-chauffeur's unit which I had initially telephoned would have briefed him and General Paget's complexion gradually returned from purple to its normal very dark red.

I made this an opportunity to suggest that he needed a young active ADC to do the work that I was doing and that I would prefer to gain some experience of the proper staff work which I had so recently been trained to carry out. 'Pop' Dowler came to my rescue and said he needed someone to hold the fort whilst his M.A. had some leave, and that I could do this for him until I got a normal staff posting. I moved out of Flagstaff House with a mixture of regret and relief and stayed at Shephard's Hotel during my time with him. It was great fun living in a first-class hotel with a fine cuisine. I also met a lot of people of all types as Shephard's was one of the two leading hotels in Cairo and hence one of the first to be burnt down in the post-war anti-British riots.

After a most interesting month as 'Pop' Dowler's M.A. I was posted as a General Staff Officer Grade II (GSOII) to H.Q. Palestine in Jerusalem. This was a most interesting assignment, because I had been in Palestine six years earlier getting the worm's-eye view of soldiering and was now at the hub of things with a parish which stretched to the Southern border of Turkey to the North and to the borders of Iraq and Saudi Arabia to the East. My duties sometimes took me up to Beirut, where the Free French were in much evidence, and the place had not lost its feel of a Southern Mediterranean seaside resort.

The headquarters in Jerusalem were sited on an upper floor of the King David Hotel, with a wonderful panoramic view of the Old City with its Western Wall facing our windows. Although access to our floor was well guarded from below, and we controlled the lift and the staircase, no-one had thought that terrorists could take a room on the floor below one of our offices and leave a large bomb in it. This eventually happened after I had left for England.

We had quite a high social set-up. The General's daughter was Lady Wellesley and her husband would eventually become the Duke of Wellington and she the Duchess. To keep a fatherly eye on her, the General made her his civilian P.A. (Personal Assistant); and though charming, she could be fairly dictatorial. My immediate boss was The Hon. Martin Charteris who, although he had no inkling of it at the time, was to become Private Secretary to Princess Elizabeth and later when she became Queen, her Assistant Private Secretary. When Sir Alan Lascelles retired, he became the full-blooded Private Secretary to the Queen. The Staff Captain 'A' was Lady Stuart-Richardson who I sometimes met at a dance or party. She eventually carried out all my documentation when I went home. A certain Brigadier Turnbull, who commanded 'Raiding Forces' used to drive up to escort her to parties. I mention this now, as both were due to enter my orbit three years later, arriving at different times in Addis Ababa. He was always known as 'Bull Turnbull.' Had there been no threat from terrorists, there would have been little for the Operations Staff do do; but the likes of the Stern Gang and Irgum Svai Liumi had already shown their hands, and were led amongst others by laymen who later rose to high political office, were blowing up roads, setting booby traps and carrying out attacks on military targets.

There were no Officers' Messes available for Staff Officers to live in, and we all had to find accommodation in the various 'Hospices' which had sprung up in peace-time to cater for the many pilgrims who visited the Holy places in and around Jerusalem. I stayed in one less than half a mile from the King David. It was comfortable but over-crowded and we had to share double rooms. These hospices varied a little, but by and large they were not as comfortable as a two star hotel, but better than the average British boarding-house. The food was quite good and plentiful.

On of my responsibilities was the provision of adequate smoke screens for every British based airfield in Palestine and the Lebanon, which gave me complete freedom to order a staff car and drive up to Haifa or Beirut. After being stuck for so long on a tiny island, it was good to be able to spread my wings a bit, and at times I also had to do the drive across the Sinai Desert and liaise with my opposite number in Cairo.

Fairly early on, I discovered that although extremists from both Jews and Arabs were planting bombs at vital spots to kill V.I.P.s, there was no interchange of information between the three Armed Services amongst themselves, or between any of these and the Palestine Police, although all these four forces had bomb disposal units of their own: the R.A.F. for their airfields, the Navy for the ports – mainly Haifa and Jaffa – and the Army and Police interwoven with one another in the countryside and major towns and cities.

I had a talk with Martin Charteris and suggested that we should run a couple of courses to make sure that all those risking their lives on bomb disposal duties would at least know everything that all on our side had discovered. Endless ingenuity had been used by terrorists to produce fairly accurate timing devices to explode bombs.

Examples are a detonator connected to a short length of slow-burning fuse which had the other end wrapped in a french-letter and dipped into a small ink bottle filled with strong sulphuric acid. The acid would slowly burn through the rubbery latex until it was finally dissolved, when the acid would ignite the fuse. There was a long period when the latex had partially perished, but not enough to let the acid in. The slightest knock or shake would however cause its collapse and the detonator would explode in seconds. Another was a primitive but accurate wrist-watch device for use with an electrically activated detonator. One wire would be wrapped round the winding handle of the watch, and the other to a small screw which had been screwed into a hole in the perspex face, which acted as an insulator. By removing either the hour hand or the minute hand, the remaining hand could be set to hit the screw in anything up to around 59 minutes, or just under 12 hours by the hand hitting the screw and completing the circuit.

All the Services and the Police responded positively, by making their top bomb disposal officers available as instructors on the courses, and I soon found a suitable building standing near some waste ground as the location of our temporary school. As the senior officer and general co-ordinator I became the Headmaster and was soon in my element. After a few days, when each instructor gave details of any unusual devices he had encountered or heard about, I drew up a syllabus and we prepared the props for the practical work. By this time I had invented and tried out a device which it was virtually impossible to dismantle without blowing it up. It was based on an internal pendulum not touching a ring within which it hung and the main secret was how to set it without the setter blowing himself up.

On the last day of each course we used live detonators on all the realistic situations which we had set up, and no main charges. The detonators were all bound with cloth, so that at the worst someone might lose a finger. I felt that the first time a newcomer to bomb disposal was given the job of defusing a live device, with the attendant tension that that entails, it was better that only a finger and not his life should be at stake.

There is always a know-all on all types of course, and on these the 'Butler Special' was saved to the last and given to the big-head. It was never defeated and the worst that happened was that the blast blew the plug off the top of the metal pipe which was the bomb, and took the big-head's cap off.

The biggest contributor from the instructors was Inspector Elson. He was known as 'Grip' Elson, because he so often carried a small grip containing the tools of his trade. These included a pencil sized torch for looking through small holes, various pliers, cutters, mirrors, insulating tape, etc. etc. When the courses were over we five instructors had become firm friends and I was issued with my own bag of tricks and given the King David Hotel as my special responsibility.

On the evening of the last course the three Service Instructors, 'Grip' Elson and myself had a monumental party. After eating and drinking too much we all piled into one jeep, which merely meant two people in the front bucket seats and the others sitting on the hood at the back with their feet on the rear seat. We finished up driving all round Jerusalem singing all the full and vulgar words of all the Rugby songs we knew. Starting with "Oh what a pity, she's only one titty to feed the baby on" and then deteriorating from there onwards.

We had built up a great rapport in a very short time, built on respect for each other's qualities, most of which we shared. It was a sad feeling parting at the end of the evening, but we agreed to be on call to help each other at any time we felt the need. I knew that I was likely to see more of Lt. Morgan, the Army Instructor, as our paths were bound to cross.

One day before my arrival a suspicious parcel had been found in a loo at the far end of our floor of the King David. The whole place was cleared, a light grappling hook attached to a long line was draped over it, and it was pulled to an area where closer inspection could be made. It turned out to contain nothing more offensive than a used sanitary towel!

Very shortly after we had all dispersed from the bomb disposal school the Army was ordered to clear all the mines which had been laid on the beaches of the Gulf of Aqaba, and Lt. Morgan immediately contacted me. Because some mines were below the low water line we felt that the Navy should be represented, and because of our warm inter-Service relations we felt that the Airman and Policeman should also be allowed to come! It was obviously going to be a most enjoyable trip. I managed to clear things with the Police, Navy, R.A.F. and the long suffering Martin Charteris, and off we went in two 15 cwt trucks, one a Dodge and one a Bedford with all the mine-detecting equipment, sleeping bags, food and a plentiful supply of drink. Both trucks were driven by Sapper N.C.O.s picked for their all-round abilities.

Our plan was to drive down to the Dead Sea and then up to Amman for the first night. It was the first time I had descended below sea level into the lower Jordan valley, or had crossed the River Jordan and entered what was then Trans-Jordan. In Amman we stayed in what had been Speke's house. In his earlier life, Speke had been a well known explorer of darkest Africa. The second night was spent on the high plateau desert between Amman and Ma'an. We cooked our supper in the usual Service fashion by making a ring of stones to take a frying pan, pouring some petrol into the sand in the middle and lighting it.

After sitting in a circle and dipping into our extremely adequate supply of alcohol, we turned in with blankets inside our sleeping-bags, as it was cold at that height after dark. I shall never forget the rich pattern of the myriad of stars forming a bright ceiling over our heads and the frequency of the shooting stars which one rarely sees in such numbers unless in clear, still air with no other lights anywhere.

"…we turned in with blankets inside our sleeping-bags,… I shall never forget the rich pattern of the myriad of stars"

We were up with the sun the following morning and by noon we were near Ma'an. We had been following the desert track which runs roughly parallel with the old narrow-gauge railway running South to Ma'an from Damascus. It is only a short distance from Ma'an to Petra, "Rose Red City half as old as time", and we vowed then and there to visit it on our way back. It had not long been re-discovered, having been lost for centuries, and we looked forward to exploring it.

After Ma'an the desert track began to descend until we reached Naqb Ashtar, a sharp turning by our track to the South East at the very edge of the high plateau. The view from Naqb Ashtar was breathtaking. We were looking down around four thousand feet at a vista which has never been equalled for quality of colour during all my subsequent travels, although these have included vistas of the Himalayas from Kashmir, the Victoria and Niagara Falls, Kilimanjaro, the Alps, you name it. The sandy plains below us were not of the usual sepia colour but a pale lemon yellow. The distant hills which rose from them, with peaks of varying height were, in that light, a misty powder blue, and one was looking down on them as from an aircraft. Along the edge of the high plateau there were eight peaks of over four thousand feet, and four of those were well over five thousand feet. The closer hills which lay immediately below us, rising to one or two thousand feet, were of brown rock slashed with vivid red. This was undoubtedly the same rare rock strata which gave its colour to the buildings of Petra. I got out my sketching pad, did a pencil sketch, and using the most accessible white plate (which I still do) as a palette, I opened the little flat cigarette tin which contained a few tubes of water colour paints, mixed a small quantity of the powder blue, the lemon yellow and the red colours and painted in one or two areas of each colour, for me to finish off when I got back to Jerusalem. The final picture is a bit of a mess, but I may try and get it included in this book for its genuine veracity, colours and unusualness.

We wound our way down the escarpment to the flat plains which we had seen from above and looked back. It was very hot down there and the dust flew up and kept the second truck at quite a distance from the leader. I was glad I had bought an agal and kaffieh which not only protected me from the sand but also made me look like a real Arab. We reached Aqaba in time for a swim in a tiny area which we first swept with mine detectors before settling down for drinks and supper. We were sitting on the veranda of the bungalow that Lawrence had used before going up North to ignite the spirit of the Arabs. There, in the general area through which we had driven, he welded them into an effective fighting force against the Turks and led them in support of General Allenby's campaign in World War I.

"The closer hills which lay immediately below us… were of brown rock slashed with vivid red"

"We were sitting on the veranda of the bungalow that Lawrence had used"

The bungalow was approximately halfway round the Northern apex of the bay at the top of the Gulf of Aqaba, with the old Arab trading port to the East and the then embryo town of Eilat to the West. Eilat is now a thriving tourist resort which we visited in 1980. The bungalow is still as we left it in 1944. The old Port of Aqaba was the gateway from the Far East to the cities of Jerusalem, Damascus, Beirut and Ankara.

The long caravans of camels followed the route which we had taken, and I feel sure that the story of Ali Baba and the forty thieves is based upon the secret city of Petra, whose entrance from the East is so well hidden by folds in the rocks, which begin the fissure which separates the basin in the hills in which Petra nestles from the high flat plateau which leads North. It seems certain to me that the forty thieves were not pure fiction, but the bad-hats from Petra who crept out and raided the camel trains carrying riches and spices from the Orient, only to vanish into the mysterious hillside like thin air.

When we had lifted all the mines, removed the detonators and blown up the main bodies in batches, we returned via a detour into Aqaba's picturesque Arab town and port, and then up to Nag-eb-Ashtar. This time we went into Ma'an to call on the local post manned by the Arab Legion, arrange for a guide to lead us to Petra and hire horses for the trip. The dusty trail on hard local saddles was a most uncomfortable experience. We had not originally planned to make this pilgrimage and none of us had protective trousers. Our knees lost a lot of skin and I, who seemed the only member of the party to have riding experience, was reduced to riding with my knees stuck out clear of the saddle, like all the others.

One hundred yards away from the deep crack in the mountain face, which extends for about a quarter of a mile, there was still nothing to indicate any fissure, as the entrance was like a giant overlapping hospital screen. At ground level there was an area of tall shrubs which helped with the camouflage.

Having dismounted and left our horses with the guide's assistant, we followed him along this fissure which not only overlapped vertically, but even overhead, so that at times we could not see the sky. Cut into the rock of one side of the fissure was a well preserved aqueduct, which must have carried water to the ancient city and was still running.

As we rounded a sharp bend we were suddenly confronted with a magnificent and well-preserved building cut into the solid rock. It was not built cut stone on cut stone, but a cave had been cut in the form of an enormous square hall with access by a single noble door. The fascia of the building was, however, carved in the rock face in the style of an ancient Roman building with cupolas supported by pillars, and ornamental windows with pillared sides. The main entrance door was flanked by pillars supporting a semi-dome and at the top of the building's facade was a huge ornamental pot, probably around six feet high. It was pitted with the scars of the many bullets which had been fired at it by Bedouins believing that it was filled with gold coins. In fact it was carved out of solid rock, was part of the rock face, and was in fact itself solid. Because it was protected from the hot sun, being still inside the slowly widening fissure, it was the best protected of all the fine buildings of Petra. It was known as the Treasury. The old inhabitants were known as the Nabateans and they had obviously been extremely civilised. I had been so impressed by the Treasury, that the other buildings or facades were something of a disappointment as, although many were bigger, none were so well-preserved. We all took numerous photographs.

When the local Arabs found the old city of Petra after its apparent disappearance for so many centuries, they were very cagey and superstitious about it. They would not reveal its whereabouts to any stranger, let alone a European, and the archaeologist who eventually gained access only did so by posing as an Arab for years and pretending he had come from the East. This he could do as that is where had he been working, and had genuine local knowledge, and eventually he accomplished his quest. I believe that they now run helicopter trips there and hence the mystique which we enjoyed would be completely lost. In many ways it is a pity that they have not been more subtle and forbidden entry except by horse or camel trek from Ma'an, with daily numbers strictly rationed. They could charge the earth for such trips and those doing them would still feel that the cost was worthwhile.

Before returning to our trucks at Ma'an we bound our knees with handkerchiefs outside our thin drill slacks. We spent that night at the officer's Mess of the Arab Legion and made a very early start next day, driving to reach Amman that evening.

In order to see more of the country, we elected to return by a much more rugged track half-way down the Eastern side of the Great Rift, in which lies the Dead Sea, and hence on the Western slopes of the Jordanian high plateau. Every now and then we would have rewarding glimpses of the distant Dead Sea twinkling away in the sunshine nearly two thousand feet below us. To start with we continued to see layers of red and pink in the exposed rock faces.

Eventually we ran into trouble, as the Bedford began to boil and we found that the fan belt had broken. In that heat, and climbing up and down slopes instead of along the flat plain above us, we were in dire straits. We used a lot of our valuable water refilling the radiator and some knitting expert plaited a fan-belt of sorts from a ball of string which we had brought to tie along tops of posts to mark mined areas.

This excellent effort only lasted for about five miles because the string-belt had no elasticity and had to be adjusted very taut to grip enough to

"We found that the fan-belt had broken"

turn the magneto. We finally constructed a fan-belt from the two NCO's braces, which had some elasticity. By then we had used all our drinking water, nearly all our mineral water and had saved the bottles for use in case we were reduced to the ultimate fluid, our own urine. Mercifully, this was only needed once, about five miles from our destination.

We crawled into Amman very late that night, having free-wheeled down every bit of downhill track to save wear and tear on the braces and the need for more topping up. Next day we were lucky enough to be able to get a new fan-belt for the Bedford and a spare for both trucks. We knew that we had no hope of climbing the two-thousand feet from the River Jordan to sea level and at least another thousand feet to Jerusalem without sound fan-belts and plenty of spare water which, in the event, we did not have to use. As I lay in my bath in Jerusalem that evening I reflected on the pleasures that memories of even our worst moments evoked, and how you can never really enjoy a drink to its fullest unless you have been dry and thirsty, or the comparative coolness of hilly air unless you have been sticky with sweat in a hot environment.

✧

Not long after this journey I heard from Phoebe that there was talk of families being shortly allowed to return to England. It was difficult to carry out such correspondence with any accuracy, due to the censorship in force, but we got through to one another that it would be worthwhile for us to try and co-ordinate our arrival in the UK. I had a trump card to play. I had been abroad for nearly seven years, and there was a scheme called 'Python' which was based upon everyone who had served more than five years overseas being due for immediate repatriation.

Whereas Phoebe and our two children were dependent on the vagaries of the families control system, I could at any time play my trump card and demand to go home. Like my surgical boot, my repatriation arrangements had not caught up with me. In guarded terms I learned that my family might be leaving South Africa in the late summer and so I took the first steps to get my own repatriation started. The only difference was that whilst any increase in either the German or the Japanese submarine campaign could bring Phoebe's movement to a halt, once my request was filed, there was no way I could back away from it. The aforesaid was of course precisely what happened.

✧

In Jerusalem a big event took place during this period. Grip Elson telephoned me early one afternoon to say that the Police had information that a suspected explosive cache of mammoth proportions had been reported in the modern area of Jerusalem, not far from the King David Hotel itself, and that he would appreciate my help. The other three instructors were too far away for immediate availability, so I grabbed my little box of tricks and joined him at his headquarters. We proceeded to a quarter which was slightly squalid and found a small single storied building already cordoned off by Police.

Grip was the first to enter the front door, which had been left ajar, with me rather foolishly too close to his heels. He peered through the crack in the door with a torch, to see that it was not wired or booby trapped with some movable object and gently pushed it open. We both entered the dark room, whose windows were all shuttered, and shone our torches round. There was an enormous pile of what looked like builders' sand rising to about four feet in height, and the walls were lined with what, in the dim light appeared to be bricks stacked against them. About two feet from the threshold lay a khaki haversack. Elson made no attempt to pick it up or to undo the flap. He very gently slid his hand under the flap and slowly moved his fingers left and right, feeling for any suspicious wires. He duly found them.

"It's a booby-trap all right," he said, "if you shine your torch in through the gap in the flap, I'll cut the wires one by one if they're single." (If wires are double, then pliers join them electrically and act as a switch). When we had eventually made the booby trap safe, we discovered that it was set so that the floor itself pressed up a wooden rod which projected down through a hole in the base of the haversack. This rod was surmounted by a piece of flat metal, thus forming a 'T' which was poised above the positive and negative terminals except when the haversack was on the ground and the rod and plate forced up and away from them. To lift the haversack without first disconnecting or cutting the live wires meant curtains for the lifter; and in our case countless lives and many buildings. We removed the charge and detonator and passed them gently to the nearest policeman who was, very sensibly, not too near the door!

We then opened the doors wide and took a good look around. The actual pile was not sand but ammonal, a grey and highly explosive powder. The things which had looked like bricks, stacked against the walls, were prepared hand bombs, each consisting of four sticks of gelignite, bound together with sticky-tape, with a detonator thrust into their centres already fitted with a short length of safety fuse. The floor was littered with tubular brass detonators, showing that a very hasty exit had been made. If, in the dark, one of us had trodden on one of them, it would not have been a case of losing a few toes, though we would have done, but a very large number of houses would have gone up with them. We would have been non-existent.

The explosion of just one detonator would have set off the bottom of the pile of ammonal which was spread over a wide area, and the first flash or spark to touch just one of the safety fuses would have set off its four sticks of gelignite, which would have set the whole lot off.

Moving slowly and methodically, we gradually cleared the floor of all detonators and then began passing the prepared gelignite bombs out to the police helpers, who were now becoming braver and more inquisitive. We decided that it would be prudent to defuse all the gelignite bombs by hand at an area far enough away from the cache to be relatively safe.

The job of defusing them was not highly skilled. It was simply necessary to use no force, to draw the detonators slowly from the bunch of four sticks, then remove the safety fuses from the detonators, and finally place the gelignite sticks on one pile, the safety fuses on another, and the detonators, each separately, on laid-out pieces of soft cloth. I think there were three of us on the job in the end, and that we did around twenty bombs each. I did not know before that if one handles enough gelignite, one gets the most appalling headache. Next day I added a pair of rubber gloves to the contents of my little suitcase. Grip Elson, who was a brilliant and fearless bomb disposal expert seemed to lead a charmed life, and I was humbly proud to have been instrumental in passing on his knowledge and experience to others who made good use of it.

He was one of the people to whom I paid a warm and meaningful farewell when I eventually left Jerusalem two months later. After nine years, when I again met John Fforde, who by then had become the Commissioner of Police in Lusaka, Rhodesia, I asked for news of Grip Elson and learned that he had been killed 'on the job', mercifully almost instantaneously, not long after I left Jerusalem. A sad loss for the Police and all his many friends in Palestine. Since writing the above I have learned that his reputation was of international proportion.

✧

A few weeks before I left Jerusalem, Martin Charteris was posted to Cairo as a GSO II. He came back for a week-end two or three weeks later, as a major, for a party which included Bull Turnbull and Kate Stuart-Richardson, who, as Staff Captain 'A', had been helping to try and co-ordinate my return to England with Phoebe's return from South Africa. In the event, what with U Boat scares in both the Cape area and the North Atlantic, I got home in September 1944 and Phoebe and our two children not until January 1945.

I was dined out in some style by my fellow staff officers at the restaurant of the King David Hotel. One of them, Pat Hunting, re-appeared in my life only four months later, as a fellow student at the Staff College, Camberley and flattered me by buying a picture of an Arab village which he kindly returned for me to copy and appears opposite page 37. He was soon to become Chairman of the Hunting Shipping Line and later Hunting Airways. Having bid my farewells to all and sundry, I drove back across the Sinai Desert.

Approximately half-way between Gaza and Ismalia, and in the middle of this almost featureless desert, there was one solitary military outpost to break the monotony of the one hundred and fifty mile journey. It was a detachment of the Royal Electrical and Mechanical Engineers, whose job it was to attend to any breakdown on this long narrow and seemingly endless desert road, and if necessary to recover any vehicle which could not be repaired 'in situ' and to carry out the job in their workshop.

They were as pleased to see me and my driver as we were to see them when we suggested that a cup of tea would go down very well. I got talking with a Corporal about their lonely existence and wondered if they lived for the day of their relief.

"Not a bit of it Sir" he replied, "We all love it here after the first week and fight like hell to stay here. The complete silence and solitude of the desert soon gets you and you begin to feel a part of it. Every sunrise is different and every sunset. You should see some of the fiery sunsets we have. I wish I could paint."

I was most impressed. Instead of being an untidy dump, which such a place could have been with little senior supervision, they kept it as tidy and neat as if a fiery Sergeant-Major had been breathing down their necks. The desert had got them, and they had willingly succumbed to its subtle charms. Even by day, apparently, an hour or more could pass with no vehicle going by and at night there was practically no traffic at all.

I was able to understand their feelings and when we resumed our journey and our road stretched ahead endlessly for mile after mile, the mesmerism of the solitude of the desert was rammed home to me. No wonder Mahommet went alone into the desert to seek distraction-free inspiration from our Creator, and Jesus to the wilderness East of Jerusalem, which is but a rocky desert instead of a sandy one.

After staging in Cairo, I took the train to Alexandria and boarded a troopship bound for the United Kingdom. To my dismay I found that I was once more to experience an alcohol-free journey. We continued to steam West after passing through the Straits of Gibraltar and played cat and mouse with German submarines, finally finishing up at Gourock. I had completed an overseas tour of nearly seven years, approximately one quarter of my whole life. That same evening I boarded a train and on my way South to London, masses of gliders and transport planes flew Eastwards across our path. It was our Airborne Forces on the way to death or glory at Arnhem.

Chapter XII

Ten months in Wartime Britain

On arrival in London I headed straight for Maidstone and reported to our Regimental Depot. I arrived late in the evening, having had a bite at Charing Cross Station. There were quite a few 'birds of passage' at the Depot. People like myself from overseas, people returning from leave and others between jobs awaiting postings. I knew about a third of them and after a few drinks in the ante-room we all knew each other and gossiped until midnight. The next morning I was granted two weeks immediate leave and given a first class return rail warrant to Colchester, where my parents duly met me. So much water had gone under the bridge since they had last seen me on my wedding day more than five years earlier, that I felt rather like the prodigal son returning and looked forward to eating the fatted calf (wartime version) and seeing them hanging on my lips as I recounted my adventures. They were obviously very pleased to see me, but their gaze, particularly my father's, roved up and down the platform.

It was evident that someone else was expected, and eventually my father's eyes lit up as a blonde American officer of the fair sex, in her middle thirties, stepped down from the far end of the train, looked around and then waved at us. This was their expected, and for me unexpected, guest. She had been one of his conquests during his three years service as a doctor in the Merchant Service, and I feel that his story should be told.

Having doctored on until I was safely launched on a military career, he had looked forward to many summers of cruising the seas in the Sailing Yacht Phoebe. In the event, he only had three and then World War II came along and he was forced to lay her up. He had always loved the sea, and just as I had learned from him, so had he learned to sail from his father. When he qualified as a doctor, the first thing he did was to enlist as ship's doctor on a tramp steamer sailing all round the Mediterranean ports including Istanbul and Beirut. In 1939 he felt that he was probably too old to be taken on in a sea-going appointment, but wrote to the British Medical Association as a recently retired doctor who was 100% fit and anxious to serve his Country in any way possible.

To his utter amazement, forty-eight hours later he was opening a letter instructing him to report forthwith to the offices of the City Line in

Liverpool, where the S.S. City of Nagpur was now awaiting his services as ship's doctor.

He packed his bag and went straight off in his yachting clothes and did not get his uniform, with its three gold stripes on red, until after his first voyage. He went all over the world and qualified for the Atlantic and Pacific Stars. It was whilst in America that he met Helen Schuyler, the blonde on the station platform, due to his Captain having known her from his regular visits to the U.S. and Canadian ports. He was a Norwegian and a mere 28 years of age when my father was a mere 72. I got a much fuller story later, because Helen asked me to look her up next time I was in London. I was thrilled to learn what a wonderful time he had had, as being born a Victorian, he never let his hair down 'en famille', was most abstemious and almost too good to be true. Helen told me that this was not the man who went on the tiles with his Captain and First Officer. As soon as their ship docked in New York they would come and call on her and her fellow feminine officers and take them out on a binge. On one occasion they decided to hire a car and drive about eighty miles to some popular hotel. The young Captain insisted that they stopped and had a drink at every watering hole. I injected "my father must have found that rather boring". "Your father" she retorted "he was the worst of them and I remember when we passed one because the others were looking the other way, he made them turn round and go back".

I was so pleased that he had this fling in the Autumn of his years. I still saw no sign of it in our home at West Mersea and although I would have loved to have pulled his leg, I realised that he was also a Victorian, and that Victorians kept to the edict 'not in front of the children.'

He was however prepared, after a little persuasion, to talk about some of his adventures. He had by then left the Merchant Service but still helped out at the local surgery and read every issue of the Lancet from cover to cover, to keep himself up to date.

He was obviously a man of great mental and physical courage. The following incident says everything. The City of Nagpur was eventually torpedoed and sunk in mid-Atlantic. My father twice went back down below into the sinking ship just as he was about to descend into a lifeboat because someone had shouted up for something to be saved from their cabins. Eventually after she sank they were all in open boats, in winter, for 24 hours before being picked up. He was back at sea within a fortnight in another ship having contracted a severe chill. He had written to apologise for being so long in reporting back, but that "he had sustained a slight chill." He lived on to his ninetieth year and was universally loved by young and old, and indeed all who knew him.

I soon learned that I was posted as GSO II to South Wales District in Abergavenny. Because petrol coupons were so scarce for civilians but more obtainable by servicemen, my father lent me his car. It made all the difference to my travels because the wartime rail service was slow and unreliable. At Abergavenny, known to very few people indeed we held Rudolph Hess in relatively comfortable imprisonment. After his air flight to the United Kingdom to try and negotiate an acceptable cease-fire with the British Government, our Security Services deemed it wise for his whereabouts to be known only to those with a 'need to know.' Few people, even at our own headquarters were aware of the distinguished prisoner in our midst.

One of the occupants of the General Staff Office was my fellow GSO II Andrew Cruikshank. I was GSO II Ops and he GSO II Training. He was a charming and entertaining companion, but having served abroad for so many years, I had never heard of him as an actor. He subsequently had many leading parts as in 'Dr Finlay's Casebook' and many Shakespearian roles. I last saw him in a West End Play in the part of a Judge, and went to his dressing room in the interval for a drink and some reminiscences. He was still wearing his full robes for the part and carried the air of dignity and authority quite effortlessly off-stage. He died only two years later. There was only a small Officers Mess at Abergavenny where occupants were mainly unmarried junior officers. Most married officers had their wives with them and married field officers (majors and above) whose wives were not with them were put up in good hotels, with adequate local allowances. In my case I stayed at the Angel Hotel which was a three star hotel and extremely comfortable. There seemed little shortage of food and drink.

I shared a table for two with a Lt. Colonel in the Royal Engineers who had just returned from a stint with the Iraq Levies. Instead of coming home having converted some of his men to Christianity, they had done a job on him and he returned a devout Moslem. He used to wear a coloured skull cap and pray on a small prayer mat turned to the East.

Having spent a few years by that time in Moslem countries, I was fascinated by that religion. Mohammet was influenced by Christianity and accepted Jesus as a Prophet but there were certain facets of the Christian religion which did not fit the Arab way of life. Monogamy for one thing was a problem. The Arabs produced far more girls than boys and the surplus of women produced a social dilemma.

Mohammet, following the example of Jesus, decided to go off on his own into the desert and pray to God for guidance. Away from the distractions and hurly burly of daily life he was able to concentrate on his communion with his Creator and mentally a pattern of suggestions entered his mind and formed the basis of the religion which bears his name. Since all the main religions in this world are monotheist and pray to one God, it does not stretch the mind much to realise that they are all looking up to one God, our Creator, whatever they may call him. I personally have felt the same feeling of sanctity and the presence of our Creator in all places of worship irrespective of whether they were Protestant, Roman Catholic, Moslem, Jewish,Coptic or Buddhist. They all pray to our Creator.

My tablemate and I had interesting discussions and he was a much better informed and fervent believer in his religion than someone born into it. He had been converted and gave up what he had been taught in the gullible days of child-hood. One of the things which I could not understand was the purpose of Ramadan, the ninth month of the Moslem year, during which no food or drink is permitted during daylight hours. This is a hot month, and for outdoor workers presents considerable hardship. "Its perfectly simple" he said, "its purpose is to encourage and to maintain self-discipline, something so important."

How right it is to encourage that virtue, and how lacking it is in this present day. Almost all the ghastly rapes of defenceless women and little children would be halted if self-discipline could be re-installed in our society. With no effective legal deterrent and little notice taken of religious teaching there is virtually nothing to prevent the spread of every kind of crime. The Public Censor has been abolished and the Church condones buggery which is against its own teaching. My first letter to Dr. Runcie on this subject, when he was still Archbishop of Canterbury, were carefully answered by staff who could not be specific. When I wrote to him a second time saying that I wanted to know what he thought, and not what they thought he thought, they again replied with extracts from a speech which he had made on this subject in which he said in effect that homosexuals had problems and that it was the job of the Church to help people with problems. My fertile mind began to visualise certain types of curates helping choir-boys with their problems.

✧

As a professional soldier I was slightly worried whether my staff qualifications from my Sarafand course would have adequate standing in peace-time, and asked to be considered for the Staff College, Camberley. My General duly recommended me and I was granted a vacancy on the Course assembling in January 1945. I hence spent only three months in Abergavenny and left in December 1944 for Christmas leave before joining. It was during this leave at West Mersea that I was asked when I would be available for the investiture of my MBE. The Beatles and the like had not been similarly honoured in those days, and in any case the Military Division has a different ribbon and I was quite proud of it. I had thought of asking for my investiture to be postponed until my wife had returned from South Africa and explained to my parents that as I would only get two tickets for the ceremony, only one of them would be able to come. They both looked at each other and said in complete unison "you go darling."

I made up my mind then and there to see that they both attended. I had a hunch that something might turn up for the capture of Rachi Ridge, and that Phoebe would have a chance to attend at a later date. I decided to push out the boat in a big way to show my appreciation for all that they had done for me and booked them a suite at the Ritz Hotel the night before and was their host at dinner. I then belonged to the 'IN and OUT' (Naval and Military Club) which is only a hundred and fifty yards from the Ritz and so could not have been more conveniently situated.

At the ceremony, I made an unfortunate blunder. After moving up a red carpeted ramp to the level of the King we were supposed to turn right, bow and then take a pace forward to be shaken by the hand and the decoration hung on a temporary hook which was placed above the appropriate ribbon already on our chests. I turned right and forgot to bow, took a pace forward and then remembered that I had not bowed. I therefore bowed, and then took a tiny pace forward. King George VI looked aghast and had to sway back and take a tiny pace to his rear to accommodate this unexpected manoeuvre on my part, but was kind enough to appear not to notice it.

By December 1944 the 'Python' scheme, whereby everybody was posted home after five years service abroad, was well established. It is probable that King George VI, who was known to be a shy man made this an easy talking point to everyone. After hanging on my decoration he asked me how long I had served overseas. "Seven years Sir" I replied. "Seven years" he ejaculated. "All bar three months" I conceded. "Well you're home now anyway" he said brightly and the brief encounter was ended. I bowed and took a pace to the rear, did a left turn and marched down the second ramp. I now begin to wonder whether he said to one of his aides "Don't let that man come here again if he ever gets another medal"; because when that moment was due eighteen months later I received a small registered parcel which, when opened by me with disinterest, I found within a Military Cross and a printed letter from the King apologising that he was unable to present it to me personally. I had therefore made a gross miscalculation in 1944 and Phoebe never attended an investiture.

At the end of my leave I duly reported at the Staff College, Camberley and found that I was sharing a room with Ben Stoneham, a member of my Regiment about two years senior to me. We had never met before, because he was in India when I joined. He was a pleasant companion with a great sense of humour, but not a great exponent at the planning aspects of military life. He had been in a series of backwaters during the war and was even more bemused by the great variety of weapons and equipment then in use and the variety of new names given to them than I had been when I left Malta. The courses at Camberley were then divided into four periods of six weeks, after which all the syndicates were re-shuffled so that we all had new instructors and a new set of faces with which to work.

The other thing that happened was that anyone who was too obviously finding it difficult to keep up with the very great pressures to which we were subjected were returned to their units. It very rarely happened, and was usually taken so badly by the victims that, already under great mental strain, they committed suicide rather than face their brother officers. After one or two such cases, it became the policy for anyone receiving this bad news being never left unaccompanied until they had left the College precincts. It is sad to relate that some even shot themselves during their subsequent journeys.

Poor old Ben had been muttering to me that he was finding it a bit hard to cope, and that he feared getting the chop. I did my best to reassure him that we were all under pressure and that we would all have the greatest sympathy for anyone who was sent away, and in no way look down on them. In the event Ben did suffer this fate, but was most phlegmatic about it. He was rather like Eeyore in Winnie the Pooh, but with a sense of humour and a natural self deprecation which cushioned the blow.

He became the first student to face the World with his head held high and we respected him for it. Having started this new fashion, no more suicides took place, although students on subsequent courses were put under less pressure, because the War ended in Europe in May of that year, and the same syllabus was stretched over a year for future courses.

Neither Ben nor I knew that Phoebe and his mother-in-law were sharing a cabin in the S.S. Andes, then sailing from Capetown to Liverpool, or that he and his wife Beryl were eventually to settle down in Tunbridge Wells only a stone's throw from my sister Mirabel's house.

Owing to the need for security, I had very short notice of Phoebe's imminent arrival with Michael and our daughter Jill, whom I had never seen. I did a careful exercise, taking all factors into consideration, when choosing a hotel to take them all for the night when their boat train arrived at Euston. Fate was on our side, because my enquiries revealed that the Euston Hotel was the last big London hotel to be completely re-decorated and refurnished when war broke out and was therefore about the only one which did not now have threadbare carpets. I was lucky enough to book a large room with a double bed, a single bed and a cot in it, so when they all arrived looking utterly exhausted, they only had to walk across the main hall and there was our quite (wartime) luxurious hotel. They even supplied good wine and food and a couple of glasses of vintage port after dinner. I had, after considerable pressure, managed to get 48 hours leave and was therefore able to drive them down to Shawford, near Winchester, where Phoebe's parents had bought a house to live in when Asfordbye had been taken over and turned into a 'Wrenery'.

We stopped at the Ely Inn on Hartfordbridge Flats for lunch and I was red with embarrassment when Phoebe held up a nappy to air by the fire of the dining room which was alongside our table. Having shepherded them for days on South African Railways, weeks on a troopship and then down from Liverpool, she had become a hardened and thick-skinned traveller. I am ashamed to admit that even to this day I have never put on a nappy. The Ely Inn had a romantic connection, as it was into the car park of the Ely Inn that I pulled on the way back from that Sandhurst dance in 1936 to kiss Phoebe for the first time.

In preparation for Phoebe's return I had scouted around for a house to rent and finally found one in Kings Ride currently rented by a namesake, Tom Butler of the Grenadier Guards, who with his wife Rosemary was awaiting a posting. This house became available a week or two after Phoebe's return and thus gave her just the right amount of time to unwind and enjoy the re-union with her parents whom she had not seen for over five years. Part of the deal with the Tom Butlers was that we had to take on their dog, an attractive wire-haired terrier bitch called Bim. We changed this to Jane, which she accepted immediately.

I struck up a close rapport with Jane, who was obviously a man's dog, and she used to embarrass me by following me to the Staff College every morning and then sitting outside the door of whatever room I was working in. I used to turn round after leaving our house and see her following me, and she would obediently stop and obey my order to go home; but she would then slink back onto my tracks and I would find her once more lurking in my wake. Obviously we soon kept her shut in for a while after I had left each morning, but eventually she would get out and appear in my hall of study or even at a lecture.

Unfortunately my syndicate instructor at that period was rather humourless and even threatened disciplinary action unless I kept her under proper control, and I was each time ordered to walk her home and lose working time. Eventually she had to be gated for at least an hour each day after I had left the house. She never ceased to be a source of amusement and concern. After I had left the Staff College to go to Burma and she accompanied Phoebe and the children back to Shawford, we and all our neighbours found that the tits were breaking the silver tops of the milk bottles and drinking the top of the creamy milk. This was what they thought

The elusive Jane with Michael and Jill

until one day a bottle was knocked over and Jane was seen scampering off with her tail down. She must have been extremely clever all those other days to bite off the tops without disturbing the bottles. It has occurred to me since writing this that tits may have given her the lead and opened the odd bottle and that Jane, smelling the milk, finished off the job and continued the thieving habit. Eventually Tom and Rosemary Butler asked for her back. Phoebe missed her, but was probably well off without her.

So many interesting things happened on that course. To start with, it had drawn together officers with experience of every kind of warfare and every conceivable theatre of war including Norway, N.W. Europe, the Aegean, the desert, Italy, Burma, Ethiopia and East Africa. The Directing Staff were all experienced and the lecturers chosen for their first-hand knowledge of their subjects. Our syndicate D.S. were around our own ages and sometimes even younger, and high spirits prevailed. Because I could draw a little I used to do a topical cartoon almost every morning on the blackboard to greet the arrival of my last D.S. who was Anthony Kershaw, later to become Parliamentary Private Secretary to Edward Heath, when Prime Minister and now Sir Anthony Kershaw M.P.

Great excitement was engendered by the Victory Day in Europe and we all went up to London to join the crowds outside Buckingham Palace and to see Churchill appear beside the King and Queen on the balcony, to the deafening cheering of the crowd.

During my last two weeks I had the misfortune to lean out of my 15 cwt truck to see that the small column which I was leading on an exercise was keeping up. The catch of the canvas panel, which acted as a side door, gave way and I rolled onto the tarmac road at 30 mph and broke my right wrist. The pain kept me awake all night and the next day it was strapped up and felt more comfortable; but it was never X-rayed and was later to cause problems in Burma. Although protected from further overseas service by the Python Scheme, I volunteered for Burma, where the fighting continued, as I felt that I had lost so much experience of mobile warfare whilst in Malta that I should 'follow the sound of the firing' for the good of my career.

At the combined 'End-of-course Dance' and 'Victory Ball' at Camberley the organisers used the ideas in my topical blackboard drawings and asked me to do a number of rough sketches with amusing captions which one of the clerks, who was a cartoonist in civil life, blew up into coloured life-size cartoons, which decorated some of the walls. I remember that one caption simply said "Report at crossroads 428 147 at 0900 hrs, Dress Battledress". The cartoon showed not a single officer properly dressed in battledress. There were sheepskin jackets, pale yellow suede desert boots, kilts, corduroy trousers of many different hues, turbans and you name it, all accurately portraying our motley collection of warriors.

One of my problems in getting to Burma was getting up-graded medically to fitness for active service. I still had a 'dropped foot' which tired very quickly and would not pick up. I hoodwinked the Medical Board by brushing the whole thing aside and saying that the leg had been sound for simply ages, and jumped up and down on my right leg to prove it. My calf muscles had returned to normal but I did not let them know that I could not raise the foot. After a short leave with the Sawyers and with my parents at West Mersea, I found myself once more leaving the United Kingdom for an indefinite period. It was sad to be parted so soon from Phoebe and the children, with whom I had been re-united for so short a time. They stayed on at West Mersea for the rest of the summer.

When I took off for Burma I learned that because we had such a full load we were going to fly for almost three days just to get as far as Karachi. The first night we staged at Malta, where I left the R.A.F. mess as soon as we had dined, borrowed a jeep, and drove round all the spots which held such memories for me. It proved to be a most nostalgic evening and I returned quite late that night. In the morning we took off having trundled within a few hundred yards of the quarries where I had had such varied experiences. After refuelling in Cairo, we flew on, and on that second night we landed at Sharjah in the Trucial States and had a midnight meal in a white fort which looked like a scene from Beau Geste. That evening, before landing, we heard the amazing news that Winston Churchill's Government had fallen and that Attlee had become Prime Minister. A hush fell over the aircraft when it sunk in that the British people who had thronged the whole of Central London on V.E. Day (Victory in Europe), and demanded his presence on the balcony of Buckingham Palace, were so fickle that they were prepared to throw him out before the war with Japan was over. It was, for me, the beginning of a disillusionment about the 'Great British People' which has continued over the years with increasing intensity. I heard stories of women saying "I am going to vote Labour, as long as we still have Mr. Churchill" and that most voters would have liked to retain him but thought that the Labour Government would get the troops home sooner.

Chapter XIII

Burma; War, Peace and strange adventures

On arrival at Karachi, instead of staying for a day or two, we were held up for around three weeks, which gave us time to assimilate the Indian scene, it then being part of India, and to get suitably bronzed. I was able to do some sailing and even rowed in a very scratch eight a few times.

We eventually took off for Ceylon, but were forced by appalling thunderstorms to do a wide detour to the East and we eventually landed in Madras. During the earlier period of some intense buffeting we unfortunately learned, from the airman acting as steward, that on the previous day an identical Dakota had broken in two and that all the occupants had been killed, some still strapped into their seats, and others near the break had fallen to their deaths as individuals. This was not the sort of cheerful chatter that a modern air hostess serves up and every time our Dakota shuddered, I wondered if I would be in the front half, the back half or a single lonely body when I hit the earth.

Madras was extremely hot and sticky and we were all delighted that after refuelling and having a meal, we were proceeding on to Columbo in Ceylon. There, we found ourselves in a pleasant camp under rubber trees and a very short distance from the sea and a delightful, almost white sandy beach.

We were all destined for different appointments, some at the Supreme Headquarters in Kandy, some in Burma and some in Malaysia. However, there seemed no hurry and we would swim, drink at the mess bar in the shade of rubber trees or take a taxi to Columbo town and have a meal and drinks at the Gaul Face Hotel.

There seemed to be plenty of Wrens in Columbo, presumably based at the Naval Headquarters, and we found them very attractive and uninhibited. I remember a party of five of us drinking out in the garden of the Gaul Face, each with a Wren on his knee, being taught by these charmers the entire words of 'Cocaine Bill and Morphine Sue' which I had never heard before. In those days drugs did not seem a problem because only a few weak-minded idiots seemed to be affected. I do not believe that any of us suspected that the drugs problem would eventually change the whole moral structure of the world, break up lives, break up marriages, affect the very structure of governments and cause addicts to commit crimes including murder to feed their coffers or satisfy their cravings. The words of the song foretold so accurately the troubles now descended upon almost every nation on earth. The 'sniff' in the poem represents a sniff, not a word, when the ditty is sung.

> Cocaine Bill and Morphine Sue
> were walking down Fifth Avenue
> Oh Honey have a sniff have a sniff on me.
> Oh Honey have a sniff on me.
>
> She had no Morphine and had had no coke
> because the pair were just plain broke.
> Oh Honey etc
> Oh Honey etc
>
> They went to every joint in town
> and every one just turned them down.
> Oh Honey etc
> Oh Honey etc
>
> Said Cocaine Bill to his Morphine Moll
> "There ain't no sense in alcohol".
> Oh Honey etc
> Oh Honey etc
>
> Now in that graveyard on the hill
> Lies the body of Cocaine Bill.
> Oh Honey etc
> Oh Honey etc
>
> And in the graveyard by his side
> Lies the body of his morphine bride.
> Oh Honey etc
> Oh Honey etc
>
> The morals of this story tell
> If you fall for drugs
> You will end in Hell.
> Oh Honey have a sniff have a sniff on me.
> Oh Honey have a sniff on me.

⟡

During a week of gaiety and sunshine in Columbo two or three officers a day were summoned up to Kandy to be interviewed at

Mountbatten's Headquarters and receive their postings. The journey up by train to the highlands in which Kandy nestles is as beautiful as almost anything I have seen or experienced before or since. The train puffed up valleys, winding its way round the bends and exposing new views at every turn. Ceylon gets that admixture of sun and rain which ensures luxurious growth, and every little patch of cultivation on the hillsides was surrounded by lush groves of leaved trees and palm trees, arranged by nature as well, if not better, than an experienced landscape gardener. Every now and then we would come across elephants working, or even grazing under supervision, to lend enchantment to the scenes. I sat in a warm and bemused trance.

Kandy itself is very beautiful as it nestles in a confluence of several valleys and one seldom went any distance on the flat but always down a slope and then up the other side of another. Just as I had been lucky to bump into Bill Oliver as a Brigadier in Cairo, in Kandy I found that the Major General, Administration was Jimmy Riddell, who had been a captain with the party from our 1st Battalion at Haifa who had been dropped off from India to join our 2nd Battalion when we came out from England. I called on him and found him stripped to the waist, as everyone was in their offices during the heat of the day. It allowed the sweat to evaporate and keep one cool, and prevented that itchy condition known as Prickly Heat; a rash of red pimples caused by blocked pores.

After my interview with the Military Secretary's Department I returned to my transit camp and learned on that very evening, and for the first time since the Japanese war began, the ornate 'Festival of the Tooth' was to take place. One of the Buddha's teeth is kept in great reverence in one of Kandy's temples, and is carried in procession in a gold casket on the biggest domestic elephant in the area. The whole procession was at least two miles long, proceeded by half-naked men cracking long leather whips to drive away evil spirits.

I booked a table in the restaurant on the first floor of the Tooth Hotel with a view of the street and was just settling down with a long drink in my hand when Malcolm Dewar appeared. he had been one term junior to me in the same company at Sandhurst and was dressed as a Lieutenant Colonel. He was a great all-rounder, having represented the Suffolks at eight different athletic events, played tennis at Army level and rugby football at trial level. We had run against each other at the Eastern Command Championships at Colchester in 1937 which we won, and later at the Army Championships at Aldershot. When we took over from the Suffolks in Malta, both regiments served long enough together to coincide with the Athletic Championships. so we, Malcolm and I, found ourselves once more digging in our holes together for the 220 yards.

Having joined me at my table we both proceeded to enjoy the spectacle which had been in abeyance for three years. Just as country towns here run summer fetes with decorated floats, on flat-topped lorries,and London outdoes them with its Lord Mayor's Show, so did the people of Kandy decorate their elephants to represent various themes. Not only were the howdahs intricately carved and decorated, but the caparisons were decorated with coloured silks and semi-precious stones. The sides of the heads of the elephants were stained with bright colours, stretching down the sides of their trunks. The climax of the procession was the golden casket carrying one of Buddha's teeth, ensconced in a miniature temple complete with dome, all on the back of the largest elephant I have ever seen.

It took quite a long time for this long procession to pass, and by the time it had Malcolm Dewar and I had finished our dinner and were well sustained with refreshments. We wandered down to the road and decided to take a couple of rickshaws and tour Kandy. After wandering along side by side for a bit we urged our rickshaw boys to do some trotting and eventually to have a race. They were obviously not trying to outdo one another and kept more or less level. We decided unanimously to halt them and change places with them. We then took off and soon worked up to almost sprinting speed whilst the rickshaws lurched from side to side and nearly overturned to the sheer delight of the crowd and at the anxiety on the faces of the new passengers. When we eventually ran out of puff we pulled up,called it a draw and held out our hands for payment; more laughs all round. I don't suppose such a scene was often enacted for them by a Major and a Lieutenant Colonel.

Next morning I returned by the picturesque mountain railway and soon received my posting order to 17th Indian Division then stationed at Pegu, about fifty miles North of Rangoon. I was required to proceed by train to Trincomalee which is in the North East of Ceylon and travel from there to Rangoon in an Aircraft Carrier, H.M.S. Bulwark. The route taken by the railway enabled me to see even more of the beautiful island as it started round the Western side of the main central highlands and then bore North East to Trincomalee.

H.M.S. Bulwark had a motley crowd of people from all three Services on board and with the Japanese war approaching its end, spirits ran very high. There was no rationing of drinks in the Ward Room for officers not on duty, and we hitch hikers were never on duty. We used to play five-a-side hockey on the flight deck, and as there were no rails or stops of any sort at the sides it could be quite an exercise in self-preservation when the ship was rolling a bit. One of my fellow passengers was an Old Oundlelian who could play the piano by ear and seemed able to pick up any tune if one hummed it to him a couple of times. I determined to achieve this social asset one day and can now struggle through most tunes by ear. The trouble is that nowadays people of my vintage no longer seem to have become involved in such enjoyable occasions, nor do so many houses have a piano. Sadly I am very rarely asked to play, harp or no harp, but sometimes it happens.

Having got to know quite a few Arab countries and spent a few weeks in India and Ceylon, I was quite unprepared for the splendour of the Shwedegon Pagoda which could be seen in Rangoon before we had even got alongside. The parts of India that I had seen were mainly Moslem or Hindu. Only Ceylon had hinted at the majestic splendour of Buddhist temples and effigies, but I had seen nothing like the golden domes of the temples and gigantic statues of Buddha which existed in Burma.

Soon after docking, I was ferried by Truck to a transit camp. Because H.Q. 17th Indian Division was only about 50 miles up the road I was almost immediately sent on my way in a jeep which had been sent down to collect me. I was touched by this sign of welcome but was quickly disillusioned on arrival. The Lieutenant Colonel A and Q who was to be my boss met me in the Mess, shook my hand warmly and said "we are always delighted to welcome visitors". This was a somewhat shattering remark to make to someone who had signed away his Python rights and travelled nearly half way round the world to continue the fight against a savage foe. He went on to explain that he had spent most of the afternoon trying to put off my posting with Corps Headquarters, because the Indian Captain who was my Staff Captain 'A' had been recommended to be promoted into the job I had been given, and everyone was as sick as mud that I had arrived before this could be promulgated. The officer in question, a Captain Satarawallah was polite and courteous, but did not exhibit sufficient warmth to thaw the icicles in my breast. I felt very sick at heart.

In the event I gained a lot of very quick staff experience, because after a final battle with the Japanese troops crossing through the Pegu Yomas hills and cutting our Headquarters off from our Southern Brigade, all the British Staff Officers went touring the Divisional Area paying farewell visits to friends and staying away for several nights before heading for Rangoon and the United Kingdom. There was very little work to do at Divisional Headquarters except the processing of the departures of British Officers for the United Kingdom. We used to sit in a circle in someone's tent after lunch at weekends drinking Hayward's Gin, a local brand, until nearly tea-time. On one of these days because it was my thirtieth birthday, more than usual was consumed, and the Assistant Provost Marshal and I went for an evening stroll to clear our heads near the Japanese lines. At one point these were only a quarter of a mile away and we thought we had spotted some Jap who had come forward beyond the agreed boundaries. I climbed up the lower branches of a tree to get a better view, slipped and fell and landed on the right wrist which had been damaged at the Staff College. This time the break had moved and the wrist had to be properly plastered right up the fore-arm. Two weeks later the resulting immobility nearly cost me my life.

Events had moved very quickly. The two atom bombs on Japan, the surrender of the Japanese and the beginning of the demobilisation scheme which the new Labour Government had promised to speed up. I once found myself wearing four hats and answered the phone with the words "Colonel AQ, DAQMG, DAAG and Staff Captain 'A', otherwise known as Pooh Bah, what can I do for you?" General Crowther the Divisional Commander, who was the voice on the other end of the line was not amused and made this clear.

✧

Later as a Lt. Colonel in Kenya I used to see General Crowther quite often at the Nairobi Polo Club, as we had retired to Kenya. I once told him of my hostile welcome from his Lt. Colonel A & Q and he was appalled and most apologetic. We subsequently got on very well as he tried to make amends and would insist on buying me a drink whenever we met at the Polo Club.

✧

Behind the scenes my immediate boss was still working to get Satarawallah my job, and eventually I was posted up to Kalewa, which is right up the River Chindwin. With the Japanese war now ended, there would be no more battle experience with 17 Indian Division and my subsequent travels to Mandalay, Kaymo, Kalewa and right up to Imphal and Kohima would not have taken place if I had stayed with them.

I duly set off with my belongings in a jeep, with an Indian Army driver. I had by then heard of all the battles which had been fought by the 17th Indian Division in its progress down from Mandalay, and I was to pass through all these battle grounds in reverse order. The monsoons were still going strong, any roads not re-enforced by gravel or tarmac were impassable. The countryside in general was not unlike the flatter areas of Ceylon, but had less rubber trees, green and lush valleys landscaped by Nature with clusters of tropical trees and palms on the low hills or mounds, but more rice growing in the flat fields. At this time of year however everything was a rich green. Small villages could often be seen through the trees on these mounds.

On arrival at Mandalay I reported at the Area Headquarters to learn that my proposed route from Mandalay to Kalewa was impassable due to monsoon flooding, and that I was to proceed by a landing craft, towing a steel barge on each side, in four days time from a remote village at the confluence of the Irrawaddy and the Chindwin rivers called Moneywa.

I hence became a tourist seeing the beautiful scenes in Mandalay, dominated by the Fort which stood in a moat rich with water lilies in flower. It is supposed to be unlucky to have a statue of Buddha in one's house, but this is only because anyone who steals one from a temple comes under a curse. I therefore went to one of the Buddha-makers on the outskirts of Mandalay and bought a small statuette of Buddha carved in the smoothest polished alabaster or white marble about six inches high, which had never been sanctified in a temple or a curse put upon its thief. It now stands in state in our drawing-room, next to a handsome Chinese bowl on one of those very ornate black and gold Chinese lacquered chests; most suitable.

I had heard of a marvellous hotel up in the hills at Maymyo East of Mandalay, which had been turned into an officers leave camp. There was usually a waiting list for it and I was lucky to get in for the two middle days of my sojourn in the Mandalay area. I was allowed to keep my jeep and driver until I finally embarked; and enjoyed the drive up through the hills. Maymyo certainly came up to every expectation, it was high enough up to be cool, extremely picturesque, and only 150 miles from our ally General Chang Kai Chek's China border. The friendly atmosphere of a good country hotel had been maintained by the WRAC major who ran it. It was with some regret that I finally pointed my 17th Indian Div. jeep down the hills for Mandalay at the end of my two days and resigned myself to 130 mile trip up the River Chindwin, always to be against the monsoon current and always travelling only by day; since movement by night in the strong currents in complete darkness would have been impossible.

I was appalled to see the meagre rations provided for me which consisted of very little except mainly tins of bully beef, hard Army biscuits, tins of milk, tea and sugar. There were a few tins of luxuries like jam, butter and marmalade, but very little of the goodies I thought might be available, like steak and kidney suet puddings and treacle pudding etc. included in 'compo rations' as a rule.

On reflection, I realise that I was no special friend of a strange quartermaster at the Area Headquarters in Mandalay, or his equally strange sergeant. They had given me the minimum and that was that. I reached my embarkation point at around midday. My life for the next ten days was more or less confined to a small officer's tent which had been pitched in the hold of a landing craft. This had been designed to carry two laden army lorries or one light tank. On either side was lashed a long steel barge with stores for units upstream from Kalewa stowed under tarpaulins.

The crew consisted of a Burmese skipper who had a large moustache, very white teeth and a ready smile and his mate, a clean-shaven young man who always looked very serious. Neither of them spoke any English at all, and although I had worked hard at picking up as much Urdu as possible whilst with 17th Indian Div, I could not speak a word of Burmese. Having lost my Luger pistol during my fighting in Leros, I was glad that my father-in-law had presented me with the Colt .45 Automatic which he had used in the Boer War and World War I. Although much heavier than my 9 mm Luger, it fitted into my small hand very snugly, with the second joint of the index finger at right angles to the line of fire. We were going unescorted through jungles which had been occupied by the Japanese until the previous month and I knew, from experience that many Japanese had been cut off and were making their way South Eastwards, and that some of these were even unaware that their higher command had agreed to a cease-fire. I also knew that some of the Northern tribesmen of Burma had sympathised with the Japanese and might be hostile.

At the first opportunity, when we passed through a narrow gorge which forced us close to the banks and our speed over the land was reduced to little more than one knot, I tried shooting the 45 Colt for the first time. It produced an unholy kick and it took me a few shots to get the feel of it, but when I did I found it extremely accurate and that I could hit the odd leaf lodged against the near vertical bank at ten yards.

Since the crew could not communicate with me, I had no idea what we were going to do at night until early dusk when the skipper pulled in to the bank near a Burmese village and tied up. By sign language he indicated that I might like to go ashore and stretch my legs, and strapping on my revolver and holster, I accompanied him ashore. He immediately began to negotiate with the villagers for exchanges of fresh food for his ship's stores, and I went back for a tin of bully beef and some biscuits. These produced fresh eggs and bananas which became a staple addition to my boring diet. The only cooking facility on board was a charcoal stove, a kettle and a large frying pan. The fire was lit on the metal bows of the starboard barge and my two colleagues cooked mainly rice dishes with vegetables and the odd chicken leg thrown in when they could get it; and drank tea. I shared their tea but ate my own food. Each morning I would give the mate two eggs to fry, and each morning he would succeed in breaking them, so that I finished up with an omelette-like mess.

In the day-time I used to lie on my bed with the front ramp of the landing craft lowered to a point where I had an uninterrupted view ahead. The view was always changing, always beautiful and sometimes breathtaking. The Chindwin was carrying a large amount of mud which made it a rich brown colour in the sunlight and the speed of the current varied from a few knots in the wide stretches to around ten knots when we passed through a narrow gorge, when we sometimes were almost unable to make any progress, towing as we were two heavily laden barges. The riverside villages which we passed were always built on wooden stilts, even the huts as far as two hundred yards from the river banks.

On the second evening, after tying up I again accompanied the skipper ashore. As we passed through the huts nearest the river and were crossing an open space in the middle of the village, one of the pi-dogs which barked loudly and then took cover under their owner's huts as we went past, slipped out behind us and nipped my ankle. After concluding the evening's bartering, we re-crossed the village 'centre' and passed through the river bank line of huts to the accompaniment of a renewed encore of barking. Believe it or not, the sly cur which had nipped me on the way in nipped me again on the way out. I examined the bite, which was just above the Achilles tendon and saw that the skin was broken and a flash of blood visible. This was a rabid area and I realised that we were completely out of touch with the rest of the world and that I could not hope for any anti-rabies serum for between five to nine days. I did not know how soon the serum had to be injected and hoped that I would not start barking before we reached Kalewa.

On the third evening and on all successive ones I was very careful to keep an eye on my heels as we went through the villages. I had partaken of a few shots of Haywards Gin to cheer me up and we found the villagers sitting round a camp fire and having a rather tuneless sing-song. They responded very favourably to my mellow condition and the skipper and I were invited to sit cross-legged and join them. After a while I decided to chip in with a tuneful and extremely rude after-rugby song, which I sung at the top of my voice. There was complete silence as I sang, and when I finished I wondered if perhaps I would be for the pot. Not a bit of it, the applause was deafening, laughter uproarious – although they could not understand a single word I was saying – and I continued my one man concert for a short time. At Oundle we had one of the best Bach choirs in the United Kingdom and used to broadcast every Christmas and usually cut a record; so I tried to sing one or two tuneful numbers with a good melody. They simply loved and had never experienced anything quite like it before – nor had I. Although I had set forth with an extremely good map, it was impossible to tell where I was. None of the villages were marked with any name, and even if they had been, they would have been unlikely to be big enough to have been marked on the map. The skipper knew the names of most of them and exactly where he was, but when I pointed to the map in a questioning sort of way he would wave his finger over an area which allowed a margin of error of around twenty miles.

That night I explained by sign language that I, personally, would crack my eggs next morning into the frying pan, as I was tired of the mate always breaking them. They understood this, and we all turned in. That night we had a real monsoon cloudburst and when I awoke I found that my camp bed was standing in two inches of water and that the gym shoes which I normally wore in the daytime on board were floating somewhere near the forward ramp. My clothes were on a camp stool and dry and my Army boots, with their steel studded soles and heels with 'horseshoes' of steel on them were on a wooden box with some of my gear in it as a sort of wardrobe. The mate was arranging a hose to suck out the surplus water, and I gingerly dressed cross-legged on my bed whilst the water level went down. Now came the time for breakfast; and the sun having come out, the charcoal fire was lit on the pointed foredeck of our starboard barge. I held up two eggs, pointed at my own chest to remind him that I was going to be the cook and started to climb the ladder that led onto the 'bridge' at the stern of our landing-craft, from whence one could gain access to the barge. I reached the deck, sliding about on my steel soled boots on the wet steel side-deck of the barge. Pride comes before a fall, and I was certainly very pompous as I carefully cracked my two eggs into the frying-pan without breaking them. I felt that he could now supervise their cooking and bring them aft to me on the plate which he had ready.

As the bows of both barges were square pointed, there was a triangular gap of fresh air between the raised bow and the lowered ramp of the landing craft. As I turned to jump down from the comparatively high bows of the barge to the lowered ramp of the landing craft to take a short cut back to my tent, my iron-shod Army boots slipped on the wet metal and I found myself falling headfirst onto the metal ramp. The thought raced through my mind that if the skipper had not witnessed my fall and I became trapped by the water rushing into the V created between the two vessels, I could be trapped there by the pressure of water and drowned. In that split second I also realised that if I landed headfirst onto the metal ramp I would be knocked out and drowned or break my neck. Neither option seemed desirable. As I fell I decided to do a jack-knife dive and aim at the V of water.

I succeeded in doing this without making any contact with either vessel and concentrated in continuing the dive as deep as possible to avoid being cut to bits by the starboard propeller. It was completely dark under these craft and I probably continued to swim downwards too long after I felt the throbbing of the screw pass over me. I then began to swim upwards.

To my amazement and increasing fear everything remained completely black. Although I was, I thought, swimming vertically upwards I could still see no trace of any light. I was now almost completely out of oxygen, because I was still on the one gasp of air I took as I dived in, and had expended a lot of energy trying to swim to the surface. I began to wonder if I had become disorientated and should swim in a different direction, but decided to trust to my instincts and continue swimming as hard as I could in what I believed was an upward direction. I realised that I was within seconds of drowning; my lungs were bursting and there was a roaring in my ears. I made one supreme final effort, cursing the fact that I was wearing heavy army boots and had my right arm up to the elbow in heavy plaster. Suddenly there was a dark brown tinge to the water above me which changed to a lighter brown and a second later I shot out of the surface of the water, head, shoulders and chest, completely clear. The breath of fresh air I took in was the most wonderful thing that had ever happened to me. The landing craft was about two hundred yards from me, and about half-way between it and me was a round lifebelt which had obviously been thrown over-board by the skipper or the mate when they saw me slip and fall. After half a dozen deep breaths of fresh air, I swam slowly towards it whilst the three craft gently reversed back towards me. I give no extra marks to any reader who hazards a guess that I have always reckoned that incident as the most poignant of my nine lives. It was so drawn out and so positive and the whole incident must have lasted for well over a minute. I have often wondered why there was total darkness down there and the solution has only come since I started writing this chapter. Each particle of mud would have looked brown with the sun on it and black from underneath, so the effect of thousands of these black dots above me produced a complete closure to light and hence complete darkness.

After a good rub down and putting on some dry clothes, they gave me a cup of hot tea and I ate the breakfast I had cooked so recently. Needless to say, in the excitement of the rescue they had left my pan of eggs on the charcoal fire and they were as hard and unpalatable as they would have been if the mate had cooked them in their usual broken state.

The rest of the trip was uneventful except that I felt a constant twinge of anxiety that I might reach Kalewa too late for the serum to save me from rabies. We duly arrived and I was made most welcome by the Commander of the area to whose headquarters I had been appointed. One of my first requests was for a shot of anti-rabies serum; and after consulting the Indian M.O. they looked a bit glum. They had none and were cut-off not only from Mandalay to the South, but also from the North by the monsoon rains. Eventually they wirelessed for an emergency air-drop and my anti-rabies serum was duly injected into my stomach for fourteen days of no alcohol in a jungle camp where there was nothing else to do in the evenings but drink and play liar-dice. As a result, I became extremely good at liar-dice and felt that my pride had been dented if my monthly winnings did not cover my mess bill.

With the onset of peace, and the prospect of continual movement having ceased, my fellow officers immediately tried to raise the standards of comfort to peacetime proportions. We lived in a patch of primary forest, which meant that from above in an aeroplane we would look like part of an unbroken green cauliflower, whilst at ground level we lived in a cathedral-like setting of tall trees which shaded us from the hot sun, and very little low ground vegetation. The Indian soldiers had built bamboo huts and little verandas at the front, with only the roof of tented canvas to keep out the rain. At the rear of each 'bungalow' was a screen leading to a bathroom. This consisted of a basin fitted into a bamboo tripod and a shower, consisting of a grill of stout bamboos on which to stand, over which was suspended a used petrol can with a bottom perforated with small holes. Our bearers would pour warm water into it whilst we had a good soap down and would then pour a second sluice to rinse the soap off. Finally, through another screen was a wooden 'thunderbox' which contained a bucket which was discreetly emptied by the 'Bhisti', who belonged to the only caste who would undertake such duties. Sometimes at night I thought I heard the sound of heavy breathing but could not discover the source and eventually ignored it.

We would take it in turns to play host after dinner in our various tented bungalows; which meant providing the liquid refreshments and borrowing the one leather cup and set of dice which had found its way to Kalewa. On one such evening we were sitting in a small circle inside my bamboo bungalow having a drink before playing liar-dice, when we all heard the sound of heavy breathing which I have described above. I called for silence and we all listened. There was no doubt about it, we were not alone and the noise now seemed to be coming from my veranda. I grabbed my Colt .45 from under the pillow of my bed and led the more intrepid members of my party out onto my rickety bamboo veranda. To my left, and no more than six feet away I saw two small beady eyes reflecting the light of my torch at a height of at least two feet six inches. There was the distinct sound of a hasty retreat behind me as my guests fought to be the first back through the doorway. By sheer circumstance I found myself at the back of the queue.

We had a council of war and whilst some decided that we had a tiger outside, others were sure it was only a hyena or even a large jackal. I was unconvinced, but still curious, and with a torch in one hand and my Colt .45 in the other I gingerly poked my head once more round the door. The torch settled all the arguments, I found myself staring at the head of a snake reared up in the striking position whose eyes were fixed on me. No-one could have got back through the entrance to my tent faster than I did, and I thanked my lucky stars that the others were by then out of the way.

One of our number sneaked out through the loo at the back of my tent and raised the alarm. It was by now pitch dark and we were all far too scared to initiate a well planned counter attack against an unknown species of snake which reared to a height of three feet. The Indian troops treated this as an enjoyable routine anti-snake operation, and soon lined up with tin cans rather like the beaters in a shoot. They located their quarry who proceeded to lead them quite a dance round the camp area until it finally made for home base which was, guess where, the wet stones under my shower. It had been sharing my bungalow the whole time I had been there and was the source of the mysterious breathing I sometimes heard at night. It proved to be eleven feet long but a non-poisonous python. I was still pleased that our joint-ownership had ended.

Duties at our Headquarters continued to be light and routine and I therefore asked the Area Commander if I could push off up North to Imphal and Kohima to visit Jim Sawyer's grave. Phoebe's brother had been a Company Commander in the Royal Berkshire Battalion that relieved our 4th Battalion in the great battle to halt the Japanese Army at Kohima and had been killed during some very gallant close-quarter fighting. He received a posthumous Mention in Despatches for Gallantry which, in those days, was the highest award he could have won except the Victoria Cross. In those days DSOs and MCs could not be awarded posthumously but his C.O. Lt. Colonel Bickford made it quite clear that he would have been awarded an immediate DSO if he had lived.

I set off in a jeep with a very pleasant batman/driver whose command of English was much better than my command of Urdu. I had by then managed to pick up a .303 rifle which had been lost in some battle and had converted it to a sporting rifle by removing all the heavy ironmongery from the muzzle end and all the superfluous woodwork from the front. This made it much lighter and easier to handle, and with its powerful charge and reasonably high velocity bullet could be used effectively on a wide variety of game if one was a good shot; because those rifles were extremely accurate.

I converted another later on when I went out to Ethiopia and only sold it this year when my firearms certificate was not renewed, due to a blitz on privately owned firearms.

✧

My first night stop was near Tamu, approximately half-way between Kalewa and Imphal. I soon got on to the main road which the sappers had built to carry supplies down to the Fourteenth Army in Burma during their Southward advance after the Kohima battle, which had turned the tide of the Japanese thrust up towards India. The road had been levelled with bull-dozers and angle-dozers, rolled with heavy rollers and then laid with long rolls of very heavy bitumen matting. The matting had been laid when the roads were dry and the hundreds of vehicles which used the road made the soil beneath it rock-hard. When the monsoon rains came the water just ran off the waterproof road and into the ditches on either side. Only in one or two places in low lying ground the culverts were sometimes too small and the water got under the matting which became crumpled up. There we had to crawl through the best bit of road available, or even made a detour onto the uphill side of the road. In other places the road was superb with banked bends like a motorway.

The unit I was making for near Tamu was the Elephant Company, run by Elephant Bill for so long, now commanded by a Major Finch with Claude Hann, whom I have mentioned earlier, as his 2 i/c. The camp was a wonderful sight, with lines of elephants. A number of 'trusties' were grazing the jungle in the immediate vicinity of the camp with only restraining chains joining their front legs, to prevent them running off too fast. Their wooden bells all tinkled out different notes and were individually made by their own 'oozies'.

Before sunset and in the cool of the evening, Claude took me off for an hour's game stalk. It was my first lesson in junglecraft from a professional, because he had been a game warden before the war. We saw an amazing number of tracks, including mountain bear. Tracking is far more simple and logical than one would imagine. The hotch-potch of animals' tracks at a jungle cross-roads would indeed be a hotch-potch to an untrained observer, but if one stops and looks very carefully one can read a complete story. For example if a wild elephant's tracks lead down a path to the water and his tracks have been super-imposed by a large deer passing across them, and the elephant has then returned and his return tracks are not covered by the deer's tracks; the deer passed by whilst the elephant was having a drink. The same would apply to a man's foot prints, and a knowledge of the timing of animal's habits enables an expert to put a time on the man's movements.

✧

This is the simplest possible example but shows how a complete picture can be built up. This technique was later used to determine the approximate time when men had passed across a jungle path in the Mau Mau campaign in Kenya; and from professional big game hunters, who were normally tight-lipped about their craft, I was able to get down in writing, for the first time, a wealth of jungle tracking hints.

✧

Claude and I got back to the camp just before complete darkness fell, and after dinner I heard some of the amazing adventures of the Elephant Company and of their many achievements. I recommend the book

'Elephant Bill' written by J.H. Williams, who was Finch's predecessor and who steered his loyal and powerful band into and out of many dangerous tight corners. Before I left next morning for Imphal my hosts made me promise to stay another night with them on my way back. As far as I was concerned, nothing could have kept me away.

As I set off I remembered that most of the way from Kalewa to Imphal was taking me up the Kabaw Valley, and that Kabaw was the Burmese for death. Apparently, the local brand of Malaria was extremely deadly and before the advent of Mepacrine the European members of the Bombay Burma Trading Corporation had an extremely short life expectancy. We were lucky to have Mepacrine, which one had to start taking before arrival and take a tablet a day throughout one's stay and for a month after leaving. It made us as yellow as any Asiatic and was said to make one sterile. Fortunately my family was by then complete.

I do not want to bore you with endless descriptions of the scenery, but I feel I must tell you that I never ceased to be bewitched by the ever-changing views round every bend, of the variety of greens on the hills to our left lit by brilliant sunshine almost every day, since the monsoon rains were almost over. Brightly coloured birds could be seen flying in the trees and the odd snake sometimes gave me the creeps. Two I will never forget; the first hanging from a tree which overhung the road and which I thought might drop into our jeep and the second, about fifteen feet long, on the road and apparently having a sleep which I feared might rise up and strike if I drove too near it.

We ended our journey in daylight by virtue of the wonderful sappers road, having crossed the unmarked frontier between Burma and India around midday, and I was surprised at Imphal's size and sophistication. It had a mess, a small hospital, and even an airfield. There was a pleasant atmosphere of post-war exuberance in the mess, and I was made welcome and well fortified with both food and drink.

Next morning we continued through hilly country all the way to Kohima, having climbed well clear of the Chindwin valley and up into hills with summits of around 2,500 feet. The summit of Mount Japvo to the South of Kohima is in fact 9,800 feet high and towered well above us. This was the country which helped slow up the Japanese advance and helped to buy the time for 2 Div. to relieve the small garrison of Kohima. The 4th Battalion of my Regiment was the only British unit in the original garrison before being relieved by 2nd (British) Division.

⟡

I recently had the honour of being invited to their annual dinner and I found the event a unique experience. When men have gone through a battle such as they experienced in Kohima, a bond is forged which is irreplaceable, and this is currently being disregarded by comparatively young and inexperienced politicians. The dinner was proceeded by a fairly long drinking party, and during the course of this I had the chance to talk to a large number of Old Comrades. I did not meet a single man who had not been wounded at least once, including one who had been a stretcher bearer. From the numbers there I doubt if more than a handful who had fought in the siege and survived the intervening years were not present. Some had travelled long distances.

◇

My first impression of Kohima was quite shattering. Where Imphal was on a plateau which had already been cleared of forest to re-establish the pre-war town, Kohima had been a forest hill station, built on a series of hill-tops with trees growing amongst them; but now looking like a picture of Flanders from World War I. A few wooden buildings had been re-erected, but the vista was one of a battle scarred village with jagged stumps of trees torn by shell fire all around.

The main battle had squeezed the original garrison of 4/RWK, the Assam Regiment and the Assam Rifles into a small area around Garrison Hill, which was topped by a small plateau on which had stood the District Commissioner's bungalow, the Commandant's house, a summer house and a tennis court; each on low ring contours. All the defensive positions finally handed over to the 1st/Berkshires were hence on forward slopes and under direct enemy fire. The nearest Japanese positions were near the tennis court, a mere fifteen yards from our forward posts. It was in these trenches that Jim Sawyer was later mortally wounded and where Lance Corporal Harman of my Regiment won his V.C. His older brother had been my contemporary at Oundle, and I was later to be his father's guest on Lundy Island, which the Harmans owned.

I was made welcome by Lt. Colonel 'Buster Keane' the Camp Commandant who had survived the siege and returned to his job there after the area had been re-occupied when the fighting was over. He had had few troops to command by the end of the siege because most of the Indian troops were not in a high state of training and had gradually been filtered out to the North. In any case, there was insufficient food and water for even the effective members of the garrison, who were unable to wash or shave or have more than two hours uninterrupted sleep throughout their fifteen day ordeal.

The War Graves Commission had already done a magnificent job, and the Military Cemetery had been laid out with crosses bearing the names of the fallen installed on every grave. I was able to take some good pictures of

Jim's grave and sent them off to the Sawyers on my return to Kolewa. This return journey was uneventful and over the exact routes that I had used to reach Kohima. Once more I sojourned with the Elephant Company and got in my evening and early morning stalking with Claude.

On arrival back in Kalewa I found a letter awaiting me from Ginger Stockwell, who was by then stationed in the Orkneys, congratulating me on being awarded a Military Cross. Due to the submarine campaign, they only got mail every three weeks up there, and I felt slightly piqued that none of my family or my in-laws, who had seen the letters from my Brigadier and Commanding Officer in Leros, had not beaten him to it with this exciting news. There was no M.C. ribbon in Kalewa however, and it was some time before I was able to wear it.

There was less and less work to do in Kalewa as the run down of 14th Army gained momentum, and in due course we received the welcome news that we were being moved to Akyab, an island approximately halfway down the Eastern coastal stretch between Chittagong and Rangoon. By this time the airstrip near Kalewa had dried out and everyone was flown down to Rangoon except the road transport. This column of jeeps and lorries was to proceed by road under my command, with an extremely pleasant young captain, Tony Truscott, as my 2 i/c.

The Commander then discovered that the D.A. Q.M.G., who blanched when told to prepare the Movement Orders, including detailed staff tables breaking down everything and everybody by weight into aircraft loads, had not the slightest idea how to set about this task. I was then asked if I would mind doing it for him before setting off with my vehicle column. I was delighted to have the opportunity of doing this job, as I had never been actually posted to a 'Q' appointment, and never was to the end of my army career. For the uninitiated I should explain that in those days the staff was divided into Operations (G Staff), Personnel Management (A Staff) and Supplies, Transport and all inanimate objects (Q Staff).

On the day of the move Tony Truscott and I had all our vehicles ready to leave, with two men per vehicle, so that when the last plane load left, we could just drive off. I have never seen such a sight as unfolded before me as the Indian troops emplaned. There were squawking chickens, goats and the odd pi-dog, and all manner of unauthorised and improvised furniture. Fortunately I had allowed a generous percentage of error to compensate for such things and not many items had to be abandoned after the checks on the improvised weigh-bridge. As the last Dakota took off, Tony and I walked to our jeeps, me in the leading one and he in the last, and away we rolled along the jungle tracks between Kalewa and Mandalay. This was all new territory for me, having completed the Northward trip in the memorable landing craft. We had hoped to make

Shwebo the first night, but as the loading of the aircraft took so long, and Shwebo was well over 120 miles from Kalewa, I decided to camp in a reasonably open clearing where we could concentrate our vehicles and mount guard over them. Dakoits, the Burmese equivalent of particularly lethal 'Robin Hoods' had never ceased their activities because there was a war on; preying on British, Japanese or local Burmese as and when opportunities arose.

The night passed without incident and the next day found us in Shwebo, where things were less primitive and the two or three British N.C.O.s, the Indian N.C.O.s and men, and Tony and I were all absorbed into the appropriate messes. On the following day we found the forest road much improved South of Shwebo, and saw more plantations and other signs of civilisation. We reached Mandalay fairly early, but decided to have the afternoon off to allow Tony and some of the others to enjoy a little semi-civilisation. The rest of the journey down to Rangoon, where I was to hand in our transport, less two jeeps, was free of hassle or incident. We passed through Meiktila, Pyinmana, Toungoo and Shwegyin, following the line of advance of those units of 14th Army who moved down the Sittang River. We reported to a transit camp in Rangoon, handed in our vehicles and enjoyed two or three days of unofficial leave whilst awaiting our air trip to Akyab. I was conned into buying a diamond and sapphire ring from one of the better jewellers, but was prudent enough to have it checked by another who pronounced it a semi-fake. The gold was gold, the sapphire was a sapphire, but the diamonds were false. I was lucky enough to bump into two military police wearing my Regiment's cap badge. They were from the 4th Battalion and were delighted to see another officer of their Regiment. They were both at least six feet tall and wearing red cap covers over their normal caps with the White Horse of Kent badge. I asked them to march in behind me, where I intended to confront the first jeweller and ask for my money back. I strode in and faced him across the glass counter of his shop and told him that he would be arrested for fraud and removed, then and there, if he did not accept the return of the ring and refund the money I had paid him. He complied immediately.

I had not had a chance to explore Rangoon on my first arrival there from H.M.S. Bulwark. It was then evening, it was raining, and my jeep and driver from 17 Ind. Div. had been waiting for some time. I just got a glimpse of some of the ornate temples as we drove past. Now, Tony Truscott and I had time to explore the city and to spend some time in the Shwe de Gon Pagoda with its spire-like roof covered with real gold leaf. We also visited some interesting temples and holy sites outside Rangoon, notably The Lying Buddha. Situated within driving distance North of Rangoon, this enormous effigy of Buddha lying full-length on his side, with his head cupped in one hand, must be around half the length of a full size football ground, but still ornamental and embellished to the last detail.

✧

The Buddhist religion is interestingly close to the Christian religion. Both were founded by holy men; in the case of Buddha a prince born in great luxury, but prepared to devote his life to the religious ideals he believed should be followed. The second similarity is the end product. The Christian religion has adopted the Jewish Ten Commandments. The Precepts of Buddha resemble these closely. For example – the Buddhist 'Respect your elders' has virtually the same instruction as 'honour thy father and thy mother'. Buddha himself did not wish to be deified and worshipped as a God, but there are probably as many statues of Buddha as there are of Jesus on the cross. I do not believe Mohammed wished to accomplish more than to guide the minds of his followers towards Allah's wishes, and would have been appalled at the way in which the Moslem faith was forced upon non-Moslem people to the East of Arabia on pain of death. It is likely that all the three founders of the great monotheist religions would have been displeased with many of the subsequent actions of their followers, including Christians torturing disbelievers or variants during the Spanish Inquisition.

✧

We sampled the food in Rangoon restaurants and found it much nearer to Chinese food than Indian or Ceylonese. The time came when a Dakota was finally made available to take us and our two jeeps to Akyab. The aircraft had been adapted to carry vehicles by cutting a wide door on one side. The ramp was set at an angle almost parallel with the aircraft and one drove up it and down the inside. Our drivers had somehow found some local livestock and we had certain things which our Headquarters had ordered by wireless. After an uneventful flight we started to descend on Akyab's small airfield; not long enough, I thought. Akyab is really the end of a peninsula with three sides surrounded by the warm blue waters of the Bay of Bengal and the fourth side being a river with a bridge to the mainland, thus making it an island.

We were met by the DAQMG who was not the brightest and best, and led along a narrow but tarmac road to our headquarters. After unloading our baggage, which consisted mainly of our valises and the odd suitcase, I thought I would pay a visit to the officer's loo on the way to the Mess. I remember that we had to walk along a raised grassy dyke to get to it, and as I turned into the bamboo built structure I was so appalled by the odour that when I reached the target I was seeking I was unable to restrain myself from vomiting straight into it. How and why my opposite number had been able to put up with it I shall never know. The Commander had his own privy and would never have allowed such a state of affairs to exist. By that same evening great changes had taken place!

Akyab was like a small Indian Military Station, with its hospital, club, wooden chapel and bungalows and gardens of a size appropriate to low and middle ranks. There was very little work to do as the names and priorities for repatriation to the United Kingdom had already been sent off, and there was no question of building things up in the structural sense as everything was being run down. We had by that time become a Sub-Area.

The beaches facing the afternoon and evening sun were splendid, and we made surfboards from any old planks of wood to ride the medium-sized waves. I learned to surf without a board, with my chest hollowed out and my head poking out through the front of the wave. The effect of one's whole body being involved with the turbulent water was most exhilarating. At Christmas we had a water carnival in a long freshwater reservoir. I remember that the programme included water polo, relay swimming races and individual championships. I managed to win the 100 yards by not trying to win my heat. The first two in each heat went into the final and the winner of my heat was quite the best swimmer of us all. He was however so keen to give me a clean pair of heels that he exhausted himself, and as we were the last heat he had still not recovered enough to beat me in the final.

On New Year's Eve 1945 there was a dance at the club attended by virtually all the nurses from the hospital which was a large one for so small a station, but had been built up to take the heavy casualties expected from the final battles for Southern Burma. I could have done with quite a few weeks of this tropical paradise, but the powers-that-be who had allowed Captain Satarawallah to take my job in 17th Indian Div felt that it was time I did something more taxing and effective and I was very soon posted to Jhansi in the Central Provinces of India.

Chapter XIV

The long, long trail to Jhansi

There was an attractive 'Sanders of the River' type port at Akyab with wooden jetties and I duly embarked in a small coaster which I reckon was not much over 1000 tons. I was the only officer passenger and fed in the small officers dining room which was presided over by the Captain at almost every meal. The voyage was uneventful, but for me was most enjoyable as everything was new to me. I loved seeing the long coast of Burma, which we hugged fairly closely. I even did a quick water colour of one pretty headland with a lighthouse on it. My immediate destination was our first port of call, which was Chittagong. This is about 200 miles East of Calcutta, but separated from it by all the many estuaries of the River Ganges. I spent one night in Chittagong and enjoyed being back in India where the people were so much more colourful. I then took a slow train due North for 80 miles to Comilla. There I detrained and took a very primitive train for around 50 miles due West to Chandinir. This was the end of the branch line, and to my amazement I was invited to get aboard a large petrol driven launch or waterbus which was a river link with another branch line many miles down-stream on the West bank of the River Burak, which rises in the foothills of Assam.

My fellow travellers consisted of a few officers and British servicemen and a small number of Indian merchants. The driver, who sat at the front of a long bus-like cabin, was a Burman who could speak no English or Urdu. I remember a notice pinned above his head saying "If the driver cannot understand you, it is no use shouting louder because he still won't". Time had already begun to mean nothing mentally, but my stomach kept asking me when I would get my next meal. Eventually a wooden jetty hove into sight and we disembarked and carefully followed the porter who carried my own baggage until it was unloaded into the only first class carriage of a really primitive train. An ancient black engine of the nineteenth Century and four wheeled carriages. Surprisingly, a simple meal was available in the first class carriage and the ancient locomotive groaned into action for a tedious journey of another hundred odd miles to Calcutta. We arrived after dark and it was with both surprise and relief to find that the officers transit camp was in none other than one of the most comfortable hotels in that great sprawling city, The Grand.

To reach my final destination, the railway junction and British Military Station of Jhansi, I had to face a further rail journey of around 900 miles Westwards to Delhi and then another 250 odd miles South. After enjoying a very comfortable night and first class food and drink, I looked forward to my forthcoming rail journey because I knew that the rolling stock would be more modern and comfortable, and I was still a green enough traveller to enjoy the ever-changing scenery which I had been experiencing to date. I could not have been more wrong.

As far as I can remember there were two well-appointed first-class sleepers with a restaurant car in between them. By day the beds folded up and the carriage became a comfortable four seater. I was lucky to find myself in with three pleasant companions, and to discover that they all enjoyed playing mediocre bridge. As we puffed out of Calcutta and cleared the taller buildings, I took in the general scene which I had missed in the darkness of the previous night. To the right at all times, the high ground leading up to the Himalayas dominated, whilst to the left the flat plains of Northern India stretched into the distance. Every two or three hours we would stop at some small town where sometimes the engine would be watered and refuelled. I noted that most houses were flat topped and single storied, whilst there was an area of larger two storied houses for the more prosperous. There was also a Mosque and minaret. At our first stop I took it all in with great interest. The second town was so similar in appearance, that I rubbed my eyes and wondered if we had not gone back to the last one. I then realised that the scene was unlikely to change hour after hour and day after day for the next three days and two nights which it would take us to reach Delhi. The hills to the North were sometimes further away and allowed provocative glimpses of the snow heights beyond, but usually the foothills intervened. To the South the flat plains stretched endlessly. They were by now already a parched yellow as the monsoon rains had finished over two months earlier. We soon stopped looking out of the windows and played bridge all day, pausing only to go to the restaurant car for meals, or to have drinks in our compartment. I do not remember anything more about the trip; it seemed so endless and boring, and maybe we hit the bottle rather hard. My mind never registers things which do not interest it, and I do not remember the names of my companions or what they looked like, nor do I have a positive memory of our seats being turned into two bunk beds on each side. Perhaps it was done whilst we had a lingering dinner, suitably augmented by beverages.

As was to be expected, we arrived at Delhi in the dark and were driven in Army vehicles to the Delhi Transit Camp. I remember the huge walls and impressive gateway. There was no privacy within, and even Field Officers slept in rows in what had been, I believe, a hospital ward. I was now firmly in the hands of 'Movement Control' and was told what to do and when to do it. This meant breakfasting, reporting at a pick-up point and being ferried in mid-morning to the railway station from which trains departed for Jhansi, via Agra where one of the most beautiful buildings in the world still lies in well-maintained splendour, the Taj Mahal.

✧

I was all agog to catch a glimpse of the Taj Mahal as our train passed through Agra. It is one of the Wonders of the World and I was still young and naive enough to want to be able to say that I had seen it! In the event Phoebe and I did a trip to India, Kashmir and Nepal in 1979 and we did a day trip from Delhi down to Agra and spent several hours in the grounds and the buildings of the Taj Mahal. It was not until that trip that I realised that my 'transit camp' in Delhi in 1946 had been none other than the famous Red Fort, and that our hotel in Calcutta was The Grand, which I had stayed in on our way back from Burma.

✧

I arrived in Jhansi in the early afternoon and had my first experience of a well run pre-war Military Station which had not been much changed by the War as Karachi had been. I was met at the station and driven to the Mess to be allocated a bungalow. I was there told that the bungalow that was earmarked for me would not be vacated for two or three days, and that I would have to go to a 'single captain's' quarter in the Mess. At that moment Malcolm Dewar walked in, and after we had greeted each other and he heard my news he said "I knew that you were arriving soon and has just come in to arrange for you to share my bungalow until yours is free". So my belongings went straight from the Mess veranda to his bungalow, which had two bedrooms, and we took up our stories from August 1945, when we raced our rickshaws through the streets of Kandy in Ceylon.

Malcolm had had a number of fascinating jobs in South East Asia in the interim, taking over various islands from the surrendered Japanese. Having had interesting religious discussions with my Moslem (but English) colonel in Abergavenny, I now had illuminating talks with Malcolm on the Roman Catholic religion. He was a charming and repetitive sinner and I wondered how he reconciled his lifestyle with what I had always believed to be a very strict faith. He proved to be a very sincere Catholic and explained that the system of confession and penitence was a thing that he could live with. He admitted his errant ways and said that he had come to an arrangement with his Father Confessor to pay a handsome sum annually as a fine for a year's unconditional sin. Since my own belief is that we are all a part of our Creator and that all religions are striving to create and maintain a spiritual link with Him, I was not in any position to argue or criticise; but I have noted that the Roman Catholic religion does seem more firmly rooted in quantity amongst poor populations and those with below average I.Q. I am also aware that Jesuit Priests all hold Doctorates of Philosophy, and I shall later describe my mental sparring with one, when I was trying to seek religious respectability within his faith.

Jhansi was a fairly large station which in pre-war days probably accommodated a brigade of four battalions and the appropriate supporting arms and services. It was now the home of an organisation responsible for the records and administration of all British troops in India. The job I had to do however was Top Secret and only known to three other people other than myself.

Because the early partition of the North Western part of India, which was mainly Moslem and now known as Pakistan, from the rest of that great sub-continent was being hurried forward by a Labour Government not versed in the control of Eastern peoples, those who had such experience predicted the most appalling outbreak of violence and bloodshed. It was not ruled out that the British civilians in India could well be involved if we withdrew the British elements of the Indian Army and the British Battalions serving in India prematurely. Even Lord Louis Mountbatten with his strong personality and Royal connections seemed oblivious to the fact that casualties greater than those in World War II were likely to be suffered if we pulled out prematurely.

There were large numbers of Indian Army personnel serving in Jhansi and a few all Indian units stationed in the vicinity. The one which exercised my mind most was an Indian armoured regiment equipped with American tanks only 30 miles down the road!

Since we did not want it to be generally known to either British or Indian troops how soon and in what manner we would withdraw, I was given the task of preparing three Internal Security Defence plans. The first assumed that all India personnel were loyal and could be incorporated into any Internal Security Scheme. This involved organising all Military personnel, including all those normally doing clerical jobs, into three small battalions.

Since no-one could be told about this, I had to work out the whole structure on paper, give an actual name to every appointment and then write a brief instruction for each individual telling him what his appointment was, who his Commander was and where he was to go.

The first scheme envisaged a large area with a perimeter of around three miles, a safe central area, which included the hospital out of small arms range from every part of the perimeter.

Across the old cemetery to Jhansi Fort

The second scheme was an all-British force with a minuscule perimeter and nowhere, even in the centre, out of small arms fire.

The third scheme was a last ditch effort to avoid us all being massacred if the nearby Indian Armoured Regiment turned sour and came trundling up the road from its barracks.

Every British officer therefore had three orders addressed to him in sealed envelopes, and people who were company commanders in Scheme 1 would be platoon commanders or even section commanders in Scheme 2 etc. All this work took place in a large room where I and two senior British clerks operated under the highest security. We all had keys, and the room was permanently locked whether we were in it or not.

Meanwhile, after duty I enjoyed the social scene of a peace-time Indian Military Station. Once I was settled in my own bungalow I started to take part in the various activities available. These included riding and organised game hunting. There were still too many tigers around in those far off days and some of them were man-eaters. At the request of my bearer, whose village was being terrorised by one of these, I allowed myself to be taken out to a tree near that village that evening around full moon, where a platform called a machaan had been built.

At last light a goat was duly tethered to a nearby tree, my friends departed and I pulled up my rope ladder. I had a bottle of ready-mixed whisky and soda, some sandwiches, a powerful torch and the converted game rifle I had used in Burma.

The goat, with whom I had great sympathy and something of a fellow feeling occasionally bleated. This I thought was a definite bonus as far as attracting the tiger was concerned, and I found that the light of the moon was bright enough for me to see the goat very clearly. If I moved my position now and then to keep moonlight on my rifle sights, I could also see them well enough to shoot accurately. I vowed to try and ensure that the goat did not get hurt. It was as nervous as I was and was constantly doing poos! I had agreed to stay up there for five hours which meant that they could return for me around midnight. After what seemed ages and the dusk midges were still active, I stole a look at my luminous watch and found that it was not even eight o'clock yet.

With nothing to do except keep quite still the hours dragged by interminably. Three times I heard movement and got all keyed up. I knew that my enemy was quite ruthless because three weeks earlier he had broken cover when an 'on foot' tiger beat, which I had not attended was advancing in line abreast through scrub and had gone down the line like a flash and mauled four officers with open claws as he went past, one very severely in an arm which needed endless stitches. No-one had got in a shot because he was so quick and they were afraid of shooting each other.

This episode did nothing to calm my nerves as I realised that climbing trees was part of a tiger's relaxation!

I realised then that the tiger might prefer me to the goat and practised getting into a position where I could point my rifle down the tree. This meant projecting quite a bit of myself over the platform and made me feel quite insecure. I vowed to shoot the tiger before it got into a position under my machaan under the tree, ate two sandwiches and had a slug of whisky and soda. My watch then told me it was only eight thirty five.

I do not know how I got through the remaining three and a half hours, but stiff and tired I and the goat were duly relieved around midnight. I vowed never to repeat this performance on my own although I did take part in one of those hazardous line abreast efforts a week or two later, and took care to be one of those in the middle of the line.

Having learned a bit about individual stalking from Claude Hann in Burma, what I enjoyed most was riding off into the blue, completely on my own on a bicycle with my converted .303 rifle across the handlebars. I would turn off the main road from Jhansi into jungle country and then follow tracks which, in the dry weather, were quite cycle-worthy. When they ceased to be so I would dismount, hide the bicycle in a bush, take a long and telling look around noting the position of the sun and then slip silently into the rather sparse jungle of that area.

There were several types of deer around and it was considered fair to shoot a large peahen if one could surprise one by a silent approach. Etiquette demanded that one should only aim at the head so that one either killed it, stunned it or missed it but never sent a wounded bird to die later in the bush. I kept well clear of all thick cover which might be concealing a tiger's lair and in a holster in my belt carried my Colt .45 which at short range could stop even a tiger.

It was during one of these solo trips that I found myself thirsty and resorted to the ploy which, I am told, Boy Scouts are taught; namely if you dig down in the middle of dry stream-bed, you will eventually come to water. This I did in the middle of nowhere and far from any village. Using the pointed end of a round of ammunition to loosen any large stones, I managed to scrape out a hole and reached water after only about fourteen inches of depth. It was absolutely clear after I had allowed the grains of small sand to settle, but was lukewarm and tasted pretty foul. Nevertheless I felt like a melange of Stanley, Livingstone and Sanders of the River, and had i been a dog I would have wagged my tail. It was one of those experiences which make up the rich pattern of Life; but more anon.

On Saturday evening, the Officer's Club was enriched by two of the Nursing Sisters from Akyab whom I remembered and who had only arrived that afternoon. Since there was a dance that night, I thought it would be a good idea to make up a small party and to include them. About three hours later, when we all assembled, men in gaberdine service dress and ladies in long frocks, all went well until a fellow member of the mess who was joining us appeared. He was not particularly sallow, had an English name, but wore the uniform of the 'General List' which has a badge of the full Royal Coat of Arms and was worn by officers entering the Army from civil life who had not been assigned to a specific unit. Because he had a slightly Welsh sounding sing-song in his voice both the sisters from Akyab vanished into the ladies loo and one remained there for a long time until eventually prized out by someone a little more broadminded. It transpired that he had a British father and an Indian mother, and in those days even young women who had not grown up under the strict separatist pre-war conventions had caught that attitude. In those days even the most well educated Indians always spoke with a slightly Welsh accent. I believe that everyone should be judged on their merits, and that in all social contacts people should be free to choose their friends.

I also believe that marriage between ethnic groups who have very great differences are not desirable and that their offspring do suffer disadvantages. No proud people wish to be overwhelmed by an influx of strangers and this has happened to Great Britain. It is part of the Laws of Nature laid down by our Creator and the wild ideas of the silly billies who framed the Race Relations Act who may still live to regret it. A lesson is now being enacted in Bosnia.

When I joined my Regiment the Regimental Quartermaster Sergeant had African parentage and my groom Indian parentage. Both were nicknamed Darkie and both were extremely popular. When I ran a manufacturing company, one of the best welders was a full-blooded Jamaican who was liked and respected by both management and his fellow workers. By injecting hundreds of thousands of Jamaicans into this country, millions of normally tolerant and broad-minded citizens have now become hostile to immigrants of all colours. Mainly because they were thrust upon us with no mandate, and a law was passed forbidding us to utter or write unfavourable comments upon people of other races, however truthful. This law is contrary to the Common Laws of England and should be amended. Speaker's Corner at Hyde Park was a deliberate safety valve whence people could let off steam. If they talked sense they were listened to, if they poured out a load of codswallop they were laughed at. In those days politicians appeared to have more wisdom and experience than most of those in Westminster today who must have given many foolish bills a majority.

A few days after my experience at the dry stream bed,my posting home was confirmed and I only had two or three days to be on board a troopship in Bombay. I had applied for repatriation on the grounds that I had served nearly seven consecutive years abroad and on arrival home had been protected from an overseas posting, but had volunteered for service in Burma because there was still a war on. Now that the war was over and that I had been posted to India, and that my right (writing) hand was still in plaster, it seemed a fair request to apply for a home posting. In fact my plaster came off shortly after my application was recommended by my boss and passed on to the War Office, but the other factors remained valid.

There was very little packing to do as I only possessed what I had taken to Burma by air, plus a few purchases. I sold my rifle for a fair sum to an extremely wealthy Anglo-Indian family who had been generous hosts during my stay in Jhansi. I had not been feeling well for a day or two with a slight temperature and some enteritis, and felt extremely groggy. However, I thought, once I was on that train it was next stop Bombay, and on to a troop-ship, so I brazened it out and somehow made the train. There were four of us in a first class carriage and I remember nothing about any of them except that every now and then one would lean forward and say "are you sure you're alright old boy". With the thought of a first class trip to England to buoy me up my muttered reply was always "I feel a bit tired, but I'll be fine as soon as I get on the boat". Eventually, after a few hours one of them leant forward and put his hand on my forehead and said "You've got a roaring temperature, we're all sweating in this heat and you're bone dry." I still persisted that I could make it to the boat at Bombay.

Two of them disappeared down the corridor and came back with a Medical Officer who happened to be travelling on the train. "We will soon be going through Deolali" he said after he had taken my temperature which was 104°F, "there's a big Military Hospital there and I am going to get you taken off the train and admitted there." I argued that the ship was bound to have a sick bay but he was adamant and by then I had lost all my will power and ability to argue. My last memory was being helped down from the train and being assisted by two of my former companions, one each side, to stumble into some room at the station. My next memory was of waking up in a large airy room which had a fan going hung from the ceiling and that, in spite of it, everything seemed very hot.

I was apparently suffering from a particularly lethal form of Infective Hepatitis. A virulent amoeba was attacking my liver and eating it away. Yellow bile was being discharged into the blood-stream, hence my pee looked just like Guinness. The other thing looked as if it had been fashioned from white brick-dust. Just to make things more difficult, the temperature inside my room was around 104°F, so even if I clung onto the metal head of my bed it did not cool me down.

One morning the sweeper came in from the veranda which ran along outside the senior officer's rooms and announced brightly "The Colonel sahib in next room die in night sahib." Since I was feeling like death, I could have done without these tidings, and closed my eyes and continued to hold onto my bed-head, which during the night and early morning was a few degrees cooler than me. I remember nothing more about that day or the succeeding night except that I felt restless but too weak to toss and turn. On the following morning my sweeper friend blew in again, this time with an almost triumphant expression "The major sahib in the room on the other side die early this morning sahib" he declared brightly.

"My God", I thought, "the Great Reaper has got a short bracket on me and today it's my turn." That afternoon at around 2.30 pm I was at a very low ebb and breathing very shallowly. The afternoons were always peak temperature time. The day Sister came in routinely and took my temperature, felt my forehead and declared "You're frightened aren't you?" "What of" I muttered. "I think I'll go and crush a couple of aspirin tablets in half a glass of water" she replied, and duly hurried off.

She soon returned, propped up my head with one hand and held the glass to my lips with the other one. I drank the tepid mixture and lay back. I must have dozed off for a few minutes, because I don't remember breaking out into a sweat, but found myself wringing wet. I found the electric push-button switch which was taped to my bed-head and heard the bell buzz in the Sister's office. She appeared rather quicker than usual, I thought, and said "are you alright?" "I'm wringing wet" I replied, "but I'm feeling terrific." She sponged me down, dried me and then took my temperature. "You're already down to 100" she cried, "you've made it." "You made it" I replied and drifted off into a long and relaxed sleep.

I never looked back after that dose of two aspirins and within 48 hours my temperature was normal and I had the strength to get up and walk to the loo on my own. I do not know how long it took me to regain enough strength to be considered fit enough to be discharged and put aboard a troopship, but the whole stay at Deolali was around four weeks. I still believe that the caring Sister saved my life and cannot understand why no-one had thought of trying aspirin before. The moment I got onto the gangway of the troopship at Bombay I began to feel better, and after about three days at sea in the company of a wonderful mix of charming hard-drinking people, I began to regret that I had been firmly instructed not to touch any alcohol for three months. The liver is apparently a most wonderful organ which when injured regrows to the correct size, but takes time to do it. Being a British ship, there was no question of it being in any way dry, and I really suffered watching all my friends downing their drinks whilst I sipped lemonade. Eventually, when we reached the Red Sea, I decided to have half a glass of lager to see what happened. I dreaded that the ghastly feeling that prevails when one has anything wrong with one's liver would return, and waited to see what would happen with great trepidation. There was no reaction whatsoever and after that I used to have a full half-pint of lager as my tipple each morning, at evening drinks time, and with meals. It did not seem to affect me and doubtless, because I never gave the liver an overdose of work to do, the gentle exercise it had was perhaps even beneficial for it.

A large number of passengers were civilians from companies like the Bombay Burma Trading Company and various oil companies, who had either been interned by the Japanese or diverted to India to await the end of the war. Many had the most interesting stories to tell. Inevitably we formed circles of friends and I was lucky to be amongst people with a great sense of humour and from every walk of life. One of the most amusing was a Scot who, before the war had owned an enormous ranch in Patagonia and could not wait to get back to his livestock, his horses and his South American gauchos.

After the nostalgia of passing through so many places I had known, such as the Suez Canal, Alexandria and Malta, we eventually docked at Southampton. The local military authorities granted me two weeks leave and I contacted Phoebe by telephone. She felt it unwise to leave the children all night with a nineteen year old au pair girl, and arranged to meet me at my club the following morning.

Chapter XV

Life at the War Office and at Fulmer, Bucks.

I made my way to London and booked in at my club, the 'In and Out' in Piccadilly. The next morning Phoebe joined me. She had gravitated to West Mersea, where my parents still lived, and had rented a spacious houseboat which was none other than the 'Hispania', King Alfonso's former 'J' class racing yacht. The standard of fixtures and fittings was very high, reflecting the taste of her former royal owner. She could only be reached by a long catwalk of planks and we dreaded that one of the children might fall into the water, or worse still, at low tide into the mud.

In those days West Mersea, an island surrounded by the sea or mud and in the bracing East Coast air, was always a tonic to me. I soon began to feel really fit once more and, all too soon, I received a posting to the War Office. It was said to be one of the rungs on the ladder which all officers who aspired to reach the top must climb. Phoebe started house-hunting to the South West and West of London, where pleasant countryside could be reached with the shortest commuting time. We cut out London as being unhealthy for children to live in permanently. I duly moved as a temporary resident into the In and Out and hoped that my sojourn there would not be too long.

I acquired a small Standard drophead coupé which Phoebe used in her search for a home and eventually came up with a dream house near Fulmer in Buckinghamshire, between the Piccadilly line terminus at Uxbridge and Gerrards Cross. The house, Orchard Cottage, had been especially designed and built by a young architect who had married a German girl whilst serving in Germany at the end of the war. It was in the Bavarian style with an interior of unpainted pinewood panelling. To reach it one had to drive for the last quarter of a mile, partly through woods and rhododendrons which were all in full flower. When Phoebe and I drove down for me to see it and give it the final seal of approval it was a lovely sunny evening in early June, and the beauty of the countryside there, and the setting of the house amidst woods, copses and fields completely overwhelmed me. We were able to move in almost straight away.

A bonus was that the widowed mother of the owner, who had a temporary job abroad for three years, said "there are lots of rabbits about now as there is no-one shooting here at the moment, so shoot rabbits whenever you like, but don't go shooting my ornamental golden pheasants." She went on to explain that they had been installed just before the war, and left undisturbed, had established themselves well.

In 1946 there was still rationing in a big way and coupons were needed for most items of food, clothing and petrol. The latter necessity was solved in a most extraordinary manner. My father had been generous enough to present me with his yacht the 'Phoebe' as he was by then beyond sailing her himself. I was duly listed in the Lloyds Register of Yachts and by the Board of Trade who supplied special coupons for shipping. One day I received a formal letter, enclosing many more petrol coupons than I received for my car, saying "please find enclosed 12 petrol coupons for training Sea Cadets." I had never trained a Sea Cadet and felt rather shifty about this. I felt that perhaps I ought to go out looking for one, for I could always teach him a bit about navigation without using any petrol. However, I kept quite quiet, as we were around a forty minute run from my office at Hobart House and sometimes needed to use the car in emergencies, or if I was delayed too much to go via the Piccadilly line, which took over an hour to Hyde Park Corner. Four weeks later I received a further supply of coupons with the encouraging note, written in ink, saying "do not hesitate to let us know if these are insufficient." I never had the neck to apply for extra coupons, but we went on receiving our quota throughout our stay in Fulmer. The winter of 1946/7 was the one of the big freeze and S/Y Phoebe was laid up on the hard at Mersea until at least April 1947.

Our charming 'au pair' girl who had been taken on by Phoebe before I arrived home from India came to Orchard Cottage with us and stayed for a few months. When she left, Phoebe had her hands very full with two small children and we took steps to replace her. Such help was hard to come by, and eventually we were forced to accept a South African girl with a child who had been married to a British seaman who was in prison for deserting his ship in Cape Town to be with her. Because I worked in London, I was duly despatched one day to collect her from her digs near King's Cross station after work at my office in Hobart House. Phoebe was going to meet me with our car at Uxbridge station.

When I arrived by taxi at her digs, I climbed the narrow stairs to her room and knocked, she opened the door about an inch and said "Oh." "Weren't you expecting me" I asked. "Yes" she replied, "but I'm not sure I want to leave London now." I said "You can't let my wife down now, she's counting on you." She then took a sudden decision. "Alright I'll come" she said, "I'd better get packed."

She had made no preparation for the move and proceeded to put two suitcases on her bed, opened them and then folding nothing, she emptied her drawers and cupboards into them, just pressing everything down hard.

The inevitable result was that they filled all too quickly and half her belongings, the boy's few clothes and all his toys were thrust into paper carrier bags, not plastic ones that one uses today. Amongst the toys in one bag was an electric iron. I had left the taxi with its meter ticking away all this time, as they were as scarce as gold at that hour. We carried all the cases and bags down in one shift as I explained that we must be able to do that on the underground. I felt really embarrassed, being in uniform, as we still were at that time, and being seen with such strange companions. The six year old child, who was not the son of her present husband, had to carry two of the paper carriers. The scene as we were dropped off at Knightsbridge Station and made our way to the ticket office was indescribable, but worse was to come. When we were half-way down the escalator the bag that I was holding in one hand in addition to one of the suitcases, split open, and led by the iron, its contents went tumbling down the moving stairs. I have never moved faster on a staircase in my life and I rushed down the steps two at a time, overtook the avalanche of toys and hardware and just had time to put the other bag and the suitcase down and field the avalanche of goods as they reached the bottom. We had to repack the torn bag with soft clothes and put the toys etc in the sound bag that had held the clothes. No-one lifted a finger to help us and I had to re-arrange my porterage and get them to the platform for Uxbridge, scarlet in the face, and hoping no-one would recognise me.

Once in the train the child spoke in a very loud voice, and we were soon the focus of everyone's attention. A complete silence prevailed except for the child and his South African mother. I longed to stand up and pronounce that I was not the father and had mercifully never seen either of them before that day. Phoebe met me at Uxbridge station some 40 minutes later, but not realising my problems, did not come down to the platform, and so I and my two charges had once more to load ourselves up with parcels like three octopuses. It was raining when we reached the entrance and Phoebe was sitting in the car. I prefer to forget my words of greeting.

My job at the War Office was extremely interesting and very complex. I found that I took all of the "four to six weeks" to master the complexity of that Headquarters which everybody said was needed, and I learned a truth then which subsequent experiences verified. The work of running a large military headquarters was done entirely by the staff-trained majors. The majors were at the peak of their brain-power, and in their early thirties. It was they who thought up all the ideas which were put into practice and wrote the papers which brought them to reality and function. The captains were just too young and were all working to get to the Staff College, whilst Lt. Colonels and above seemed to supervise their branches and tidy up papers that needed polishing. Brigadiers and Generals attended conferences and took the ultimate credit. Sometimes I think that they really believed they had thought of the original ideas. My own tiny empire was called AG1(b), and believe it or not, my responsibilities included:-

The selection and posting in the U.K. to 'extra-regimental appointments' of all officers and other-ranks in the U.K. other than Staff Appointments, which were the responsibility of the Military Secretary's Staff.

The preparation of all 'Army Council Instructions', known as A.C.I.s, the circulation of their drafts to all departments of the War Office for approval or amendment; and finally the organisation of conferences at a senior level to pass A.C.I.s for publication.

The co-ordination of the arrangements of all functions requiring action by more than one Service or Arm. These were endless, and included such tasks as forming the Polish Resettlement Corps to absorb the Poles who had fought with us so gallantly, or providing men and vehicles to deliver milk during a strike.

My pièce de résistance was to use all my guile and experience to ensure that Princess Elizabeth's escort of Household Cavalry on her wedding-day was attired in full dress. Because the Brigade of Guards had not yet re-acquired enough bear-skins and scarlet jackets to clothe the large numbers involved, they were playing dog-in-the-manger and trying to prevent the Household Cavalry from wearing their breast-plates and plumed helmets. By this time Tom Butler, whose house and dog we had taken over in Camberley, had become Brigade major, Brigade of Guards. I rang him up and said sweetly "Good morning Tom". "What can I do for you" he countered. "I'm sure you're looking forward to our lovely Princess being escorted to Westminster Abbey by a Household Cavalry escort in full dress" I said "I certainly am" he replied. "Well" I said "you're not going to see it because one or two of your generals are playing sour grapes and saying that as the Guards lining the route can be provided with grey overcoats but no bearskins, the whole parade must be dressed to the same standard. You've got to use all your cunning to make them back down and I'm sure you'll succeed."

To his eternal credit Tom Butler did succeed and the glowing young Princess was duly escorted in the proper manner. Phoebe and I drove up from Fulmer for the day, which was a holiday, and tried to get a reasonable view by walking across Green Park from my club in Piccadilly. The crowd was at least twenty deep and we had little hope until, with Michael sitting on my shoulders, I held onto the tail of a police horse which was being urged right through to the front. I had complete confidence in their training and did not let go until we emerged at the top of the Mall, just East of the fountain. We had the most wonderful view as the bride's procession went past on her way to the Abbey. Phoebe had had less good fortune and was left with Jill, who happily collected waste paper and put it in one of the waste paper bins. Having held Jill up as the bride's ornate coach came past, she asked her what she had seen. "I think I saw Windsor Castle" she replied!

◇

After a few months at Hobart House I was rewarded by people who had arrived later than me coming to ask me how to set about doing this or that. "I believe you know better than anyone else how this bloody place works" they would say. I could not stand the awful pale dung-coloured walls inside Hobart House and suggested that my office needed redecorating. The walls of all the rooms had been pasted over the years with notices and instructions and many brown and dog-eared with age. Once I had won my point I said "if you're going to distemper the walls anyway, why can't I have them pale green?" This was duly approved and my vast staff of two captains agreed that we would stick no notices on them, but hang a few water-colours. My office soon became known as the most civilised room in the building and I sold one or two of my water-colours.

◇

Back at Orchard Cottage we were feeling, as everyone else was, the effect of the food shortages. I used to exercise my stalking expertise to get down-wind of rabbits and pick them off with my 22 rifle. Phoebe and I, who had not become involved before with the gory side of shooting, soon learned to skin a rabbit; and later when I shot the odd non-golden pheasant, to clean and pluck it. We had acquired a super little black and white Welsh Springer called Sally. I used to throw a ball and get her to enjoy retrieving it and later a dummy bird, which was no more than an old sock with some feathers stuffed into it for scent and then rolled up into a ball which she also retrieved. She meanwhile came with me when I went round with my gun and got used to the bangs. There came the day when I decided to try her out and I managed to bring down a cock pheasant about forty yards from where we stood. Having sat completely motionless, the moment I said "fetch" she was away, brought the bird back, laid it at my feet and then looked up into my eyes. I was so moved that I suspect that they were moist.

At weekends Phoebe and I would drive down to the Black Horse at Fulmer for a drink on Saturday evenings or sometimes Sunday mornings. There we met quite a few celebrities and got to know some quite well. Being near Denham, we met a few members of the film fraternity. John Mills had just made a film with Stewart Grainger and had to do a fight scene. Stewart had apparently thought that he might cause him a few problems, so John did some secret training and gave him quite a surprise on the first day they faced each other in front of the cameras. John Snagge was another regular, and at the peak of his period as a commentator. In those days, with virtually no television, the job of the commentators was most important and his calling the time of the strokes at the annual Boat Race will be remembered "Oxford are now striking thirty four, in-out, in-out" etc. His wife was a very attractive dentist. I remember him saying "It's useful to have a wife who earns money, but a bit off-putting when she puts one of her patient's plates on the breakfast table before going to her surgery."

Another less known but equally prestigious drinker was Cecil Peel, the current boss of the hand-made boot makers. He would say, after quietly sipping a drink or two "I was measuring Princess Elizabeth's feet this afternoon in Buckingham Palace." Peter Proud, another regular who was a producer for Arthur Rank, made a big impact on me as he seriously suggested that I gave up the Army and took up a job in the Rank Organisation as his Production Manager. He had seen some of my water colours and I had sold one to the landlord of the Black Horse. Apparently I combined an artistic sense with organisational abilities, and these qualities were rarely both available in one person in his profession. I enquired what the job meant and he gave an example. "If I made a film in Ceylon, you would go ahead, find the most suitable site, rent it for the period you deemed necessary, recruit all the local extras – and elephants if required – and have the whole set-up including accommodation for the cast, animals and technicians ready for our arrival."

It was just the sort of free-thinking, challenging and all-powerful job I would have liked, and the pay was high. I thought long and hard about it but realised that there was no certainty about the future. I decided, however that I would take it if I did not think that I would become a brigadier or higher, but the signs then were that I would, so I turned it down.

The gravel road which ran so picturesquely through the woods to Orchard Cottage passed near a gamekeeper's cottage which possessed no 'facilities'. The couple who rented it, Claude and Georgie Mouncey, had only a spade and limitless woodland for their sanitary requirements and an old wood-stove for cooking. He had a job at Denham Studios and used to ride to work on a bicycle usually sporting his Westminster tie. They were both heavy drinkers, and fought at times like cat and dog. He was tall and elegant and Georgie very shapely and attractive. If Claude came home too much the worse for the wear she would bolt him out and the noise, even a hundred yards from our house, was quite alarming; especially when he tried

The Mounceys' Home

to break his way in with logs of wood as hammers. One day when they came to drinks they brought their tame goat. It was house-orientated and liked to curl up on a sofa but not 100% house-trained. We asked them if they would mind leaving it behind next time they came. They were however an amusing couple and we owed Georgie a great debt of gratitude for rescuing Jill from their water-butt and possibly from drowning... Since I wrote the above, Phoebe has pointed out to me that Georgie was supposed to be in charge of her that morning!

Jill wanted a cat and we got her a kitten, black and white to match Sally. She had recently acquired a pink doll's tea-set, and when we asked her what she would like to call the kitten, she said 'Pink Cup'; so as 'Pink Cup' the kitten was always known. I was determined to make them friends and decided to do it quickly and by force. I sat in the middle of our sofa with Pink Cup held by the scruff of its neck in my left hand and Sally by her collar on my right. Sally struggled like mad to assault Pink Cup but I managed to hold her back. Pink Cup was very gallant and with her tiny claws outstretched she hissed and spat like mad. I gradually allowed them to get nearer and nearer together until their noses were only two inches apart an they could get each other's smell. I also did a lot of talking to them. After another five odd minutes I let them touch noses and almost immediately that battle was over and they both relaxed. That night, after Sally had gone to her basket, I quietly came up with Pink Cup in my arms and talking reassuringly to Sally, gently lowered her in. From that night onwards they always slept together, and both being black and white, we were never able to tell where one started and the other finished.

A memory of Pink Cup which I will never forget is when she got her head stuck up the bottom of a gutter down-pipe. Phoebe pulled until her neck was stretched like a Disney cartoon, but to no avail. She was eventually released by pushing her head up and down the pipe using soap-suds to lubricate the inside of it, and the head was finally pulled out.

The winter of 1946/7 was one of the coldest I remember, and everything was frozen-up right until the Equinox. I spent my entire Christmas leave chopping wood to keep a roaring fire in our drawing room and the boiler going to heat the water and the kitchen. In spite of this, when we had people to a meal they always arrived in overcoats and kept them on. We used some of our nautical special victualling coupons to acquire a seven pound tin of tongue, and with wine virtually unobtainable, we threw a beer and tongue party which was an enormous success. People were really short of food, particularly meat, and so as there was no shortage of beer or meat on this occasion, everybody tucked in ate and drank as much as they could, a rare luxury in those days.

Nobody seemed to lose weight in those days, however, and I forbore from telling them what it was like to really get down to skin and bone as we almost were in Malta in 1942.

✧

Boots Stanyon reappeared into my orbit by getting a job at Hobart House, having been a P.O.W. since Dunkirk. One day he threw a big birthday party at the flat which he shared with his girlfriend; rather avant-garde for those days. I drove back to Fulmer to change and collect Phoebe, so we arrived rather late. Everyone was already a little noisy when we got there and Boots produced two drinks for each of us, insisting that we knocked the first one straight down to catch up and were then allowed time to absorb the second.

We went on to the Berkeley Grill and finished up at the Astor Club to dance. I found myself talking to a chap in uniform who was just off to Palestine the next morning, and found that his parents owned the estate next to that in which our cottage was situated.

He insisted on my drinking champagne at his table, and this does not go well with whisky at any time, and that is what I had been drinking. I decided that it would be prudent for me to stop drinking and go out for a breath of fresh air before returning to our table. This is course fatal because it was during the cold weather in early 1947. I was poleaxed by the cold air and soon felt much worse instead of better. I staggered towards Shephards Market, which led towards my Club, instinct telling me to avoid getting lost.

Meanwhile Phoebe had noticed my absence and sent Boots out as a one-man search party. He came upon me already heading back towards the Astor and took my arm. There was a really hard frost and the roads were a sheet of frozen snow and ice. I started to slip and tightened my hold on Boots to steady me. Down we both went and found ourselves lying side by side in the gutter. We both roared with laughter, and Boots, remembering the Sandgate evening when we had been subalterns at Shorncliffe, said "just like old times old boy."

We eventually struggled up and made our way back to the Astor. I was not the most popular person with Phoebe, and there was a serious discussion about how we were going to get home. In those days there were no breath tests, and it was just a matter of deciding whether one could if stopped, persuade a policeman that one was fit to drive. "I think I'll be alright after I've had a glass of water, and a few minutes sitting down to gather my wits." I began. "Over my dead body" said Phoebe, "and that's what it probably would be."

In the end Phoebe drove the car, but the problem was that she had never actually driven the car out of London, but had always been a passenger and not necessarily taking much notice of the roads. The moment I got into the car I fell fast asleep, but I knew the road so well that every time Phoebe slowed down and asked for directions I was able to open my eyes, have a quick look round, and know exactly which way to turn. Eventually we drove through Shepherds Bush and turned South towards the White City and then into Western Avenue. Then suddenly the motion of the car began to irritate my insides and I decided that I must part with some of the alcohol. Phoebe pulled into the kerb and I lurched out of the door and went into someone's front garden, was sick and then lay in the snow. I vaguely remembered Phoebe coming and shaking me by the shoulder and being rightly, but painfully abusive. She was getting desperate, because she could not leave me to freeze in the snow and I was turning a deaf ear to the insults. Eventually a lorry came along and pulled up in front of our car. "Can I be of any help" said the driver as he put his head in our car". "My husband is lying in the snow in that front garden, rather the worse for the wear, do you think you could persuade him to get up and come back to the car?" "Leave him to me lady" said the kind lorry driver "I'll soon have him back with you."

This conversation was reported to me later of course and all I remember was a kind voice saying "Excuse me Sir, but I've got a small problem with my lorry, do you think you could give me a hand to get it started." This of course did the trick straight away. "Of course I will" I replied and with the minimum of assistance I was soon up and walking out through the garden gate onto the pavement. Our friend then deftly guided me to our car which had the front passenger door already open and before I could gather my wits together he had slid me into the front seat and slammed the door. "Step on it madam" he cried "and don't stop for anything or anybody until you get 'ome." Phoebe duly accelerated away and from then onwards I made a steady recovery. On arrival home I was soon fuelling our large boiler with large logs of wood and feeling more than a little ashamed. The lessons to be learned are, do not mix whisky with champagne however hard your head, do not go out into the cold from a warm room when you have had a skinful, and do not insult a drunk or he may get pugnacious, but a kind word will win him over in no time.

⟡

When the summer eventually arrived in 1947, we made the most of it and soon had the Phoebe launched at West Mersea. We used to go there for weekend sailing with the children, and sometimes I would have an all-male crew from friends at the War Office. For part of my summer leave we left the children with my parents at West Mersea and Phoebe and I set off with 'Boots' Stanyon for Ostend.

Once we had got half way across the North Sea, having turned Eastwards from Brightlingsea, we found ourselves suddenly in calm waters. The waves were still high from the strong wind that we had been experiencing and we rolled like a sow. I was unaware that we were in fact in the eye of a low, and with both Boots and Phoebe asleep below with open portholes, to make the best of the still air, I was concentrating on trying to keep the boom from being flung from Port to Starboard and yet maintain an apology of a course. Suddenly I felt a blast of air, as hot as when one opens an oven, blowing in my face. The S/Y Phoebe shot forwards like a startled duck, and with the boom crashing into the wave-tops and the Port deck awash, there was a real danger of water pouring in through the open portholes. I shouted down for all portholes to be fastened and for Boots to come up and give me a hand, as I was fighting with the tiller and had little chance of getting the main sheet in quickly. Boots had been a dinghy sailor all his life and had no experience of getting in a reef in the dark and in a rough sea, nor did I fancy giving him the helm. I decided to turn to windward and let the wind spill from a forty-five degree boom and we went like a train. I paid no attention to what our course was, survival being the main priority. After about an hour we must have passed into the storm centre again, or perhaps it was one of those whirlwinds which eventually get sucked upwards, because we were not to feel another breath of air until we reached Ostend.

More adventures were to follow, because to start with I had no idea where we were when the dawn finally broke. The waves took a long time to subside and Phoebe took to her bunk. I decided that we should try and get our 6 horsepower Stuart Turner engine going.

Although the Phoebe had been well fitted-out after all those years in her mud-berth at Mersea, her spotless engine had not been run. She had always been a good starter and I had no worries. The trouble was that the normally reliable skipper who my father had organised for me had not drained the engine before her seven year holiday. Being a two-stroke engine, which ran on a petrol/oil mixture, the fuel had separated into tar and a pale green and probably highly volatile fluid. Even the carburettor was gunged up.

I have an average to good 'sea-stomach' and although the engine was situated under the forward part of the cockpit, the carburettor was only got at by lifting the companion ladder away and removing a low vertical panel. This I was able to do and to remove the carburettor and strip it down. The main jet was completely solid and after I had found a needle and freed it, and then blown and sucked at it, the diesel-like fumes began to nauseate me. Eventually, every time I crawled back to the engine I was violently sick, and was reduced to lying on my bunk, and carrying out short sorties to get just one or two more turns on the carburettor or jet until everything was assembled. I then had to siphon out the filthy brew in the tank, starting the flow by sucking the fuel end of the rubber pipe until my mouth was half filled. Need I say more? Eventually we poured a fresh and correct mixture into the tank and got the engine going.

I reckoned that we had been swept off in a Northerly direction and set a course due South, feeling that I was bound to hit land somewhere between Zeebrugge and Ostend. Eventually we spotted a fishing smack ahead going our way, hailed it and found that they were heading for Blankenberge which was only a few degrees to Port from my roughly estimated course for Ostend. We arrived at Ostend around late lunch time, having had no breakfast, and within a minute of our entering sheltered water Phoebe stirred herself and came up on deck. It was always seemed to me incredible how quickly sea-sickness vanishes; whilst my few experiences of air-sickness have lasted for many hours after reaching terra-firma.

We motored right into the innermost quay in Ostend and tied up alongside. We then tidied up the decks, changed our clothes, shaved and went ashore for an omelette and coffee.

At times mistakes can be amusing in retrospect; such as when sailing up the Scheldt from Flushing to Antwerp, I had gone below to study my charts and when I came up for a check, I found that we were passing red buoys to starboard. "Why on earth have you gone about" I demanded. "We haven't" replied Boots. I looked to port and saw green buoys and then red ones in the far distance. I then looked way out to starboard and saw green ones. I realised at once that we were sailing over an island of 'middle ground' which was only covered because the tide was three quarters up, but falling. We failed to make it to the Port side channel before running aground and were lucky to be able to motor slightly 'downhill' to get into it, carving a deep rut in the mud. By the time we returned to England I had a feeling that it was easier to sail single handed than to enjoy a superfluity of unskilled assistance.

On returning from our trip to Belgium and Holland, Phoebe and the children stayed with some Mersea friends, a Dr. and Mrs Llewellyn-Jones. A polio scare had started that summer, and whilst they were there, both Michael and Jill started to feel ill and had temperatures. My father, who only lived a short distance from the Llewellyn-Jones, briefed us on all the steps one had to take in case it was polio, the most important being complete rest and taking no exercise of any sort. Being a disease of the nerves, it is important to give them as few messages as possible to relay from brain to muscle, as too much electricity flow down the infected nerves can burn them up and produce partial or even complete paralysis. The knowledge imparted to me then, including the type and place of the initial headache was invaluable to me some years later in Nairobi, where I became infected.

Life at the War Office continued much as usual except that I moved into the Club whilst the family was at Mersea and we shut Orchard Cottage up for four weeks.

My Section of the War Office varied with spells of intense activity and occasional quietness. During the latter I and my staff sometimes took slightly alcoholic lunch hours, usually on draught Worthington E, and came back rather somnolent. I remember once being unable to keep my eyes open once settled comfortably at my desk, and eventually put an imposing-looking document before me with my right hand between two pages on the table and my left supporting my head. I closed my eyes for a moment or two. The next thing I heard was the noise of some footsteps. I opened my eyes but had the sense not to look up. I quietly turned over a page and after a few seconds glanced up and pretended to have been taken aback by seeing a senior officer standing over me. "I'm sorry Sir, I exclaimed, I never heard you come in". We proceeded to do some business and I was able to answer his questions. He thanked me politely and there was no funny twinkle in his eye. I think I got away with it.

By the end of my tour at the War Office, at the end of 1947, quite a number of changes had been made to social life. As in pre-war days, uniform was no longer worn at the War Office, and we turned up in lounge suits. Evening dress became the order of the day in the better watering holes and those who had not possessed them in pre-war days, or who had lost them as I had, usually found that they could scratch together enough clothing coupons to acquire new dinner jackets. Many people even sported tails on appropriate occasions, and in my case I was lucky, because although all my Malta wardrobe had been pillaged, I had left my tails at Mersea before going to Palestine, and could still struggle into them. I am reminded about the tails because we wore them at some function at the Ritz and my fellow section boss at Hobart House had his wallet pinched out of his tails rear pocket whilst doing the Conga round the Ritz ballroom. One thing which did not improve much was the food, and rationing remained severe. One of my Staff Captains was however a farmer's son who had already begun to farm actively with his father before joining up for the War. He seemed to have an endless supply of duck eggs which are full of nutrition but cannot be stored in Waterglass. One therefore had to eat them fairly smartly. They were rather strong as boiled eggs but wonderful fried on fried bread or as omelettes.

⇦

My greatest triumph before leaving the War Office was when I was secretary to a very high-level meeting to decide upon the future of the Infantry. My own ultimate boss, the Director of Organisation was sponsoring the meeting which was to get general agreement to abandon the Regimental system in the Infantry and have a Corps of Infantry with numbered battalions like some continental armies. Apart from a senior civil servant, who was all for the scheme, and myself the Secretary of the Meeting whose sole job was to take accurate Minutes, all the others were generals or brigadiers representing all the Arms and Services and relevant branches of the War Office. They all seemed intent on wiping my Regiment and all the others off the map. There was no question of just making cuts, as they are today, but changing the whole structure. Only the Director of Infantry, my old boss 'Pop' Dowler from Cairo days, fought against them and was losing. My adrenalin flowed strongly and I took advantage of a pause to interrupt uninvited. "Could I possibly say a few words Sir" I said turning to my boss who as Chairman was sitting at the head of the table with myself on his right. "I know that I'm only here to take the Minutes, but I am still a serving infantryman and the only person here who is actively affected by the decisions now being made." "By all means" he courteously replied "go ahead."

I then proceeded to tell them how I had passed high enough in my Army Entrance Examination to go to Woolwich and become a Gunner, a Sapper or a Signaller, but that I wanted to join a County Regiment, which was like joining one of the best clubs in the world; small enough for everyone to know each other, yet big enough to ensure that somehow, wherever one went in the world one would find a member of the Regiment doing some sort of job, and however high or low his rank compared with one's own, the Regimental bond would ensure friendly hospitality. I said "in war, which is what armies are kept for, men are asked to risk their lives and sometimes to give their lives, to achieve important objectives, and they will not do that unless they are part of a unit which has instilled a loyalty which only centuries of tradition has built up.

"Armies who have numbered units into which men are drafted in and out run away when things get hot. We don't. When our Fourth Battalion was finally relieved in Kohima there was hardly a man, including the stretcher bearers, who had not been wounded.

"We cannot just throw away this priceless quality which can never be replaced."

When I finally sat down feeling rather red in the face, I noticed that many others in the room also looked red in the face. I believe that it may have been with shame, because after a very short period of muttering and nattering the meeting voted against the establishment of a numbered Corps of Infantry.

The time eventually arrived when I could start planning to get back to regimental duty, having had two confidential reports at the War Office.

I immediately contacted the Infantry representative who used to attend the weekly 'Exchange and Mart' meetings. "I want to start a move to get back to regimental duty" I explained. "I want to be posted to an overseas station where they still have servants, and I don't want the heat of a place like the Sudan. There must be somewhere a few thousand feet up where one enjoys cool nights and full domestic services."

David Appleby went away and said he would do his best, and returned two days later with a broad grin on his face. "How about this" he said, handing me a draft.

To my surprise it was to post me to the British Military Mission to Ethiopia as Chief Instructor to their Officers Training College, which was 30 miles outside the capital Addis Ababa. This was Emperor Haile Selasse's mini-Sandhurst. "It really fits all your requirements" David Appleby went on "it counts as regimental duty, it is at eight thousand feet, and Ethiopians are Coptic Christians, so their womenfolk can be trusted to look after your children."

Field Marshal Montgomery, who was currently the Chief of the Imperial General Staff and hence my ultimate boss at the War Office, had recently returned from a tour of Africa which included Addis Ababa. He had found the British Military Mission to be in an appalling state of inefficiency, with no-one with much knowledge of the subjects which should have been taught to the Imperial Ethiopian Army. Not a single officer there was even staff-trained; not even the General, who had arrived there at the end of the Italian-Abysinian war as a Major (temporary Lt-Colonel) and had finally found himself a Temporary Brigadier, local Major-General, because he got on well with the Emperor. The report on Monty's visit became known as 'Addis in Wonderland' and Monty decreed that no-one was to be posted there in future without his personal approval. I immediately telephoned Phoebe to get her reaction to a posting into the wilds. She misheard the word Ethiopia for Albania and looked it up on the map. She phoned me back and announced that Albania seemed to have plenty of hills! When we got this sorted out and I explained that we would have a house-boy (butler), a cook (male), a nanny (young widow), a kitchen-boy and a groom, she agreed that I should accept at once, which I did.

I was duly passed by Monty and after hearing that one could expect to get some polo and game shooting proceeded to get some white riding breeches made by Hawkes and bought a .375 medium game rifle from Cogswell and Harrison in Piccadilly. Phoebe kitted herself and the children out for temperate and hot-weather clothing, as at 8,000 feet it was cool in the shade even at mid-day but very hot in the sun.

We terminated our rental of Orchard Cottage and stayed with the Sawyers at Shawford for my embarkation leave. It was made clear that I was required fairly urgently, but that there was no accommodation for my family at present although I should have little problem in sorting something out once I arrived. I began to understand why the Mission, known as the B.M.M.E. was known as Addis in Wonderland, and learned that I was the first officer to be allowed in following Monty's visit.

Chapter XVI

Journey to Addis in Wonderland

My leave ended and Phoebe duly drove me up to Blackbushe Airport, which was still an R.A.F. airfield, and from whence I flew in a four-engined York for a night stop in Malta. A few hours later we swept along the runway at Luqa and past the quarry where I had suffered my Laurel and Hardy experience with the rock on my ribs. Within two hundred yards of my former gunpit there was now a large R.A.F. hutted camp, with officers and Other Ranks messes and full Transit Camp facilities.

It was by now late afternoon and after being shown to a room I formed up to the Adjutant and explained my earlier connections with Luqa, only four and half years earlier as it happened. I borrowed a jeep and drove round the old haunts such as our first house at Balzan, Christopher's grave, St George's Barracks and our bombed house at Sacred Heart Avenue, which had been rebuilt. Rebuilding houses was not a big problem in Malta, as the main materials, the sandstone blocks which must have averaged around eighteen inches long, twelve inches high and nine inches thick were usually intact and simply had to be re-erected with a minimum of mortar. I was in trouble when I returned for keeping the jeep for so long but the station Commander, to whom I had to explain the reason, was most understanding.

When we took off for our next stop, which was Ismalia in the Canal Zone of Egypt, I was for the first and only time in my life nervous at take-off. We were loaded to capacity and using the shorter of the two runways, but I think it may have been that I was still haunted by the fear with which I had lived for so many months when I was in the area of the most bombed place on earth. I knew that Mike and Mary Read were stationed at Ismalia, and the first thing I did after landing was to try and contact them by telephone. I stayed the night with them and we had many experiences to exchange. I had not spoken to him since we were in Samos, and had had only a fleeting glance at him moving with his company along the lower slopes of Rachi Ridge during the battle of Leros. He had been badly wounded and left Leros in a German hospital ship from which all British prisoners were 'rescued' by a British destroyer; not quite within the terms of the Geneva Convention; but at least an act of mercy and not one of the unspeakable breaches of that Convention perpetuated by the Germans such as shooting all the Italian Officers on Leros in cold blood after the cease fire, although they had only been obeying the orders of their own Italian Commander-in-Chief to co-operate with the British after the fall of Mussolini. Mike thus missed the journey from Southern Greece in cattle trucks and the humiliation and boredom endured by most officers captured in Leros in German prisoner of war camps. He never fully recovered full movement of his right arm after the severe wound in his shoulder.

Next morning I flew to Asmara for onward transmission to Addis Ababa by Ethiopian Airlines. I was met at the airport by a British major in Movement Control and informed that I would be staying for some time in Asmara as the frontier with Ethiopia had been closed due to a Cholera outbreak. I had not been specifically inoculated against Cholera and was not allowed to fly into Ethiopia until two weeks after inoculation. This meant that I had to stay in the Officers Mess at Asmara right through the Christmas festivities, as it was then the thirteenth of December. I soon got to know the regular inhabitants of the mess and the married officers, who would bring their wives in for lunch-time drinks, and nearer Christmas, to the inevitable Christmas parties.

The Area Commander of the Asmara area was a Brigadier Gamble. He had been one of the instructors in No.3 Company at Sandhurst as a senior captain who had fought in World War I. I got to know him quite well, and he had paid me the compliment of offering me a firm vacancy in his Regiment, The Sherwood Foresters. I duly called on him at Flagstaff House and he and his wife made me extremely welcome. He was a keen polo player and made one of his most reliable polo ponies available for me each day to 'stick and ball', which is the first step a polo player must take if there is no wooden horse from which to learn to hit a polo ball. I was very grateful for this as it enabled me to start playing polo shortly after arrival in Ethiopia.

In due course I took off in an Ethiopian Airlines plane for Addis Ababa. On landing and passing through customs I looked around for the inevitable jeep and a major or captain to contact me. To my surprise I saw a Rolls Royce with a Union Jack flying from its bonnet and a Major General walking towards me and saying "You must be Butler, welcome to Addis Ababa". He then told his chauffeur to put my suitcases in the boot and waved me into the back seat, and off we went. After we had exchanged the usual pleasantries, General Cottam cleared his throat and harumphed a couple of times and then said "I was talking to the Emperor yesterday and he said that our Military Mission was doing a good job turning promising young cadets into young officers, but that we seemed to be neglecting the higher forms of training required by senior commanders and staff officers.

He wants me to start a Staff College, but the trouble is that we have no-one here who is qualified to teach them at that level. I see that you are P.S.C. (Passed Staff College), do you think you could do it?"

I forgot all about the fact that I had not done a day at Regimental Duty since being wounded on Rachi Ridge four years earlier and that I had specifically told David Appleby to ensure that my next posting would be, or count as Regimental Duty. The challenge of setting up a Staff College from scratch, and then being responsible for teaching, was more than I could turn down. "Oh, I should think so" I replied quietly. "That's settled, then" replied Algy Cottam (as he was always known behind his back). "You must come and stay with me until we can get everything sorted out."

The journey form the airport to the General's house was short, but took us through the outskirts of Addis Ababa to the sprawling British Military Mission, which consisted of a number of buildings and houses which covered a wide area. The town itself was a fascinating mixture of round African one-storey huts, and tinroofed square buildings. The latter a legacy of the Italian occupation and European merchant enterprises from firms like Gelatly-Hankey, who specialised in overseas expansion. The General's house was an imposing, stone-built house with a gravel drive complete with lawn and flagstaff. It had been the residence of the Italian Commander-in-Chief. I was shown into a spacious room after a warm welcome from Mrs Cottam.

Having celebrated Christmas in Asmara, I was about to celebrate New Year's Eve in Ethiopia. We dined 'à trois' that evening, the thirtieth of December 1947 and after dinner, Algy Cottam spent the rest of the evening describing the state of the B.M.M.E. and, in a sense apologising for it. It was only natural that once the Italians had been defeated, the valuable fighting troops and trained staff officers were moved to other theatres, mostly the Western Desert or Egypt, and only comparatively unskilled administrative troops were left to cope with the Ethiopian Army. The only officers of calibre were the three majors who were allocated as advisors to the three Ethiopian Divisional Commanders, and a Lt-Colonel, a major and three captains who ran the Officers Cadet Training College around 30 miles to the East of Addis Ababa at a place called Holletta.

"As a result of the Field Marshal's visit" explained Algy, "I am having to make a few changes and am bringing in Gray Reid from Dessie to command the Cadet School and you were to have been the replacement as Chief Instructor." I realised that the writing was on the wall that once more I would find myself in a Staff Appointment and that my two years Regimental duty would go out through the window. However the prospect of running my own show and being answerable only to the General appealed to me and I welcomed the challenge. I did not then realise that nothing had been done at all and that they had not even decided where the Staff College was to be.

I decided that it would be far better if the Staff College was well away from Addis and all its distractions and the General agreed. Holletta had been the country residence of Emperor Menelick who had had a palace built by Indian craftsmen. "There are several buildings round the actual palace" said Algy, "you'd better drive down there and see what you think." "If I'm the only staff trained officer" I explained "there will have to be very limited numbers on the courses, in fact only one syndicate on each, so we will only need accommodation for about twenty." He agreed. "The Army is too small for more than twenty of the brighter officers to be away from their formations and units at one time" he added.

It having been decided to set up the Staff College at Holletta, my next moves were to write to Denis Jackson, my former protegee in Palestine and one of my platoon commanders in C Company in Malta; who was now an instructor at the Staff College Camberley and ask him for copies of the Six month War Course at Camberley, and then to make a reconnaissance of Holletta itself and look at the buildings available.

As my car wound its way out of Addis Ababa, the facade of civilisation fell away, the Greek and Italian shops giving way to colourful native markets, and the brick buildings giving way to the round house traditional to Ethiopia. However large, the Ethiopian houses were built on the same pattern of a central pole and a circular building. Some buildings were quite palatial inside and divided into several spacious rooms. They were all called Toucles, and those in the outer suburbs had more space around them and cultivated plots growing maize, or a ground crop producing small millet-like seeds known locally as Teff. At times the 10,000 ft mass of Wachacha dominated us to our left, but its peak was too far from the road for us to see it.

As both Addis Ababa and Holletta are at around 8,000 feet anyway, it was only 2,000 above us. A tarmac road, a rarity in Ethiopia, had been built by the Italians the whole way to Holletta. The countryside we drove through was not at all typically African, because being cool at night it was more like somewhere on the North side of the Mediterranean, and being mid-winter, the grass was green and not dried up. At that height the air was always pure and cool but very hot in the direct sunlight. One had only to find the shade of the smallest tree at midday, and the temperature could be quite chilly. When the road eventually emerged from the pass through the Wachacha Range, which separates Holletta from Addis Ababa, I caught my first glimpse of the wide plateau which runs on the Eastward side of the range in a Southerly direction. The land on either side was cultivated with various crops, but with no marked boundaries between the

The outskirts of Addis Ababa

different 'fields'. My first sight of Holletta itself did not come until we were almost at the Holletta turning, as we had driven through a belt of giant Eucalyptus trees.

We turned left and South and the tarmac on the main road ceased abruptly. Unfortunately the tarmac also ran out along the 'Holletta track' as everyone called it. It was a real bone-shaker and spring-buster and in places we jumped from rock to rock. Holletta was dominated by a small hillock, on top of which stood the former Emperor Menelik's old palace; known by its Ethiopian name the Ghibbi. It was a two storied building with a veranda running round the upper floor and stood in a high walled garden of about three quarters of an acre. On the left of the Ghibbi was a mimosa wood and copses of very large Eucalyptus trees. To the South were the large buildings of the Cadet School which included a big gymnasium, barracks buildings and a grass parade ground. The track went between the barracks and the Ghibbi and circled round the far side of it in a climbing curve. On the Southern side of the hill lay the village of Holletta which was typical of most African villages for squalor, and housed a number of lepers, many with no fingers on their hands.

One of the larger buildings about a hundred yards South of the Ghibbi was un-occupied. It had two large rooms, which could be used as a lecture room and an Officers Mess. There were a number of small rooms which could be turned into single bedrooms for officers, and the whole set-up was obviously a basis round which adequate kitchens and staff quarters could be built. I returned to Addis Ababa and told the general that our problem seemed to be solved and that I felt that I should go at once to base myself in Holletta to supervise the preparation of the buildings and the syllabuses. He agreed and I left the next day. The brightest of the three captains was allocated to me, one Nigel Evans, who had been a prisoner with the Japanese. The big problem was the time element as it had been planned to start the first course in May which gave me four months to prepare a six month course; and it takes more than an hour to prepare a one-hour lecture. A bombshell then descended on me in the form of a signal from Jacko in Camberley, informing me that no Staff College Syllabus was allowed to be sent outside the Commonwealth. I therefore had to prepare a six month course from nothing in four months, and at the same time supervise the structural changes in the new Staff College building; even finding myself designing the wooden beds for each room, as they all varied in size, and the beds had to be tailored to the maximum length to squeeze into them. Thus tall officers got slightly larger rooms with slightly longer beds and short officers the smaller rooms. I was appointed a very intelligent and helpful English-speaking major as assistant and interpreter named Haile Bakadene, and I had to explain the whole syllabus to him as it rolled out of my brain; and he had to prepare all lecture notes, and everything to do with the syllabus in Amharic, the most common language in the country. He also had to invent Amharic names for military terms and items of equipment previously unknown in their country.

I had had a fair amount of experience at lecturing; starting at the Command Tactical School in Malta, and later when I was a member of the Directing Staff (Lecturers) at the Eastern Command Pre-Staff College courses; but had never lectured before through an interpreter. Haile and I built up a great rapport and I was sure that we would get by smoothly after four months of working side by side.

Due to this close rapport I was able to detect the likely weaknesses of our future students and cater for them. Mathematics was a real weakness, and I could see Haile's eyes glazing over when I tried to get him to translate anything mathematical. Since Staff work is very concerned with timings and quantities of men or stores etc, it is vital that Staff Officers can really cope with at least elementary mathematics; and so this subject became part of the syllabus. Concentration and brain-work was another weakness, and when the students finally arrived and work started, I realised that I would have to win their trust and then be quite blunt about their short-comings.

Fortunately, Ethiopians have a great sense of humour and I was able to make them laugh by saying that their heads were full of cotton wool and that my first task would be to extract it before we could get down to real work.

I then forced them to do the most simple sums and then stepped them up fairly quickly until I had them doing simultaneous equations. Once they had started to get their brains working the glazed look left their faces and they very quickly became intelligent pupils. I was finally able to announce that I had now extracted all the cotton wool from their brains and this was greeted with roars of applause and laughter.

There were the usual hiccoughs from naturally lazy people being made to use their brains, and I reacted to this by playing on their sense of humour. I learned that I was known as 'Uncle Butler' and turned this to my advantage by saying that they were therefore my nephews and would hold out their hands to be beaten by a wooden ruler for all idleness and misdemeanours! This was a great joke, but the victims did not like it and I laughingly hit them really hard; but they had to take it well because their fellows were all laughing.

They had a problem with the contour heights when map-reading, so I bought four panes of glass and sixteen flat india-rubbers. By putting four rubbers on the corners of a large sheet of paper the size of the glass and drawing contours on each pane at a time with a chinagraph pencil, gradually getting higher and smaller circles, as each pane is raised by its four rubbers, one gets the effect of a real hill and can produce a valley coming into it and a cliff in one place by putting all the lines there almost one above the other. To them it seemed like a miracle as it was so lifelike – as indeed it did to me when I first saw it done. The reader must remember that I was working with Haile for four months before my first course of students arrived, and in the meantime, I was getting integrated with the British Military Mission and particularly the small circle at Holletta. I was also getting acquainted with Sam, a large smooth haired mongrel, probably half Yellow Labrador and half African Pi-dog. He had been hanging round the Officers Mess at Addis and longed for a proper home. I decided to adopt him, and have never seen a dog look more proud than Sam was when I put a brand new collar on him and he looked up at me, wagging his tail.

Whilst preparing for our first course I lived in a partly converted flat on the upper floor of the Ghibbi as a temporary measure. On one of my visits to Addis Ababa I had been introduced to a Canadian civilian who appeared very intelligent and well informed. We got onto religion and I discovered that he was a Jesuit priest wearing normal civilian clothes, doing a teaching job in a Roman Catholic school in the capital. We soon became involved in friendly but sincere and interesting arguments, and he was fascinated by my strong ecumenical views. He promised to visit me in Holletta and bring some books which might persuade me to become a Roman Catholic. I was still feeling rather spiritually naked, being rather out on my own with sincere beliefs, and welcomed the idea of becoming a convert into an active and recognised religion. He duly arrived one afternoon, and we spent around two hours whilst I explained how my own beliefs had evolved and listened to his Roman Catholic arguments which he presented well. After all, Jesuit priests all take a degree in Philosophy as part of their training for full priesthood. We agreed to meet again in a week, by which time I would have read his books. One was by Arnold Lunn, the founder of the travel company of that name. I duly read the books, but found myself in no way convinced that on a Sunday morning during Holy Communion the thousands of gallons of Communion wine being offered at altars all over the world had become the actual blood of Jesus of Nazareth. I also found that I could not believe that the physical body of Mary, mother of Jesus, was somewhere in space in its earthly form.

When my friend and I had further discussed these matters on his second visit I expounded my own beliefs to him and he found great difficulty in faulting them. He agreed that the books he had lent me might not convince non-Roman Catholics to join his faith, and gave me two more books to read. I did my best to become a conformist, but it was no good. His arguments on his third visit were very hesitant, and I had the feeling that his training as a philosopher was causing him to accept my logic and the sincerity of my own beliefs. We parted as good friends and he never came again.

I believe that many people in their hearts are not entirely happy with the way their religions are presented to them, but have not the courage to say so. Many priests even go over the top and make things worse for anyone with logical thinking powers.

About a year after this event Phoebe, who had by then arrived, and I attended an Easter Service at the BMME Church in Addis Ababa. The visiting Padre's sermon was centred on St John the Divine who had led a hermit's existence on the Aegean island of Patmos. I have since visited that lovely island and seen his cave. Because he once had an odd dream about Jesus and imagined him with a sword instead of a tongue and eyes like balls of fire, our Padre assured us that we should stop thinking of Jesus as we may have done but realise what he was now like, "with eyes like balls of fire, and his tongue a bright shining sword". "Remember" said the Padre, "St John was the last man to see him and that is what he must look like now". I was unconvinced, and when we were all having an after-church drink in the General's house, I cornered him and said "Don't you ever stand up again and talk such rubbish to a captive audience. All of us have dreams and illusions, and St John was a very old and bigoted hermit. But to suggest that the whole Christian World must now believe that Jesus looks like he suggested, and would decapitate anyone who stood too near him if he turned his head too quickly, is turning fancy into farce. Don't you ever dare do that again!" He blanched, and had the look on his face of a man who believed that I was talking sense to him. I doubt if he ever repeated his mistake.

✧

The Ethiopian story from December 1947 to August 1950 could fill a book, so I will try to confine my tales to those which made the greatest impression on me at the time. Since the small staff at Holletta was separated from the bright lights of Addis by thirty miles of winding road, and official transport was restricted to one vehicle per week, unless we bought and used our own cars, our lives became centred around Holletta and the four main occupations, our jobs, horses, entertaining each other by dinner parties and bridge. These tended to merge and to develop as we would often ride in the evenings in a small group and then after seeing the horses stabled, someone would invite the remainder to have a drink before the evening bath and dinner and we would sit around until it got dark.

The initial cast consisted of Lt-Colonel Gray Reid and his wife Con (for Constance), Captain Pug Roberts and Cherry, and Captain Rex Carey and

Joss, a Dutch girl. All except the Careys had children. Phoebe did not join me until just after my first course had started in April 1948. She and the children had travelled out in a troop-ship to Massawa and thence by rail to Asmara and plane to Addis. On the boat she discovered that she had been at school with a fellow passenger Violet Orr, the wife of Colonel Orr who was coming out to be the Deputy Head of the British Military Mission. They later became our firmest friends who came to live, on retirement, only a couple of miles from our house in Sway.

Any readers who may have formed the opinion that I had been, seemingly, too pre-occupied with the consumption of alcohol is now in for a shock. I had never previously been much of a drinker, but enjoyed over-indulgence when there was something to celebrate. Ethiopia produced a new dimension to Butler's drinking habits. Because we were in the middle of Africa, and at 8,000 feet at that, the delivery of all goods tended to be extremely expensive. Everything had to go by ship to Massawa, by train from Massawa to Asmara and then be flown from there to Addis Ababa. The result was that a pint bottle of beer, delivered Addis Ababa cost (then) six shillings and sixpence a bottle. To get prices in perspective, a pint of beer in England then would have cost around a shilling. Most of our groceries and drinks came to us through the Navy, Army and Air Force Institute; known as the N.A.A.F.I. British officers, however, had long made arrangements with the British Embassy in Addis to acquire wines and spirits at duty-free prices. This meant that we could buy a bottle of Gordons Gin (at export strength) for only six shillings a bottle. It does not require much imagination to know what happened. No-one ever dreamed of drinking beer, and we became enthusiastic gin drinkers. Lime juice was extremely expensive through the N.A.A.F.I., but limes were abundant in Ethiopia, so we all drank gin and freshly squeezed limes. Liqueurs and whisky were also available from the Embassy, so we were well equipped with Cointreau and VSOP Brandy.

Being ordinary humans we soon accustomed ourselves to this splendid situation and were not only generous to ourselves, but also to anyone who happened to drop in after a ride. For example, sometimes we would be all sitting drinking after a long pleasant ride round the countryside and find that it was after 8.00pm. The drill then was for our guests to send a message to their cook to send their food over and they would join us for dinner. Even today if Phoebe and I hear a bottle going glop, glop, glop into a glass we exclaim "that was a Holletta tot."

During my spell as a grass widower I had bought a good two year old Vauxhall 14 and was fully mobile. I had been told by Algy Cottam that the Emperor was going to reward me for taking on the job of starting the Imperial Ethiopian Staff College by sending a pre-fabricated Italian bungalow out for me to live in when my wife arrived. What is more, I was given a free choice of site on which it was to be erected.

Outside the walls of the Ghibbi complex there was a small mound, and on this I decided to have my new home erected. I sited it very carefully, and to the South I had a view which stretched for around 35 miles. To the West I had a view for a mere 15 miles. To the East my view was restricted by the Ghibbi, but beyond it towered the summit of Wachacha, some 2,000 feet above us. To the North was the Holletta track and a view of no more than a mile or two, but we could at least have warning of any vehicles bumping their laborious and painful way along it.

My bungalow had a full veranda on one side and a half veranda on another. I elected to have my front veranda, which stretched the full length of the building, facing South and a view stretching for 35 miles, whilst the shorter veranda, which made a dog leg with it, faced the setting sun and a view stretching for around 12 miles. The roof covered both verandas and hence they were sort of outdoor rooms.

We lived there for nearly three years, longer than anywhere in our marriage until my eventual retirement. Unfortunately the bungalow was not quite ready for occupation when my family arrived. It had been completed structurally, including a brick fireplace, but had not been repainted. We also had to get together a motley bunch of furniture, carpets, beds etc before we could move in; because both we and the children had nothing but our clothes with us.

During the two or three weeks whilst we were waiting to move in we occupied a 'flat' in the upstairs floor of the Ghibbi. One half was occupied by the Careys, and our half had never been properly completed. There was a fairly large living room, and a plywood walled room with no windows as a bedroom. The plywood was only six feet high, and there was no roof to it, except the main roof of the Ghibbi about twenty feet above us. This was occupied by a family of owls who used to spit out tight balls of feathers and bones onto us. These were the regurgitations of items which their digestive systems could not cope with.

The open lid of our 'Box' provided plenty of light as long as we did not try and read in bed. The children slept in a tower-like structure approached by a six foot bridge. Part of this had apparently once been Emperor Menelik's loo, which was still in working order and our family loo. I suspect that the china one we used was post-Menelik and that the big drop system of sanitation was used in his day.

Michael and Jill sitting on the steps of our newly-erected bungalow

Chapter XVII

About horses and Holletta

Because more of my leisure time in Ethiopia was spent on horseback than on anything else, I have decided to consolidate most of my equine experiences into one chapter rather then feed them in in chronological order with other happenings. I should therefore give you the equine cast of the Butler household.

Sayed: My first purchase; a snow-white grey; extremely comfortable, a safe jumper and able to play polo. He was quite fast, but not up to racing in Addis. He thought it rather undignified.

Tamu: (The Swahili for sweet) A perfect bay with black feet and not a white hair anywhere. A beautiful little pony, brave as a lion, quick to learn polo; a careful jumper and a fast sprinter who could also stay for a mile.

Cossack: A natural jumper who never refused and gave me great confidence. Faster than Tamu over sprints and enjoyed playing Polo.

Borderer: An all-rounder who did not like jumping but was fast over a mile and could play polo. He matched Cossack for height when I used him for polo. I had a half share of him and he lived in my stables.

Ras: A powerful dappled grey who jumped well and was fast over long distances. I had a half share of him and he lived in my stables. On him I rode and won my first race of fences.

Friend: A child's pony; docile, lazy but very safe. Michael learned to ride on him. Was strong enough to carry twelve stone.

Toby: Jill's donkey: a honey

Foray: A polo pony 'par excellence' who was small, like Tamu, and paired with Tamu for polo so that I could use the same length polo stick with them both. At most gymkhanas there was always a mounted bending race for polo ponies. I was always leading after going down the line of poles, weaving left and right of alternate poles, but lost to the same member of the Imperial Ethiopian Bodyguard who whistled round the last pole like a flash, whilst Foray and I overshot and lost two lengths on him before the return run. I got to know him quite well and he told me that when he went stalking in the jungle, they were so much on net that his pony followed him on his hocks when he crawled through a game tunnel. Before the last Imperial Gymkhana, Foray and I practised the sharp turn round the last pole and I found that using my voice but not my legs was the answer. I still have the cigarette box presented to me by the Emperor.

On Phoebe's first evening we went for a hack and Sayed, who was normally a very comfortable and safe ride, played the trick that many horses do with a new rider, namely give them a trade test. We were cantering through a mimosa wood and he managed to weave her into one of the trees. Luckily she was not badly hurt, but very shaken. He was a great character and could pull like a train if he felt like it. Not long after this Phoebe thought she would try him with a jointed pelham with a fairly slack chain. He hated it and shook his head the whole time. She dismounted to loosen it by one more link and he then refused to let her mount again and she had to lead him the whole way home.

I always rode all my ponies on snaffles except when playing polo in order to keep their mouths soft. There were all types of equestrian pursuits to follow in the Holletta and Addis circles, the latter having an International flavour owing to the Embassy staffs. Although we were only riding polo pony sized mounts, most of them had some strong Somali blood in them and were good weight carriers. It was just like one-design sailing, inasmuch as if the mounts were much of a muchness, it all depended on the riders and their ability to train and ride them and to bring out the best in them. At the Embassy gymkhanas there were all the jumps one finds at Badminton, including water jumps, but the hurdles were of Eucalyptus, and the poles for obstacles like triple bars were again white-painted roughly-hewn Eucalyptus and not precisely turned smooth poles.

The Emperor was all for giving his blessing to European-style sports, and the Imperial Polo Club and eventually the Imperial Racing Club sprang up. Both the latter were started by us from Holletta who formed a Polo team which challenged the Police which were run by a British Commissioner, and the Imperial Bodyguard which was run by the Swedes.

I have always been very attracted to horses, and before leaving Ethiopia had built a long lean-to stable against our side of the Ghibbi wall which eventually housed no less than seven horses. I usually kept a minimum of two polo ponies at the British Military Mission stables (always known as the BMME) as all important polo was played on an enormous flat plain on the outskirts of Addis, known as the Jan Meda. It had once been used as a ceremonial parade ground, was now encircled by the race course, and had the Polo ground in the middle, together with an area used for jumping events. The French Embassy and the BMME used to run 'International' gymkhanas on their own territories and the Emperor Haile Selasse would often honour us by presenting the prizes.

Although 'Friend' was a very safe pony, he was so lazy that in the end we used him as a spare pony for grown-ups who could kick him into action.

General Turnbull receiving a rosette from the Emperor. The author next in line?, Ghibbi in background

To start with I used him when I taught Michael to ride. Before Michael's first lesson I made a pompous speech explaining that everyone fell off horses now and then, but that it was just part of the game and didn't hurt. We made good progress to begin with when I was on my feet and leading Friend at the walk and trot with Michael on board. When we first started to canter, Michael continued to make good progress and sat down well in his saddle. The trouble was that I found it rather a bind to run fast enough to make it interesting and eventually started riding alongside him with a leading rein. Friend soon discovered that he could have a free ride and be pulled along by Foray, who was the horse I had been using for these lessons. The moment I slowed down Friend would stop dead. On one such occasion, when Michael was doing particularly well and had been sitting very firmly in his saddle, he shouted to me "I'm falling Daddy". I looked round and slowed down, whereupon Friend stopped dead, Michael shot onto his neck and rolled off, and Friend trod on the inside of his left thigh, missing his future prospects by about an inch. He was very brave and after I had inspected the damage, a horseshoe shaped bruise, I said "Mummy will be so worried about you now, I think it would be best if I lifted you onto Foray and I'll run alongside him". Michael was splendid and settled down well, and the arrangement was obviously a success.

I had soon started riding alongside him on Cossack and we went from strength to strength. Unfortunately, after two such days, I had to go into Addis and Phoebe took on my job that evening riding on Sayed with Michael on Foray. All went well until they passed our watercart, which drove daily down to a local well, pumped itself full of clear water and then topped up all the water-tanks of the various bungalows. On this evening, just as they were passing, its pump started and Foray, who was normally a very steady pony, jumped sideways away from it. Michael came off and broke his arm. For a chap who had been told that it didn't hurt to fall off a horse to experience being trodden on in his first fall and to break his arm in his second was too much. He gave up riding with my complete blessing and did not mount a horse again for another seven years. He refused to go into Addis to have it put in plaster until I came home to accompany him, and so when I arrived back I had to turn straight round and drive him back to Addis. Once he took up riding again, this time in Kenya, he never looked back, and since marriage he has seldom been without his own horses.

Racing started at Holletta when Pug Roberts acquired a very fast horse which he claimed would beat Tamu, my fastest all-rounder who had never been beaten. There was a long earthen road which ran South from Holletta for about six furlongs, and we decided to race along this track. The challenge somehow captured the imagination, and soon Phoebe and

Cherry were sewing colours for us to wear and someone suggested that we invited a few friends from Addis and that someone should run a book. To make it all worthwhile we decided to have a Visitors Race and a Ladies Race and interest grew and more people came from Addis.

In the end it was a good afternoon's fun, where picnics were eaten, much gin and lime was drunk and Tamu gave his rival a good hiding. The Holletta races continued to be run at around monthly intervals until the Imperial Race Club was formed and racing took place on the Jan Meda. Bull Turnbull took over the organisation of the racing in Addis and a racecourse was laid out with proper rails. Major Tony Irwin was taken off normal duties and employed full-time as his assistant. By this time we were wearing silks and 'paper boots', which are riding boots made of the finest thin leather with one millimetre soles and hollow heels. I never quite threw off my Malta enteritis, which returned in warm countries, but in a benign form which kept my weight down to around nine stone four. I used to lose a few more pounds by having nothing to eat or drink on the day of a race, having had a tiny supper the night before, and only a small glass of sherry about half an hour before the first race.

The Emperor's Racing Stable was run by an Armenian/Ethiopian named Kosroff. He knew all the tricks of the trade and had the best horses in the country to choose from – if he found them first. I was lucky to have an eye for a horse and eventually owned or had a half share in four potential winners, which Kosroff was always trying to buy from me. I did not and still do not believe that a whip should be used in racing except early on in a race to wake up a fresh but lazy horse. I always rode a finish with my hands and voice, sometimes shouting a quickening pace into the horse's ears. "oy, oy, oy". I once shadowed an opponent and then moved steadily past him as we neared the finish and unconsciously eased, but found him coming up as we came to the post. We were neck and neck and I threw the reins loose and we fell forward and won by half a nose. If a horse starts to tire before the end of a race, it means that he has not been trained for the distance and it is his trainer who deserves the whip. I had early experience of the seamy side of horse racing in Addis Ababa and decided to supervise the feeding of my horses and be entirely responsible for their training. I reckoned that all the rules of training I had learned to coach human athletes should apply to horses, riding them longer distances at a slower pace to build up stamina and shorter fast gallops, preferably slightly downhill, to build up their speed.

I also disapproved of the idea of separating the long-distance work from the jumping which some trainers did. I wanted my mounts to be able to clear their fences safely when slightly tired and hence would finish a two mile gallop at three quarters speed by going over some jumps.

One day whilst doing this on Ras (the Ethiopian name for Lord) as the last work before a race, I was using a numnah saddle, made of thick felt with a shiny piece of leather just in front of my knees. Ras took off for his usual flying leap which normally gained him half a length at each jump, but being tired he hit the fence and shot my knees forward along the slippery leather and onto his withers. I was still firmly on and quite vertical and whispered to him "steady boy", but he suddenly swung left and then stopped dead. I was slowly rotated to the right, and in slow motion dropped vertically onto my head. I was fairly badly concussed, and our M.O. motored out from Addis and decreed that I must lie in a darkened room for two days. It had been the final Wednesday gallop before the race on the Saturday, but I sneaked out of bed on the Thursday morning before Ras was taken into Addis and put him over a couple of fences to restore both our confidences in one another.

On the Saturday I was to ride in three races, two on the flat and the third over fences. My headache had gone by the Thursday evening and I felt that I had no problems. In the event each race had its own particular problem. My first race was on Borderer, who having long legs was in a high gear and better at running fast downhill. The finishing straight at the Jan Meda was slightly downhill, hence the far side of the roughly oval course was slightly uphill. I kept Borderer in touch for the first half of the race, knowing that we would have a good fast swoop going down the final straight. However, the field bunched very tightly as we rounded the bend at the top of the rise and I found myself completely boxed in as we started to go slightly downhill. All I saw was a mass of horses bottoms. I worked my way gradually forward, taking advantage of every gap until I was held up by four horses in a tight row in front of me, and one a length or two in front and slowly pulling away. Suddenly the two middle horses parted for a moment and Borderer and I shot through the gap and began to gain ground on the leader. We just failed to catch him and were a good second. It was however a very exciting race, and I felt that Borderer would have beaten any of them, including the winner, in a two horse race. His jockey had failed him in the early stages; I should not have left him so much to do and avoided being trapped.

My second race was unique, I believe, and certainly unforgettable. I was riding Cossack in a four furlong sprint. I have already explained that he had a deep chest, high withers and no stomach and was hence wedge shaped with the thin end aft. He was a wonderful starter and he watched the starter's flag like a hawk. As soon as the flag dropped he bounded forward like a stag and I saw the whole length of his back surge forward from me, whilst the saddle and me on it slid to the rear where there was a smaller circumference and the girth became loose. I managed to retain my balance and my lead for about fifty yards whilst the horses to the left and right pounded along just behind me. However, my weight was in the wrong place and I realised that I would get nowhere and probably fall off any minute. I decided to leap for his withers and ride him bare back and succeeded in doing this and we began to make ground again; but then I heard some clanging from underneath his stomach and realised that the saddle had slid round and that the stirrups were clinking against each other and probably hitting his back legs. We pressed on and three horses passed us, but we finished without shedding anything, but with a very exhausted jockey. I rolled off after pulling him up after crossing the line and lay on the grass completely exhausted after Phoebe and Pug Roberts came up with his groom and led him away. I puffed at them "For God's sake tell all our friends not to back me in the next race", (which was Ras over the fences) "because I feel so weak that I'll probably fall off at the first fence."

Many of our friends had backed all three of my rides and would have put a lot on Ras in the last race. In the event, I soon felt stronger and by the time I had sat down for five minutes and then paraded in the paddock I felt as fresh as paint. I was second over the first fence, pulled up to lead as we cleared the second and then went on to win by about twelve lengths. No-one had put any money on me and I felt a complete idiot. The next time Cossack ran was with Phoebe in a Ladies' race. He had been so put off by the odd start that he had had with me that he danced around and gave her a bad time before getting going. Phoebe finished absolutely exhausted and just failed to get a place.

✧

Whereas in Europe and America races tend to be geared to the quality of the horses running, the Imperial Race Club divided the runners into three main classes; Ethiopian horses which were of mainly Somali stock, pure imported Arabs and enormous horses from New South Wales originally imported by the Emperor to pull his State Coach, which was an ornate copy of our gold State Coach. They were pretty wild when they first arrived and a crew member of the ship that brought the first batch had his finger bitten off as he innocently rested his hand on the rail of their compound on deck. They were called 'Walers'. The two Australian vets who came with them were great characters but they never got their pay. In the end they fled the country with some funds they had been given for some other purpose, and managed to get out into Eritrea.

I was lucky enough to be asked to ride other people's horses sometimes and rarely failed to win a place. In my last year the Imperial Racing Club produced a properly printed monthly Racing Calendar and before leaving I looked up the 'past races' and found that, scoring 3 for a win, 2 for a second

"Phoebe finished absolutely exhausted"

and 1 for a third, I was second to the Emperor as an owner, to his man Kosroff as a trainer and to his leading jockey as a rider. I was the champion white jockey. A big fish in a very small pond, but it was great fun at the time.

Feeding our horses could have been a problem, due to lack of European type food. The Ethiopians did not often make hay, bran was difficult to get, and few oats were grown. To compensate for this, local horses were used to living out at grass. There was plenty of grazing, and as there was an abundance of sunshine the grass was always growing. It was yellowish in summer, but always there; hay on the hoof! Barley was however always available, and in the end became the staple food for producing the protein for horses being worked hard, i.e. at polo or racing. We hence allowed them free grazing and they never developed grass bellies. We regulated their moistened crushed barley and salt according to their needs, plus a little linseed. They did very well on it and always looked in good shape and had shining coats.

Horses have far more character and intelligence than usually credited to them. If a human being was chained to a wall with nothing to occupy his mind whenever he was not being exercised, he would not be all that bright! Ours were never chained to anything, but had to be brought in at night due to the danger from hyenas. Because we were more horse orientated at Holletta than most, Addis friends tended to ask us to look after their horses when they were away for some reason, in exchange for our free usage of them. Leonard Figg, a Second Secretary at the British Embassy (now Sir Leonard Figg, a retired Ambassador) once lent us his horse named Cerberus. He had obviously been maltreated by the Italians and hated anyone with a white face. He ran straight at you with teeth bared and kicked forward with his front legs. An Ethiopian syce (groom) had to hold both sides of his bit, facing his front, whilst a white-faced rider mounted him. Once aboard, he was the most comfortable ride I have ever had. One could sit down at the canter and feel that one was on a smoothly drawn sledge on soft snow. He had a good mouth and impeccable riding manners. His one snag was that one could not dismount until one found someone with a dark face to hold his head! Phoebe once got lost on a long solo evening ride and knew that the one thing she could not do was dismount until she had found her way home. Because there were no horse-boxes available or even existent in Ethiopia in those days, the interchange of horses between Holletta and Addis was solely by riding and leading, and I or our groom would take a mountain route over a grassy pass through the Wachacha range, which cut the distance down from approximately thirty to fifteen miles. This took about five hours, an average of three miles an hour including halts to rest and change horses, and resaddle the one whose turn it was to be ridden.

Tamu was still very fiery, and I never allowed him to do this trip except when I rode him. He had been a country horse from birth and purchased from a well-to-do Ethiopian as a four year old. He was seen riding him near Holletta with a wicked bit with a square bar with unrounded edges, so that his tongue and mouth were cut if he pulled. Blood was pouring from his mouth. In addition to this the shanks (side-bars to which the curb chain is fixed at the top and the lower rein at the bottom) were around five inches long. There was no provision for an upper rein. He was bought on the spot by Gray Reid's predecessor and I bought him from him when he left after a few weeks to hand over to Gray by which time his mouth had healed. On the day that I took him over Wachacha to Addis, with no lead horse, it was for his first race in Addis, he was extremely fit. We cantered gently and effortlessly whenever the going allowed it, as I felt it would shorten the total time of the trip at not too great a cost of energy.

By this time I had got well into my first course at the Staff College, and the word had apparently got round the villages that there was a very understanding teacher in Holletta who was working miracles with their brains. When I reached the highest village up the Western slopes of Wachacha I thought I would give Tamu a chance to graze for about half an hour and drink some water. The villagers somehow immediately identified me and I was treated with unbelievable respect. Tamu was unsaddled and taken away to be watered and fed and a chair was produced for me to sit on. A ring of curious villagers quickly formed, all squatting on the ground, and then a dignified old elder with white hair strode forward. I had my left leg crossed over my right knee, with the toe pointing forwards. The old man bowed low and lightly put his hand under the toe of my boot and kissed it. I was embarrassed and overcome by this extremely sincere gesture and stood up, took his hand, and asked for another chair. I remained standing until a chair was brought and would not sit down until, protestingly, he had done so. It was the best that I could think of doing under the circumstances to indicate to his villagers that I regarded him as an equal. Few people can have had such an experience.

After our short rest and watering Tamu and I continued up to the top of the Wachacha Pass and soon had a view of the sprawling city of Addis Ababa on the plain below us. The mountain track by which we descended eventually ejected us into a street in the suburbs which had a tarmac road and a variety of traffic, including horses and carts. Tamu, who was a country horse born and bred, had never seen anything like it, panicked and tried to bolt. I managed to restrain him whilst he skidded about on the unfamiliar slippery tarmac surface, and after a lot of reassuring words he eventually settled down.

The BMME was on the Western side of Addis, and so we did not have to get into the thicker traffic that day. He was an intelligent little horse, and very quickly adapted himself to urban life. Someone from Holletta had driven in to meet me at the BMME and drive me back. On the following day I drove in to see Tamu to give him a short walk and a hundred yard gallop as a pipe opener. The five hour trek had taken more out of him than I expected and on the third day when we raced at the Jan Meda he was second for the first time in his life, beaten by a very fast horse from the French Embassy.

It was on Tamu that I had the first and only experience of being dragged. I had been giving him some practice starts the day before a race in Holletta, and had dismounted and loosened his girth. I remounted and then let the girth out another hole because I intended to walk slowly home. I passed Rex Carey riding out from Holletta and he called out "How did he go?" "Like a train" I replied, "Just watch this". Forgetting the loosened girth I dug my heels in and Tamu took off. The saddle slid round and I found myself being dragged at full gallop. It was an unforgettable experience. My left foot was trapped in the stirrup and I was being dragged feet forwards on my right shoulder, my face being only a few inches from Tamu's rear hooves. If I had dug my right heel into the ground, it would have swung my head under them. By the grace of God the ancient stitching of the old second-hand saddle gave, and the saddle crashed to the ground and Tamu disappeared in a cloud of dust. Rex helped me onto his horse because I was more than just shaken. Luckily I had been wearing a jacket and we had been on grass, so that I was not badly skinned, but my riding muscle and crutch were painful.

I retired to bed on arrival back at Holletta and our Medical Officer, Ronnie Houston, was telephoned and asked to come and see me on the morrow. He duly arrived and strapped me up and announced that I had torn a muscle and also suffered a slight hernia. What was worse, he ordered me to stay in bed for two days and not ride for a fortnight. I spent all next day in bed, and got up on the following day and gently walked around. I felt very stiff in the affected areas but things improved as the day wore on. I had two more days to pick up a bit more strength, and quietly vowed not to take a decision to ride until the morning of the race.

It was only a Holletta meeting, but we had quite a few people coming out to ride from Addis and a larger number of their supporters. After breakfast on that day I decided to give it a go and Tamu and I went into our normal race-day routine. When one has any form of crutch or riding-muscle strain, there is a proven technique of lashing one's thighs together with a spare rein just above the knee. This has the effect of holding the knees firmly against the saddle. This I duly did and saw no sign of Ronnie Houston as I went down to the start. One forgets muscular discomforts once on the job, and with the adrenalin flowing I rode a normal race. The first face that I registered after passing the post in the lead was Ronnie's.

He had arrived just in time to catch me red-handed, and handed out a public and embarrassing rocket as soon as I had dismounted.

✧

Cut off from civilisation as we were at Holletta, we had to do virtually everything ourselves, and this included running a school for our children. There had to be two classes, one for the over five year olds, and a kindergarten for those under five. The wives were the teachers, assisted later by a nanny who had become a permanent fixture with children who no longer needed one. The teachers' appointments were, in typical Army fashion, graded in accordance with the rank of their husbands. Thus the Colonel's wife was the Headmistress and Phoebe the Assistant Headmistress. They did in fact run a very efficient show and joined the P.N.E.U. who sent them a syllabus. Fortunately there was a linguist among them and someone who understood the rudiments of mathematics.

There was a wonderful air of nonchalance about the teachers. Every now and then a 15cwt truck would go into Addis for supplies, and one of the 'teachers' would hear about this and send a note to Elspeth saying "I'm going into Addis in the truck today, do you mind taking my French class". Elspeth would then send a note to Cherry saying "Phoebe and I are going into Addis in the truck, do you mind taking my geography lesson". Eventually the news would reach Con Read's successor, Enid Elliott, and she would send everyone a note saying "The School is closed today, and Nanny will look after the children". They would then all pile into the truck and have a day's shopping!

They would invariably finish up at one of the Greek grocers' establishments, Vaporidis or Politaridis. The respective owners would regale them with glasses of locally made Chianti while one of their employees was sent to the native market to haggle and get the best price for the fresh fish and vegetables they wanted. The proof of the pudding was however in the eating because when the children returned to schools in England after more than two years away from normal schooling, they were more or less up to standard. Michael was even top of his form at his pre-prep school after his first term.

The older children would be let off early and would go down and play in Ballilla's 'Aladdin's Cave'. Ballilla was an Italian mechanic who had been a Prisoner of War when we defeated the Italians and drove them out of the country. He had been stationed at Holletta and retained there after all the other soldiers had been shipped away as Prisoners of War because he was the only person who could work the ancient diesel engine which kept the entire complex's lights going. He was dressed as a civilian and paid as such, but it had been made clear to him that he would never be given a visa to leave the country. He tried once to get away, but was returned and warned of dire retribution if he did it again. His 'Aladdin's Cave' was the enormous workshop cum warehouse cum living quarters where he lived his life out. He was a charming man with a fair smattering of pidgin English and the children adored him. They would appear with all sorts of bits of metal-ware after their raids on his dwelling, and every now and then he would get in a frenzy if they had pinched some vital part of his machinery.

Life in Holletta with all its freedom was paradise for the children, and they always looked back on those days as amongst the happiest of their lives. It was only possible because the Ethiopians were sincere Coptic Christians and there was absolutely no danger of rape or indecent conduct as there is in Britain today.

After we left we had news that Ballilla had at last made it into Eritrea and thence to his beloved Italy. It was a matter of Ethiopians taking revenge on the wrong man. Ballilla was one of Nature's gentlemen. More unpleasant Italians had pushed Ethiopians who had displeased them out of aircraft at 2,000 feet above the ground. They executed every Ethiopian who was educated, and their yardstick was that anyone who spoke a foreign language was well educated. My second assistant, Haile's successor, was a Major Tesfa Desta. He escaped to Djibouti by hiding in the water of the tender of the steam engine hauling a train down to the Red Sea with only his mouth sticking up above water level. Tesfa was a fastidious dresser and always carried a rolled umbrella, even when in uniform!

My courses lasted for six months, after which we had at least a month's break. The mini-Sandhurst's courses were of different duration, which meant that every now and then the entire British Staff would be on holiday at the same time. We thus arranged picnics to local beauty spots or expeditions to remote areas where there were plentiful Black Duck to be shot. These duck were obviously related to Mallard, were the same size, and had the same blue and white coloured patch on each wing, but their bodies were charcoal grey instead of beige. We were only given the secret of these little-known spots after winning the friendship and confidence of our Holletta friends. No-one in the Embassies knew where they were.

The best of these was a whole day's riding from Holletta, and we therefore had to take tents for the night and food for a camp-fire dinner and breakfast the next day. The spot was a fairly deep zig-zag stream running through an open plain. The Amharic for duck is, unbelievably, duckie, and the word for many is boozoo; hence this hallowed site was always known as 'boozoo duckie', as this was how it was described to us before our first visit. The journey there involved gradual gaining of height, and we probably finished up at around 8,750 feet above sea level.

The drill for these shoots was that we halted in a hollow about four hundred yards short of the stream and dismounted. The wives took charge of our horses, and they and our house boys, who had been shadowing us by bounds in our 15cwt truck containing a large tent, our camp beds, food and cooking utensils, started to organise our camp and evening meal. The four guns crept off to positions round the boozoo duckie. On the firing of the first shot all the duck would get up and fly in formation up and down the valley and our two end guns would take on the leaders and send the main body back down the valley. Our best bag totalled forty two and a half brace (85 duck) and all of them of edible size.

Our first trip to the boozoo duckie was during the colder weather, and at around 9,000 feet, even in the tropics, it freezes at night. We wore jerseys and jackets as we sat around the camp fire that night and enjoyed our barbecued dinner. In our case we had not brought our house boy but our cook, Mocra. He was an all-rounder who was not a bad cook and could turn his hand to anything, including care of horses. The answer was that he had travelled up to Kenya during the war and had fought with the Kings African Rifles. Turning his hand to anything was perhaps an unfortunate expression, as future events will show. He also had the habit of 'chewing the leaf'. I do not remember which particular drug was present in the 'leaf', but it was known as 'bang', and made the chewer pleasantly inebriated when taken in moderation, and almost incapable if overdone.

After our meal under the stars, and enjoying the perfect peace which I remembered on the high plateau of Jordan only four years earlier, we took to our camp beds in our clothes and well wrapped up in rugs and blankets. Not one of us had thought of putting a sleeping bag in our luggage when we packed in England to go out to Ethiopia! In spite of the fact that we had the tent flaps closed to keep out hyenas, as well as the cold, we found we needed all the warm clothing and rugs we had got. In the morning Phoebe found that not only a bottle of milk, but even the cooking oil was frozen solid under her camp bed!

The carcasses of the duck were well preserved by the cold air, but there was always a panic to get them back to a cool environment through the heat of the day on the journey back to Holletta, and thence by road to Addis for sale to the two main European hotels, The Ras and The Imperial. After our last trip to the Boozoo Duckie we did not get them into Addis until the afternoon of the following day, by which time they had all gone 'off' and had to be destroyed. I vowed then and there never again to shoot for more than our own pot or pots. Of course there is a tremendous pleasure in achieving the skill to pull off a 'right and left' and bring down two duck from the same formation, but it can be nothing but uncivilised to kill game which is not going to be eaten, just for pleasure.

After a few months Gray Reid and his family were posted home, but not before, under the inspiration of Con Reid, we put on a very laudable performance in Addis of 'The Importance of Being Earnest'. In those days Ethiopia's annual rains could normally be depended on, and during two or three months, riding was restricted by the sogginess of the ground. Con Reid decided to take the advantage of the lull.

◇

There was a religious day called the Feast of Mascal, which was to celebrate the end of the rains. By some extraordinary miracle the rains often stopped on the Feast of Mascal. On that day the whole countryside went yellow, carpeted by millions of Mascal Daisies.

◇

All the cast of 'Earnest' were able to play parts suitable for their approximate ages, as the younger wives, Elspeth Evans and Cherry Roberts were still in their twenties, and Nigel was just right for Algy, while Con made a splendid Lady Bracknell. We were rather nervous on the first night and took a lot of liquid courage. The recipe was just right and we sailed through with flying colours. On the second night I remember saying "We must drink exactly the same amount tonight, because the result was perfect". There is no such thing as certainty however, as because we were not in the slightest bit nervous our brains did not require as much assistance and all of us were forgetting lines, driving the prompter crazy, and slurring our words when we did remember them. We seemed to get more laughs the second night, but I suspect for the wrong reasons!

The Reids were replaced by Tim and Enid Elliott, and their children Nicky and Joanna. The name of the former can be seen on television, as he is now a leading T.V. producer. Tim, a Sherwood Forester, had lost a leg below the knee during the war, but refused to let that alter his life. With the ability to move the lower leg undiminished, the disability can be minimal; but on long rides the metal callipers which are required to hold the artificial foot up to the stump used to chafe his knees on the inside and he suffered agonies.

One of these rides was a visit to the Sandfords in which Tim, Phoebe and I were the sole participants. The Sandfords lived well past the Boozoo Duckie area, which took all day. I was riding Cossack and leading Tubby, who was on loan from the Ethiopian Army. His saddle had had the stirrups removed and impromptu saddle bags tied, one on each side, with our change of clothing and washing things. To start with Tubby was not happy at being led and tended to need dragging along, rather like the wretched Friend. Eventually, when we were well on our way, he came up alongside Cossack and was as good as gold. "I think I'll let him run free now" I called out, and unfastened his leading rein. After about ten paces he was round in a flash and heading for home. Cossack and I soon caught him and he had to return to the leading rein.

My own situation that day was not exactly a happy one, as the girth stitches on another of our old second-hand Italian saddles went as we hopped over a tiny stream. Being absolutely miles from anywhere I had no intention of walking in my Polo boots, which would have been purgatory, neither was I prepared to ride bareback on Cossack's knife-edge withers. I therefore removed the girth altogether, got Tim to hold the saddle, and vaulted on. I thought that we would be reduced to walking, especially with Tubby in tow, but Cossack soon realised what the form was and we finished up by cantering quietly with the others, but never changing direction at the canter. We did not arrive at the Sandfords until early dusk, by which time one of Tim's legs was really raw and he was in agony.

Brigadier Sandford had been, like Algy Cottam, one of the people personally involved with the physical reinstallation of Emperor Haile Selasse in Addis Ababa after his years of exile in England following the Italian/Abbysinian War. Just as he had rewarded Algy by insisting that he was made head of the British Military Mission, he rewarded Sandford, who was retiring from the Army, by granting him a wonderful piece of land on the edge of one of the escarpments which separate the high plateau on which Addis stands from the hot plains below. This meant that he was able to live in the comparative coolness which one enjoys at 8,500 feet, and grow tropical crops like bananas and dates on the plain immediately below him which was part of his domain; strawberries and dates all growing in the same large garden!

Tim struggled out of his saddle and walked in great pain through the front garden to the Sandford's house, muttering that he couldn't wait to get a really strong drink inside him. There, after the usual welcome and handshakes, Mrs Sandford brightly asked him if he would like a nice refreshing cup of tea. Tim's face was a study of unbelievable conflict between politeness and disbelief. It was by then half past six and nearly dark, and the sun had not only 'passed over the yard-arm' but had for some time been shedding its light on other lands. After we had been duly refreshed with some very good tea, we were shown to our rooms, as we were still hot, sweaty, and covered with the dust which rises when cantering on dry soil. While Phoebe had first crack at our primitive but well organised shower, I sneaked into Tim's room. He had made no attempt to change, and was making inroads into our jointly owned whisky bottle. I enjoyed a tot but did not claim my half share – Tim needed it!

We devoted the following day to rest and recuperation. We had a good lie-in, a late but splendid breakfast, followed by a guided tour of the estate by the Brigadier's son and daughter-in-law. It was fascinating to be, seemingly, in an English rose garden with an English vegetable garden alongside it, but when we looked over the edge of the escarpment, we were gazing at tropical vegetation. Tim returned to the house to rest his sore leg and we were invited to climb down the rocky track. I hope my reply was polite – it would have taken all morning, and we faced another mammoth ride on the morrow.

The return journey was fairly uneventful. There was no way of getting my girth stitched properly, but the Sandfords kindly lent me a surcingle which bound my saddle on quite firmly, and Tubby was quite happy to be pointing for home. Tim's legs were bandaged up to reduce the rubbing, but I know he suffered uncomplainingly for most of the second half of the trip. When we did get back to Holletta he didn't ride again for over a week.

We organised a number of group picnics during periods when our students holidays coincided. These either took the form of all day rides to beauty spots, with a truck meeting us with food, drinks, and rugs to sit on, or miniature safaris when tents would be brought out and we would all sup around a camp fire. The best mid-day picnic was to a cedar forest which grew on the lower slopes of the Wachacha range. It was about a three hour ride, and we would all set out on horseback, walking, cantering or trotting, and because we rode so regularly a total of six hours a day in the saddle meant nothing to us. We would arrive amongst the beautiful, stately cedar trees feeling pretty warm, and select a picnic spot in some glade, where our house boys, who had been following in a truck, would lay out our picnic rugs and we would form a circle, drink the six shillings a bottle gin, and cool off. The views to the West were superb, because the whole landscape was gradually falling away, the whole main Ethiopian Highlands being like a gigantic slice of cake, with its Eastern side running parallel with the Red Sea, as the thick end of the slice, with the vertical sides dropping thousands of feet, whilst the Western side fell gently for hundreds of miles to the lower lands of Central Africa.

Our favourite place for longer picnics, reached by trucks and gravel tracks, complete with tents and camp beds, was down in the forests to the West, and was known as the Jum Jum Forest. There we saw many species of birds and animals which were already scarce in other parts of Africa, such as black and white Colubus monkeys, and black birds the size of large pigeons with scarlet slashes on their wing feathers and bright red wattles like domestic cockerels, similar to, but not the same, as the black jungle-fowl in India.

Because so few of the locals had any form of transport and there were not many Europeans around, we seemed to have the whole world to ourselves; we were in fact experiencing true paradise, with no noises by day but the

"The best mid-day picnic was to a cedar forest which grew on the lower slopes of the Wuchacha range"

The Emperor Haile Selasse leaving the Staff College followed by myself and General Turnbull

songs of birds, and silence by night except for the occasional calls of animals and chattering of monkeys. This sense of paradise was emphasised by the fact that the trees were not growing as thickly as in most African Equatorial rain forests, and hence provided numerous little sunny glades. This, combined with the fact that all the Holletta families had become firm friends, planted happy memories of the Jum Jum which none of us will ever forget.

Other memories which we are unlikely to forget are the occasional visits by the Emperor. He enjoyed the dignity of his position and whenever he was on a journey all cars had to stop, and the occupants dismount and bow as he drove past.

At Holletta we were treated to a more relaxed performance but we still pushed the boat out in our own way. On his first visit after my arrival Tim and Enid Elliott were in the saddle, and Enid arranged the one rather ornate chair they possessed as a sort of throne for him to sit on, placed on one of our better rugs. The plan was to offer him light refreshment of his own choice, which was biscuits and a glass of Perrier Water. Both the packet of biscuits and the cork and silver foil of the Perrier had to be opened in his presence. He knew a thing or two about poison as I was told that he had gained the throne in the first place by poisoning his aunt!

We were each to have a few minutes audience with him, and although he could speak English quite fluently he was better at speaking French. He therefore insisted that our audiences were conducted in French, which put most Englishmen at an immediate disadvantage. When he was settled with what pomp and ceremony we could muster, it was decided to offer him refreshments before the linguistic ordeal began.

Enid Elliott then remembered to her horror that the Perrier Water, especially ordered for the Emperor, was in a corner cupboard behind the Emperor's 'throne', which could not be opened without asking him to move! This contingency was not covered by our careful planning, and the means of dislodging him had not been considered; nor had the means of informing the others that a change of plan been worked out. A lot of strange movements took place round him as people whispered to one another, and he began to look a little apprehensive. Perhaps he thought some terrible conspiracy was about to unfold. Personally I would have told him a half truth, very politely, explaining that the Perrier Water had been placed behind the throne until the last minute to ensure that it could not possibly be tampered with. Enid however decided to move on to Phase II, which was a walk in the Ghibbi garden which she and Tim, plus their garden boy, had made extremely attractive. Since she had only just asked the Emperor if he would like to refresh himself after his tiring drive before touring the garden, it made no sense to him and he showed signs of panic. Maybe he thought we had all gone barmy; and separated from his bodyguard as a compliment to us, this must have been most unsettling! Somehow he was eventually bundled out into the garden where plans had been made for him to do a tour and then sit on a seat in a leafy nook where our children would be presented to him. The out-door team were naturally taken unawares by his early appearance and did not know that under Plan B he was going to do a short tour, go back for his Perrier Water and then made a second exit to talk to the children. He must have been quite mystified by all the nods and winks and whispers which went on and probably thought we definitely were barmy, but hopefully harmless!

When the children were eventually presented one by one, he was absolutely sweet with them and had each on his knee in turn – and spoke to them in English! He asked Michael if he could speak Amharic and Michael replied in Amharic with the word "Yes", and then proceeded to count in Amharic from one to ten. Fortunately at this moment the Emperor, most impressed stopped him. I wonder whether he realised that Michael could not have gone much further anyway.

By and large we had by then seemed to please the Emperor and he went off in due course all smiles and French felicitations.

✧

Meanwhile Monty's orders to upgrade the quality of officers in Ethiopia were taking effect, and a trickle of well-trained and presentable officers were arriving. Quite early on, I heard that a Major and Mrs Stephen Bassett had arrived in Addis Ababa. The former a Third Hussar who was to be adviser to the commander of the Ethiopian division based in the capital. When I first met them I was delighted to find that Mrs Bassett was none other than the former Lady Stuart-Richardson, whom I had known in Jerusalem and who had, as Staff Captain 'A', arranged my posting home in 1944. Stephen and Kate were to become our close friends who turned up again when we were later stationed in Nairobi. We kept up with one another after our retirements, and still visit them whenever we go to Spain, where they now live. Stephen was a great asset to our BMME polo team once we had discovered that he really could ride.

To start with he made every excuse not to join us for an evening's hack when he stayed at Holletta, and we thought he might be a paper Hussar. The truth was that he had ridden so much, that unless riding a horse for a specific purpose such as polo, riding over fences, or show-jumping, plain hacking was boring to him. He had had the good fortune to be stationed just after the war in Jordan with the Trans-Jordan Frontier Force. Apart from the Household Cavalry and the King's Troop of the Royal Horse Artillery, the TJFF was virtually the only unit where one rode on duty, and they used to patrol vast areas of hilly country to keep the peace.

With Jerusalem the nearest place where the TJFF officers could meet and relax with other Britons, it was there that he met Kate, who was already estranged from her husband. The Bassetts lived in an enormous toucle on the Addis side of BMME. It had plenty of rooms, all built round the large central room with its 'tent-pole' going up to the middle of the roof. Not long after the Bassetts arrived, Algy Cotton was relieved by Brigadier Turnbull with the similar rank of Local Major General. Having known Kate in Jerusalem, Bull became a regular visitor to the Bassetts until his wife Andrea arrived to join him. Stephen told me that he felt rather like a father whose daughter was being courted by an unwelcome suitor. He used to sit and read a newspaper whilst Bull Turnbull tucked into his whisky and chatted up Kate.

Back in Holletta our isolated existence continued. Usually the single telephone line to Addis was out of order and so we were completely cut off from the outside world. We received the Airmail Telegraph, but it often used to arrive in batches of as many as ten, and sometimes even the latest would be more than a week out of date. The result was that to plough through thousands of words to get completely up to date was just too much, and we would tend to glance through the last copy and leave the rest. To give you an idea of the completeness of our isolation, we were quite shattered to learn that, unknown to us, there had been a major airlift to keep West Berlin supplied with food during a typical Soviet blockade.

We had so many local problems to deal with that we did not notice our isolation at the time. One day Tim Elliott passed the word round that the Ethiopian driver who daily drove a motorised water cart to a well over a mile away, had reported that some ill-wisher had done to our well what ill-wishers so easily can do. Some can spit in one's beer when one has left the room. Others can do far worse things to one's well! We were told that all drinking water, which was filtered anyway, must also be boiled for five minutes, and believe me, that is what we religiously did. After about a week I decided to ride out and look at the well and make sure that there had been no second helping delivered.

To my horror I discovered two objects floating in the well, and they didn't look new. I galloped back to Holletta to spread the news and Tim sent for the driver and demanded to know why he had not reported this new development. "It not new", he replied. Why did you not remove it when you first reported it?" shouted Tim. "You not ask me to do dis", replied the driver! I was appalled when I learned that Tim had not only failed to order the thorough cleansing of the well, but had not been to inspect it and check that this had been properly done. For the first time in my life I lost my temper with a senior officer and shouted what I thought of him. From then onwards we always boiled the water, and the well was regularly inspected.

Since Bridge is one of those games which exercise the mind, and at which one is climbing heights which can rarely be reached, it never fails to hold the interest. None of us were all that good when we came to Holletta, but because it was the only mental recreation we had, we played it after dinner when guests were one man and wife. On one of those evenings we were playing with Pug and Cherry Roberts in the bungalow, which was inside the Ghibbi's outer walls. We had a liver and white spaniel called Minnie and the Roberts had a black spaniel called George. Minnie had been left in our bungalow which I called 'Banana Ridge', because it had a few banana trees around the back of it and along the outside of the Ghibbi walls near us, and Mocra was guarding it from a position on the veranda where he would sit with a Panga across his knees.

Silence reigned as the after dinner Bridge four was on, except for the usual hubbub between hands when we would be offered a top up of gin or whisky. Suddenly George growled and was told to shut up. He then started barking loudly. "For goodness sake shut up, George", shouted Pug, "You'll wake the children". George prowled round the room and eventually Pug opened the door of the sitting-room to see if anyone had got into the house. All was quiet. The only other door led into the Roberts' bedroom, which had no outside door, but a high window at least five feet from the ground. George still growled now and then, but was silenced until the last rubber was over and we bade our farewells. Mocra was still on guard on our veranda and I sent him home. We had not been back in the bungalow for more than five minutes when Pug reappeared and asked if he could borrow a couple of blankets and pillows. "Whilst George was barking and being told to shut up", he explained, "we were being burgled by someone who crept through the window in spite of its height above ground. All our clothes have been stolen, and even our pillows and blankets!"

Our faith in our impregnable system was shattered and the local police were called and the so-called experts from Addis. Eventually some of the stolen property was tracked down to Mocra's pad in the village, and he was put away for a couple of months. Most of the stolen clothes and bedding were eventually returned. Mocra must have organised the raid with his inside knowledge, but probably did not participate.

We had a rather poor cuisine while Mocra was away, and selfishly looked forward to his return. His sense of loyalty was such that he would have never stolen even a pin from us, but anyone else was fair game. Although he sometimes chewed bang, he was a good cook. I believe he was nervous if we were having people to dinner and we were having special dishes, and he chewed bang to give him courage. Before one lunch party he was in such a bad way that he could hardly stand, and his eyes were really bloodshot. He could however just speak. Phoebe said "I've lost my temper with Mocra – you go and cope. I'm going to have my bath". I went out to the kitchen, and he said "Sorry Sah, but all main dishes cook. Just sauce to make. You make it Sah and I tell you how much you mix and cook". I was then completely inexperienced at the finer arts of making sauces, although I had learned basic roast and vegetable cookery with my father on our yacht.

Mocra guided me through the operation, slurring his words but being quite positive about quantities and time of stirring etc. I remember him saying "A little now Sah, just a little now, now stir Sah, more stir Sah, now a little more".

The occasion was a lunch party for the French Ambassador and his wife, and I had impressed upon Mocra its importance. In the event the food, and our jointly prepared sauce, was perfect. Other imperfections did however creep in. Our houseboy Berou was very short sighted and always spent hours peering at our table mats to see that the hunting scenes had the horses with their feet on the ground and not pointing skywards. He had not noticed that one of the table napkins had an enormous hole in it and it was placed for the use of Jacques de Blessant, the Ambassador. As he opened it up he saw the hole and with a broad grin thrust his head through it with the biggest overlap hanging down like a baby's bib. This set the tone for the rest of the meal, and the locally made red Chianti which the Italians had taught the locals to make, tasted like the real thing from Tuscany!

Whenever I saw Mme. de Blessant, who rode the one horse who beat a weary Tamu, I always thought of Manchowe, the First Secretary at the Egyptian Embassy. He always said that Mme. de Blessant looked 'constipe' when she rode a race. He was a charming host and we were told to drop in at his flat in Addis at any time and help ourselves to a drink, whether he was there or not. If we did find him out we either waited for him to return and join us, or left a little note of thanks.

Sometimes we organised joint Holletta lunch parties for a number of Addis friends and each Holletta family would do one course, and the guests would be shunted from bungalow to bungalow. Often a few plates knives and forks had to be quickly washed and smuggled into the next host's kitchen by the houseboys.

At the end of it all we usually finished up by playing a couple of chukkas of 'Holletta Polo'. This was a two a side affair played on the large grass parade ground of the Cadet Training Wing. Unbelievably we played all out and always seemed to hit the ball cleanly in spite of our blood count, which would not have passed today's police tests. Two of the visitors were always warned what was to befall them and to bring breeches and boots. Two a side polo is very good for one's game because one's team-mate is always at a two to one disadvantage when one passes to him and the hitting must therefore be accurate. It was considered a social uplift to be invited to a Holletta lunch and the various phases which this involved. Everyone turned out to watch the polo, which we played, as I say, all out. We would then return to the Ghibbi area where the participants could have baths, and everyone normally had drinks in the Elliotts very large drawing room in the main building before setting off for Addis in the early evening. Our accommodation was too tight to have guests in our bungalows, but because we stayed so often with Cecil and Violet Orr in Addis, we repaid their hospitality by having a small marquee erected on the grass between the Ghibbi wall and our bungalow, where they took a week's holiday and fed and rode with us in the daytime and played Bridge in the evenings.

✧

A tragedy befell us towards the end of our stay which neither grown-ups or children will ever forget. Minnie, our spaniel, had a litter after an arranged marriage with George, and the puppies were born in strange circumstances. We had taken Pat and Peter Harrison, who ran the British Council Office in Addis, for a picnic lunch. After lunch we had gone for a stroll and as we crossed a stream Minnie slipped and became wedged by the running water between two boulders. We managed to extricate her and dry her off, and when we got back to the car she was placed between Michael and Jill, then aged around seven and five. Soon after we had started to lurch on the bumpy tracks Jill announced "Minnie's being sick". We looked round and Minnie peering at what appeared to be a shiny bit of liver; then she bit it gently, and out came a puppy's head. Minnie proceeded to give birth to five baby spaniels, three of which took after their father George and were black. They were a healthy litter and quickly became active crawlers. Minnie was a splendid mother and the puppies soon became house-trained – much sooner, it seemed, than the average puppy today. They were duly distributed around, some to Addis, one to the Roberts, and one, a black male called Ben, we kept. He had a delightful character and we adored him, not just because he was a puppy but also because of his personality. Then tragedy struck. Ben went down with some kind of illness and became very weak. Minnie was a wonderful mother and he slept in her basket. One morning when Minnie had nipped out to spend a penny I saw Ben struggle out of his basket and stagger towards the open door to the veranda. He collapsed and I ran forward to pick him up and carry him out. I felt his little heart feebly beating against my fingertips and then suddenly, as I was going down the steps on to the lawn, it stopped. His neck went limp, his head dropped, and he was dead. Michael and Jill were mortified and so were all of us at Holletta. Within forty-eight hours the Roberts' puppy had bitten Micky in the groin and drawn blood.

Ronnie Houston, who by his training was best equipped among us to be our vet, tested the Irwin puppy and diagnosed Rabies.

All Holletta dogs were shut into the tennis court and no one was allowed in there, by Tim's orders, except me, who was told that Bull Turnbull had ordered that all our dogs must be shot. Anyone who has lived in the wilds of Africa knows that rabies is rampant and is carried mainly by the movement of jackal packs and hyenas. We knew that every now and then a village dog just below our mound had become rabid and was destroyed, but somehow we felt that it would never happen to us. As I had a Colt Automatic pistol, I was given the unenviable task of shooting all our pets whilst the entire British community took off for Addis for their first anti-rabies injections, and to get them away from the gruesome events which were to take place in Holletta.

I felt that I just could not go into the tennis court and shoot the dogs in the presence of their canine fellows, so I arranged with the various house-boys for the favourite meal of each dog to be prepared and put in a bowl in the garden of the dog's home, out of sight of the tennis court. They then fetched each dog in turn. I started with Sam, my first canine acquisition, so that he would not hear the shots and feel any fear. I shot each dog in the head while it was enjoying its food. The last dog but two, a half-bred Alsation, was probably the most intelligent, and somehow put two and two together and refused to be caught. I was obliged to give it a heart shot from three yards and then shoot it through the head as it was still twitching after falling. The last two were George and Minnie, and after they had witnessed this execution I could not bring myself to put them down. I ordered the 'boys' to feed them, give them water, keep them shut in the tennis court, and then to make a large bonfire to cremate the dead.

I then drove off to Addis for my own treatment with any of the 'boys' who had been in contact with the dogs, feeling sick at heart. We officers and our 'boys' had to make this journey each day thereafter, while the wives and children stayed in Addis until the course of treatment was over. Ronnie Houston had quickly reverted from vet to doctor and had prepared a serum from the brains of Tony Irwin's puppy and there was enough to provide serum for all of us who had been in any form of contact with any of the puppies. The injections under the skin of our stomachs would not have been pleasant at the best of times, but somehow it made it worse to know how the serum had been made. We prayed that Ronnie had carried out the instructions in his Medical Manual correctly, as he had never done it before. He got it right however, and some of us probably owe our lives to him. The children were very brave and were all told to set a good example to the others and never to cry, even when there seemed to be no new space left in their tummies to stick the needle. Only Bridget Roberts, who was two years old, was allowed to cry, and in a way this was a good thing, as the others were reminded that they were no longer babies!

We adults suffered from being unable to drink alcohol during the treatment, but to me it was even worse to hear what awful rubbish other people talked when they had a drink and I was stone cold sober.

Chapter XVIII

Addis Incidents

Because there were so few Europeans in Addis we all got to know everyone fairly well, except for the Russians. They only left the huge Embassy compound which covered several acres, to attend formal functions. They came and went in their Embassy cars except for those working in the Russian Hospital and the agents who slipped out to build up a Communist network among the Ethiopians. Considering the fact that the Russians had previously had little contact with Ethiopia before World War II, no trade and no common frontiers, they had to be cooking up something to be there in such numbers.

What they were in fact doing was founding the Mau Mau movement in neighbouring Kenya and laying the foundations for the revolution in Ethiopia which placed their Communist converts in power and imprisoned the Emperor, his family, and all the nobility they could get their hands on. The Emperor was to 'die' in captivity in the course of time.

Because the BMME had no dentist in its establishment, Phoebe had a crack at the dentist at the Russian Hospital. Needless to say he was extremely skilful; a shop-window man whose like would be rarely encountered in Mother Russia. Dentists here still rave about the quality of her Addis stoppings and ask her who did them.

✧

The other nationalities were also representing their countries, but in a more open manner, and we made many friends. In an effort to impress the International Community the Crown Prince and his brother The Duke of Harrar gave sumptuous evening buffet parties. Except for the Russians we would all turn up in our dinner jackets and long frocks and sample French wines and champagne and European cold dishes. Sometimes there was dancing. Sometimes we were treated to a buffet of genuine Ethiopian fare. This consisted of Wat and Angira, which interpreted means unleavened bread and curry sauce with squares of raw meat, which were again dipped in a curry sauce.

We were warned not to touch the raw meat if we wished to avoid getting worms. On one occasion the Emperor held a formal reception which entailed the Embassy Staff wearing their gold braided tail-coated uniforms, and the Military their blue uniforms and medals. Tim Elliott found that he had forgotten his hat and wrote to his Saville Row tailors to send one out. A round box duly arrived and when he opened it he found they had made an error and sent him a hat for an officer of the Gloucesters, which had a second badge at the back so that he could not get away with it by wearing it back to front! It was also two sizes too small so it perched on top of his head. As we carried our hats inside the palace with our left arms curled round them it did not insult the Emperor in any way, but Tim would insist on wearing it on his head in the queue before going in, and later on the steps when we paused for someone to photograph our party coming down them. Ladies were required to wear white gloves and their shoulders had to be covered by short sleeves. Phoebe had made do by cutting material from the hem of a long evening dress, but this material was unable to do more than cover the exterior of her shoulders and she had to keep her arms, down to her elbows, held firmly to her sides.

The Emperor had abandoned the giant round toucle which he had used before the Italian invasion, and moved into the palatial stone building which had been built by the Italians for their Military Governor and Commander-in-Chief. I was tickled to see a large oil painting in the palace of Emperor Menelik wearing a leopard-skin cloak and holding a spear. Some palace official had felt that it was slightly degrading for a former monarch to be portrayed with bare feet and had ordered a pair of large black British Army boots to be painted over them. To emphasise them the artist had turned them out like Charlie Chaplin although his knees were pointing straight forward. No socks or leggings were portrayed and the tops of his boots were much wider than his slender ankles.

Phoebe and I saw this at the same time and both had to suppress silent laughter. As soon as we tried to do this we became inflicted with a fit of giggles, which one somehow cannot suppress. I must make it clear that the Emperor Haile Selasse had his feet firmly on the ground and was endowed with his full share of African cunning. This was made very clear when Phoebe and I were invited to stay with Count von Rosen and his wife on the shores of Lake Bishoftu, a volcanic lake of very deep clear fresh water about an hour's drive South of Addis. He had been an air ace in the Swedish Air Force, and just as the British ran the Police and the Army, the French ran the Imperial Bodyguard and the Swedes the Air Force.

Von Rosen told us that he had found problems getting sufficient areas for airfields due to the corruption of the Minister of Lands, who demanded bribes. Von Rosen asked for an audience with the Emperor and it was granted. "Your Majesty" explained Von Rosen, "I am having great difficulty in acquiring sufficient land to do justice to your Imperial Air

Force, due to the corruption of your Minister of Lands. Do you not think it might be wise to retire him and appoint a new Minister". "I am well aware", replied the Emperor "of the corruption of this man, and it has taken me years to discover how much he takes and exactly how he manages to take it. But now he has filled his family coffers and is hardly taking anything. If I appointed a new man it would therefore be a most expensive exercise, as being new he would be comparatively poor and would need to make quite a lot of money. It would take me a long time to discover how much he was taking, and his particular methods of obtaining it. So you see, it is much better to go on using the present Minister as long as he continues his reduced corruption". Von Rosen turned to me and said, "So you see, he certainly has his finger on the pulse."

The Von Rosens were an entertaining couple, but it took quite a while to get used to their eating habits. They were both wiry and slender but extremely fit. We were woken the first morning with two trays, each bearing a cup of rather watery tea and a small plate with what I would expect to eat at a cocktail party a small bit of salt fish on a piece of toast about one and a half inches square, a piece of asparagus wrapped in a roll of very thin ham, and a tiny round cake about one and a half inches in diameter. We had been well lubricated the previous evening and I did not feel like spoiling my breakfast, so I just nibbled at my cake and drank the rather weak continental tea. We duly bathed and went down to breakfast, but could not find our host and hostess. We eventually found them sitting in the garden and received a warm and smiling welcome. By this time I could have done without the preambles, my bath and shave having got my juices going and I was fully ready for breakfast. After further polite conversation Von Rosen asked if we would care to stroll down to the lake for a morning swim. Suddenly the penny dropped. We had had our breakfast, and I had only eaten a third of it. No wonder they both had such good figures.

✧

There was always an endless variety of personalities and of activities going on in Addis. At Christmas and New Year time there would be every kind of Ball and children's party, one of the latter being given by the Emperor, who would appear for a short time. I remember the French Embassy children's party well because for a long time my children would not allow me to forget it. A Christmas scene was enacted, and when Santa Claus was led in on a huge mule at the far end of the room, this real mule did a real poo on the rich Embassy carpet and of course really brought the house down!

We at Holletta made a point of attending the BMME New Years Eve Fancy Dress Ball as a team, to compete for a prize of champagne. The first year we went as the cast of Cinderella, complete with the 'ugly sisters' played by myself and Pug Roberts. Phoebe played Cinderella dressed in rags, and danced round with a broom. After we had paraded the judge said: "The Holletta team can fall out". Since we had been wildly overacting and Pug and I as the ugly sisters had made some rather vulgar signs we thought we were being ordered off in disgrace. I remember Cherry Roberts turning at the door and saying "We've been thrown out of better places than this". We went to our cars and opened a bottle of champagne. Eventually someone came and found us to inform us that we had won the first prize, which was why we had been ordered off the floor. They had seen enough, we had won, but looked as though we would go on for ever.

The Harrisons ran a Variety Show for charity at the British Council and I did some conjuring. John Whitty, who was talented in so many directions, had taught me some sleight of hand. These tricks, together with my having spotted how a professional conjurer had done a trick at a concert in Malta, and found that I could do it, led to my getting to know a member of the Magic Circle on board the ship coming back from South Africa. I was able to teach him two tricks which he did not know in exchange for two of his, one of which was a way of sawing a woman in half. I duly did this at the British Council with Phoebe as the volunteer, and needless to say well rehearsed. Unfortunately I had the 'coffin' made too flimsily of plywood on a light wooden frame, and when the saw was only about three inches from coming out the other side, having gone well past Phoebe, the blade stuck firmly and could not be moved. I did my best by getting volunteers to carry the coffin down the aisle so that everyone could see that she had been well and truly sawn, but I felt very deflated as I was becoming rather professional, having been told by my former instructor that he would sponsor my membership of the Magic Circle if I could think out an original trick. This I have done, but have lost touch with my friend!

When Bull Turnbull first arrived he made a big point about everyone being equal on the polo field, and that we could call him anything we liked in the heat of the battle. In an American Tournament when my team was playing one captained by Bull, Tony Irwin, who was in Bull's team, was having rather a bad day and they were not doing too well. Bull was giving them hell to the extent of embarrassing us all, and then suddenly he abused a member of my team who had done nothing illegal, but had merely successfully ridden off one of his team who looked set to score. I was quite near to him and shouted 'You've lost your temper and shouted at your own team, kindly don't shout at mine'. He rode up to me and hit the top of my helmet as hard as he could with the head of his polo stick! This began a feud which never ended.

✧

We made a number of interesting trips to places well remote from the Holletta – Addis Ababa area. One of the most notable was to stay with Jerry Pink, who had been the Lt. Colonel A/Q at BMME when I arrived, and had retired to become the British Consul at Harrar. He had been a few terms senior to me at Oundle, and we naturally got to know each other. He very generously invited me with the entire family to take a break from the 8,000 feet altitude at Holletta, at a time when he in turn was going to drive across the Ogaden Desert of British Somaliland to visit his outpost at Berbera on the coast. We flew down to Harrar by Ethiopian Airlines, whose planes had extremely ornately painted exteriors. I was told that all the paintwork, which included enormous golden 'Lions of Judah' increased the drag by at least twenty knots. We were relieved to note that they had American pilots.

Harrar is a walled city, and a relic of the days when the tribes from across the Red Sea in Arabia had pushed the Hamitic African peoples back from the Western shores of that Sea. All primitive Ethiopian paintings, mainly on the walls of their Coptic Christian Churches, faithfully depict the Ethiopians as a mixture of brown and black people. This they claim is the result of the well publicised liaison between King Solomon and the Queen of Sheba. I think that the Arabs of those days who pushed Westward through what is now Somalia, were responsible for far more pale skins than those descended from King Solomon.

In addition to the inhabitants of the walled city, a fairly large township of relatively modern construction had sprung up outside the walls, due to the Italian occupation. Harrar being the second most important town after Addis Ababa. Consulates had sprung up and one or two extremely comfortable modern hotels. These were picturesque rambling one-storey buildings with whitewashed walls embellished by mauve and red Bougainvillaea, with tennis courts and swimming pools. There was also an outpost of the BMME run by Major Guy Campbell. His job was to advise the Commander of the Harrar Division of the Ethiopian Army, assisted by two captains, one of whom was a mad Irishman. They lived in a fine Mess with a spacious drawing-room on the first floor which had a view all round. Phoebe and the children spent a very happy time with them each day during the period when Jerry and I were away on our trip to the coast.

Before we left, Phoebe and I explored the old walled city and at the main market-place I bought some hot red chillies which were laid out on the ground on a rush mat. Most Officer's Messes serve 'chilli peppers' with soup and I still have mine now. They have lost their strength and heat, which lasted for about twenty years, but still produce a flavour after forty four years; the bottle having been topped up with endless bottles of sherry. Frank Spragg, who used to coach the Rugby XV at Oundle in my day, and who subsequently became housemaster of St Anthony when Michael was there, told me that he reckoned you could serve up dishwater at a dinner party if it was hot, well salted and laced with sherry peppers.

The day dawned when we set out in Jerry's drophead coupé for our trip to Hargeisa, then the capital of British Somaliland and approximately half way to Berbera. The road, which was no more than a track, runs across the North of the Ogaden Desert where for centuries a few hundred tribesmen from Somaliland and Ethiopia squabbled over the waterholes and were sufficiently small in numbers to survive. Now modern medicines have cut down Mother Nature's method of maintaining stable numbers and an enormous number of people there are about to die. People who have never lived in some of these remote places take well-meaning decisions and over-rule the advice of those living on the spot.

Jerry and I only just made Hargeisa before dusk and were glad to wash away the dust of the journey from our bodies including hair, eyes and ears. We were guests of the Somaliland Scouts, and I found Roly Hill of the Dorsets there, who had been on my course at the Staff College.

We spent the next day socialising. A lunch party was later followed by an informal polo game, where I played abominably due to being used to the smaller ponies of Addis, with which I had developed wrist shots which one cannot do with a long stick. That night drinks were followed by a dinner party and I remember some important person falling asleep at the dinner table, a victim of the grain on grape. We made an early start for our slightly longer drive down to Berbera and once more made it just before dusk.

Life at Berbera was unbelievable. I had thought that the Holletta pattern was pretty alcoholic at times, but Berbera was a revelation. I will describe a typical twenty-four hour period from midday to midday; but first the cast. There were only four white men in Berbera at that time; the British Consul, a French merchant who acted as French Consul, a Scottish doctor, and a long term guest who was staying with him. Only the British Consul had a wife out there, and she sailed serenely through the strange circumstances with poise, charm and a great sense of humour. Without those qualities she would never have survived.

At around midday the European population would assemble at the British Consul's house. This was a two storied building with the upper floor consisting of two large rooms surrounded by open terraces on all four sides. The flat roof had the same area as the lower floor and so the hot sun was unable to penetrate into the upstairs rooms. The verandas were in permanent use and furnished with beautiful rugs and cane furniture. The colour of the sea over the roofs of white Arab houses was as blue as the Mediterranean, but slightly more turquoise in shade, disturbed by only the most gentle swell. Being slightly higher than its neighbours, the Consul's house had a good view and caught what there was of the sea breezes.

We would sit round in great comfort with well charged glasses and, very shortly, a house-boy with a red fez and immaculate white Galabieh would appear bearing a large bowl of succulent oysters, plucked from the sea that very morning. We would then all be passed a small bowl and he would silently glide round and serve us all with a huge curved gravy spoon. From a youth spent holidaying at West Mersea, where the renowned Colchester Oysters were reared, I had acquired an appreciative connoisseur's appetite for fresh succulent oysters. They were all prepared with tomato and paprika sauce, and slid down easily as these delicacies can.

The trouble was that they slid down all too easily and after two days the bowl suddenly reminded me what a spittoon in a T.B. ward of a hospital might be like, and I not only felt I had eaten enough oysters for that day, but was put me off them for about eight years by their sheer volume. I prefer my oysters sitting in their shells and putting my own exact quantities of lemon juice and cayenne pepper etc on each.

To continue; this morning party would last until about half-past three or a quarter to four; the conversation having covered every topic under the sun and many amusing stories being exchanged. We would then all troop downstairs for a curry lunch of immense variety and size, washed down with chilled lager. This meal and the soothing effect which the constant intake of not too much and not too little alcohol engenders, would last for around two hours and we would disperse after drinking some extremely good coffee not long before sunset. Jerry and I would make our way to the guest house about two hundred yards away right on the edge of the beach. I would have a dip in the sea to cool me and clear my head, and then lie on my bed for an hour's sleep. Whoever woke up first would call the other and we would slip down in the twilight for another swim before changing for dinner. We would turn up at the Consul's house between half past eight and nine and once more meet the rest of Berbera's Europeans for drinks on the upper terrace. Dinner would be served between nine-thirty and ten and the evening would finish up with a final quiet drink on the terrace. The most unpleasant smells of camels and local cooking would drift up from the Arab houses and the sound of voices gently murmuring, interrupted by the call to prayer from the top of the minaret of the nearest mosque, which would remind us all of how much more time is devoted to religion by the average Moslem, compared with the average Christian. There being no distractions found in Mediterranean and similar seaside resorts, Jerry and I would find ourselves climbing into our beds around midnight. On each of the nights we spent there I sneaked down to the sea for a final dip.

We would awake with the rising sun lighting up the Eastern horizon and would soon be brought tea. We both swam before breakfast and after breakfast read some local English language newspapers, which I imagine had arrived by road from a night run from Hargeisa. Breakfast would be followed by another swim, and then we read some magazines which had been thoughtfully provided before the veranda of our bungalow, which was not as airy as the Consulate, became unbearable. Jerry disappeared for around three quarters of an hour one morning, to have some consular discussions with our host, but apart from this he did not appear over-worked.

At half-past eleven we swam again, washed the salt off our bodies and got into open necked shirts and slacks for our appointment with our host and his hospitality at twelve. In my case this did not include the further consumption of oysters. Perhaps this verb was too well chosen!

I gathered that the British Consul always played host at these gatherings, because the others did not have big or airy enough houses for the other regulars, who repaid hospitality by gifts of drink and anything special in the food line.

It seemed a wonderful way of passing the time, but I doubt if I would have retained my sanity for more than a week if I had lived there permanently. Jerry and I had an eventless return trip to Hargeisa where our visit included another game of polo and dinner party. On our final leg to Harrar, during one of my spells at the wheel, I managed to knock off the draining plug of the oil sump on the uneven desert track. We did not notice it until the engine temperature soared. Luckily Jerry had a reserve can of oil, and we managed to screw a cork into the sump hole.

Phoebe and the children had enjoyed their stay with Guy Campbell and his officers and we were not to know that on our next overseas tours Guy and I would find ourselves serving alongside each other in Nairobi as Lt. Colonels.

Our flight back to Addis proved rather trying, as it was a freight flight for Indian merchants taking their wares to the markets in Addis. The seats were bench seats along the sides of the hold and most of the merchants, some of whom had families, bundled their sacks of peppers and betel nuts under their seats and sat on the bulging parts which projected. We were the only Europeans and as much their focus of interest as they were of ours. They chewed betel nuts and reeked of garlic. Being an afternoon flight the ground was hot below us, and we had lots of bumps. However some of the scenery was spectacular. Having no comfortable sacks to sit on we had to endure the hard seats, and the time certainly did not fly.

As we approached the mountainous area around Addis the bumps became more pronounced, and the aircraft would suddenly drop twenty feet or shoot up twenty feet. Michael and Jill began to look rather white and when we saw Addis in the distance, Phoebe murmured a few words of encouragement: "We're nearly there darlings", she said, "There is the airfield, only about a mile away. Hold on to it and don't be sick now". They nodded numbly and did their best. The Captain's voice came over the speaker. "I am afraid we are not being allowed to land for another five minutes because an aircraft has been delayed on take-off". He banked steeply and there was another of those drops of greater depth than before, because there were more hills and valleys surrounding the airfield area and the heat of the hot land was much nearer to us. Both the children gave way to airsickness and Phoebe and I did our best to comfort them. Then one or two of the Indian passengers threw up, and the stench of regurgitated garlic was more than Phoebe could cope with and she joined the children. As we banked again and again at slow speed with flaps down I found myself beginning to swallow, and was within about two minutes of joining my family's plight when we finally touched down!

Soon after our return from Harrar we had the sad experience of saying farewell to the Elliotts. They had been very good friends and Tim never pulled rank. He once pulled my leg by giving me an adverse report and then tearing it up and giving me the proper one. He said it was not an adverse failing he had brought up in the first one, but he felt I ought to know about it. What he had enlarged on was the fact that I could do anything well if I was interested and wanted to do it, but was quite useless at doing something which I did not want to do. I am afraid he was absolutely right. He let his hair down completely in our social life and once called Enid a "bloody old cow" when she failed to return his suit a bridge! We kept up with them after Holletta and exchanged visits, although they lived then in Northern Lincolnshire.

Tim's successor was a very different type of soldier. He was a little man who rushed round trying to change everything before he discovered why it happened that way. A typical example was that British officers, including the General, did not wear webbing belts with their battledress because the Ethiopians, who were fitted out with British weapons and uniforms, did not have separate belts to wear with battledress. Our newcomer insisted that we wore belts. Once I was able to explain this to my little friend he calmed down and cancelled the order and then bore me a grudge for having made him appear in the wrong. I suppose I did enjoy deflating him a bit and that I was perhaps foolish enough to let him see it!

The next thing that happened was that when I sent for the Staff College file to look up the lectures for the following week I found that the file contained a letter from him to the General saying that he was not happy with the way the Staff College was being run and that he did not even believe we had a syllabus before his arrival, as the one presented to him "had obviously been freshly typed"!

I didn't even bother him with my views but drove in to Addis and had a talk to the General. I reminded him that only a few months earlier he had asked me if I would agree to an extension of an extra year to my tour as I had produced such good results and achieved such rapport with the Ethiopian Army. He replied "I am not prepared to accept an 'either he goes or I do' attitude, and you will just have to sort it out with him". I returned to Holletta and had a clearing the air session with my persecutor, explaining that I had indeed had our syllabus, which I had frequently updated and changed to suit local requirements, retyped for him as a matter of course and courtesy, and that I strongly resented him going behind my back to the General without a word of criticism to me. We then agreed to a wobbly truce and he offered to sell me a half-share in Borderer, which he had bought from Tim, if I would agree to ride him in Addis Race Meetings.

A few months later I was approached by Tesfa Desta, a student on the first course and my interpreter on the second, with a message direct from the Emperor to the effect that His Majesty believed that our General's conduct at formal and semi-formal functions, such as the dances and receptions given by the Crown Prince and his younger brother the Duke of Harrar, set a very bad example to the officers of his own Army, and he would like him removed and replaced. (After he had had a few drinks the General would behave badly, pinching women's bottoms, and even going round hoovering up other people's half empty glasses!). Tesfa also said that senior officers of the Ethiopian Army were pressing him to ask for the removal at the same time of my own local bête-noir, who had succeeded in rubbing every Ethiopian up the wrong way. He seemed unable to accept the fact that his job was to advise senior officers diplomatically, and that he did not command them. The only Ethiopians he commanded were the officer cadets of the Cadet School and their instructors.

I was placed in quite a serious dilemma. Normally one would pass such a message to one's superior for upward transmission, but he was a target. The next one up was the General, who was also a target. I decided that I had no alternative but to request a private and confidential interview with Dan Lascelles, our Ambassador. We were after all a Political Mission and this was a very sensitive matter of both political and military importance. Dan Lascelles was very understanding, realised the need for confidentiality, realised the dilemma in which I had been placed, agreed that I could not possibly remain in my job, and assured me that I had done the right thing. In due course I learned that he and the General had boarded a plane for Cairo, and felt very sick at heart at the part I had been forced to play. I did not expect to see the General again.

A day or two later I learned that the General had returned. There was no reaction for a time except that my new boss at Holletta was becoming increasingly unpleasant and must have heard what I had passed on to the Ambassador. I became desperate to get away and could find no way of achieving this until the Brigadier (Operations) at GHQ Cairo paid a routine visit to Addis and I was able to mutter to him at a cocktail party "You've got to get me out of here as soon as possible. As a result of my passing on the Emperor's wishes to the Ambassador my position has become intolerable". A posting home for me duly arrived from Cairo. I was then summoned to Addis by the General and invited to sign an adverse confidential report. I refused to sign it as it contained not one word of truth. "It was you who asked me if I would agree to serve on here for another year", I pointed out. "I've changed my mind", he retorted, and told me that the Ambassador had told him that I was the Military link in the chain between the Emperor and himself. "If you do not sign this report I will keep you here, and your wife and children will leave without you", he thundered. I signed the report. The truth is that I learned something from every course and that these continuously improved. At the same time my technique of lecturing through an interpreter was also improving as I learned when to make the right pauses for effect, and stretched the length of each sentence or sentences in accordance with my Ethiopian officer/colleague/interpreter's increasing memory and fluency.

I now could not wait to get away from the 'new look' Holletta and the uncomfortable atmosphere which now prevailed, and Phoebe and I prepared for our move and the round of farewell parties which were thrown for us. These included the De Blessants, who gave a sumptuous dinner party for us at the French Embassy, and Dan Lascelles, who gave a lunch party for us where Phoebe occupied the place of honour at his right hand. I never discussed his breach of my confidence with him. The most touching farewell party was that thrown by the Staff College graduates who all got leave from their various staff appointments, some over a hundred miles away, to attend. I knew that they were all pretty broke and underpaid, but they gave a dance in our honour complete with band, and the speeches were embarrassingly touching and sincere. Then there was a call for silence and the senior 'old boy' came forward and presented me with a beautifully made gold and ivory cigarette-holder and a cigarette case. It must have been specially made by some European firm, probably Cartier, and the Imperial Crest and the wording which is normally engraved on such presentations was in relief in solid gold. I was almost rendered speechless, which is not normal for me!

We finally departed from Holletta with mixed feelings; memories of events which had brought fulfilment of purpose, excitement and happiness tinged with relief to be leaving a changed and strained atmosphere. We drove down the sloping track which encircled the Ghibbi in the Vauxhall to spend the final days as guests of Ian Bell, the First Secretary at the British Embassy, and his wife Ruth. They had been wonderful hosts on many occasions and we kept up with them after my retirement from the Army.

Chapter XIX

The Drive to Massawa

My final adventure was to drive our two year old Vauxhall to Massawa for shipment home, as post-War cars were still difficult to get in England. I chose as my co-driver Alex Napier, who was representing De La Rue and trying to get the Ethiopians to invest in a new set of post-War bank notes. His family had escaped with their lives from Russia early on in the revolution and both he and his brother had been brought up as Englishmen; public schools and Brigade of Guards. The Emperor was a great prevaricator and kept people waiting for weeks at a time between appointments. I suppose the idea was that they would get so tired and frustrated that they would lower their prices rather than go home empty-handed. The dispute with Eritrea had already reared its head and we could not be guaranteed a safe journey. I was given no escort, but my network of former students was by then in staff appointments and deployed country-wide. The word was passed along that I was not to be molested. At the end of the line was the Commander of the Area containing the frontier post with Eritrea. From thence convoys with strong military escorts ran the gauntlet to Asmara twice a week, and we thus had a 'train to catch'. We left the British Embassy before dawn one Saturday, well wrapped-up against the cold night air which prevailed at that altitude.

There had once been a tarmac road all the way between Addis and Asmara with concrete culverts over all the streams. Sadly the Ethiopians had done no maintenance whatsoever and the surface was worse than a bad gravel road as the potholes were not like shallow basins with sloping sides, but had vertical sides of concrete round places where the ground had subsided under the concrete surface and a solid hunk of concrete had dropped between four and eight inches. Virtually all the culverts were intact, but most of the approach slopes had subsided adjacent to the concrete structures which again provided a vertical obstacle to be taken extremely slowly.

The Vauxhall 14 of those days was a fine six cylinder car with good suspension, but the front wheels' suspension was by torsion bars. These had a trailing arm fitted with the stub-axle which twisted the bar every time it went over a bump. This meant that we had only to hit one bump too hard and that wheel would vanish into its mudguard and bring the car to a standstill. We had to face around six hundred miles of difficult and completely varied terrain, passing through forests, climbing escarpments rising to peaks over thirteen thousand feet high, and crossing deserts populated by an extremely warlike tribe called the Danakil, whose womenfolk ensure that none of their wounded enemies can have children for evermore.

Alex and I worked out a drill whereby if in grave danger the passenger would slide back the sun-roof and stand up on the front seat with a Colt .45 Automatic which had four large magazines. There was also a light game rifle which was accurate up to 200 yards and whose bullets would travel less accurately up to 1,000 yards. It turned us into a sort of armoured car, with the man standing with his head and shoulders above roof level having an all round view and a reasonably long range weapon; certainly we could outrange the Danakil who were blowpipe people, but we were not too happy about Eritrean guerillas.

In order to catch our armed convoy near the border with Eritrea our general plan was to drive for three days, and if necessary at night, non-stop except for halts for meals and nature. A large soft pillow against the left-hand side of the interior enabled the resting passenger to doze comfortably by day and sleep by night without his head rolling about. We had a box containing easy food, including cake and fruit, and plenty of tinned milk, sugar, tea and coffee. We also had enough water and a petrol Primus which did not need pumping. Changes of clothing suitable for hotels in Asmara and Massawa were in suitcases in the boot, together with cans of spare petrol. We agreed to an immediate fine of one Ethiopian dollar, to be handed over on the spot, for hitting a pothole or culvert too hard and endangering the front suspension. Having dropped down through the forests East of Addis and then up the incredible zig-zag which climbed the Abuya Myeda escarpment, we stopped at the top where the road runs very near the edge to admire the awesome view which stretches for over two hundred miles across the desert to the Red Sea. At the edge of the cliff the first thousand of the eight thousand foot drop to the upper desert is practically vertical. We crawled cautiously to the lip and peered down with feelings of vertigo. Suddenly we found ourselves under fire from a volley of large stones and small rocks, some about the size of half a brick. We were round in a flash and found ourselves facing a troop of some thirty dog-nosed baboons. These are as heavy as a small man, and rather evil looking, with eyes set very close together. They are also quite good shots with a rock! We acknowledged defeat, ran for the car and drove off. I should have known better, as I had once had a similar experience when driving to Dessie with Phoebe; but there had been no sign of them when we got out of the car and walked towards the cliff edge. They must also have been masters of the art of ambush and concealment.

The road gradually distanced itself from the edge of the high plateau, climbed even higher and eventually at a height of around 11,000 feet entered the famous Mussolini Tunnel and headed for the pin-point of light at its Northern end. On emerging we were rewarded with a similar view to our right, but could now see the small town of Debra Sina lying about two thousand feet almost vertically below us and enjoyed wonderful scenery with the peaks of the lower mountains on our left. When I say we, I should say 'when passenger', because the driver's eyes had to be permanently glued to the hazards of the unmaintained road surface. The road then began to descend and crossed a tributary of the River Awash, which South of Addis Ababa and, in the rains, runs across the Aussa Desert to what was then French Somaliland and the Somali port of Djibouti. The road was blasted out of the sheer rock on the side of the cliffs and followed parallel to them, doubling back with hairpin bends which made the hair stand on end. I knew this stretch of road and was determined to be at the wheel when we negotiated it. I could not contemplate going down it as a passenger. Alex was very stoical and silent! At the top of the pass we had been wearing pullovers and jackets but we were pulling everything off on the first bit of straight road at the bottom, finishing up with no more than Aertex vests and pants. The road here was the worst we had encountered and we were rarely able to drive more than twenty yards without slowing right down for a pothole. At our first village with a cafe we pulled up. These were known as Tedj Beits. Tedj is a local drink brewed and tasting not unlike the English mead, and a Beit is the Amharic for 'house'.

The road then changed direction from North East to North West, and we found ourselves gradually entering wooded country not unlike the New Forest, with open green glades and quite different from the Central African thick jungle. The heat was such that we stuck unpleasantly to the leather seats of the car. We passed the ruins of what had obviously been a small town. It was completely deserted and not re-occupied by locals. I later discovered that the Italians who had built it suffered so much from mosquitoes that they abandoned it and built another town on higher ground. They had obviously intended to colonise Ethiopia and settle there permanently. But for World War II they would doubtless have succeeded. As the road gradually rose we found ourselves in scrub-covered foothills. The local houses were now quite different and looked like tall beehives. They were made by planting a ring of poles and pulling the tops together to form a point.

We decided to stop at the next Tedj Beit we came to, but as so often happens, after another hour we had still not passed one. We pulled in off the road and decided to make a meal of bread and butter, some sardines and a glass of beer. There was no-one in sight as we squatted down on a large round rock and started to munch. Suddenly I spotted a slender figure leaning on a five foot staff and contemplating us from the other side of the car. Neither of us saw or heard his silent arrival. I addressed a greeting in Amharic but he was absolutely motionless, not even his eyes seeming to move. I gave it up, we finished our food and got back into the car; still no movement. As we drove away I watched him through the driving mirror and when we had driven about a hundred yards he took a couple of slow, measured steps and picked up the sardine tin, examined it and put into a fold in his garment. To him it might have been a good water-tight container and something to value. One cannot measure wealth in such disparity of life-styles.

The light began to fail soon after this and it became more and more difficult to see the potholes. To make matters worse the road surface between the potholes deteriorated and the stones in the road became much larger. Our lights were now needed, but they tended to pick up and brighten the road fifty yards away, but not the bit just in front of the wheels. Suddenly there was a loud clonk under the clutch casing and then a noise like a child running alongside park railings, clicking them with a hard stick. As I put my foot on the clutch to come to a halt, the noise doubled. I crawled under the car and Alex passed me a torch. I found that a sharp stone, which must have been quite large, had knocked a hole in the comparatively thin clutch casing which was actually touching the clutch. I managed to get a large screw-driver into the hole and lever the sharp points round the hole away from the clutch. After some trial and error we got the jagged points away from the clutch except when it was fully withdrawn with pedal down. We pressed on into the darkness, taking great care and depressing the clutch as little as possible when changing gear. To our right and well below us we could see a bush fire burning. It looked as if an army of torch-bearers were moving forward in a straight line half a mile long. Every now and then there would be a big flare up as some dried bush or tree went up. It was an awesome sight and we were glad that we were well above it and did not have to go through it. The big rains were due in the following week, so the scrub and bushes were at their driest.

The next hour seemed interminable as we crept ever upward and tried to avoid further damage to the car. We also had to make sure that we did not miss a left fork where the road led up to Dessie and not a right fork which would lead us to French Somaliland. As we reached the zig-zag bends which climbed up towards Dessie we found the darkness rather comforting, being unable to see the ghastly drops on the down-hill sides of the road. The lights of Dessie eventually appeared and we reached the house which was the Officers Mess of the two BMME advisors to the Dessie Commander. We found that my signal announcing our arrival had not reached Dessie, and that they were on tour. The good news was that they had left behind to guard the place none other than my old friend Mocra, whom I had recommended to them under pressure from my fellow officers at Holletta. They, and particularly their servants, did not wish to risk another Mocra organised inside job! He soon had a fire going in the living room and a hot meal on the go in the kitchen. He was really pleased to see me and grinned from ear to ear; a likeable rogue.

The warmth and hot food soon restored our spirits, but at the back of our minds we still worried whether there was a mechanic at the Ethiopian Army Headquarters who would be able to sort our clutch out satisfactorily. We were up early the next morning and as soon as we had had breakfast I drove the car onto a smooth patch of grass and had another look underneath the clutch casing. In the bright sunshine I was soon able to see which jagged edges of the hole were catching the clutch and managed to prise them back into their proper positions using a screwdriver as a lever. Eventually with all the points back in place the hole was almost completely closed. We decided to give it a go and loaded the car, drove into town and found the only petrol station open and were on our way by ten o'clock.

Dessie is built at two levels, the upper part being where we had spent the night and the lower part well below the towering old town. The Italians had built a typical Europeanised suburb at the lower level with comfortable bungalows standing in their own spacious gardens and shaded by tall groves of Eucalyptus trees. Amongst them was the inevitable C.I.A.A.O. Hotel, the local equivalent of a mini-Hilton. After delivering a letter from our friendly Greek grocer Vaporidis to his brother who ran the family branch in Dessie, we struck North along the Asmara road.

Our way led us through a succession of green hills and valleys which resembled my idea of fairyland. Picturesque little villages nestling on the hillsides, fertile cultivated valleys and everything somehow in miniature. The tops of the little hills were in fact nearly 9,000 feet in height but as the road runs at over 8,000 feet the impression one got was of friendly little hills a few hundred feet high. To our right we caught glimpses of a large lake with an island in the middle containing a quaint looking monastery – most of the Ethiopians are of course Coptic Christians. The road surface here was on the whole good, having a top surface of rolled gravel. This we found had worn far better than tarmac whose potholes tend to grow when not properly maintained. Our system of fines was still in operation and we were each of us just in single figures. We proceeded in this fashion until about four o'clock, when we stopped for a late lunch at Waldia. The old Ethiopian town of Waldia lies half a mile away from the main road across a valley. The Waldia that the main route passes through was just a collection of Italian built cafes where lorry drivers could not only get a meal but also doss down for the night. It lies at the Southern end of the Riya Plain which is low lying, malarial and populated by the Danakil, whose gruesome habits are often (and very wrongly) attributed to all Ethiopians. To Southbound travellers Waldia is therefore a welcome oasis after the heat, mosquitoes and other inhabitants of the Riya Plain. In our case it was the kicking off point.

When we finally did kick off, after omelettes and chianti – in my case too much chianti – Alex was driving and I quickly fell into an alcoholic doze. I awoke to find us down in the plain and the sun burning my face through the near-side window. At the first Halt to change drivers I stripped down to my 'aertex order'. This was now grey with dust and stained purple here and there from having spilt chianti on it whilst drinking with the car in motion; we made a point of always taking the unconsumed portion with us after stopping for a meal. The Riya Plain seemed absolutely deserted and the road surface fair, so we made fairly good time for several miles. We then came across a dried out river bed about half a mile across. The rains of the previous year had evidently deposited hundreds of tons of sand and stones across the road to a considerable depth. This had now been bulldozed and we passed through a sort of cutting with high banks of old river bed which the machines had thrown up on either side.

After another half hour we passed a column of small donkeys carrying blocks of rock salt. One of them had sagged down to the road under its heavy load and was unable to rise. Its owner was spearing it in the back with a pointed stick. This was more than we could stand and I quickly stopped the car and Alex and I began to remonstrate. With no common bond of language the only answer was action. We untied the blocks of salt which were fastened with leather thongs which cut deeply into the donkey's belly. This was evidently what the owner wished to avoid, as being one continuous strip it would take a lot of unwinding and putting back. The blocks of salt were then distributed singly amongst the other animals in the column with tremendous opposition from the other owners who had up to this moment been enjoying the whole spectacle. The stricken donkey, once relieved of its load and assisted by us to its feet, quickly escaped into the bush. The owner fastened me with a menacing scowl. Alex remarked on the pastimes of the inhabitants of the Riya Plain. I looked down at my flimsy aertex pants. Alex and I said "good afternoon", retreated with dignity to the car and drove smartly off.

Soon after this we were passing the small village and fort of Alamata which gives its name to the famous Alamata Pass. The gradients and bends on this pass made the Mussolini Pass seem real kindergarten stuff. There were no appreciable foothills and so the Italian engineers just zig-zagged on and on until they reached the top of the escarpment. We halted two thirds of the way up and took a photograph of the mass of hairpin bends which disappeared almost out of sight below us. The car was boiling furiously and so we took ten minutes off to smoke cigarettes and admire the view. To the South the Riya Plain stretched as far as the eye could see; a thin straight line marking the road we had just travelled for about ten miles and finally disappearing into the haze. About seven miles away, looking from here like an ant-hill in a smooth meadow, stood the small hillock near which we had assisted our donkey. I wondered if they had managed to catch it yet.

On reaching the top of the escarpment we found green grassy undulating plainland. We were back on another part of the same gigantic plateau on which Addis Ababa and Dessie stand. Within twenty minutes of reaching the summit we sighted the town of Quoram. It would soon be getting dark and as there was little prospect of a meal for another two hours driving we stopped for a cup of coffee and some food in a local tedj beit.

It was as we opened the car doors to get out that we met 'Sally', or rather that 'Sally' met us; for she proceeded to hop straight in and sit firmly on the front seat. "Seems to be used to driving in cars" said Alex. "Must have been left behind by some passing Europeans" I commented, as I took in her liver and white markings and long dangling ears. There were probably not more than a dozen spaniels in the whole of Ethiopia; all imported. We made our way across to the tedj beit and ordered coffee. Alex and I were both thinking the same thing and not saying it. I broke the silence as we were finishing our coffee. "I hate the thought of leaving this dog here, she is obviously used to cars and is asking to be taken back to her old way of life". "I was thinking the same thing" said Alex. "Didn't like to mention it as it's not my car". A small boy then appeared and pointed out that we had his dog in our car. I could not speak enough Amharic to ask him how he had come by a spaniel bitch in such an outlying spot but merely told him to wait a bit. Alex and I finally decided that no amount of arguing would get us anywhere, that our duty was to rescue the dog and find it a home in Asmara; and that the best way of accomplishing this was to saunter nonchalantly back to the car and then suddenly jump in and drive off. This we did, but not without our young friend running alongside for twenty yards screaming at the top of his voice until our gathering speed literally forced him to let go of the door handle which he had been clutching. We both felt very sorry for the boy but as we looked at Sally our sorrow receded, and we felt a mixture of Don Quixote and St George as we began another descent.

"Alex remarked on the pastimes of the inhabitants"

"We stopped for a cup of coffee and some food in a local tedj beit"

"The Riya Plain stretched as far as the eye could see"

We were now somewhat behind schedule and decided not to stop for the night but to press on, taking it in turns to sleep. The 'passenger' merely put a pillow against the near-side window and leaned his head against it. Sleep of a sort was possible but it was usually light enough to extort the standard fine for bumping the front suspension. Both our dollar fine scores were now well into double figures. We stopped for a break at the foot of the Amba Lagi Pass and I ate some very tough meat. Alex couldn't face it and gave all his to Sally. As we drove off we could see the lights of a diesel lorry high above us negotiating the bends of the pass. When we ourselves approached the summit our headlights picked up scores of skeletons of Italian Army vehicles scattered all over the hillside, which bore silent testimony to the Allied bombing during the last great stand of the Italian Army against the British and Dominion forces. Overlooking the road at the highest point of the pass we could make out the rocky summit in which the Duke of Aosta had blasted a large bomb proof headquarters with a private cave for his own motor car. Amba Lagi was also the scene of a much later action in 1943, when the people of the Tiogre rose against Emperor Haile Sellese and were finally quelled by his newly formed army under British leadership. The rebels then had rolled gigantic boulders down the hillside to block the reinforcement route of the Emperor's forces. The two largest boulders, one of which was two or three yards in diameter, still caused traffic to take to the edge of the road in order to pass them, some thousands of feet above sea level.

We were too sleepy to record much of the countryside after Amba Lagi other than the fact that the native architecture had again changed, this time to small square stone built houses with flat roofs. Two hour spells at the wheel became too long and were reduced to an hour and a half. Around midnight we stopped at Quiha to stretch our legs and make ourselves some hot coffee. The directions for working our Primus said "Warm the main tank by holding in the hands for a few seconds. Petrol will then begin to ooze out of the nozzle". Our hands were so cold that nothing happened and we were obliged to hold a lighted match underneath the main tank to produce the required "ooze". The coffee warmed and revived us and we were soon on our way with Sally now in possession of most of the front seat. We passed two small towns in complete darkness and had not the foggiest idea where we were but imagined that we were still in Ethiopia as the road was still bad. In fact we had passed near the town of Adowa where Emperor Menelik defeated the Italian Army in the nineteenth century. One comfort was that we could not go wrong as there is not a single major fork or cross-roads in the hundreds of miles between Dessie and the Eritrean frontier. Dawn came and with it the normal waning of our fatigue and at around six o'clock we saw the town of Adigrat in the distance, and well to the East of our route.

We halted the car half a mile short of the town and by juggling about with the kit in the back I managed to get fairly horizontal, whilst Alex took the front seat for an hour or so of sleep. Bright warm sunshine woke us up at half-past seven and we lit the Primus for coffee and hot shaving water, and changed into more formal garb for the passage of the frontier post.

At a quarter past eight we drew up at the barrier across the road. No-one seemed to be about so I got out and examined it. It was fixed with an enormous padlock. I had just re-entered the car when an Ethiopian policeman appeared from nowhere with the number of my car scribbled on a dirty piece of paper and a desire to know where Sally had come from. Had we picked her up in Quoram? There might be only a single telephone line to Adigrat but it evidently worked!

We were escorted to the Yard of the Police Station and things did not look at all good. The dog belonged to the Governor of Quoram. My Amharic could not possibly stand up to the strain of explaining the mental processes which had led us into believing that we were 'doing the right thing' in making off with Sally (who was quite obviously not Sally at all but someone quite different!). In the end I left the Police Station virtually by force and drove to the local Brigade Headquarters of the Ethiopian Army. There I was lucky enough to meet a very charming Colonel whom I had known well in Addis Ababa, who could vouch for the fact that I was not the common dog-thief type, who knew I had two dogs in Addis Ababa, who could speak perfect English, who understood my story, and who finally assured me that the Governor of Quoram was married to the sister of this very Brigade Commander, to whom he promptly introduced me. He furthermore undertook to return the dog the following day on his way back to Dessie.

The Ethiopian official does not like accepting responsibility. In spite of the assurances of these two comparatively senior officers my Policeman friend would not let me out of his clutches until he had received the official counter-order by the superior officer who had ordered my arrest. We sat down in the telephone exchange where an unshaven old rascal rotated a handle for minutes on end shouting telephone 'signalese' which he had picked up from Italians and British with a few Ethiopian oaths flung in for good measure. We finally got through to Makella, the biggish Ethiopian town near Quiha which housed the Police Headquarters of Northern Ethiopia, to find that the superior officer concerned was out at the time. Things looked very black until the Brigade Commander put over a superb bit of oratory in which he pointed out that the Governor of Quoram's dog was to some degree the Governor's wife's dog, that the wife concerned was his sister and that therefore he too had some claim on the dog. After final assurances that I was in any case not fleeing the country but flying back on the Thursday plane to Addis Ababa, I was released from the hands of the Police and transferred to the mercies of the customs officials. After willingly paying everything I was asked for including stamps and the paper on which the triplicates were typed, we were free to go on our way. We were however in honour bound to stand drinks to our military friends. We were panting to get on our way, felt certain that we would miss our convoy, which we learned would leave Senafa, the Eritrean frontier post twenty miles to the North, at half-past two, but could not afford to offend these people who had been so kind to us.

I am very bad at drinking bottled beer quickly. Alex was appallingly slow. We were saved by our hosts who fairly sucked it down and were not in the least offended at the idea of helping us out by drinking the unexpired portions remaining in our bottles. But the rounds had to be bought in full and returned in full.

We finally left Adigrat hiccuping slightly and cursing all dogs in general and bitches in particular. Sally had deteriorated from "must have quite a pedigree don't you think" to "that bloody little mongrel" and "typical spaniel, gets into anybody's car". We were now in a no-mans-land away from official protection from Ethiopia and twenty miles from the start of the British protected convoys. We remained very alert, particularly Alex, who had had nothing to eat since the omelette at Waldia the previous afternoon. I think the bottled beer had revived him. An hour's drive brought us to what appeared to be a deserted barrier in the middle of the road, but of the formal type which one can pass to the right or left by turning slightly off the road. We passed it to the right and saw no sign of a soul. After five minutes I began to feel uneasy. I had received firm instructions to contact the Eritrean Police and join a convoy. If I didn't play the game other people might suffer. "Don't be a fool" said Alex, "Drive on, they don't care". "You're alright" I retorted, "but I happen to be in charge of the car". In the end conscience prevailed and I sheepishly turned round and went back to Senafa. Luckily there were no Europeans at the Police Guard Room by the barrier and the native Corporal could only say "Yes". "Has the convoy left?" "Yes". "A long time ago?" "Yes". "If I start now can I catch it?" "Yes". "Is it alright if I go on then?" "Yes". The poor chap never guessed that I didn't come from the South I suppose, as my car was pointing as if it had come from Asmara. "Come on Alex", I said, "We have had official permission to proceed". So off we went.

Our next worry was petrol. All our stock were now in the tank and the gauge told us that if we did 25 miles to the gallon we would probably make it. We could not guarantee this with the constant hill climbing, and decided to free wheel down all the hills. This resulted in our never catching the convoy, though we desperately wanted to tag unobtrusively on to its rear and pretend we'd been there the whole time when it entered Asmara.

The roads were now like billiard tables and the car felt like a Rolls. It all seemed so civilised this side of the frontier that we quite forgot about bandits. Suddenly two trucks swung round a bend, coming in the opposite direction. Two or three figures with rifles leaped into the road as they slowed down and took up positions of readiness. The leading truck stopped alongside us and out stepped our absent host whose house we had used in Dessie. He had a sten gun slung over his shoulder. The convoy was about ten miles ahead of us, he said. There had been no incidents for a week or so but this was just the spot for them when they did occur.

We thanked him for the use of his Dessie house and we both proceeded on our way. As soon as they were out of sight Alex and I both began cursing each other for not reminding each other to ask him for a gallon of petrol. It was too late. We continued coasting down all hills and arrived in Asmara at tea time with the petrol gauge registering zero. We bought petrol at the first filling station to make certain of reaching the centre of the town.

As we drove into the courtyard of the spotless C.I.A.A.O. in Asmara the fine score stood at 21 bumps to 20. Alex paid me a dollar. Any one of those forty-one bumps might have left us stranded in the middle of nowhere for goodness knows how long. Tea in the C.I.A.A.O. was Alex's first meal for 27 hours. He ate a piece of toast and two cakes.

Next morning (Tuesday) we made arrangements for getting convoyed down to Massawa. It was too late for that day's convoy and Wednesday's was a 'slow' convoy for heavy vehicles. An acquaintance at the club advised us to start two hours late and catch it up at a point where the danger of 'shifta', the local name for bandits, would be over and we would be allowed to drive on ahead in our own time. I have never before encountered such illogical logic, and of course we took his advice! Our next trouble occurred with the immigration authorities when we were trying to fix our passages for Thursday's plane to Addis Ababa. They wanted to know how we came to be requiring permits to leave Eritrea when our papers said that we hadn't even entered it. This took a little careful explaining but the explanations were nearly stalemated when I failed to resist the temptation of asking an official sitting at the next table which had nothing on it – not even an inkstand – if he was straining himself.

We left the Immigration Office with our task accomplished and declared the rest of the day a holiday. I met a friend who was soldiering out there and stationed adjacent to the airfield. He was none other than Pat Leeper, whose flat I had forbade him to enter after we had played the Devons at Rugby in 1936 and failed to realise that he was my host! We accepted an invitation to lunch with him on the Thursday before emplaning. We found Asmara a fine well laid-out town with good shops cinemas and restaurants. It is a good example of the result of the better type of Italian Colonial Administration and we learned that many Italians were still doing the same jobs that they had done when their country ruled Eritrea.

On Wednesday morning we bowled past the Massawa convoy rendezvous point an hour and a half late and began the long descent to the coastal plain. It was most interesting to follow the course of the railway which snakes its way from sea level to Asmara's 7,000 odd feet by a slightly different route; presumably because it required a gentler gradient. Every now and then the road and railway crossed either by bridge or level-crossing. A heat haze prevented our seeing the maximum distance, but even so the views we got into the plains below must have covered distances of from twenty to thirty miles.

Towards the bottom of the long descent we joined up with the rear of the convoy; great lumbering diesel lorries blowing filthy black smoke out behind them. One by one we passed them until we came to the main convoy halted by a large cafe. The temperature had risen a good fifteen degrees and I regretted that etiquette denied us our 'aertex order'.

A sweating corporal announced that the faster vehicles were to be allowed to proceed on ahead escorted by one man with a sten gun who was to sit in the rear vehicle, a bus. I announced the presence of our modest armoury and so we were given the job of leading the convoy, which included two other private cars, thus taking a total of four vehicles. We spanked along the excellent road and the hot air blew in through the window as if from an oven door. The bus never lost a yard on us and both Alex and I were thankful we were not travelling in it.

At last Massawa came into sight and we were soon crossing the long bridge which leads to the island on which the Port stands. At a quarter to one we were swimming in the fine sea water pool of the C.I.A.A.O. Hotel with its vast canvas canopy to keep the sun off the water. To us, accustomed to the comparatively cool climate of the Ethiopian Highlands, Massawa seemed unbearably hot and we spent all our time in the pool except when drinking, eating or doing business.

In the cooler part of the evening I made arrangements with the shipping agents and was distressed to find another car which had left Addis Ababa months earlier still sitting there. I hastily arranged for my car to be shipped by coaster to Port Sudan and then onwards from there. It appeared unfashionable for big ships to call at Massawa any more.

Our mission was thus accomplished and we seemed set fair for catching Thursday's plane for Addis Ababa. Wednesday night was spent buying sponges at a shilling each and eating oysters by the dozen at a waterside cafe. On Thursday morning, bright and early, we caught the Littorino, which is a diesel driven tram which tears along the railway line at high speed and lots of gear changing. This landed us in Asmara in time for lunch at the airport and answered the perplexities we had had on the way down as to where the railway had disappeared to every now and then. After a lunch which was too well lubricated and full of reminiscences, the big hitch occurred. The truck which Pat Leeper had laid on to take us and our luggage to the airport did not turn up. After frantic telephoning it was announced as being "on its way". With only five minutes to go before take-off the truck arrived. We bundled everything in and roared off. As soon as we stopped at the main entrance I began to run to the airport customs buildings determined to hold the plane whilst Alex coped with the luggage. The authorities did not look at our tickets or our passports but when I burst onto the tarmac the plane was revving up with doors closed and step ladder moving away. Luckily the second pilot spotted me out of his window, the revs died down, the steps were replaced and the door re-opened. At this moment Alex appeared with the luggage and our harassed looking host. We tore across the tarmac and up the steps. The door was closed and away we taxied. At six o'clock that evening Phoebe and I were sipping cocktails at the British Embassy in Addis Ababa. I had breakfasted in Massawa and lunched in Asmara, which made our long and exhausting car journey seem rather remote and belonging to another world.

✧

The Bells took us to the airport and saw us off for Aden, where we had to wait for several days to catch a troop ship home. It was extremely hot and we spent most of the time at an Officers Club beach in a small bay which was guarded by shark-proof nets. Half of it was permanently shaded by a huge sun-proof canopy, which enabled us to swim and sit around without getting fried.

The most memorable event took place during our departure. Half way from the jetty to our Troopship, which lay invitingly a few hundred yards offshore, surrounded by sunlit ripples, Phoebe suddenly went a bit white and tight lipped. It wasn't seasickness because the launch was purring steadily and smoothly along. "Are you alright?" I asked. No reply. The moment we had climbed the ladder and reached the boarding deck she could not wait to rush to our allotted cabin and await the arrival of our suitcases. As soon as they arrived she fell upon hers, tore at the locks and opened it. "Oh my God, they're not there" she cried. She had left her jewel case at the hotel. I had approximately 35 minutes to find the officer of the watch, organise a launch to take me ashore, sprint along the front to the Crescent Hotel and up the stairs to our room. It had of course already been ransacked by the staff for any pickings, who counter-attacked me by saying that one of the wire coat hangers was missing from the hanging cupboard and they were sending for the Police. I did not have their damned hanger but was not in a position to prove it. I retreated as fast as I had arrived and no doubt increased their suspicions. They had won game, set and match. I was glad at that moment that Phoebe had lost the diamond and platinum regimental brooch, which I had given her as a wedding present, at a dance in Addis Ababa. At least it had fallen among friends. In those days family moves for soldiers were one of the perks of military life, a wonderful free cruise with nothing to do except relax and relish the fact that spirits were around sixpence a tot, or forty gins to a pound. No wonder we all developed bad habits which took quite a few years of civilian life to shake off.

Chapter XX

Return to Shorncliffe Camp

Shortly after our arrival home and my being granted a month's leave, I went to the War Office and explained how I had again been diverted from regimental duty in Ethiopia. I pointed out that I must be brought up to date by serving a tour of duty in the British Army on the Rhine (BAOR), where one of our Home Counties Brigade's regiments, The Royal Fusiliers, was serving. It was agreed that this posting would be arranged and I was granted indefinite leave until a vacancy occurred.

I also informed the Military Secretary's Branch that I had signed my adverse report in Ethiopia under duress and that it was blatantly unjust. The officer who interviewed me assured me that this had been assumed and that it had been ignored; and that my name had already been put into the Grade I pool, which was the list of officers recommended and qualified for Lt. Colonel's staff appointments. He took the opportunity of trying to get me to enlarge on the failings of the general. I refused point blank and told him that I had fulfilled what I had believed to be my duty at the time and would say nothing further.

We had just settled down with Phoebe's parents at Shawford, near Winchester, as their house at Bishopstoke had been taken over at the beginning of the war as a 'Wrenery' for thirty Wrens. Since our exact future was uncertain, we decided to send Michael to Eastacre, a Winchester pre-prep school which Phoebe's brother Jim had attended. The tragic loss of Christopher made Michael even more precious and my heart bled for him. Eight is very young to go to a boarding school, but it was normal in those days, and he knew that his home-from-home with his grandparents was only five miles down the road, and that he would be with them at half-terms and holidays, whatever our future movements might be.

I was so anxious about his welfare that on the day following the one when we threw him in at the deep end I drove into Winchester, parked my car a short distance from the school, and crept up to a stretch of the boundary fence which had a hedge which provided cover and which also enabled me to peer through the gaps. I selected the time of their mid-morning break and was relieved to see him playing happily with another boy with whom he had obviously made friends. The headmaster Mr Beale was an extremely kind and likeable man and all the boys called him Bir, which was a mixture of Sir and his name.

My forebodings about the uncertainty of our future proved valid. Firstly Phoebe's appendix blew up. It had been grumbling in Holletta, but a course of penicillin had quietened it and we thought the infection had subsided. We were proved wrong, and she was whipped into hospital in Winchester. Secondly within days my 'indefinite leave' came to an end.

The simultaneous wars in Korea and Malaya had caused a reorganisation of the 1st Battalion of my Regiment, which had to split into two major units. It had to go off and fight in Malaya, and to leave sufficient officers and men to continue its current duties of training reinforcements for Korea. It had been hotch-potch of officers and men from all the seven regiments in what had become, for administrative and training purposes, the Home Counties Brigade Training Depot. All those who were members of my Regiment plus a few others to make them up to strength, were posted to 1/RWK, and officers from the other regiments in the Home Counties Brigade were posted in to the Home Counties Brigade Depot to make it up to strength.

Having just returned from overseas I was destined to be one of them. The War Office was really human and understanding. The officer who had promised that I would be posted to Germany rang up to explain that I had been asked for, by name, by Tony Martyn, who commanded 1/RWK, and that since I had completed my official four weeks leave I was available. He also pointed out that the Brigade Depot was training re-enforcements for Korea and that I would in every way be engaged in regimental duty.

I duly arrived at Moore Barracks, Shorncliffe, which was adjacent to Napier Barracks where I had first joined my Regiment. It had then been occupied by the Royal Berkshire Regiment with whom Phoebe's father and brother had served. It was strange to be living in a mess once more and for longer than we expected, as Phoebe's surgeon made it clear that she would need time to convalesce. I set about looking for a quarter and was able to find one at New Romney, currently occupied by a captain who was leaving it before Christmas. I attended to all the details of the forthcoming take-over, including the purchase of any odd bits of furniture he had bought to supplement the existing inventory. I then got on with life at regimental duty, which I had not experienced since getting wounded in Leros seven years earlier.

I was soon appointed President of the Audit Board and found one or two skeletons in the cupboards. I had a talk to Tony Martyn and asked how he wanted things handled. I wanted to give him a chance to get things sorted out and re-presented but he said, quite rightly, that there was to be no covering up.

The Regular Non-Commissioned Officers (NCOs) who were training men for Korea were first class and the recruits, many of whom were National Servicemen, responded well. Many had held quite responsible jobs between leaving school and their call-up, and possessed more intelligence than regular recruits. I was put in command of the Advanced Training Wing, and I concentrated on things which I knew would stand them in good stead in Korea, particularly quick accurate shooting and the ability to move quietly and confidently at night.

As far as games were concerned, I observed wistfully that Rugby Football was being played and had always believed that my Rugby days were over. The outside of my right leg was still super-sensitive as a result of the sciatic nerve injury at Leros, and some of the nerves had grown down into the wrong channels, so that if I tickled the outside of my calf, I would feel it in my toes or the side of my foot. I also felt as I was walking on a walnut the whole time and having been on the staff for seven years had not worn boots for the entire period. I wondered, however, if I would get away with it if I played on the right wing, where I would tend to be tackled from the left as I ran down the right hand touchline. In the end I decided to give it a go and captained the Training Depot against my Regiment.

I discovered that I could still run like a hare and side-step at full speed. A tall 2/Lieutenant was playing full back. He was the son of 'Swifty' Howlett who had been a fast bowler who played for the Army and had been a captain and company commander at Napier Barracks when I joined the Regiment. His son was to win the Military Cross in Malaya and to become a full General and a NATO Commander. I am appalled to realise that he is now a knighted retired officer and wonder what I am doing in this world! By the time Phoebe joined me I was once more a hardened infantryman, but had still never been seen in a pair of boots. We had a good Christmas at Orchard Cottage, New Romney, but it was bitterly cold and any dripping tap caused icicles.

Early in the new year of 1951 we were able to move to a quarter in Hythe, which was near the road which winds up the hill to Shorncliffe Camp, missing out Sandgate. It reduced my daily turn-round mileage by twenty-five miles and Phoebe and the children, who were with us for the Christmas Holidays, were no longer so cut off. She frequently drove me up to the Barracks and could then use the car for shopping and socialising. We found a Convent School for Jill which took day girls and boarders. My front door was only eighty yards from a wicket gate which led to the Hythe Golf Club and about ninety-five yards from the nearest green. As a result I joined the Club and could nip in and practice chipping or play a few holes any time I pleased in the evenings. In those days less people played golf and most clubs were pleasantly under-subscribed.

After my Regiment had left for Malaya early in 1951 I took over the Rugby at the Home Counties Brigade Depot and we built quite a useful team. One of our sources of players was the Junior Leaders Wing, to which all National Service recruits who were considered potential officer material were channelled. Many had played in the First Fifteens of good Rugby playing schools and needed little help from me. The threequarter who played inside me on the right wing was John Rae. He was eventually commissioned and then went to Cambridge and just missed his Blue as a flank forward. He went on to become headmaster of Westminster School, and is now a television personality. Another good player, Jumbo Wood, had already been commissioned and was an almost unwilling newcomer to Rugby Football, but had too good a physique to be overlooked. He was six foot three inches tall and weighed fifteen and a half stone. He made very quick progress and never regretted being press-ganged. The following season I got him accepted by Blackheath, and he went on to lead the Army pack. In his third season he played in the prestigious Army/Navy match.

One of the unwelcome additions to the hazards of Rugby, which had rarely been encountered before World War II, was illegal violence off the ball. I was very much against the usual tit for tat behaviour which only escalates the violence, so I laid down 'organised reprisal'. One of our flank forwards was six foot two and fourteen and a half stone, named Corporal Tyler. He was a member of the training staff and packed a lightning punch. He was known to the troops as 'The Bosun'. If anyone was illegally kicked, punched or trodden on he was to let Corporal Tyler know at the first opportunity but do nothing else. The Bosun would pick a moment when his victim and the referee were separated by a loose scrum and lay him out stone cold. He would then be seen bending over him and asking him tenderly "are you alright old chap?"; a better system than constant fights.

Throughout the Summer of 1951 I was hard at work supervising the training up of reinforcements for Korea. In the evenings and at weekends I tried to improve my golf, and eventually was able to play a round about fourteen over par. During this summer Guy Sawyer, Phoebe's father, came to stay with us and was able to witness the Hythe Carnival Week 'Venetian' Regatta. This was a procession similar to those run in most towns with decorative floats sponsored by various societies and retailers, but in this case on narrow barges, not lorries, which glided down the canal only twenty yards from our front door.

In the late Summer I learned that we were being moved to Canterbury, and I was asked how many rail tickets I would require to move my Advanced Training Wing, which included the Junior Leaders, to their new home. On the spur of the moment, remembering that the Infantry should not forget their legs, I said "None thank you, we'll march". I had in that grandiose moment forgotten that the days of horses were over and that I would either have to march myself or lose face. I went into secret training and was still never seen in boots, but wore them in plain clothes for solo walks of five miles, nine miles, and twelve miles in successive weeks. The distance to our barracks in Canterbury was around sixteen miles.

I had quite a problem with my right foot, which had tender points which I had not been aware of when wearing shoes, but by fitting pads in one or two places I got round the problem, and when the great day arrived I appeared in boots and gaiters for the first time in public. A lot of eyebrows were raised, and even Company Sergeant Major Saddington, who had not been let into my secret, allowed a flicker of surprise and pleasure to light up his craggy face. I took command of the parade of over 300 officers and men, plus the Corps of Drums of one of the Home Counties Regiments, and marched them off. There was tremendous applause from a welter of spectators as we marched through Shorncliffe Camp and past the Brigade Colonel Joe Parry, who took the salute. We had formed up as a two company battalion, with Saddington acting as the Regimental Sergeant Major; so for the formal march-pasts we were strung out with him and the leading company commander following me in single file with pomp and ceremony.

I had picked a route which avoided the main roads and went up to Etchinghill and then up Stone Street, an old Roman road. As soon as we were clear of the built-up area we formed a 'three' and I set a good pace the whole way. I learned later that a certain amount of money changed hands between those who thought I would not make it and those who felt I might. The Drums were a great help and we only took six hours including hourly halts and one twenty minute halt for haversack rations.

After our final 'march to attention' with sloped arms as we passed through Canterbury with drums and fifes in full song, had inspected our soldiers feet and vanished into the Mess, I was able to have a peep at my own. In spite of my training I had gained a few blisters, but what was worse, the athletes foot germs which had been lurking in my boots for eight years had sneaked out and into my toes. I still have to powder them daily with Mycil or Mycota powder to keep the scourge at bay. East Kent is a vast peninsula between the Thames Estuary and the Channel, with Canterbury in its centre, hence the surrounding countryside leads to nowhere, is unspoiled and dotted with picturesque oast-houses and orchards; the Garden of England.

We were allotted an extremely good quarter in Old Park Barracks along the Dover Road which housed the Depot of the Buffs. There were three of these well built houses near the Buffs' Mess and we had the end one. The middle house was bigger and occupied by the Brigade Colonel and his wife

"Our final 'march to attention'... we passed through Canterbury with drums and fifes in full song"

"...dotted with picturesque oast-houses and orchards; the Garden of England"

Brenda Parry, whom we got to know extremely well. The official title of my quarter was No.3 M.O.Q. (standing for Married Officers' Quarters). I immediately christened it Old Park Lodge and had a fine hardwood board painted with this new title screwed to our front gate.

My place of work was at the barracks at the North side of Canterbury, quite near the Cathedral and over a mile away from our house. I looked round for a Rugby ground and discovered that no such thing existed. I insisted that we should have one and gained immediate support from Joe Parry who had played Rugby Football for the Army. I managed to get a good hockey ground converted, and remember saying "and lets have decent high goal posts and not some of those which look like a soccer goal which has grown short horns". We finished off with a splendid ground with towering posts, and my recreation then became to build up a team worthy of it.

The story of the 1951/2 Rugby Season is a saga in itself. 128 teams are entered for the 'Draw of the Inter Regimental Cup', and the enthusiasm which I exuded caught on with the whole Depot. Our first match was against the Life Guards at Windsor and there was much fast beating of hearts in the bus on the way there. I had heard that their officers tended to wear their hats at meals but was quite unprepared to witness it. I wondered whether they only did it when strangers were present, because only a few wore hats; perhaps as an act of defiance.

Their Rugby XV were impressively large, and I wondered how our young side of almost schoolboys would handle the situation. I need not have worried. They tore into them and gave them a good walloping. This was just what we needed to settle us down. The enormous list of 128 teams was down to 64 when we received the next draw, and after two more matches it was down to sixteen. We were suddenly only two matches away from the semi-finals if we kept winning; and we did. In those days a regimental pack which averaged over twelve stone was considered reasonable, but our success brought volunteers from officers and men who had given up Rugby prematurely through lack of incentive, and we finished up with a pack which averaged thirteen and a half stone. In the middle of the back row was Pte. Campbell-Lamerton, who weighed sixteen and a half stone and was very fast. Once he had learned to tackle and throw his weight about, he became a formidable No.8. I had told him that if he would unwind he could become an international. He finished up as a Scottish International and captain of the British Lions.

We went on to make the semi-finals and were drawn against the RAMC. Although they were numerically large and had a world-wide strength of playing doctors they were allowed to enter the 'Inter Regimental'. Anyone who has seen the finals of the Inter Hospital Cup will know what a wealth of hard playing medics are around, and there were a number of County players lined up against us. We had a half a stone per man advantage in the scrums and were leading 12-3 half way through the second half. I had even begun to relax. Then one of our backs was carried off with a torn leg muscle and Corporal Tyler was taken out of the scrum to take his place as a centre three quarter.

Our half a stone per man advantage became half a stone lighter with the remaining seven losing over fourteen stone, and the difference was soon felt. Likewise, Tyler as a three quarter lacked the finesse of the injured player, who had played for Bristol University. We finished up with a draw, and under the rules of the competition had to play ten minutes each way of extra time. With a man short in the pack the forwards began to tire and we lost by one try.

The game was played at Blackheath and all the officers and the wives of married officers turned up to watch. Even Bill Oliver, who was by then Chief Instructor of the Imperial Defence College, was on the touchline. It did my reputation no harm and I later learned on the grapevine that, although only 36 years old, I was one of those short-listed as the next Commanding Officer of our First Battalion.

On the re-organisation following our move to Canterbury I found myself commanding everything except the recruits from the various Regimental Depots being groomed for entry to Eaton Hall, which was a mini-Sandhurst for National Service officers. We seemed to have far more men than at Shorncliffe, and I found myself spending more time in my office.

C.S.M. Saddington was replaced by C.S.M. Whitlock. He had been one of the fastest and safest drivers of 15cwt trucks in the Palestine days and we were old comrades in arms. To gain any further promotion it was necessary for him to pass his First Class Certificate of Education, and he was one of those people whose proper understanding of mathematics had eluded him. We used to have lessons in my office when the pressures of our duties allowed, and I put him through the Ethiopian routine of simultaneous equations and the like. He was successful with his exams and has never ceased to be grateful. He keeps in touch and I have stayed with him. He has made a mint of money in property deals and even owns and manages blocks of flats.

The history of my endless shifts from proper regimental duty continued. Joe Parry summoned me to his office and asked me to accept the appointment of Brigade Adjutant. This was a newly invested major's job and was technically regimental duty; but Joe was not commanding the regiments in the Home Counties Brigade, merely the amalgam of Depot and Training Centre. I explained to him how I had been successively diverted from regimental duty into staff appointments and the need to get an up to date recommendation for command. "My dear Robert" he replied, "The appointment is classified as regimental duty and as I shall be writing your confidential report, you need not worry". I bowed to this logic, was flattered by his offer and delighted that I only had to walk eighty yards to his office each morning and that Phoebe would hence have full use of the car. I accepted without worry or reservation. I soon found that there was very little work to do in this job and my brain nearly went to sleep. It did however give me much more time to concentrate on coaching and organising the Rugby Football, and to devote more time to my family during school holidays.

   A telling example of how my brain did not function unless it was properly occupied is that when I first went to my new office with Joe Parry, I switched on because it was a new job and needed studying. I remember Joe looking on with admiration when I was able to take an incoming telephone call whilst already talking on another line, and talked to two people on different telephones, one to each ear. I carried on separate conversations, covering the mouthpiece of one alternatively to block the conversation with the other, but listening to both simultaneously. Three months later when I had realised that there was not really more than two hours real work a day, my mind switched off and when I made a long distance call, and in those days the operator would ask "what is your number please?" I would have to look at the instrument to see what my number was! I went to the Medical Officer and asked if I was going barmy. He gave the question careful consideration and replied, "You are suffering from boredom and have the sort of brain which shuts down when not exercised. Believe me, when you get any challenge your brain will spark at once, not gradually". I was not sure that I believed him, but he was quite right, and this is precisely what happened.

   I was asked for by Eastern Command to be an instructor at their pre-Staff College courses and had to go and live in London for a few weeks. I slipped straight into a tight schedule, with students' papers to be corrected and taken back to my club, where I lived for that period, and would mark them for two or three hours every evening. I did not even notice that there was a problem of concentration and rejoiced in the pressure of work in a martyred sort of way. My annual confidential report came up on my return, and I was genuinely surprised at its contents. Both Joe Parry and the General commanding our District, who was based in Dover Castle, wrote in glowing terms; but the icing on the cake was the accolade from the C in C Eastern Command who ticked the box containing the words "Is he fit to rise to the highest positions in the Army?" or words to that effect. In those days we did not see our reports unless they were adverse and needed to be initialled by the victim; but Bill Oliver, who was Chief of Staff at Eastern Command, sneaked me a photo-copy.

Joe Parry and I had a splendid social life, being chauffeur-driven by an Army driver round to all the seven regimental depots where we would be feted and generally fawned upon by the Depot Commanders. The driver, named Watts, was the son of one of our Captains and Quartermasters, and he would listen to our conversations in the back and forget himself and chip in. We would give him a rocket, but he never lost the habit. Sometimes he corrected us and was infuriatingly right. We would pick our date for visiting the Royal Sussex Depot during Goodwood week, and the Royal Fusiliers at the Tower of London on some suitable London social occasion such as Trooping the Colour, when we had VIP seats on Horse Guards Parade.

When King George VI died, we and our wives were allotted VIP seats on Horse Guards Parade to witness the funeral procession. I was very moved by the forlorn figure of the Duke of Kent, then a boy at Eton, and the only senior mourner following the gun carriage on foot in a morning coat, as opposed to some military uniform.

Down at the Barracks in the middle of Canterbury a diverting problem was being enacted. The Kray brothers had been called up for National Service and duly arrived with a batch of recruits. They had no intention of laying down their lives for South Korea and soon made this plain. They simply refused to obey any form or order which displeased them. They soon found themselves serving a short sentence in our own guardroom but this meant nothing to them. They would not even pick up a broom except to threaten someone with it. They eventually received a longer sentence which transported them to a proper Military Prison. They won their battle of dodging all drafts for Korea and were eventually released to prey upon the British public and become hardened criminals, now still serving life sentences.

A more pleasant experience for me was to receive an invitation from Bill Oliver to make up a party of three to be the guests of Martin Coles-Harman, the owner of Lundy Island, to cull some of his older stags. Harman had built up a rapport with my Regiment after his second son had won a posthumous V.C. at Kohima. It was a coincidence that I had visited his last resting place when I photographed Jim Sawyers' grave and that I had been an exact contemporary of his older brother at Oundle.

We duly met in London to take the train to Ilfracombe, from whence we were flown by helicopter to Lundy. The Lundy trip was an unforgettable experience. Harman was a millionaire who had done a stretch of 'porridge' for his part in the Harman and Hatry swindles and was now an almost paranoiac defender of his rights over his island, which he regarded as his independent kingdom. Although there was only one modest mansion in which he lived, a pub and a few cottages which were called 'the village', the local currency consisted of coins of his own minting with his head on one side and the appropriate number of puffins on the other, one puffin being worth one penny. All mail leaving Lundy also had to have a one puffin stamp on it in addition to the appropriate British postage stamp. Although we had one formal meal with him at the mansion, we were put up at the small pub in comfortable rooms and with full board.

We were invited to stalk and shoot around a dozen of the older Sika and Red Deer stags. The proposed routine was that we would rise early each morning and stalk and shoot before breakfast. In the event, because the few local islanders had nothing to do in the evenings except go to the pub, and more so when there were new faces, voices and hands dipping into pockets to buy rounds of beer, we found ourselves climbing up the rickety stairs in the small hours and waking up too late to reach the best areas before sunrise. After two of our 'early' mornings our score was Bill one, me one, and Dicky nil. On the third morning I really was up early as I felt that we were letting down the Regiment, and both Bill and I added one more each to our score. I could have had two, but just as I was about to fire at a stag that I had stalked to little over fifty yards, it must have heard me and looked up, and we stared eyeball to eyeball. By my own rules, which are that I had lost the stalk, I lowered my rifle and went back to breakfast. I decided to go out on my own after breakfast when I realised that we had only shot a total of four stags, and I managed to surprise a red stag which walked across my front only forty yards away. My first heart shot had absolutely no effect on it and it just continued to walk. I couldn't believe it. My second shot, which aimed slightly further aft, produced the same effect. I aimed my third shot another inch and a half aft of my second shot, but believed that something must have gone wrong with my sights. To my relief the stag dropped stone dead. When I reached it I found there were three holes, each one and a half inches apart. I was using my converted .303" game rifle with normal ammunition. The first two shots had passed clean through the rib cage just in front of the heart without hitting bone, and the third had pierced the heart after hitting a rib.

After getting over this extraordinary experience I did not expect to have any further success, but moved to another valley overlooking the sea and surprised a grazing Sika stag in low heather and dropped it with a single shot. Another stag got up from the heather about twenty yards to its right and started to gallop towards a track which would lead it round a cliff path to the next valley. I knelt down and took aim at a point on the path just ahead of it, and was lucky enough to get my timing right. It was bowled over and rolled down the cliff and into the sea. Luckily the current carried it along the steep cliffs and it was eventually washed up on a beach near

Harman's mansion. The result was that we produced a score of seven stags, which was far more impressive (or less shameful) than four.

Harman presented us with the antlered heads which we had earned and a haunch of venison each to take back to our families. I was fairly stretched financially at that time and could not afford to have my five heads mounted. I had however learned from my Indian days that if one plants the heads so that only the antlers stick out, mother Nature's inhabitants of the earth will pick off everything except the bone. For three months a row of antlers grew in our small vegetable garden, and at the end of that time my Indian tutors had proved themselves correct.

Another interesting interlude was a Battalion Commanders course with the French Army at Sissonne, near Reins. Major Tony Lewis in the Dorset Regiment was the only other foreign officer on the course, and we teamed up and travelled together.

It was an interesting experience, some of the instructors having fought with the Free French in the Eighth Army being well up to date, and others having collaborated with Marshal Petain and the Germany Army having a different viewpoint and an inferiority complex which made them rather prickly.

Tony and I found the hours of work trying, as we would breakfast at 7.0 am with a croissant and a cup of coffee and then at around 10 am be absolutely ravenous, having missed our eggs and bacon!

On one such morning we were out on an exercise and slipped into a village cafe for some ham sandwiched between two slices of baguette and some red wine. In walked another syndicate with some of our friends who had fought in North Africa. "What are you doing Robaire, drinkin red wine with 'am? You mus' drink white wine with 'am". Whereupon he shot my red wine through the open doorway into the road and bought me a glass of white wine. This was the beginning of my education as a wine-buff which has continued to this day and developed an expensive palate.

Just as the Royal Navy produced a daily rum ration, so the French Army received a vast wine ration. This was pooled in the Mess and we were served with the correct wine at every course. Sometimes no less than four carafes of varying sizes would be served at dinner.

One week-end we went to Luxemburg and enjoyed the delights of that beautiful Principality, including a sumptuous lunch at which we both ate snails for the first time. To our amazement they did not taste earthy in their garlic flavoured butter sauce and we loved them.

On our second free week-end we went to Paris. The Arc de Triomphe was being run at Longchamps, and we found ourselves being invited on to the top of a coach owned by one of England's leading bookmakers, which was sited in with all the other coaches in the centre of the racecourse. We were fed with cold chicken and limitless champagne.

Before we left Sissonne the Assistant Commandant, who was an Eighth Army man took us out to dinner and treated us royally. I remember tender frogs legs as a starter and that the main dish was a very young veal cooked in cream and washed down with still champagne with unforgettable flavour.

The Military Attache in Paris was Brigadier Sir Geoffrey MacNab who had been our Brigade Major when I first joined at Shorncliffe. He arranged for us to spend a whole week in Paris at the end of the course so that we could be properly debriefed on our impressions of the French Army, and arranged for us to be made honorary members of the French Officers Club. This meant that we were able to live in first class accommodation in that expensive city for a mere pittance. We took the opportunity of getting our wives to join us. Sir Geoffrey has always been a great friend and admirer of my Regiment and our comparatively rare stays at the Rag in St James's Square happily often coincide with his. he is one of those rare men who has no enemies and deserves none.

In due course I received news that I had been allocated one of the seven Infantry vacancies at the Joint Services Staff College Course starting in January 1953. The first thing I did was to buy a reliable second-hand car for Phoebe, as I would need mine to drive from Latimer, near Amersham in Buckinghamshire every weekend, or see nothing of my family for six months. I found that bigger cars which had been more expensive when new were better value and more reliable, and with petrol still quite inexpensive it made sense to buy one. Phoebe enjoyed the reliability and comfort of the large Morris saloon which I bought her, but was obliged to hear some of the soldiers shout "Taxi!" as she drove through the barracks. It was senior enough to have a rather square look form behind.

Not long after hearing that I had been selected for the JSSC, Bill Oliver telephoned me and invited me to lunch with him at the Imperial Defence College in London. I felt flattered and drove up in my dark London suit and highly polished black shoes. After a drink of sherry from a cabinet in his private office, Bill took me into lunch with the students, who were all comparatively senior officers. We then went back to his office where coffee was served and he came to the point. After a couple of 'harrumphs' he suddenly said "I want you to make friends with the Admirals and Air Marshals of the future whilst you are at Latimer. You are a future Colonel of the Regiment". For the uninitiated, the honorary office of Colonel of a Regiment is normally held by a General, or the most senior officer or retired officer available. I naturally took this to heart and left on 'cloud nine'. My future seemed assured and it was reassuring to know that the remarks made in my last confidential report seemed beginning to be realised.

Chapter XXI

Joint Services Staff College

The Joint Services Staff College (now called the Joint Services Defence College) was, and probably still is, a 'must' for any Army Officer who was going to reach the top. It cost thousands of pounds per officer per course and opened a new door to one's global military awareness and thinking. The Naval Officers thought it "an important step", but one of the RAF Officers confided to me that they regarded it as the "kiss of death". This was probably because they would certainly face desk jobs after the course rather than flying jobs, but for some it might have been because they found themselves out of their depth and were better at flying than planning. Our last big individual exercise was a paper on the Soviet Union's current global strategy, and was complicated by Stalin's death in the middle of the course. The slant was changed to a brief on the above to his successor.

Buddy Rogers, who was an RAF Group Captain and became a great friend of mine, said he would teach me to fly in exchange for letting him crib my paper, and he faithfully carried out his part of the bargain. His speciality was flying training and he was a wonderful sportsman who had played both Rugby and Cricket for the RAF. He was one of those who abhorred paperwork! We used to fly a Chipmunk two-seater trainer from Booker Airfield, which was only about ten miles from Latimer and two from High Wycombe. He put me through the lot including stalls and finally said that had I been flying legally in the RAF he would have sent me off solo. I then put in some twin-engined training in an Oxford with Group Captain Dicky Abrahams, who also took a lot of trouble and would cut out an engine when I was flying to make sure that I reacted correctly. He once did it very shortly after take-off, and I could have done without that.

The syllabus was all-embracing, from the planning and paperwork side to practical experience of the weapons and equipment of all three Services. We also had a very distinguished set of lecturers. I was, I suppose, a born 'enfant terrible' and could never resist having a crack when a lecturer seemed to need sharpening up or correcting. When Sir Vincent Tewson, the then TUC boss, asked the usual "any questions?" I asked him if he did not agree that the British Trades Union movement had sprung up in the last century to correct the exploitation of low paid women and child workers, and rightly so; but not to interfere with dock workers in East Africa, which they were then doing. He used the old trick of talking off the point for about five minutes, and when he finally stopped with an unctious smile of satisfaction I stood up and said coldly "You have not answered my question". There was tumultuous laughter from the audience and he turned a little red. With Labour governments in power for so many years after that, I wonder if my leg-pull backfired on me and blocked my later promotions. Another victim of mine was the Director of Staff Duties, who was trying to explain why the College might have to be closed down for financial reasons. I stood up and made a good case for its retention. He riposted by asking me the sort of question utilised by the Pharisees in the New Testament: "If you were in my position", he said, "and you had to choose whether to disband your regiment or this College, what would your answer be?" "Someone else's regiment" I answered in a flash. Once more there was laughter all round, in which the General reluctantly joined.

Our visits to Service demonstrations and civilian establishments were fascinating and included living aboard an aircraft carrier, carrying out an exercise in a submarine, flying in jet aircraft, attending debates in the 'distinguished strangers' gallery at the Houses of Parliament, and even a trip down the Thames to see the various points of interest. I could have done without the visit to the Sewage Works where raw sewage is filtered, purified, and finally offered in a clear state for drinking out of a glass. Although assured that all London drank it, I felt that I was too close to the source and turned down their offer. I never drank water as such in those days except in tea or coffee.

The aircraft carrier HMS Eagle, which was our home while we were based at Portsmouth for several days, had the misfortune to be our host for the Coronation Review of our Queen. I say this because whereas all the ships, including the foreign contingent, had their crews in spotless uniforms all sized in perfect rows for HMS Britannia, with the Queen on her bridge, to glide past, HMS Eagle had a motley collection of chaps in turbans, glengarries and the odd trilby belonging to the odd boffin, mixed up with the service caps of the officers of the three British Armed Services on the course. We were not sized and must have looked awful. Our wives were also honoured guests on that day but were hidden below for the sail past. The wife of one of the crew, who was also on board as a guest, gave birth to a baby when our guns fired their salute as Britannia sailed past, and was later appropriately christened Aquila.

I have a vivid memory of the first evening on the Eagle when Dick Schaeffer, an American Air Force Colonel, discovered that gin was only two pence per tot and remarked "Say, the whole time we're not drinkin we're losin money!" Another incident which I will never forget was when we were exercising at full speed with a destroyer racing alongside. We had been invited to observe from the flight deck, which has no railings anyway. Someone then fired a rocket, which was attached to a light line, at the destroyer's bridge. This was caught adroitly by one of its crew and they then hauled a heavier line across from HMS Eagle which our crew had attached to the middle of the light line. It then had two lines aboard and made the heavier one fast to their bridge. A bosun's chair with a roller above it was then suspended from the heavier line and hauled into a position overhanging the sea. Because the carrier and the destroyer were both rolling a little it was not possible to make our end fast so it was handled by ten sailors wearing non-slip gym shoes and a Petty Officer who was the 'coach' of this 'tug of war' team and waved them back and forth to compensate for the rolling.

The Captain then called for a volunteer from the visitors to be hauled across to the destroyer, where he would be refreshed with a large tot of rum. We all blanched at the thought and waited for some idiot to go forward. I felt that we should not let our distinguished College down, and like at Oundle when I was beaten for hanging on the changing room rails when everyone had done it, I found myself walking forward like the village idiot. The moment of getting into the bosun's chair with the grey sea below me was bad enough, but the sight of the team of sailors moving forward to stop the line from being snapped and then pulling back was even worse. Two sailors on the destroyer began to haul me across, using the light line. Once half-way across I began to feel better, until I realised that if my tug of war team slipped we would all go into the drink and I would drown as I was tied to my chair. Eventually I reached the bridge of the destroyer and the Captain shook my hand and made a sign for someone to come forward with a glass of rum. "Can't I get out of this damned chair first?" I pleaded. "No, you're going straight back" he replied. "Drink up before the sea gets worse". I knocked back the rum and did not enjoy it one bit, but Navy rum in those days was very strong and before I was half way back I was already beginning to feel braver. I was heaved aboard the carrier complete with chair, to loud applause from my fellow students. Better, I now felt, than the icy silence of the fifty guilty boys at St Anthony who had funked their beatings.

We had quite an adventure when we had a day in a submarine. We were supposed to be trying to manoeuvre into a position to fire a torpedo at a target ship, whilst a number of corvettes and destroyers hunted us. Our course had been split up into groups of around thirty into various submarines, and these were in addition to the normal crews. We were invited to wander round wherever we wished and to ask any questions we liked. I was standing near the control centre, where the captain or officer of the watch could see what was going on through the periscope and plan our moves. Suddenly we started to point down at the bows and the Captain ordered the forward hydroplanes to bring the bows up. We still went down and I saw the depth indicator needle moving steadily in the wrong direction. The Captain suddenly shouted "Stop engines, blow forward ballast tanks" but we still descended. I had become slightly claustrophobic about being trapped under water after my Chindwin experience and thought for an instant "Oh my God we're in for a harrowing experience". At that moment the penny dropped in the Captain's head and he shouted on the tannoy "All visiting officers move aft from the bows immediately". We apparently had around a ton of visitors up forward and they had nearly put the cat amongst the pigeons. The needle I had been watching reversed its direction and I breathed a sigh of relief.

Another spree was a visit to a Royal Air Force station in East Anglia. We were all flown in various aircraft and in my case a Meteor. Owing to my very few recent hours of flying training I was allowed to fly dual and soon made myself feel airsick by giving myself too much 'negative G'. This means flying an outward forward curve instead of an inward forward curve as in a loop. One's stomach is pressed upwards and I was solely responsible for my fate. Whereas sea-sickness usually vanishes as soon as the movement ceases by entry into sheltered waters or going ashore, air-sickness goes on and on for hours after one reaches terra firma. I was not even physically sick but just felt awful and could not face tea or even dinner hours later. Fortunately I had been able to fly moderately low over our house at West Mersea before climbing up and doing myself that bad favour.

In order to further the cause of 'International Détente' I invited Dick Schaeffer and his wife and children to spend a weekend with us at Canterbury. I though that the grown-ups would be interested in the history of the Cathedral, as the centre of the British Protestant Religion, and the bloody end of Thomas a Beckett. Phoebe gallantly played nanny to the two children, who took her for a real ride, saying that they were allowed to do this and that including using their beds as trampolines. Meanwhile, as guide, I did my stuff with their parents, even showing them Thomas a Beckett's small house in the town, which has been preserved as it was in his time. On the way back Dick turned to me and said "Say Rahbert, who was this guy Thomas a Beckett?"

Towards the end of the course, when I received two tickets for the 'distinguished strangers gallery' of the House of Commons, I thought it would be a wonderful opportunity of repaying the hospitality of Harman at Lundy. No gift that I could then have afforded would have meant much to him, but the debate on offshore islands around Britain's coasts could not have been more appropriate. To complete the occasion I found myself sitting next to the Crown Prince of Ethiopia on my left, whom I had known moderately well only three years earlier, and was able to present Harman to him with a feeling of one-upmanship. Sitting between a current Crown Prince and a current millionaire made me feel as if I really was a distinguished stranger.

At the end of the course we were asked our preferences for future postings by countries and types of appointment. Because I have always felt happy in France and enjoy keeping my French going, I asked for a posting to Supreme Allied Forces Europe (SHAFE). I wondered why they had bothered to ask for a preference when I received a posting to Nairobi in Kenya, where the blood-letting Mau Mau underground movement was in full swing.

Chapter XXII

The Mau Mau Campaign

Phoebe and the children went once more to stay at Shawford with her parents and I flew off to my beloved Africa. Kenya is immediately South of Ethiopia and has a common frontier with it, so I was almost going home once more. My first official title was GSO1 (SD and Training) and after full briefings from Jim Hammersley, the GSO2 (SD) and Mike Oakley, the GSO2 (Training), I realised that when Phoebe joined me it would not be possible for her to be left alone in a house, even in the suburbs of Nairobi. Most houses stood in over an acre of well shrubbed and well wooded gardens and were out of sight of one another. Even loyal African servants had, under pain of death, entered dining rooms carrying the next course followed by Mau Mau thugs with pangas. After the resulting slaughter they had deserted and were forced to take the Mau Mau oaths or die themselves.

Pistols were carried at all times and were alongside plates at dinner tables. I had already bought a .25 Automatic, (which we called Little Arthur) for Phoebe's use before I left England and immediately wrote to her to take a crash course in shorthand and typing so that she could get some job in a safe part of Nairobi when she joined me, and we could both drive in together each morning. I then went out and bought a 6 year old Dodge, the largest private car in Nairobi. It was a 7-seater with two folding seats and a rear seat wide enough to take three fat men! I could not have made a better choice, and it later took us all over Central Africa from Mombasa on the Indian Ocean in the East to the Belgian Congo in the West.

I tried to get a new feel of Kenya under the Mau Mau. Everything was different in some way from anything the British Army had taken on before. Malaya was probably the nearest thing to it but there were so many differences, even from Malaya.

The Malayan enemies were well armed and equipped by the Communists. The Mau Mau were poorly armed. In Malaya the climate was warm in most fighting zones, and troops could sleep in the open. The forests of Kenya rose up to high altitudes and extra clothing was needed at night. The enemy in Malaya was under a unified command. The Mau Mau had little cohesive command and really primitive communications. I decided to give some clear and independent thought to the best tactics to defeat our particular enemy and the best form of training to carry out those tactics.

It was fortunate that Lt. Gen. Cameron, who had recently been succeeded as C in C by General Erskine was about to pay a farewell tour to the Governors and Military Commanders of all the countries in East Africa, and Geoffrey Rimbault, the Chief of Staff, thought it was a good opportunity to provide General Cameron with a senior staff officer on his travels and also to give me a chance of meeting them all and sizing up the enormous size of our 'parish', which stretched from Ethiopia to the Northern borders of South Africa and included Kenya, Tanganyika, Nyasaland, Northern Rhodesia, Southern Rhodesia and Uganda.

General Cameron was an entertaining and informative travelling companion and I was able to learn how Mau Mau and our efforts to counter it had developed. Our visits were fairly stereotyped, consisting of staying at the various Government houses where there was normally a dinner party given for us, followed by a private pow-wow between the respective Governors and the General next morning, whilst I was driven round to see the sights and meet the Commanding Officer of the local King's African Rifles Regiment (KAR).

There were small variations, inasmuch as Peter Bathurst-Brown, who had been my closest friend at Sandhurst had left the Army and was now a Government officer in Lusaka, and I was lent a Jeep to visit his house; and at Salisbury, Rhodesia I stayed with Tony and Polly Lewis of Sissonne and Paris days, who took me to a local dance.

In Nyasaland I found that I knew the brother of Sir John Colby's wife from ocean racing contacts and was persuaded to eat my glass at the dinner table in front of everyone, when it was discovered that this was one of my parlour tricks. In those days I really did chew up and swallow the glass, less the stem, with no apparent ill effects, but I was later advised to get rid of it by pushing it into a handkerchief with my tongue, under the pretext of delicately wiping my mouth.

One of the things which horrified me during the conversations I had with General Cameron was the brutality of the murders which the Mau Mau had inflicted on the settlers of outlying farms and our failure to catch the culprits. Much effort was expended herding innocent Kikuyu into Reserves where they could be watched and guarded, but the bad hats were getting away with it.

The barbarity of some of the murders was appalling. When Ruck, a white farmer, was out on patrol as a Kenya Police Reservist, his entire family was butchered. His pregnant wife, who was found having a bath was sliced open then and there and left to die with her unborn child. Her little toddler had his hands and feet cut off and was left to bleed to death. The bloody marks of his stumps were found on the wall of his cot as he struggled to stand up before bleeding to death.

On our return from the trip I made it my business to find time to have long talks with Rodney Elliott, who was a game warden in the area North of Thomson's Falls and Rumuruti. He had been recommended to me as one of the best European trackers in the country. He explained to me that all the White Hunters who had worked for the tourist industry were, in a sense, in a state of professional rivalry and cagey about their secrets. He agreed however that they might be persuaded to pool their knowledge to defeat a horrific and murderous secret movement like Mau Mau.

After our first two-hour session I turned to him and asked "How many Mau Mau did you personally kill last month with your own rifle, Rodney?" He paused for a moment and I saw his fingers moving. "Eleven or twelve" he finally replied. "Do you realise" I said "that Lord Thurlow's entire Brigade of three regular battalions had a score of only two, which is not even one per battalion! We must obviously arrange specialised training so that every battalion can deploy highly trained jungle fighters capable of beating the Mau Mau at their own game."

Knowing that every County Regiment has its share of gamekeepers and poachers with built in skills at fieldcraft, I was certain that with a higher load of intelligence than the Kikuyu, they could be quickly turned into first-class forest fighters; particularly if they were allowed to share the secrets of the trade from the pool of expert knowledge.

By this time Major General 'Slim' Heyman had taken over from Geoffrey Rimbault and from our first meeting supported my views. He agreed that the training emphasis should be on skilled fieldcraft and that every battalion should have at least one specialist combat team and preferably up to four. He also agreed that we should profit from the lessons learned from the Indian Mutiny and have an all-British force available in Nairobi; all the British battalions being currently deployed in the forests.

Shortly after this Stephen and Kate Bassett had appeared in Nairobi. Stephen had served out his wartime commission as a Major in the Third Hussars and, as a qualified vet, had been granted a Regular Commission in the Royal Army Veterinary Corps. Being both intelligent and imaginative he soon had tracker dogs and infantry dogs available with skilled and trained RAVC handlers.

The forest Mau Mau undoubtedly had sharper senses of smell and hearing than the Europeans but those of a dog were far and away better than even an African. Dogs could hear a mile away a sound that an African could not hear more than 80 yards away. We thus overcame the one factor where Africans might have had an advantage over us.

We worked out the ideal composition of a tracker/combat team based on tracker dogs and their handlers to follow Mau Mau gangs, human/African trackers to determine which tracks were to be followed, and patrol dogs to warn patrols of the approach of others when the patrol was halted. Because the Mau Mau were poorly armed and seldom operated in large gangs, the fire power of tracker/combat patrols was limited to one Bren gun and one 'EY' rifle, which could fire a hand grenade over a hundred yards to augment the rifles, sub-machine guns and pistols carried by the remainder. The only contact with civilisation was by one wireless set which talked to an aircraft, which would fly past a position arranged on the previous day's contact, and receive notification of the patrol's probable position and ammunition and food requirements for the morrow.

Meanwhile at the more elevated strata of GHQ, Slim Heyman was trying to persuade the C in C to abandon large scale forest operations which were yielding nothing. General Erskine had commanded a motorised Brigade very successfully in the Western Desert and found it difficult to adjust to a completely different concept of war. He once ordered a whole Brigade to 'drive' a stretch of forest in a line about two miles wide. Stops were sited to catch all the Mau Mau who were expected by him to be finally chased out into the open. In the event not one single Mau Mau appeared; but we later heard that they had been having a whale of a time following up the line from the very start and had been living luxuriously off all the unconsumed rations which had been left behind from our troops' suppers the night before.

I began to realise that my spell of living with a bunch of very senior officers in Cairo would probably prejudice my future. I had appreciated their fallibility and I could not bring myself willingly to participate in a policy which was so obviously wrong. I was not 'suffering fools gladly'.

One of my jobs was to be the Secretary of the periodic 'Defence' Meetings of the Governors of all the countries in East Africa Command, the C in C, the Heads of Administrative Staff and the police Chiefs. All these brought various advisors and senior subordinates so that we finished up like the scenes one sees today on television; a huge circle of tables at which the elite sat, and an outer ring behind them with piles of files under their chairs for instant reference. The outer circle would be hissing hints and answers to the ears of the heavy artillery in the middle, and I was the hisser in General Erskine's as well as having to lay the whole thing on.

On one of these occasions after about an hour I began to feel a splitting headache at the back of my head and spreading down the back of my neck and felt very ill, wanting to vomit. I remembered that Michael and Jill had suffered high temperatures some years earlier when they had been staying at West Mersea, and that they had been in touch with a child who was found to have Poliomyelitis. In those days this was a frightening experience as the anti-Polio vaccine had not then been fully developed.

My father had advised that they were kept in bed until they were completely normal and to take little exercise even when they were normal and allowed to get up. He explained to me how Polio attacked and weakened the nervous system and that the messages sent by the motor nerves to the muscles could destroy these nerves if violent exercise was demanded and could then cause paralysis. I also remembered that I had visited a Major Minshull-Ford a few days earlier. He was still in bed whilst recovering from a bout of flu. His wife and I were both sitting on his bed in his bungalow and we all had a drink. He seemed cheerful and making a good recovery. Within forty-eight hours he was dead and it was discovered that he had died of Polio. Incubation is two to five days, so I was well inside the bracket.

As I sat behind the C in C, producing answers to whispered questions I realised that I had probably picked up Minshull-Ford's Polio germs. The hygiene of African servants was less than perfect and my glass could have been rinsed in a luke warm cauldron of tepid water containing glass and crockery that he had been using. I managed to survive until the meeting broke up just before lunch, and remembering to walk very slowly I walked back to my Mess and retired to bed.

My 'Staff Duties' appointment meant that I had a finger in every pie and the doctor who came to see me knew that if he certified me as having Polio, most if not all the people at GHQ would have had to have been quarantined. He bravely stated that I had a feverish cold and that I must be strictly confined to bed until my temperature came down.

After two or three days I began to feel better but I thought it very wise to wander very slowly down to my office, have sandwiches brought for lunch and then meander back at teatime and retire to bed. On the fifth day, as I got out of bed my left leg gave way and I fell to the ground. I reported this to the M.O. and he reluctantly decided to give me a lumber puncture. This is a gruesome performance when spinal fluid is drawn from one's spine with a bayonet sized needle and syringe. After this one has to retire to bed with blocks under the bottom legs to prevent the brain suffering from the reduction of spinal fluid. A day or two later I was told that the test of my fluid had shown that it was "almost normal". This was not surprising as by then over a week had passed and the crisis was virtually over. I fell twice more after this, once on the verandah outside my office and once leaving a table in a restaurant, when I keeled over onto the floor on my left side. I have still not officially had Polio although my left calf is now one and a half inches smaller than my right calf!

Whilst all these events were taking place both before and after my 'Polio', I had sought and found a suitable home for Phoebe and the children for the one free trip for the year that the Army provided. Jacaranda Drive was a bungalow on the Ngong Road, which leads from Nairobi to Naivasha and Nakuru, and just short of Dagoretti Corner, where the road forks left along the Ngong Hills to Karen.

It was an idyllic spot with over two acres of gardens. The main drive was lined with large Jacaranda trees and all the other trees dotted around were exotic types with colourful flowers, some like giant Tulips and Orchids. The front verandah was flanked with Poinsettia shrubs which grew around eight feet tall and a Golden Shower creeper spilled down from the hardwood shingled roof.

In the middle of the front lawn was a very beautiful pepper tree which had a mass of tiny green peppers. Mrs Harrison, the widowed owner, was proposing to spend two years in England and the timing could not have been more suitable. Another bonus was the presence of two black Alsations, Rocket and Puppy. The latter was five or six years old and his mother had been half black labrador; he was more heavily built than Rocket and had a job keeping his ears up. As a pair they were fearsome and no African other than Mrs Harrison's own boys, who I took on, would go near the place. Even Europeans usually remained in their cars until the dogs had been restrained.

My own experience was no different. After my first three visits to discuss details with Mrs Harrison and I had fondled and made friends with the dogs, which were to be mine for two years, I was left on a sofa whilst my hostess left the room to get me a drink. Puppy sat down about six inches from my knees and growled and bared his fangs if I moved a muscle until she returned.

Just as Staff Officers at Major Headquarters relaxed after office hours, even in wartime at the War Office and at GHQ Cairo, so we tried to take some exercise and fresh air after we left our offices in Nairobi. Owing to my love of horses and polo I had soon joined the Nairobi Polo Club and had bought a couple of Polo ponies. In fact I played my first game of Polo only forty-eight hours after I arrived in Nairobi as the guest of the father-in-law of one of my friends from Latimer, who had told me to look him up. The Nairobi Polo Club had a cosmopolitan membership which varied from a local garage owner to General 'Loony' Hinde who was organising Kikuyu resettlement. My ponies were half-sisters, one a dappled grey, the other a strawberry roan. I named them Mercury and Venus. Mercury soon became one of the best Polo ponies in Kenya, and I felt obliged to lend her to General Loony, a very high handicap player, for important matches such as Nairobi -v-The Rest of Kenya. Venus did not enjoy her Polo and would swerve away from the ball just as one was about to hit it. I had to get rid of her eventually and had to get an untrained pony which I called Jupiter. Mercury was a great character and loved Polo but hated practising, but unfortunately I needed it even if she didn't. One day when I was practising she put her ears back and deliberately kicked the head of one my Polo sticks with her offside rear hoof.

On my first Christmas in Nairobi I was invited up to Sotik in the Western Highlands to stay with Tony Irwin and his wife Paddy. He had moved from Ethiopia to Kenya, resigned his commission and bought a farm. Sotik was around 7,000 feet high, and so everyone there was slightly barmy as we were in Ethiopia.

I offer three typical incidents. On my first morning I woke up late after my long drive the previous day, and at 10.30 had just finished breakfast in my dressing gown. Like everybody else in Sotik at that hour of the day, I had a hangover. In through the open door walked a perfect stranger. He walked to the sideboard, poured himself a drink and sat down on the sofa. I said "Good Morning". He looked up, took another swig of Gin and Tonic and then replied "Any chance of making up a four for bridge". I wandered off to see if the Irwins were still around. They were but didn't wish to become involved and said that they would phone round and see what they could do. Eventually three other people turned up as a result of their efforts and after I had enjoyed a bath and a shave and had walked round Tony's tea plantation and he had shown me the system for planting, nurturing and picking tea it was nearly lunchtime; certainly drinks time and the four bridge players were in full session. None of them were members of the Irwin household or their guests!

On Boxing Day the Irwins arranged a dance. Black ties and long skirts were the order of the day. All surplus furniture was removed from their large sitting room. In the course of dancing someone had been careless with their wind and soon everyone became aware of it. In Sotik embarrassment was unknown. Tony stationed himself on one knee in a corner with an aerosol spray and as each couple passed he said "tut-tut" and gave them a couple of squirts of aerosol.

The day after Boxing Day was my last before returning to Nairobi, and we were among lunch guests of the local Master of Hounds and his very glamorous wife. The food and drinks were superb and it was half past three before we left the table for coffee. Our hostess produced a tray of coffee and our host as he made for the door of their bedroom remarked "I think you will find Port and Brandy on the sideboard, we'll see you in about half an hour". Whereupon he closed the door on them both.

The three incidents during an unforgettable weekend should convey to you the relaxed, natural and happy atmosphere which pervaded Sotik; but as far as I know all the people I met in Sotik, including the Irwins and the MFH divorced their partners and remarried happily. It was the beginning of the end of the 'Happy Valley' era, but obviously not quite the end.

Once Phoebe had seen Michael and Jill off to their respective boarding schools in Seaford, she made tracks for Nairobi and arrived at the end of January 1954. By this time I had moved into Jacaranda Drive and had won the loyalty and affection of Rocket and Puppy. They were still wary of strangers and imposed caution on all visitors arriving by car.

Phoebe was naturally a shade nervous at first in living in an apparently isolated house and having to sleep with an automatic under her pillow. I still use the heavy Colt .45 which Colonel Sawyer had given me to take out to Burma; as 'Little Arthurs' elder sister she was known as 'Big Bertha'. For the first few weeks Phoebe would gently rouse me every time our wooden shingle roof creaked, which it did all too often.

There was every reason to be cautious as there were a number of 'incidents' during our tenure. One night both the dogs kicked up an awful rumpus. I turned on all our lights, looked through windows to see that our verandah was clear and went out onto our lawn armed with 'Big Bertha' and with the dogs on leads. They seemed satisfied after a while and I returned to the house and bed. The next morning I learned that a large gang had used our garden to form up before raiding the Old Cambrians Sports Club, which was just across the Ngong Road, tying up the night watchman and stealing the cash and anything else of value.

On another occasion Phoebe gave me a tiny tug and I was wide awake immediately. A scraping noise was coming from inside my study-cum-dressing-room which was next to our bedroom. It was pitch dark and the door was wide open. I mouthed "Phone the Police" into Phoebe's ear, grabbed 'Big Bertha' and began to creep silently towards the doorway. I intended to hold the automatic in front of me and probe until it touched whoever was there. Suddenly I realised I had not cocked it, which meant pulling the top half back against a heavy spring. This would be heard by the intruders who would doubtless react by slashing at the area of the click with a panga.

I tiptoed back to the bed and cocked it under my pillow, hoping to deafen the sound. It still made a loud click and the response from my study was a crashing of masonry, a scraping sound from the ceiling and then complete silence. My hair must have stood on end as I re-entered the open doorway. As I moved forward infinitely slowly holding the pistol well in front of me, I reckoned that if it touched any intruder first he would be blown apart, but if he heard me first, or I shone a torch I would be sliced in two. I spent a long time probing around in complete darkness, taking care to avoid the table in the middle of the room and other furniture. I eventually reached the window and found it intact. I shouted to Phoebe to turn on the light and found that the upper flap window was open and found that a pile of bricks was lying tumbled against the outside wall of the house. There were scratches on the ceiling.

All that had happened was that a 'pole fisherman' had been having a go, had needed a pile of bricks to stand on to get his pole through the upper window and had caused them all to collapse when he heard my automatic cocked and quickly withdrew his pole; hence the scratching noise and the marks on the ceiling. Pole fishermen have a long pole and hook and fish for clothing which is hanging up or anything which has a handle like a cup or teapot. They fix razor blades along the pole to prevent people from grabbing it.

Nevertheless as far as I was concerned I had a complete adrenal response to a belief that there were some Mau Mau inside my house and that I had to win a struggle for my life and Phoebe's against them. Such a short but intense episode is more wearing than a whole day's intensive work.

Phoebe had three quite different jobs while we were in Nairobi, the first being at HQ which enabled us to drive in to work each morning. Since we were only 10 minutes drive from GHQ which was also on the Ngong Road but nearer the town centre of Nairobi, we usually drove back together for lunch.

Our first long trip was a weekend at Amboselli, the large game park East of Kilimanjaro and approximately half-way between Nairobi and Mombasa. There was a well organised hutted camp off the main road with light and water in all the living huts and a central dining and recreation room. In those days the elephants were well protected and numerous and one was certain to encounter small herds of elephant, rhino and prides of lion, in addition to the mass of wildebeest, warthogs, zebras, giraffes and every kind of gazelle. I was able to photograph lions, rhinos and elephants from quite close quarters from the safari wagons which were driven by African guides. Private cars were not allowed to swan around in the game park unescorted, nor was any form of weapon allowed to be carried, and I had locked up our pistols in my office the night before.

An amusing interlude happened when we happened upon a pride of threequarter grown lion cubs. Our driver stopped his safari wagon only a few yards from where they were having their afternoon nap so that I could get some really close-up pictures. In looking out of the window, his smart ranger's hat with its imposing metal badge at the front, fell onto the ground. The lions took a great interest and I remarked "It looks as if you'll have to say goodbye to that". "Me not allow to lose that" he replied "or big trouble for me".

At that moment one of the young lions spotted the red hat, pounced on it and ran off with it. We pursued in the wagon and the whole pride joined in the fun. When he eventually stopped and put the hat down we had the problem of someone getting up to pick it up without being devoured by the

"We eventually returned with plenty of photographs of game including rhino, lions, and elephants from quite close quarters"

mother lioness who was carefully monitoring the whole situation. It took a lot of juggling to manoeuvre the Safari wagon into a position where the lions and the hat were on different sides, and the driver, who seemed more frightened of the wrath of his superior than he was of the lions, was able to nip out and retrieve it. We eventually returned to Nairobi quite late with lots of memories and plenty of photographs of Kilimanjaro, and game including rhino, lions, and elephants from quite close quarters. There was a sting to the outing; as we got back so late I did not stop at GHQ to collect our pistols.

We had a peaceful and quiet night, but shortly after first light Phoebe gave me one of her urgent tugs. There was a black face framing the window. I sat up, knowing that my pistols were at HQ, put my hand under the bedclothes as if I was reaching for a pistols and quietly said "Jambo", which means 'Good Morning'. The face vanished like lightning and the bluff worked.

Rather like life in England, when staff officers returned home every evening and became civilians, so it was in Nairobi. There was the Nairobi equivalent of the 'Neighbourhood Watch', which we have regrettably now had to establish in our village of Sway, Hampshire. I changed from one of my three Army hats to a civilian hat and used to patrol at night the semi-urban area where we lived with my nearest neighbour Bill Stubbings. He and his wife Peggy lived only about a hundred yards away and we got to know them quite well. My close ties with Bill Stubbings proved a blessing one evening after we had gone to bed and had been sleeping for at least an hour, when the telephone rang at Jacaranda Drive from Karen which was a few miles along the South-Eastern side of the Ngong Hills. The call was from the girlfriend of one of my officers and indicated that the Happy Valley days were still alive, even if in their death throes. "Please come at once, Colonel" she blurted out "All hell is being let loose here and James has been shot." "I will be with you in less than half an hour" I replied and got on the phone to Bill Stubbings. "Bring your gun" I added. "There seems to be a shooting match going on".

In about three minutes I was out of my pyjamas, into shirt, slacks and a pullover and roaring up Bill's drive in the Dodge, with 'Big Bertha' on my lap. Bill was already framing his front doorway and ran to meet the car. We drove like the wind to Daggoretti Corner and forked left down the Karen Road.

I had been to the house before for a drink and knew exactly where it was; I also knew that James's wife had flown out to try and save the marriage. I wondered who was shooting at who and whether anyone had fired back. We shot up the drive and braked with a shower of gravel. The house was quite quiet by then and Bill and I approached with caution fearing some terrible tragedy. I peeped through a curtain and took in a quiet domestic scene except that James's wife was putting a bandage round his left hand. We entered with a friendly "Hi, there" and took stock. Everyone spoke at once, but I was eventually to glean the information that they had all had much too much to drink – and it still showed – that James had decided to return to his wife and that whereupon the girlfriend had said "In that case, I'll shoot myself". Getting out her equivalent of 'Little Arthur' she walked to the door, cocking the pistol as she went, and put it to her forehead. James leapt forward to grab the gun just as she pulled the trigger and the bullet went through his wrist without hitting bone or nerve.

After the bandage had been secured Bill and I were more than ready to accept a strong whisky each and I tried to comfort the girlfriend who was now weeping on a sofa. The house was in fact her mother's and that lady was the only person who was behaving rationally. We decided to take James and his wife home to spend the rest of the night at Jacaranda Drive knowing that the mother would get her sad daughter to bed.

When we got back to Nairobi, Phoebe had to be roused to organise the spare room, which had a large double bed. I do not think that either of them slept a wink and there were around thirty cigarette ends to be cleared up in the morning. James and his girlfriend had been very genuinely in love and always used to go to church together every Sunday. Love triumphed in the end and James's wife had to return to England empty handed whilst in due course James married the girl who had nearly taken her life when she thought she had lost him.

I felt that the whole performance was a private affair in the lives of private people and I decided to take no military action and to report nothing. James turned up at the office next day with a neater elastoplast dressing which I applied. I have not kept up with them but I believe James and his new wife were very happy together. It was also her second marriage.

On the military side, my work-load increased considerably. My earlier reasoning that there should be an all-British unit in Nairobi was accepted and I was ordered to form and then command a unit to be known as The Emergency Battalion. This Battalion was to be composed of three Companies. A company was formed from GHQ troops. All the officers were regular Infantrymen who had battle experience from World War II which had only finished around eight years earlier. A second company was formed from Pay and Records, many of the privates being potential officers who had failed their selection boards but were bright, intelligent and thrilled at the prospect of seeing a bit of action. The third company came from REME and Ordnance, who had among them some Armourer Sergeants who could fire a Bren gun with one hand.

My Adjutant was Captain Bill MacDonald of the Buffs, who was one of my GSOIIIs, and my Second in Command was Major Stephen Bassett, my old friend from Addis days. One of the Company Commanders was Major David Court who as my GSOII Staff Duties wore two hats, as it was his job to implement the War Establishment and regularise the issue of weapons for the new unit.

It was rather like a Territorial Army Regiment whose men normally do other duties when not embodied, except that they were all regular anyway. We got off to a good start with Operation Anvil, which was a search operation for urban Mau Mau in Nairobi itself. This was followed by being the 'Stops' into whose areas forest Mau Mau would be driven by one of General Erskine's monster drives. My troops enjoyed those days out in the forest fringes but, as I openly predicted, not a single Mau Mau ever appeared from the forest and we had to be careful not to shoot our own troops as they broke cover, particularly if they were African troops.

To encourage some Esprit de Corps we ran a football team and we also entered the Inter-Battalion Shooting Competition in which we came third out of around eight entrants. These activities were officially organised by those members of my own staff who were also members of the Emergency Battalion. I myself was finding my time too fully occupied by another extra job which came my way. This was to produce Kenya's all-embracing Handbook on running the campaign against the Mau Mau. It was to be capable of giving guidance to the Commanders and Officers of incoming units on all aspects of operating, surviving and living in Kenya's forests with as much tactical information as possible about the Mau Mau themselves.

Rodney Elliott, who had been so helpful earlier in shaping my ideas on the best way to win the forest operations, played his part nobly in getting all the old professional big game hunters to disgorge their private findings and those culled from generations of native trackers. I was able to put these down in writing for the first time.

Apart from writing some chapters, and certain sections of others, concerning forest tactics and fieldcraft, I re-wrote or amended all the other chapters from the material supplied me by technical branches in order to keep the style standardised throughout the manual. Because I was under pressure to produce the finished article as soon as possible, I found myself discussing in the day-time with the government printers on the size of the book (I decided that it should slide easily into the front patch pocket of the jungle battle dress trousers), its colour (dark fawn) and on the illustrations and their format. All this had to be fitted in with the normal load of paperwork which descends on staff officers desks. I thus found myself working night after night at Jacaranda Drive until midnight as an Editor.

I drafted a few choice sentences for General Erskine to use as a Commander in Chief's introduction and managed to keep my cool when he changed the first paragraph and wrote in the first sentence "Much assistance has been obtained from the Malayan publication…". As stated earlier, realising that almost all factors in Kenya were different from those in Malaya, I deliberately kept my mind uncluttered and never consulted the extremely good Malayan publication, and have still never seen one. The Mau Mau Handbook has since been used as a textbook at the Staff College, Camberley and has also been published in the USA by their Armed Forces as a pattern for correct control and Military/Police/Civilian co-operation, and tactical conduct of forest operations.

With the normal ebb and flow of work which my type of appointment involved, it was not always possible to take a predicted spell of leave. I managed however to get away for a few short trips and a planned two-week break when Michael and Jill were flown out to us for their summer holidays in 1954.

Shortly before the children's arrival their was a tragedy when Phoebe and I were exercising Mercury and Venus. We tried to do this most evenings after returning from GHQ and before the sun set at around 6.30pm. We were always accompanied by Rocket and Puppy who loved the long canters and their new-found freedom to roam without leads which Mrs Harrison had never allowed them to do. I believe that they had never left the gardens at Jacaranda Drive before our arrival. Because of this they were very clinging and followed rather than led. One evening, when we had stopped for a breather, Rocket got too close to Mercury's hind legs and she lashed out. Sadly, he was so badly injured that he had to be put down.

When we all set off in the Dodge for Nyali Beach, just North of Mombasa, only Puppy accompanied us. With his father gone, Puppy became much more positive and his character developed. On the first morning when our houseboy came in with our tea, Puppy took off from his bed and hit him full in the chest, knocking the tray complete with teapot, cups and saucers to the ground. Thereafter there was always a very cautious knock, and a head would appear as the boy would not enter until we told Puppy to sit. We realised that we would always sleep safely if Puppy was in our room and this arrangement continued when we got back to Nairobi.

We were accommodated in a comfortable two-roomed bungalow with a veranda overlooking the blue Indian Ocean. The Army ran the rest camp at Nyali Beach under the cheerful stewardship of Major Jack Alexander and his wife Gwen (who was not above performing a skilful and revealing cartwheel now and then on the dance floor). There was a large Club House where one could have meals or sit and drink but a circle of kindred spirits would inevitably gravitate after dinner to the Alexanders who had a very large living room where we often danced until the small hours.

The beach itself was of snow-white coral sand and well equipped with little thatched umbrella shelters. The sun was so strong that we had to wear T-shirts for snorkelling, or we would have had no skin on our backs. The beach was protected from sharks by an unbroken coral reef about 200 yards offshore and after a leisurely swim over a picturesque tropical seabed the reef provided a number of large Cowrie shells. Both we and the children, all being fair-skinned wore T-shirts for normal bathing and lying on the beach but nevertheless became slowly tanned through the material.

One day we set off early to drive up the coast to Malindi where the coral reef is much further from the shoreline and at high tides big waves came over the reef and allowed good surfing onto the beach. Half-way to Malindi the road is cut by a river at Kilifi. A chain ferry now operates to take cars across but when we were there it was a small rope ferry which could only take two cars, powered by a gang of Africans who pulled a rope by hand. It was real 'Sanders of the River' stuff, and they chanted a song appropriate to their cargo. In our case they sang "Bwana makubwa kwenda Malindi na bibi na watoto", which means 'important white man going to Malindi with his wife and children'! The manpower came not from their arms but from their legs. The African team faced aft and constantly walked, each man letting go of the rope and walking to the back of the queue when he reached the stern, thus forming an endless human belt.

We had a good day's surfing and lunch at the small Malindi Hotel. The waves were big enough to throw the experts fairly fiercely onto the beach. On our return journey I had to drive fairly fast through the jungle road to catch the last South-going ferry at Kilifi and was relieved that our progress was not delayed by one of the small herds of elephant which roam the wooded coastal area.

My first solo trip was to spend three nights with Rodney Elliott, whose field headquarters was up North of the Aberdares and Mount Kenya in the lands of the Samburu and Turkhana, well beyond Rumuruti. He had made a comfortable permanent home there with a small group of buildings which were a blend of African materials and European influence. The result was round mud walls but snow-white surfaces both inside and out, with well made windows and rooves thatched with the perfection of a well-kept cottage in Gloucestershire. As the only guest at that moment I had the best private 'guest house'.

I spent one day with Rodney and covered long distances on dusty tracks with his Landrover and two days roaming around gently in my car and from it doing mini-safaris on my feet and enjoying the silence and vastness of the undulating plains which were dotted with Acacia trees. Unlike the chattering and calling which went on in the forests, this country was a feast for the eyes rather than the ears. Moving quietly from one vantage point to another I saw distant herds of most of the game to be seen in that part of Africa, but I saw no lions or leopards. In the evenings Rodney and I dined

"I had the best private 'guest house'"

"Reward for lying really still in cover – a good close-up"

well and enjoyed our whiskies. He had certainly got both the cooking and serving staff trained to perfection. I left with regret, but knowing that I had far too gregarious a nature to live permanently in such solitude.

Another interesting week was spent with Dr Billy Hargreave-Wilson and his wife Diana on a yacht which they had chartered on the coast South of Mombasa. It was called Shimoni, which was also the name of the small harbour where we picked her up. He was one of those fully qualified doctors who had also later graduated as an osteopath. They both played polo and I first met them at the polo club. We became close friends, even allowing me to give a party in their house during the four months before Phoebe came out.

We drove down to Shimoni in their very ancient American Ford together with Diana's son George, by her first marriage. Shimoni is at the mouth of a small river which curves into the natural harbour. They had a friend there called Benjy who had a bungalow by the water's edge where we spent our evenings drinking the sundowners. A coral reef runs down the whole length of this part of Africa and with flippers, a snorkel and goggles, we became part of a giant aquarium, which was second to none. The sea was full of tropical fish of every size and colour and if we swam gently and made as little disturbance as possible they seemed to take no notice of us. I was rather relieved about this trait in their behaviour when an enormous grey shape glided past about twenty feet below me. With its side fins paddling away it seemed as if a rowing four was going past. I have never surfaced so fast in my life, even from the Chindwin, when admittedly been hampered by Army boots and one arm in plaster. There were obviously a few gaps in the coral reef!

When our few happy days were over, Diana drove the car back to Mombasa and we sailed there in S/Y Shimoni. I then realised why they had been so keen on my joining them. Billy had very little experience of deep sea navigation and was relying on my own dubious expertise. The drive back to Nairobi from Mombasa was pretty hectic as their old banger began to overheat. In those days this could be worrying as one could drive for fifty miles without seeing a civilised dwelling, let alone a garage. We made it fairly late in the evening, but despite the abuse Billy had heaped upon his car he refused to exchange it for a newer one.

He enjoyed having a car which he could drive into another and shunt it forward if it had parked too near him and rather looked down on me for having had my Dodge resprayed before Phoebe's arrival. We kept up with Billy and Diana after returning to England and shared both sailing and skiing holidays with them.

✧

"Inside Shimoni, together with Diana's son George"

One of my tasks as GSOI (Intelligence) was to keep in touch with both the Portuguese in Mozambique and the Belgians in the Congo. My GSOIII (Int) used to visit the Portuguese fairly regularly as they were also having problems not from a secret society but open rebellion.

He was once taken on a tour to their front line, where he found half a dozen unshaven men sitting round a machine gun and playing cards. He politely asked the Corporal, to make conversation, whether they had had any trouble recently. The Corporal replied "We dun hov no trobles". "None?" "Well, two week ago we hud to shoot two thousand, but we dun hov no trobles". The Portuguese were in fact sitting on a time bomb as future events were to prove.

In the Congo the story was quite different. My Belgian opposite number came to Nairobi to pay a liaison visit and we put him up in our bungalow. Before his departure he invited both Phoebe and me to stay with him at Costermansville. I checked it with Slim Heyman and he cleared it at once. We decided to drive the whole way and combine it with official visits to Kisumu on Lake Victoria, and 4KAR in Uganda.

Our first stop was at Nakuru where we spent the night with the Barclays, whose daughter Eliza had sold us Mercury and Venus. They were well established Kenya farmers whose servants had been with them for years and still treated their two grown up daughters like little girls, criticising the suitability of their dresses etc.

The routine of Kenya farmers was to sit down on their verandas when they came in from their farms and drink whisky or gin. One by one people would disappear and return in pyjamas and dressing gown, having had a bath. We duly took our turn in the only bathroom and by the time everyone had bathed the sun had set and it was twilight. We then went in and dined, lit everywhere by electricity and could hear the steady pounding of a diesel generator in the farm buildings. One nightcap was drunk after dinner and then we all went to bed. Phoebe and I were fascinated by the warmth and rapport between the Barclay family and their servants.

⬥

I was appalled to hear a few months later that even those loyal servants had eventually been forcibly oathed by a Mau Mau gang. The old man who had been their senior steward and guarded their daughters when their parents were asked out to dinner laid down his life for them when ordered to let the Mau Mau in one night. He warned his masters of the plot and then went out and committed suicide. The Mau Mau retaliated by ambushing and killing their faithful Alsation and impaling his body on one of the stakes of their fencing.

⬥

Our pleasant stay with the Barclays broke up the long drive from Nairobi to Kampala and enabled us to get there in time for dinner on the second day. We made an early start, getting away by 8.30am and drove up the Mau Escarpment and through the pleasant farming country known as the White Highlands. It was well wooded and gently undulating. The roads were fair because they were dry. They were known as Murram, which is a reddish earth which becomes hell in wet weather. We stopped at Kisumu at mid-day having covered a hundred miles in three and a half hours, bought petrol and some food to provide a picnic lunch and continued on towards the Ugandan frontier. There was a pole across the road and an African askari asleep in a sentry box. I sounded my horn and he woke up, grinned, and ambled across to raise the pole. There were no other formalities.

The roads in Uganda were much better than Kenyan roads and we made good progress to Jinja, where I was briefed by the C.O. of 4KAR on the rumbling discontent which was mounting, due to the harsh and autocratic rule of the Kabaka of Buganda. King Freddie, the Kabaka, was an Honourary Captain in the Brigade of Guards who reverted to tribal habits in his own patch and had most of the wives and daughters of his entourage in the family way. Whilst I was being briefed, Phoebe was given tea by her opposite number who showed her the bed on which our then very young Queen Elizabeth rested. She was also allowed to sit on the one 'royally sat on' loo seat; there was no other. Before leaving we were entertained by a hippo which climbed out of Lake Victoria which bordered their garden and wandered across their lawn. We pressed on from Jinja to Kampala, reaching the capital after dark but in time for dinner. We had clocked up around 250 miles, which was not bad going for the African roads of the fifties.

Next morning after I had completed my military meetings, whilst Phoebe compared the shops of Kampala with those of Nairobi, we set off round the South Western side of Lake Victoria through Masaka towards Mbarara, the last recommended stopping place before reaching the Belgian Congo frontier post Ruhenzi. ; The road was actually tarmac as far as Masaka and then good quality gravel. We had again bought food and drink for a lunch picnic and ate it in style, sitting on folding chairs and using a folding table. I always held the view that any fool can be uncivilised and uncomfortable.

The Africans who came past were much taller than those on the Eastern side of Lake Victoria and must have been related to the tall Watutsi from the Belgian Congo. The eyes of their graceful women stood out on stalks as they glided past our bushwhacking elegance! We arrived at Mbarara with two hours of daylight to spare, booked in at a typical British East African hotel and walked round to stretch our legs and explore.

The hotel had a large main bungalow and a circle of meticulously kept bandas, whitewashed circular huts with tall pointed thatched roofs. The whole setting was like Rodney Elliott's private headquarters in miniature, and I was immediately reminded of it. Mbarara boasted both a District Commissioner's House, complete with Union Jack flying, and a nine-hole golf course with really green meticulously kept greens.

We left punctually next day, and although the surface continued to be excellent, the road wound its way through wilder and more mountainous country until we had climbed right up to the bamboo forests. When we reached the frontier we were informed that the customs officer was having a day off because it was Sunday, and was climbing the local volcano which rose steeply to 14,000 feet. We were expecting a long and tedious wait, but mercifully he turned up after only twenty-five minutes and an eternity of form filling ensued.

We eventually got away and drove along a black volcanic track to Goma at the Northern end of Lake Kivu. Although the track surface was bad the whole countryside began to look more Belgian that British-looking, with avenues of trees and straight stretches of road. It worsened as we climbed higher and then improved again as we dropped down to Goma. The three hotels were rather scruffy looking and we had a job to find a decent room.

By then it was already dark and we found ourselves surrounded by three active volcanoes all belching smoke, which was lit up by their red boiling interiors. We were very tired by then, ate a light supper and went up to our room early, hoping for a good night's rest. Downstairs there was just a quiet murmur of conversation as the farmers tucked into their large weekend dinners. We soon fell asleep but were awakened around midnight by terrible crashing sounds. I went out into the corridor outside our room and walked along to the main staircase where I could look down into the dining room. The centre had now been cleared for dancing; but no-one had bothered to dance. They were all throwing tin trays about like giant frisbees. The noise was appalling. I shouted down in my most fluent Belgian a polite request for them to call it a day and allow us to sleep. There was a sheepish silence and I retired with gratification and returned to our room.

Five minutes later the racket started again and Phoebe said "Why don't you go down and appeal to the Manager?" I duly put on my dressing gown, tidied my hair and descended the stairs with dignity. I was greeted not by boos but by friendliness. A drink was pressed into my hand and I found myself drinking it. One or two chaps spun a tentative tray into the air and one was offered to me. There was apparently a target at the far end of the room (and just below our bedroom) which they were trying to hit. It was some ghastly advert that had been stuck on the wall. I had a go and got quite near to it. Lots of backslapping and encouragement followed, and then Phoebe descended ten minutes later to find out what was happening. I and all my new found friends were having a half-time drink, and one was immediately pressed on her. You cannot win them all.

We woke up the following morning with a bit of a hangover and suffering with loss of sleep. We had no breakfast, just some coffee and set off. Our road took us down to the Northern shores of Lake Kivu and the surface was again of black volcanic ash. To our right were a number of volcanoes we had seen the night before, smoking away but not actually pouring lava down. The road came right down to the lake as we passed the foot of each mountain and would then zig-zag its way up the valley and then back again to get round the next one. Sometimes the road climbed to quite a height round the side of a mountain and had no protection on the open side.

To avoid accidents the road was open to one-way traffic on alternate days, Southbound on Mondays, Wednesdays and Fridays, and Northbound on Tuesdays, Thursdays and Saturdays. On Sundays it was closed, so we had timed it just right. Sometimes the valleys were old lava fields, and the biggest we crossed was twenty miles long and two miles wide. The views across Lake Kivu were really beautiful and colourful because the hills to the East of the lake were not so steep and hence green with jungle.

We stopped for an early lunch or late breakfast and erected our table. The native Congolese were very polite and smiling and always lifted their hats to us, although many of the men wore little more than a G-string. We finally reached Costermansville, now called Bukavu, at tea-time and were quickly directed to Ernest's barracks, where he met us and guided us to his house. By this time the Dodge was beginning to show signs of the mileage it had performed for me and one of Earnest's colleagues remarked "Voilà une vielle Rosalie". From that moment she was known to us as Rosalie!

We had a wonderful three days with Earnest and his Belgian girlfriend. We bathed in Lake Kivu, which was free from crocodiles because it had too much volcanic sodium and other minerals in it. The Belgian barracks were far smarter than ours in Nairobi, all purpose built of good bricks whereas we had many temporary wooden buildings. The African Warrant Officer's quarters were far better than our average Officer's Quarters in Kenya.

The Belgians had a very sensible and workable system for maintaining peaceful Law and Order. Their Senior African Warrant Officers were well-paid and had good retirement pensions. They therefore returned to their villages and built the best and biggest hut on the highest ground and lorded it over their fellows. Just as retired officers in the United Kingdom tended to become JPs and mete out justice – and with more experienced judgement and sensible firmness than we tend to see today – so their retired Warrant Officers dominated their villages and kept the peace. They knew that their pensions would vanish if their relationship with the very efficient officers in the Belgian Army broke down; they could say goodbye to their pensions.

✧

It is sad to say that when the comparatively young King Baudouin decided to hand over power to the Congolese Africans, the thin veneer of civilisation evaporated almost overnight and the Congo was torn asunder with rape, murder and anarchy as it was when we later handed over the African countries which we administered before they had been civilised long enough for it to stick. I print a letter which I wrote during the night following the broadcast from Ian Smith in Rhodesia in which he announced that he was withdrawing from his attitude of 'not in my lifetime' and felt that he had to move with the times. I just could not sleep, I knew exactly what would happen and it did. African townships which had lived peaceably and prosperously under no policing except for an African Police Sergeant and twelve men erupted into violence and the Matabele and Mashona proceeded to kill each other. The bloodshed in the Congo goes on to this day.

The Daily Telegraph   October 10, 1976
The ordinary African is forgotten

SIR, – May I please ask for space in your columns, as one who commanded Haile Selassie's Staff College and saw the African at his best, and who prepared the Handbook on Anti-Mau Mau Operations in Kenya and saw him at his worst?

Between these extremes I know 23 African countries and formed a company in Johannesburg employing Blacks and Whites. I once dismissed a White foreman and employed a Zulu in his place.

There is one very important person who is never considered by the many Governments who trade in his affairs, and this is the ordinary African. From the dawn of time this hapless, likeable but extremely unsophisticated individual has been, both literally and metaphorically, sold down the river by his own ruthless but incompetent leaders.

Within living memory these ruthless leaders and their witch-doctor colleagues were still exploiting him to the death, and yet had not managed to raise him above Stone Age conditions. They had not discovered the wheel.

Around the turn of this century the first White men to penetrate his continent, and notably the British, removed from him for the first time the fear of famine, disease and sudden death from his neighbouring tribesmen. He received in its place a material prosperity beyond his wildest dreams, hospitals, roads, justice and peace. He was able to relax and enjoy his life, and in no less than 23 African countries I saw his smile.

By what right did the sons of his deliverers hand him back to the sons of those who exploited him through the centuries before they were ready to stand shoulder to shoulder with the modern world? Men who, with few exceptions, have condemned him once more to rule by violence bribery and corruption. In no country where the ordinary African has been handed back to the cynical rule of his own leaders is his standard of living, his medical cover, or his educational level as high as in Rhodesia and South Africa.

Although the way has been pointed out to his new leaders, they were unwilling to grasp it, and only the implements of death and destruction come naturally to them. Without the White man's presence they could not maintain more than the most primitive industry. Even as they seek power today they call for the continuing presence of the White man to provide the economic wealth and stability which is beyond their own capability.

The ordinary African does not understand voting; he simply asks his chief what he should do. He is but one of the 99.99 per cent who is being asked to suffer so that the .01 per cent can wield the reins of power and slip it quietly to enemies of democracy who are seeking world government.

Could some of your readers please grasp these undeniable facts and bring pressure on their Members of Parliament to try to slow up the coming handover in Southern Africa, so that it becomes an evolution and not a revolution?

ROBERT BUTLER, Lt.Col.
Sway, Hants.

✧

The evening before we started our return journey we and our kind hosts dined well and Ernest insisted on helping me to take out the spool of 36 exposures taken on the outward trip and insert a new spool of 36 for the return trip. I had unfortunately not reeled the last tip of the old film back into the cartridge and it somehow became replaced into the camera. The seventy-two pictures of some of the most wonderful scenery and game we were ever likely to encounter hence became thirty-six blanks and thirty-six double exposures with elephants walking across motor cars or pygmies in forests superimposed on modern buildings.

We decided to return via the Albert National Park, which meant continuing North after leaving Lake Kivu instead of turning East to start bearing towards the top of Lake Victoria. We spent Thursday night in a well run camp in the Game Park, having seen a wide variety of game, including one herd of thirty-five elephants a little over a hundred yards from us. During the night there were lions roaring uncomfortably close to us.

The whole area borders on volcanic mountains known as The Mountains of the Moon, and we passed these on our way Eastwards the following morning when we eventually headed for Masaka on Lake Victoria, where we spent the next night. On Saturday we made a very early start. We had arranged to spend the night with our old Addis friends, Peter and Pat Harrison, who had been posted to Kisumu. We made good time and managed to arrive in time for an hour's sail in their boat before dinner. On the Sunday we drove the whole way to Nairobi having accomplished a trip we will never forget and travelled around 1,800 miles, mainly off the tarmac. We bitterly regret that all our seventy-two photographs were ruined.

With such a big parish to look after, something was always happening somewhere which affected my responsibilities of Security, Training or Administration. The next one which blew up was in Mauritius. The nincompoops who compiled our Race Relations Act ought to have been there in 1954. They would have found that the importance of having a high proportion of European blood was so great that it was not only a question of Whites, Blacks and half-castes. Their communities were firmly divided into proportionate quantities down to Quadroons and Octaroons. This added up to five strata of society plus the Jokers in the pack, the Chinese and part Chinese population! It was with these that problems had arisen, and I was sent there to sort them out.

There was no British airline flying to Madagascar and on to Mauritius, and so I was delighted to find myself travelling first class on an Air France airliner. We circled really low round the peak of Kilimanjaro and then pretended to 'cross the line'. The French air crew all went mad, as if both they and their passengers had never done it before. In fact we had taken off South of the Equator which passes through the middle of the bar of the Mawingo Hotel in Nanyuki. We were all issued with certificates like those one receives on ships; much good champagne was opened 'on the house' in the first class compartment, which was in the rear, and the second pilot came in and poured one of them down between the boobs of the most sparkling air hostess.

When we landed at Madagascar for re-fuelling it was discovered that there was a defect in one engine which would take some time to repair. Instead of being cooped up in the Airport buildings as we would have been in a British Airport, we were told that we were free to explore the capital Tananarive and return in three hours. I had enjoyed chatting with an attractive Belgian woman who sat next to me and was returning to her husband after visiting her parents in Brussels. I offered to escort her during our three hour jaunt, and it was she who poured out her problems of being married to a quadroon who looked completely Belgian when she met him, but his father, a Frenchman, had married a half-caste Mauritian, which made him a quadroon. Being only one quarter Mauritian was nevertheless enough to put him beyond the Colonial French society, or that of the senior members of the British administration. She told me that I would never see her on Mauritius, and in many ways regretted her marriage although they got along very well together. I suggested that he should try and get a job in France or Belgium. I understood all the points of view, but my belief remains that Kipling was so right when he wrote "East is East and West is West and never the twain should meet".

Whilst in Mauritius I had arranged to stay with Guy and Sue De Cartaret. They were friends of mine in Nairobi and had given us their Dachshund Zinnia, whom we called Zinny, when they departed for Mauritius. As O.C. Troops Mauritius Guy De Carteret had a spacious and well appointed bungalow and had invited me to be their guest.

Mauritius is a very beautiful island and houses the little bay which prompted De Vere Stacpole to write 'The Blue Lagoon'. One afternoon we took a half holiday and drove to one of the island's sandy beaches. It meant driving through a part of the island which was completely hostile to Europeans and we were aware that if we had a break-down there, we would probably all be murdered! We drove fast but carefully through every village.

The De Carterets had invited two other couples and we went in a convoy of three cars. Our bathe and picnic were most enjoyable and we sunbathed for a while on the soft coral sand. On our return to Port Louis Sue found that she was no longer wearing her gold watch, which she had put with her clothes while she swam, and it must have buried itself in the very fine sand. I offered to escort her out next morning and we found the exact area where we had picnicked. It was however like looking for a needle in a haystack, saved by using some Naval technology I remembered from Latimer, a square search at sea. I drew out a square ten feet by ten round the area where she had been sitting and then marked out a hundred one-foot squares by drawing nine vertical and nine horizontal lines within the big square, making a total of eleven vertical and eleven horizontal lines. The watch turned up very near the middle of our outer square and in the sixth square we searched. We returned safely to Port Louis having run the gauntlet of the hostile villages each way and without the cosy feeling of being in a convoy.

The Chinese fraternity were only there 'for the money', and the meetings on this issue eventually ended in a successful compromise regarding trading rights. I left Mauritius with sadness. It really was a tropical paradise, and far enough away from the Equator to possess a Mediterranean rather than a tropical climate. On my return flight we regrettably had no champagne ceremony.

Shortly after I got back we had an unhappy experience with Zinny. She had been as fat as butter when we took her over and her tummy dragged on the ground. After a few evening rides behind the polo ponies and a sensible diet, her figure changed completely and so did her character. When she first came to us she was so idle that she was too lazy to go further than the last of our verandah steps to do her morning duties.

After a week or so she had lost a third of her body weight and, quite incredibly, kept up with the polo ponies at a mild canter. She also became more adventurous and disobedient; one day after we had taken her for a short walk in the grassland across the N'gong Road and steered her safely back on her lead, she doubled back after we had taken her lead off near the steps of our house and rushed back to something she had stopped to smell earlier on the other side of the road. We heard a scream of brakes, but after I had sprinted back up the drive I found an apologetic motorist holding her dead in his arms. We had never been anything but careful with other people's dogs entrusted to us, but we seemed damned with ill fortune.

Whilst Phoebe was still with me after Michael and Jill had gone back to their schools in Seaford after their Kenya holiday I had to fly home to represent GHQ East Africa at the War Office Establishment Committee to gain acceptance for our proposed new War Establishment. It was a wonderful chance to see the children and remind them that they did have loving parents. I remember finding London colder than I expected and having to buy a woollen waistcoat to wear under my grey flannel suit.

Not long after my return, the Kabaka of Buganda's outrageous behaviour had brought the resentment of his people to the verge of insurrection. I was sent there by General Heyman to do a detailed reconnaissance and to prepare provisional plans for the occupation of Buganda by a force of British troops. It was thought better not to involve the K.A.R., which could have sown the seeds of tribal warfare.

I flew to Kampala in what was Uganda's hot weather and was completely taken aback by the change in temperature from that which Phoebe and I encountered there on our trip to the Congo. I was having to deal with the most senior officials such as the Police Commissioner, the Resident in Buganda and Governor of Uganda. They all seemed to go in for smart tropical suits, and the first morning I had sweated away in a light flannel suit which was normal in Nairobi, some 2000 feet higher and much cooler. After lunch I nipped into the local store owned by Simpsons of Piccadilly and bought an ultra-thin Daks suit. I felt cool and smart, and it did much for my ego. I was asked to dinner by the Governor, Andrew Cohen, whom I had known as a young member of the Colonial Secretariat in Malta. I was accepted as an old friend and with no formality, and we spent most of the time in their nursery, playing with their young family until dinner-time.

Wherever I went during this fact-finding trip I was assessing requirements and solving them; so that when I finally boarded my plane to return to Nairobi, I already had almost detailed plans of how many troops seemed required, where they might have to be deployed and could best be accommodated. I even had details of water points and vehicle parks. During the flight, I used these notes to write my report for the C-in-C and handed it in to one of my secretaries for typing as soon as I reached my office, which was half way between the airfield and our house. Next morning Slim Hayman wanted to send it to the War Office exactly as it stood, but the C-in-C objected to some of my full descriptions of the Kabaka's conduct, in the introductory section, and insisted on some watering down.

My life continued to be extremely varied, due to the number of hats I wore. My official title was changed from GSOI (SD, Training and Ops East Africa) to GSOI East Africa. One of my most challenging tasks was to lecture in the place of Professor Leakey, who was a blood-brother of the Kikuyu, having grown up as the son of a missionary in their midst. He had already become famous as an anthropologist and had written books on the 'missing link' as well as on the history of the Kikuyu. I had hence secured his services to lecture on them and the birth of the Mau Mau to every new British battalion which came out. On this occasion I had only 24 hours notice to give the lecture myself as he did not feel up to it. His cousin had been buried alive in a sitting position the day before by a Mau Mau gang who had then cut off the top of his head and eaten his brains. They thought that they might gain some of his vast knowledge. Believe me, this was one of their cleanest rituals. I cannot put down in this book what went on at most oathing ceremonies.

As my lecture was given out of doors, where there were plenty of distractions from coloured birds in the trees and other movements, I expected the large audience to be either nodding off or allowing their eyes to wander. I had spent at least eight of my 24 hours notice preparing the lecture and was determined not to be too poor a substitute for Dr Leakey. In the event I was able to look into the eyes of every single soldier throughout the lecture, and the Medical Officer told me that I must know how many lectures a doctor must have had including one from Monty but that his attention had never been held so firmly. I was only passing on Dr Leakey's detailed knowledge about a subject that I had known virtually nothing about only two years earlier, and they like me found it rivetting. Dr Leakey was uncle of Ray Leakey, who taught me to play squash at Sandhurst, and went on to become a general. The occasion reminded what a small world I seemed to live in.

I was given a posting date of September 1955 to return to the U.K., and so Phoebe returned to be with Michael and Jill for the summer holidays. The time also arrived for General Erskine to be replaced by General Lathbury as C-in-C. I had known the latter during my spell at the War Office and we got on well. During the period of their handover, when both were in Nairobi, one of my Intelligence sources tipped me off that there was a fairly large Mau Mau gang in the foothills North West of the N'gong Hills. This was not thick forest, but semi-open country with grassland, Acacia trees and rocky outcrops which would have provided a measure of concealment and shelter for the Mau Mau.

I immediately reported this to Slim Heyman and he sucked his teeth for a moment because our normal battalions were all committed at that moment and there was nothing to spare. It was however obvious that if the report was correct, some positive action should be taken. I suddenly had a brainwave and said "Why don't you let me have a go at them with the Emergency Battalion?" "Why not" he replied. "I'll have a word with the C-in-C".

Within minutes he rang me up to say that he had cleared the release of all officers and men in the Emergency Battalion and that I could make my own plans for the whole operation. I was also allotted a company of K.A.R. under command and a light aircraft from the Kenya Police Reserve for air reconnaissance.

I thought it most unwise to hang around and told him that I would like the men to be available that afternoon until the same time the following day. I had decided at once to form a semi-circle round the area of the gang during the night by approaching them from an unexpected direction with the whole of my battalion, and then driving them into this trap with the K.A.R. in a very extended line abreast. This was only possible because of the open nature of the country, and the K.A.R. were ordered to take their time and search all the outcrops and Acacia clumps, keeping in virtual touch with sections to left and right and maintaining a semblance of a line.

To achieve surprise I decided not to overfly the area until my stops were in position on the morrow. They left Nairobi at dusk on the Naivasha Road under the command of Stephen Bassett, my 2 I/C, and kept the flaps of the vehicles closed until they were well clear of all habitation. This road runs down the side of the South Eastern escarpment of the Rift Valley. They debussed in complete darkness near a bridge which crosses a stream called the Kedong. They then followed the line of this stream, which runs parallel with the bottom of the escarpment. During the night they climbed the Western side of the escarpment and moved forward on the plateau to their positions encircling the North West side of the reported Mau Mau hide. The K.A.R. had no encircling to do and merely had to drive up the N'gong Road and past our house before first light on the morrow.

Meanwhile I was getting a small company wireless set installed into the aircraft which I proposed to use to talk to my three companies and the K.A.R., and arranged to meet the pilot, with whom I had flown before, an hour before dawn next day. We took off as the first glimmer of light lit up the sky over the N'gong Hills and flew towards them. Both dawn and dusk happen very quickly when one is close to the Equator, and by the time we had circled and flown towards Dagoretti Corner it was possible to see individual trees. We glided down to about two hundred feet, and by then could spot my companies on a circular line of vantage points and the K.A.R. company lined up and ready for the off.

I opened up wireless communication and ordered one of my companies to close up a possible escape route between two hillocks. All we now needed was an enemy in the place where they were supposed to be. We flew post haste back to the Airfield and I jumped into my waiting jeep and raced back up the N'gong Road to Dagoretti Corner and then up the Karen Road to a point where a track leads round the North-West side of the N'gong Hills. I could already hear heavy firing and knew we had bumped into something fairly substantial. As I reached my small headquarters I saw Stephen Bassett quietly talking to one of the company commanders with microphone in hand, and he gave me the thumbs-up sign.

The operation was proving a complete success and the gang of just over thirty were all killed by the K.A.R. or the Emergency Battalion as they ran into the wide circle of light machine gun positions manned by my companies. For me it was a great satisfaction to have been allowed to plan the whole operation and then to command it. Alex Napier, who had helped me to drive from Addis to Massawa, was staying with me at Jacaranda Drive at the time and could hear the firing quite distinctly as it was only about three miles away as the crow flies.

On the following morning I received two telegrams of congratulation, one from the incoming and one from the outgoing C-in-C. Two days later General Erskine departed and the senior Staff Officers lined up at the Airport to bid him farewell. He looked a little sheepish as he shook my hand.

Chapter XXIII

Solo to Cyprus

A few weeks later I flew home to get an up to date recommendation for command. I had not been home for long before I was summoned to the War Office. I was given the highly confidential information that the secret EOKA movement in Cyprus was proving more serious than expected and that the Governor, Armitage, was being replaced by Field Marshal Sir John Harding, currently the Chief of the Imperial General Staff (C.I.G.S.). The idea was to provide a Governor who was also a soldier who could control both the Civilian and Military situations. The Prime Minister, Sir Anthony Eden, had demanded that, pending this re-shuffle, the most experienced staff officer in Internal Security problems be sent to advise Armitage until his relief. Having just come back from Kenya, and as the author of the 'Handbook on Anti-Mau Mau Operations', I was chosen for this job. Only around half a dozen people in the whole country were aware of the proposed re-shuffle of Governors, which was Top Secret.

Within forty-eight hours I was on my way by air to Cyprus, but was told just before my departure that Armitage was being relieved forthwith, and that my job would be to advise the acting Governor Mr Fletcher-Cooke, who had been sworn in that day. During my flight I sat between Reggie Paget, the Old Etonian Labour MP for Northampton and Patrick Maitland, a Tory MP. They had been 'paired' to carry out a fact-finding tour of Cyprus. We all stayed at the Ledra Palace Hotel and every evening they discussed my movements over a drink and usually went where I had been on the following day. I found Cyprus in an appalling muddle. Nothing quite like EOKA had ever happened before. The Turkish Cypriots were very much Cypriots and lived happily and often inter-married with the so-called Greek Cypriots. Because of this Cyprus had become a quiet military backwater and a perfect haven for charming but unabrasive commanders and senior staff officers to end their military careers.

Fletcher-Cooke would ask me round to Government House for drinks and then try and pump me to tell him if he was going to be confirmed as the permanent Governor or soon replaced, and if so by whom. It was easier to pretend that I did not know than to tell him that I was not allowed to divulge this information. The General Officer Commanding (G.O.C.) the Cyprus garrison was Major General Abdy Ricketts. He received me with politeness and courtesy, but immediately made it plain that EOKA was so different from Mau Mau that I was wasting my time; and his. I tactfully pointed out that there were many similarities in the way any security problem was tackled, from the military point of view, including the firm structure of Government/Military/Police co-operation. I suggested that I should be allowed to make a fact-finding tour which would include meeting Police and Military Commanders, a look at the terrain from which EOKA operated and a brief study of the background of the Turkish and Greek inhabitants. I said that I would then prepare him a written report with any suggestions which might be useful and that he could always tear it up if he did not like it. He brightened up visibly and no doubt thought this was a splendid way of getting me out of his hair! He supplied me with a civilian car which I could drive around dicey areas in plain clothes without exciting suspicion. I did however attend his morning meeting of senior staff and a Police representative. It was an extraordinary experience. There was no written agenda, but a chat show like one would expect at a wives club. People aired their views, and sometimes two or three people got into private arguments right off the main theme. At the time I noticed that no-one was taking any minutes and when the meeting ground to a halt and the G.O.C. asked if there were any more questions – and there were not – the meeting dispersed. I asked the Major who was the secretary of the meeting if I could glance at the minutes and he replied that the G.O.C. did not think minutes were necessary. I remarked gently that no firm decisions seemed to have been taken and he nodded sagely. I do not believe that anyone in that room had left it any the wiser.

That afternoon I began my tour of the known hot spots of the Island and each day obtained interviews with Police Chiefs or Government Departments including immigration. A picture emerged that Greek schoolmasters had built up an ever strengthening Greek Nationalist feeling among the 'Greek' Cypriots, when they were in fact a polyglot of every Mediterranean race including Phoenicians, Maltese, Lebanese, Crusaders of most European countries and comparatively few Greeks. The figures from the previous year showed only eight people going to visit families in Greece, and over two hundred in London, but they all fancied themselves as descendants from the Gods of Mount Olympus.

The liaison between the Army and the Police was appalling and each jealously guarded his own information. Two days before my arrival each had learned that EOKA had planned an attack on a certain target one night and had sent out an ambush party. In the event they each saw the movements of the other and shot each other up. Fortunately for them it is difficult to fire accurately at night without special sights and no-one was killed.

Field Marshal Harding duly arrived and began to take stock. On the day after his arrival I drove down to the area of Limmasol and the local commander of a Sapper Regiment being used as Infantry was in despair because the EOKA had established a no-go area between Limmasol and the Troodos Mountains and were using it for field training. Villagers would warn them of the approach of troops by ringing the church bells and women would attack any approaching patrols with stones. The Colonel told me that he kept sending reports in about this and asking for Police to make further investigations but that no-one at General Headquarters (GHQ) took any notice of his pleas. I assured him that those days were over and that I would go straight to General Rickett's house that very evening on my return. I arrived at around half-past five to learn that he and his family were out on a picnic. After an hour's wait he appeared resplendent in white shorts, coloured shirt and gym shoes. I told him the situation in the Limmasol area and of the battalion commanders' concern, and pointed out that the new Governor would be probably at this moment making an assessment of the situation for his first report to London. I suggested that he should be told by telephone there and then. General Rickets said he felt that it could wait until morning and poured me a drink. He ruminated that a good time would be at the new Governor's daily morning meeting which took place at ten o'clock.

On the following morning I went to see him on his return from the Governor's meeting and asked him what the reaction had been. He replied that he did not feel that the moment had been appropriate. I re-emphasised that the Governor must be told that a slice of his territory had become a no-go area for his own troops and he promised to do so on the following morning. Meanwhile the two extremely influential MPs were seeing for themselves the reality of the EOKA's open defiance in South West Cyprus.

On the following morning I once more visited General Ricketts to see if he had had the courage to report the situation to the governor. It had apparently still been 'not quite the right moment'. I was staggered. I drove back to the Ledra Palace Hotel where Reggie and Patrick were having a drink at the bar. They told me that they had seen the Limmasol situation for themselves on the previous afternoon and were planning to fly home immediately to report to the British Government. I had three strong cups of black coffee and drove to Government House.

I had given no previous notice of this visit, but was shown into Field Marshal Harding's study with surprising rapidity. The Governor eyed me for a few moments and then said "You've been causing quite a bit of trouble since I sent you out here, why have you come to see me with no appointment?" I explained what had happened and he was at once all ears. He was aware of my Internal Security background in Palestine, India, and a number of African countries, and his attitude changed completely. He told me to continue my researches and preparation of a brief, which would now be presented directly to him, and shook my hand before my departure from the room. I returned to the Ledra Palace. Paget and Mansfield had already left and I steadied my nerves with a large gin and tonic, followed by lunch. After lunch I went to GHQ, to learn that General Ricketts had been sacked before lunch, and that the Commander Royal Artillery (C.R.A.) had been appointed Acting/G.O.C. I moved next day from the Ledra Palace to a smaller and less expensive hotel, as I now faced a week or two more in Cyprus. I was no longer under pressure of any sort, and was approved by the new Governor and had nothing to conceal from anybody except the EOKA.

I completed my brief for the Governor and put up a suggested Police reorganisation to the Commissioner of Police. I was able to get round the Island in my civilian car, and was relaxed enough to take a few photographs. I received much help and courtesy from all the Services and Government contacts I made, including the Legal Department. When the time came for me to leave, having completed my report, I sent a telegram to Phoebe who was staying with Cecil and Violet Orr, who had rented a house near Wantage, only a few miles from Lyneham Airfield, and 'booked in'.

I found that I was the only passenger in a Dakota aircraft which was being used for ferrying troops or supplies to and from Cyprus. We landed at Lyneham in Wiltshire and as soon as the doors had opened and steps had been pushed alongside a voice cried "Is Colonel Butler on board?" "I am", I answered as I reached the top step. A major who was standing just below the bottom step waited for me to descend, saluted and said "I have orders to inform you that you are required to report to the C.I.G.S. at the War Office at 11.00am tomorrow morning. A car will be at your disposal". I really began to feel rather important, but wondered what Field Marshal Sir Gerald Templar, the new C.I.G.S., would have to say. He had a reputation for being a man-eater, and had taken over from Field Marshal Harding after his outstandingly successful campaign in Malaya. He knew me by sight from one or two earlier meetings when I had served as Brigade Adjutant in Canterbury, and would have been briefed on my charter by Field Marshal Harding during their handover. I was however a little worried that he would descend on me like a ton of bricks for the firm line which I took in Cyprus.

I told the driver to get onto the Swindon road and then directed him to the Orrs' house, which we had stayed in before; a distance of around twenty-five miles in the right direction for London. I had travelled to Cyprus with only one large suitcase, so after lifting this out of the boot I asked him to pick me up at 8.30am on the morrow with a full tank of petrol.

We had been very close to the Orrs ever since the Addis days and had an entertaining evening. I travelled up to London in the Army car wearing plain clothes and told the driver to park on Horse Guards Parade, where I would pick him up for the return journey. I then made my way up the gracious staircase of the main War Office building, which had once been Carrington House. The offices of the C.I.G.S. and the V.C.I.G.S. were in a corner of the building with their windows facing outwards at right angles to each other. Their inner doors both opened into a large ante-room which was occupied by the desks of their respective Military Assistants. I was expected, and offered a chair. "Your report is literally dynamite", said Lt. Colonel Bobby Steel, Templar's M.A. "It's so hot that practically everyone is even afraid to handle it!" My heart sank and I almost wished I had put some blotting paper in the seat of my pants. The door to Templar's room then opened and he came in with a fountain-pen in his hand and said to Steel "Have you got any decent ink?" His eye then fell on me and, like Christopher Robin, I wished I was a 'bigly hole'.

The Field Marshal strode up to where I was now standing and said "So you're back are you?" He then slapped his hand on my back between the shoulders, not for punishment but with affection. "So you sorted that lot out", he said. "Just what they needed You'd better go and talk to Bill Oliver". Bill was now the V.C.I.G.S. and I had written to him at his private address from Cyprus to put him in the picture and warn him of my predicament. Bill then asked if he could have the copy of the Handbook on Anti-Mau Mau Operations which I had brought in my briefcase and which I have not seen since. "John Harding wants George Baker to go out to Cyprus as his Chief of Staff. I want you to brief him and will arrange a meeting between you both in a day or two".

Brigadier George Baker had been at the War Office when I was there and I already knew him slightly. He was one of those leaders who lead from the front by example and superior knowledge, and not just by leaning on rank. He became a Field Marshal and C.I.G.S. himself in due course and thoroughly deserved it. When he had been given my address and telephone number, he contacted me and arranged for us to meet informally in the saloon bar of a Whitehall pub. We spent two full hours together before he felt he had absorbed everything I had to offer.

A few days later I received a charming letter, a copy of which follows:-

23rd October 1955   Rockedge
                                                             Hook Heath Road
                                                                     Woking

Dear Robert,

It was awfully kind of you to have given me so much of your time the other day – for me it was quite invaluable and has given me an interesting background which will be very helpful – apart from your recommendations which I hope to implement.

I saw Bill Oliver a couple of days ago and asked him about you coming out as G.I. He reckoned it was not on, because you ought not to delay getting back to regimental duty for your own good!

I am more than sorry – it would have been good fun to have sorted the place out together. I'll probably write to you from time to time for your advice, if I may, when I get really foxed!

All the best.
Yours George Baker

In November 1955 I was hence able to take the leave which I started in September and duly received my posting to my Regiment in Luneberg, Germany; arriving just before Christmas and staying with Mike and Mary Read until our quarter became vacant.

Chapter XXIV

Full Circle, Return to The Queen's Own

Luneburg is a beautiful town with many medieval buildings which have survived the passage of time. Because there used to be salt mines under the town, the resulting subsidence has caused a number of these to tilt at different angles, and because of their heavy timber-framed construction they have survived. One could be walking through a Grimm's fairy tale in some parts of old Luneburg.

Because there was a large barracks formerly occupied by S.S. Regiments, firstly we had taken it over and secondly the town was full of their wives and families who hated us. If Phoebe went into some shops she tended to be ignored. The woman behind the counter would serve all her countrymen and always avoid her eye. However, we had a splendid barracks and a well-built house to live in. It was not much fun coming down to Major, which Joe Parry had promised me I would not have to do, but I never looked back at the past, and threw myself into Regimental life. I accepted the situation as a horse refusing a fence and stepping back to have another jump at it.

I took over the Rugby Football and re-started inter company Rugby, to get the young subalterns out teaching their men. From not having enough Rugby players to form a Battalion team, we immediately had $5 \times 30 = 150$, as each company and HQ company had to raise two teams in order to teach them to play. A month later we won the Divisional Seven-a-Side Rugby tournament.

In our Order of Battle we were married up with a squadron of the Eighth Hussars, which meant that each company would train and fight with the same troop and each platoon with the same tank. There was a drill for every man in a platoon to be carried on its supporting tank, which meant that the whole division could travel by road on tanks until it came under fire. It was the first time I had worked with heavy armour, which I had hoped to do when I came back from Ethiopia, and I found it very interesting. I was made President of the Mess Committee (P.M.C.) and immediately created a mess garden, as we always had in front of our messes in England. I did not like stepping straight onto a parade ground. I got permission from the German Forestry to uproot a number of young pine trees and we

"One could be walking through a Grimm's fairy tale in some parts of old Luneburg"

transported them into especially dug holes in the asphalt. We broke up the asphalt in other places and made patches of lawn and flower beds.

I took my company out for a period of defensive training in really frosty weather and we dug slit trenches which each had a small dug-out for the occupants, with enough earth on the roofs to avoid radiation from all but a fairly close tactical atom bomb. By hanging a curtain made of sandbags across each entrance we were able to survive the bitterly cold nights which were many degrees below freezing. The area was only approachable by crossing a river so we built a raft of forty-gallon drums and a wooden deck and used a slack fixed rope which was weighted and lay under water when not in use, and dug a bay in which the raft could be camouflaged from the air. This meant that no-one could visit us without our consent! In a nutshell, I flung myself with gusto into Regimental life and thoroughly enjoyed it.

Because it was the Bi-Centenary year of the formation of the Queen's Own, we were due to return to the United Kingdom that summer to celebrate the event with a Ball at the Dorchester and Trooping the Colour before Princess Marina, who had taken over the appointment of Colonel-in-Chief on the death of her husband, the Duke of Kent. We duly moved to a barracks under the shadow of Dover Castle and the smallest and worst quarter we had ever lived in. Our preparations for our Bi-Centenary celebrations were soon shattered by the Egyptian seizure of the Suez Canal under the direction of General Nasser. Anthony Eden did not relish the idea of being upstaged by this man whom he considered an upstart, and it soon became clear that he was going to take positive steps against the advice of most of his colleagues and the wishes of the White House.

We found ourselves moving to a tented camp at Bulford and seeing our vehicles painted a desert yellow. Suddenly the situation eased and we found ourselves returning to Dover. Ceremonial parades in preparation for our Trooping the Colour were once more our main occupation and our wives were shopping round for items like long white gloves for the Bi-Centenary Ball in Park Lane. On the very day of the Parade, which was to take place at our Depot in Maidstone, Anthony Eden took his decision to act. Chaos reigned. The Colour Sergeants who have such an important part to play in such parades had to revert to their wartime role and start getting stores ready for embarkation. The senior sergeants in every company had to take on their roles with no proper rehearsal and the wives who had spent the most on their ball gowns were the most aggrieved.

The Parade went off like clockwork, as I knew it would; but the wives of officers about to embark next day for Suez returned to Dover with their husbands rather than be wallflowers in London. We went to bed early, knowing we would have an early start next day, but in the event there was a banging on our front door whilst it was still dark, and Ken Dodson, the Adjutant, shouted up to me as I put my head out of our bedroom window that I had to be on parade in an hour and a half. That evening we were sailing from Southampton in a convoy of troopships for a landing at Port Said.

Although we were escorted by ships of the Royal Navy, we were also being shadowed by ships of the USA Sixth Fleet. The USA was against this intervention and behind the scenes was threatening to blow us out of the water if we did not abort the operation. The Russians took the opportunity of overthrowing the Nationalist Government in Hungary and installing a hard-line Communist regime with great brutality. Many patriotic Hungarians who escaped found their way to England and our wives found themselves helping to administer some of them.

On the morning after the Parachute Regiment's air drops and the pre-dawn assault on the beaches by our Commandos, we steamed straight into Port Said and were the first normal troops to disembark. The streets of Port Said were empty as we fanned out and made our way through to our allotted objective but we felt hundreds of eyes following us from every window.

Later that day we moved South and took over from the Parachute Regiment battalion commanded by Bala Bredin, one of my old Ulster friends. They had been halted at El Cap on the Suez Canal at precisely mid-night, after the USA had finally forced Anthony Eden to climb down. This gave our commanders no opportunity to choose a suitable place, and we found ourselves facing the Egyptian Army on a wide front, whilst we could only attack on a very narrow front. Peter Buckle's batman was wounded the first evening, but we had no other casualties. There was still a possibility that we would resume our advance and I decided to swim the Canal to the Eastern bank and make my way forward under cover of the mound which ran along each side of the Canal, to have a look at the rear of the Egyptian positions. On reflection, I was lucky that they were not patrolling the Eastern side, as if captured I would have had no clothes apart from Y-front pants.

I later flew over the Egyptian positions in a helicopter to try and see what to expect behind their front line. The RAF pilot was kind enough to let me have the controls for a while when I told him that I had flown with the RAF at Latimer, and found the controls of a helicopter strange, but possible. One makes far more use of the throttle. After landing I was told by a Canadian major in a blue U.N. beret that he had needed all his powers of persuasion to prevent an Egyptian Anti-Aircraft gun position from shooting us down, as we had strayed too far over their lines. When we were relieved and moved into billets in Port Said we went through a very dull few days, enlivened for me only by a visit to the Naval Command Ship from which the combined operation was being run – or not run! I was visiting Teddy Gueritz, who was a great friend at Latimer and who not only wined and dined me well, but also arranged for me to have the first hot bath for over a week.

As the first battalion ashore we were the first battalion to leave Egypt. Unfortunately, instead of sailing home we were told that we were going as a threat in being to -of all places – Cyprus, where I had exerted so much influence only twelve months earlier. EOKA however had not forgotten me.

After a short time in a tented camp, we were told that we would not be returning to England but would be starting a new overseas tour. We only had our battle kit and a change of clothing. In my case, knowing the form in Mediterranean countries, I had smuggled the smart gabardine suit which I had bought when in Cairo into my valise and my batman soon ironed out the wrinkles. We were all at a social disadvantage at evening social gatherings, where the permanent garrison wore civilian suits at parties and dinner jackets at the Christmas dances.

We were given an operational area at the junction of the long Eastern peninsula of Cyprus, known as the Panhandle with the main lozenge shaped island. My company was stationed at Kantara, which is on the crest of a hill with a view of distant Turkey to the North and the beaches of Famagusta to the South.

The pressure of EOKA on the military and on British civilians in Cyprus did not compare with Kenya. There were no ritual murders and the type of barbaric attacks on families which were the way of the Mau Mau. The enemy was not a natural fighter and had been goaded into guerrilla warfare by outside subversive influences.

The camp at Kantara was a mini-fortress with a double line of barbed wire and light machine gun posts covering all approaches. I never had the feeling that we would be attacked there, and we never were.

Officers took it in turns to have a day's leave in Nicosia or Kyrenia. In the case of senior officers, we would just ring up the C.O. and clear it with him. As Christmas approached, there were parties and private dances and my fellow officers were at a great disadvantage having nothing but battledress for quite a long time.

I had made a few friends during my stay on the island the previous year and had a certain advantage. Kyrenia had an up-market bar known as the Harbour Club, and I got to know the owners quite well during this second stay. The proprietors were a former singer known as Judy Shirley, and her husband was a retired Army captain. He lent me a dinner jacket for one private dance given by a couple who had rented a flat in Kyrenia. Our host was on the staff and in the Middlesex Regiment.

Evening in Limassol

I made no attempt to contact George Baker or Field Marshal Harding, but kept up with some of my legal friends. My own legal expertise was called upon on one occasion and I drove into Nicosia to consult a legal eagle, with an escort of two jeeps with mounted Bren Guns. I drove the second jeep because the driver was not very experienced. My friend Gray in the Government Legal Department studied my proposed defence and said it could not fail.

There had been some mining of roads and bombing of vehicles, and on only the previous day an order had come out that the floors of vehicles must be sandbagged. This meant a sandbag across just aft of the foot pedals and half-filled sandbags squeezed between the pedals.

We set off from Nicosia in fairly late afternoon along the Famagusta road and turned North up the winding road which climbs to Kantara. There is only one village on this road before Kantara, about half way up. As we negotiated the last hairpin bend before the village and turned into the straight narrow road running through it, I saw a bomb about the size of a large thermos flask sailing through the air from a house on the left and falling onto the road behind the leading vehicle and just in front of mine. It went off right underneath my feet, blew the offside front tyre to ribbons, and managed to propel some fair sized bomb splinters through the holes needed for the operation of the pedals. I struggled to keep the jeep moving with the right-hand tyre flapping madly and all hell seemed to be let loose as deafening machine-gun fire surrounded us. A second bomb then came sailing down from the left, landed on the right-hand side of the road and went off exactly opposite me. I felt nothing except a humming in my right ear and a real fear that we were about to be victims of machine-gun fire. We zig-zagged up the road to the end of the village, where the first vehicle had pulled up off the road well to the left. From this position it could no longer be fired on from the unfriendly inhabitants of the enemy occupied house, whose view of us was blocked by the intervening houses. My driver, who was sitting in the left-hand seat, had been hit in the leg, but had not had the open gaps for the pedals to contend with, or the blast from the second bomb, from which my body shielded him.

As I could feel the blood running down the inside of my trousers I apologised to him for claiming the first field dressing produced on the grounds that I thought I had the greater need! I started to lower my trousers and from the right thigh downwards there was a procession of holes seeping blood, each larger than the last. The lowest one was an enormous hole in the lower end of the big shin bone, just above the ankle joint, and this got the first dressing.

When we had both had our various wounds staunched I decided that we had an excellent chance of catching the bombers. They would never have done this in their own village, and therefore we must ensure that no-one left the village until it had been properly cordoned and searched for strangers.

These villages were all built like fortresses with all the outer houses joined together in an unbroken wall. It was only necessary for one man to position himself at each end of the road, and one to watch each of the outer walls, whilst I drove the undamaged jeep up to Kantara to lay on a company in double quick time. The two watching the open sides of the village were to be the two Bren gunners.

I climbed into the undamaged jeep and set off up the hill. I had not stiffened up and felt no real pain. As soon as I got to Kantara I ordered Rex Sherborne, my 2 I/C, to telephone Battalion HQ for immediate action and then allowed my batman and one of my subalterns to improve on some of the 'handkerchief' dressings with proper field dressings.

It was dark when an ambulance finally appeared to cart me off to hospital in Nicosia, and I have never felt so frightened as I did during the entire trip. The ambulance was unescorted and travelled with headlights fully on. We even had to pass through the scene of the bombing, where the driver said he saw no sign of any of our troops. They were not from my company and they had made a nonsense of it.

I was told later that under the existing regulations no troops were allowed to enter another unit's area. This was nonsensical and could mean breaking off a hot pursuit and allowing an enemy to escape. Could it have been the reaction to my discovery of the battle between Police and Army the previous year? Once made, contact with terrorists should never be lost.

I was a very long time under anaesthetic in Nicosia Military Hospital and came round lying in a ward on my back with the plaster on my right leg right up to the top of my thigh. I later counted a total of forty-two holes in various parts of my body, including one on the right eyebrow which cut the eyelid on the way but did not touch the eye. I had to add in the holes which were under the plaster from memory. There were seven.

Unfortunately the small splinter removed from my eyebrow hit the nerve which goes up the forehead and activates the area of the head where a right-hand parting would go. This all went numb and caused quite a problem a few years later, when I got shingles on the affected area including one spot on the eyeball. I was apparently lucky not to go blind in that eye. My right ear-drum had been burst by the second bomb, and this gave me perfectly balanced poor hearing in both ears!

It is extremely uncomfortable to have plaster up to the top half of the thigh for obvious reasons. One cannot lie on either side without discomfort. My face was completely black and blue and most of the holes had become infected through dirt being forced deeply into them. I was full of antibiotics and felt like death. After a few weeks it was decided to send me home to the Royal Herbert Hospital in Woolwich. This was a foul experience as when we landed for the night in Benghazi, and again in London, I was strapped down in my stretcher and if the plane had crashed I felt I would probably have been left to fry.

I eventually had an interview with the Military Secretary's Department at the War Office, and they told me glibly that I was now too old to command a battalion but would undoubtedly become, in due course, a brigadier on the Staff. I was able to see, by reading upside down one of the papers on his desk, that my mobilization role was Brigadier General Staff. I told him that I was not interested in pursuing an unbalanced career confined to a desk, and with no prospect of commanding anything.

I had heard that handsome golden handshakes were currently available for those choosing early retirement, and I duly applied for one and got it. It was sad leaving the Army, but I had experienced the best of it and given of my best to it. I had already explored one or two civilian opportunities and the grass is always greener on the other side of the fence. In the event this was to include the 'loss' of five more lives.

✧   ✧   ✧   ✧   ✧